ENVIRONMENTAL AWAKENING

The Conservation Foundation (1717 Massachusetts Avenue, N.W., Washington, D.C. 20036) is a nonprofit research and communication organization dedicated to encouraging human conduct to sustain and enrich life on earth. Since its founding in 1948, it has attempted to provide intellectual leadership in the cause of wise management of the earth's resources.

ENVIRONMENTAL AWAKENING

The New Revolution to Protect the Earth

Rice Odell

Foreword by Edmund S. Muskie

The Conservation Foundation

 Ballinger Publishing Company • Cambridge, Mass.
A Subsidiary of Harper & Row Publishers, Inc.

ENVIRONMENTAL AWAKENING:
THE NEW REVOLUTION TO PROTECT THE EARTH

Library of Congress Catalog Card Number: 80-10990

International Standard Book Number: 0-88410-630-6 (cloth)
                                       0-88410-631-4 (paper)

Jacket and book design by Sally A. Janin

Typset by United Graphics, Fairfax, Virginia

Printed in the United States of America

Library of Congress Cataloging in Publication Data

Odell, Rice.
      Environmental awakening.

      Includes index.
      1.   Nature conservation.   2.   Environmental protection.
I.   Title.
QH75.O33   333.7   80-10990
ISBN 0-88410-630-6
ISBN 0-88410-631-4 pbk.

The material in this book was drawn from several dozen issues of the *Conservation Foundation Letter*, principally from the following: "The Environmental Revolution" (December 1979, January/February 1980); Chapter 1 (October 1977, November 1979); Chapter 2 (October and November 1973, February 1979); Chapter 3 (April and May 1977); Chapter 4 (February and March 1979); Chapter 5 (January 1973, August 1979); Chapter 6 (May 1974, May and November 1976, September 1978); Chapter 7 (September 1976, June 1977, July 1979); Chapter 8 (March/April 1976, September 1977); Chapter 9 (October 1975, March 1978); Chapter 10 (October 1976, July 1977); Chapter 11 (December 1973, January and April 1975, May 1978).

*To my wonderful
and indispensable parents
Ginc and Billy*

CONTENTS

FOREWORD

Theodore Roosevelt once said, "Americanism is a question of principle, of purpose, of idealism, of character; it is not a matter of birthplace or creed or line of descent."

As one of this nation's founding conservationists, Roosevelt would have been pleased by the course of the environmental movement in this country which evolved over many decades and came to bloom in the decade now ending. It was not born simply of eccentric one-issue groups or individuals, but in a more American way: the movement was based on principle, purpose, idealism, and character. At the end of a turbulent decade, a frustrated nation called its leaders to action on Earth Day, 1970. The journey begun that day has been sustained.

A case can be made that the environmental movement is the inevitable result of American nationalism. From Jefferson's faith in the landowner through the years of Manifest Destiny to the space shuttle, we have defined success in terms of the accumulation of things: first land; then capital; now knowledge as well. We have always believed there was room enough for each of us.

Open spaces, land for a home or farm, clean air to breathe and clean water to drink were seen not as goals of a policy, but as a birthright. So were a job and a chance at economic success based on a person's own ability and aggressiveness. The two did not conflict, for there was room enough, air and water enough for all.

There was also imagination enough to invent and apply new industrial methods; create new products and, through advertising, the demand for them; find new uses for the seemingly inexhaustible supply of raw materials at our disposal.

We always derived solace and hope from a dream of an attainable better life; we trusted science and technology to find solutions to difficult problems; we relied on individual initiative to implement the dreams and apply the technology.

The bigness and nature of our land helped shape the nature and spirit of our people. Americans were able to roam free and carve out new lives and relationships with the wilderness.

Gertrude Stein, an American writer who lived on both coasts and wrote about her native country as an expatriate, said, "In the United States there is more space where nobody is than where anybody is. This is what makes America what it is."

The dreams of new land, of gold, of California, of starting over became exploitative realities. For every American who succeeded in a better life, scores more were convinced to try.

The expansion came to an end, of course. The first resource limit we were forced to recognize was the Pacific Ocean, and even then we turned to colonialism before we accepted it. We were soon to recognize more painful limits.

Not long after Frederick Jackson Turner declared the American Frontier closed in 1893, pollution had begun to kill people in our cities. Neither event struck people as greatly significant, because we Americans had begun our love affair with "progress."

We could no longer expand our country's boundaries but we could and did expand the reach and scope of our technology. From Roosevelt to Hoover, we became a nation of engineers. We built cities, public works, factories, and universities with which to carry on the American dream of opportunity.

We fought and won two world wars, and by the post-war years, there was no more fitting American symbol than the automobile, and no more American pastime than a drive in the country. But the "country" was becoming harder to find.

The competition for our limited air, water, and land resources was an unequal one. Business and industry needed those resources to fuel combustion, store wastes, and support the increases in productivity which kept America a land of opportunity.

People needed those resources, too. And America came face to face with some painful questions. Did we want to abandon the American dream of good land and healthy air? Would we be forced to choose between a clean environment and a good job? Had we become victims of our own inventiveness? Was our technology up to the task of cleanup? Or was technology part of the problem? In short, would we be forced to stop "progress" to save our people's health?

People turned to government for answers. In the 1960's, there weren't many environmentalists, in or out of government. I held a hearing on pollution in the Mississippi River in those years. One witness suggested we fence the river to stop beer can litter. So the answers government gave the people were not very good ones.

But we got better. Our scientific knowledge increased. Our understanding of the political limits of pollution laws grew. And when the people spoke on Earth Day, we were able for the first time to forge a political consensus behind meaningful pollution legislation. By the year's end the Clean Air Amendments were law. Two years later the Clean Water Amendments were law. So were the National Environmental Policy Act and Resource Recovery Act.

In those three years, an environmental ethic was debated, defined, and codified. The laws have been written and rewritten as the nation has struggled to translate goals into practical reality. Like all things shaped by the political process, the laws are imperfect.

They have been challenged by those who once were free to use our country's resources as they saw fit; by those who believe the solutions we designed are inadequate to the task; and by those who believe the limits we have placed on pollution also mean limits on economic growth and opportunity.

That is as it should be. Government and the laws it implements ought to be susceptible to debate and change when they stray from the national consensus. Those who consider themselves environmentalists ought to understand that fact. Their challenge in the next ten years will be two-fold.

First, the national environmental consensus is not assured. Every environmental gain must be rejustified. Every new proposal must be backed by the most persuasive and understandable arguments. Environmental regulation is restrictive. Business is not in business to look after the public welfare. It will resist the pressure to clean up pollution. It will win balance-sheet arguments as long as we cannot put a price on human life, or lost recreational opportunity, or open spaces saved for future generations. Environmental progress thus will mean not simply new laws, but a fresh enthusiasm for the old ones.

Second, environmentalists must become more relevant to the lives of more Americans. In the 1980's it will not be enough to save a wilderness for a few hundred canoeists with the time and money to enjoy it. It will not be acceptable to ban a poison if there is no other way to control urban rat populations. It will not be enough to talk about "alternatives" to oil without deciding which alternatives are acceptable, available, and affordable. It will not be enough to say "no" to a polluter without saying "yes" to one who pollutes less. America will not abandon its dream of opportunity. It will learn to define the word differently, perhaps. But if it is no longer persuaded that environmental concern is still relevant to social and personal progress, it could well follow a different course.

If environmentalists understand the nature of these challenges, and continue to be a positive force for change, the 1980's can see real progress. If they do not, the structure of environmental regulation may well collapse under the pressure for energy, jobs, and a more relevant government.

Edmund S. Muskie

PREFACE

Since 1966, The Conservation Foundation has published a monthly report on critical environmental problems—problems ranging from noise pollution to population control, from deforestation to automobile usage. It is called the *Conservation Foundation Letter*.

A number of people have suggested that key issues of the *Letter* be fashioned into a single volume. With some updating and minor additions, this has been done, and *Environmental Awakening* is the result. The Foundation and Ballinger Publishing Company decided to publish this book in conjunction with Earth Day '80, celebrating a decade of impressive activity. Thus the introductory chapter traces the genesis of the Environmental Revolution, its achievements, and the tasks it faces in the next decade.

I am grateful to Senator Edmund S. Muskie of Maine, an admirable environmentalist and statesman, for writing the foreword to *Environmental Awakening*.

Special thanks go also to William K. Reilly, president of The Conservation Foundation, under whose aegis the *Letter* is published; to two of Mr. Reilly's predecessors, Russell E. Train and Sydney Howe; and to Marvin Zeldin, the first editor of the *Letter*.

I greatly appreciate the judicious comments and editing of Foundation Executive Vice President J. Clarence Davies; the work of Paige MacDonald and Richard Abrams in getting the project going; the editing of Tom Blanton; and the design work of Sally Janin.

I am particularly grateful to Fannie Mae Keller for her invaluable and excellent assistance of all kinds in producing the *Conservation Foundation Letter*. Robert McCoy provided superlative final editing and production, as well as impish calm in the face of deadlines. And David

Sleeper not only wrote the section of the book dealing with the carbon dioxide problem but contributed much essential encouragement and enthusiasm.

There have been dozens of other colleagues at The Conservation Foundation over the years whose friendship, spirit of inquiry, and dedication have been most helpful and rewarding. I am likewise grateful to my family.

Finally, I must express appreciation and admiration to the thousands of people—known and unknown, individually and in heartening unison—who have carried out the Environmental Revolution, and whose actions and ideas fill the following pages. Indeed, they deserve the gratitude of everyone.

Rice Odell
Washington, D.C.
February 1980

THE ENVIRONMENTAL REVOLUTION

There is a kind of revolution of so general a
character that it changes the tastes as well
as the fortunes of the world.

—La Rochefoucauld

We have been witness to an extraordinary political metamorphosis, the
Environmental Revolution. It is the creation of a long evolutionary
process leading up to a Big Bang. A spirited mixture of people and ideas
fermented gradually over the years, then exploded into the public consciousness. The result has been sweeping cultural change. Whatever its
future momentum and direction, the Environmental Revolution has
caused a remarkable shift in United States and world history.

The environmental awakening was a rude one, indeed. It cast doubt
on some of the most cherished credos of the day—beliefs in the ever-
increasing rewards of industrial, technological, and chemical progress
and of economic growth under a free-market system. It made the future
look bleak and disappointing.

Paradoxically, the Environmental Revolution also brought a glow of
welcome reform, of hopeful change, and of prospects for a higher
quality of life. It brought a new dimension to civilization.

What was the genesis of this historical shift in thought and action,
this catharsis? Max Nicholson, a prominent British environmentalist,
has written:

> Chance seems often to determine whether some tangle of problems and
> actions acquires an accepted identity and a familiar name, giving it an
> explanatory literature and a secure place in the minds of informed people,
> or whether it stays shapeless, neglected and unidentified in limbo. Some
> problems, such as the consequences of epidemic disease, or outbreaks of
> violence, or economic breakdowns brusquely seize a place on everyone's
> agenda; others are added only through the pertinacity of people who are
> convinced of their seriousness and insist upon everyone taking notice of
> them. But others, of equal intrinsic importance, fail to win effective
> protagonists and smoulder away like a fire under peat.[1]

The Environmental Revolution undoubtedly was inevitable. Population was growing inexorably; pollution was increasing dangerously; land was being desecrated relentlessly. At some point, these excesses were bound to reach the limits of political endurance.

There were too many pressures and too many pressure points for political containment. If not as dramatically, yet as surely as a plague, environmental problems "brusquely seized a place on everyone's agenda."

And they produced the tenacious reformers to which Nicholson also referred—people fighting gallant battles, such as a David Brower pitted against construction of a dam in the Grand Canyon, or an A.J. Haagen-Smit trying to alleviate the miasmic smog of Los Angeles.

The catharsis also was inevitable because the United States is a fertilized hotbed of democracy, an indispensable locus for such a revolution to take root and grow. Indeed, this hotbed was busily spawning other changes of great social significance—the civil rights movement, the antiwar movement, the consumer rebellion, the sexual revolution, the women's liberation movement. In many ways, these fed on and reinforced each other, sharing the same skepticism of conventional wisdom and of entrenched organizations and policies, and utilizing similar political action techniques.

"There was a mood of rebellion and reform in the '60's, an iconoclasm," says Gladwin Hill, who became national environmental correspondent of the *New York Times* in 1965 and thereby played a major role himself in disseminating the kinds of reports needed to sustain any massive social change.

Wendell Phillips, the great American abolitionist and liberal reformer, said: "Revolutions are not made. They come. A revolution is as natural a growth as an oak. It comes out of the past. Its foundations are laid far back."[2]

Roots

The longest, hardiest roots of the Environmental Revolution are well known. They go back to the country's beginnings, and are reflected in a remarkable, eloquent literature celebrating man's natural surroundings and the wildlife inhabiting them. Emerson, Thoreau, Muir, Leopold, and others tapped some of man's deepest psychological and spiritual feelings.

"I wish to speak a word for Nature, for absolute freedom and wildness," wrote Henry David Thoreau.[3]

These feelings gradually developed into more concrete concerns and warnings—about preservation of park and wilderness areas, about resource scarcities and conservation, and about the specter of unrestrained population growth. The warnings rang out in such books as

William Vogt's *Road to Survival* (1948), Fairfield Osborn's *Our Plundered Planet* (1948), Harrison Brown's *The Challenge of Man's Future* (1954), Rachel Carson's *Silent Spring* (1962), and Paul Ehrlich's *The Population Bomb* (1968), to name a few with broad impact. And then there was that magazine article by biologist Garrett Hardin which somehow suddenly and dramatically clarified the nature of the ecological dilemma faced by mankind. It was called "The Tragedy of the Commons."[4]

Many other perceptive observers, concerned about the direction in which society was headed, also warned of trends and dangers. They included scientists of many disciplines, public health officials, economists, politicians, writers, and philosophers. These warnings did not fall on deaf ears—just not on enough ears. And ominous though the warnings were, they came to the public second-hand. A real revolution needs a great wellspring of public indignation, based to a considerable extent on direct experience.

Plenty of indignities to produce this indignation started coming to light, however. People began to see or sense for themselves what was happening to their environment—the hazes of pollution hovering in their cities, the filth in the streams, the maddening "No Swimming" signs on the beaches, the smelly and unsightly dumps, the urban sprawl, the interstate highways which punched through neighborhoods, the shorelines and wetlands defiled by development, the flooded scenic rivers, the clearcut and strip-mined lands, and the noise of airplanes.

Still other happenings increased public doubts about the direction of social progress. There were the mysterious threats of radioactive strontium-90; the warnings about the invasion of DDT and other pesticides; the cry that "Lake Erie is dead"; the logging of giant redwoods; and the implications of the great Northeast blackout of November 1965.

"People were hit by a whole lot of different things," says Lynton K. Caldwell, professor of political science at Indiana University, who was very much present at the creation (he played a major role in the writing and passage of the National Environmental Policy Act of 1969). Public dissatisfaction, Caldwell says, was stimulated by a "pervasive and accelerating decline in the quality of American environments."

"There was a convergence of different movements that crystallized into the environmental movement," Caldwell says. In an early book on the phenomenon,[5] he described three "sociopolitical developments"— conservation, environmental health, and public aesthetics:

> Each of these developments was distinct in origin, and although there were interactions among them and some overlapping participation among leaders and followers, not all interactions were mutually supportive.

Caldwell recalled, for example, that the "slowness of professional public health officers to redefine their mission to include recreational and
aesthetic values was a factor in the transfer of responsibility for water
quality" from the Public Health Service to the Interior Department, in
1966.

In the 1960's, there was little convergence of thought or action by the
duck hunter, the air pollution monitoring technician, or the homeowner
opposing a highway. There were separate battles to prevent the construction of dams and to preserve park and wilderness areas. Planners
tried to lay out better urban forms, and promote the acquisition of open
space. Public health experts and government officials lobbied for and
obtained passage of the first meaningful air and water pollution control
laws. Many people fought the proliferation of toxic pesticides. Others
fought noise. Population specialists promoted contraceptives, abortion, and greater understanding of the long-term threats of overpopulation. (Zero Population Growth, Inc., named with a slogan that had
great impact on public thinking, was founded in late 1968.) A variety of
offended citizens campaigned against the various forms of visual ugli-
ness that it increasingly invaded their environments—the billboards, the
junkyards, the dumps, the electric transmission lines. (The mid'60's and
the Johnson Administration are especially remembered for an emphasis
on beautification programs.)

The Big Bang

Finally, all these disparate perceptions and interests and fears began to
fuse together, and this fusion produced the Big Bang of the Environmental Revolution. It was the moment, albeit imprecise, when widely
scattered citizens realized they had common values and purposes—and a
common passion for reform. From the excitement and energy generated
by this realization came an explosion of citizen consciousness and a
surge of citizen action.

So sweeping was this revolution that its adherents concerned themselves with almost all of society's and nature's activities—from the fate
of the desert pupfish to that of an interstate highway, from soil erosion
to the sonic boom.

What was the spark that ignited the fusion and the political explosion? Who can say with any certainty? Some observers feel that a sudden
public understanding of limitations and threats was triggered by the
remarkable views of the lonely planet earth that were taken from outer
space in 1967 and 1968, and then widely displayed on TV and in the
press.

The major factor was the threat to public health, says Marvin Zeldin,
an environmental consultant. "The rivers running through the cities
were seething with foam and oil, and the air was dangerously polluted."

Many events doubtless contributed to the explosive force, and they seemed to cluster in 1969. Here is a compendium of some of the things that were going on that year:

First days of January. A barrage of letters to Congress protests the nomination of Walter J. Hickel to succeed Stewart L. Udall as Secretary of the Interior.

January 10. The federal government files suit against automobile manufacturers, charging an antitrust conspiracy to impede the development of pollution control equipment.

January 28. A blowout at a Union Oil Co. oil platform off Santa Barbara spews viscous crude oil over 13 miles of oceanfront beach and a marine sanctuary, killing many birds.

March 28. U.S. marshals seize 21,850 pounds of frozen coho salmon from warehouses in Wisconsin and Minnesota because of excessive DDT residues.

April 16. The Senate Interior Committee hears testimony on legislation that will evolve into the National Environmental Policy Act, passed by Congress in December.

April 28. Near San Rafael, California, 42 people are arrested when they physically try to block the clearing of trees for a Corps of Engineers flood-control project.

May 14. Federal officials meet with representatives of the Everglades Coalition to seek resolution of a dispute over a Miami jetport proposal threatening Everglades National Park.

June 6. A petroleum company consortium applies for a permit to construct a 789-mile oil pipeline from Prudhoe Bay to Valdez, Alaska.

June 9. A group of 24 organizations—representing conservationists, labor unions, consumers, women, and local government officials—forms a coalition called the Citizens' Crusade for Clean Water, seeking among other things $1 billion in appropriations for waste-treatment-plant grants to municipalities.

June 22. The Cuyahoga River in Cleveland, brimming with oil, sludge, and industrial wastes, catches fire.

June 30. The Minnesota Pollution Control Agency adopts water quality regulations that trigger a long legal battle over Reserve Mining Co.'s discharges of taconite tailings into Lake Superior.

July 23. The Sierra Club wins a preliminary court judgment against a Walt Disney resort development in Mineral King valley, California.

August. Inhabitants of smog-plagued Los Angeles are warned—again—not to play golf, jog, or do anything else outside that involves deep breathing.

September 23. President Richard Nixon says, "The SST is going to be built," and requests $662 million more for two test models.

October 13. The township of Ramapo, N.J., passes a zoning ordinance designed for strict control of land-use permits—thereby touching off a lengthy legal dispute and drawing attention to myriad local growth problems around the country.

One event—the infamous Santa Barbara oil spill—may well have been the single most galvanizing incident, the last straw, the final environmental provocation.

It was the kind of crisis to which the media and the public react most strongly, Caldwell notes. "It jolted a lot of people," says Gladwin Hill. "They asked, 'Who's minding the store?' "

By the time 1969 was over, the Environmental Revolution was in full swing. Its arrival was recognized and celebrated across the nation on Earth Day in April 1970. This served public notice that a substantial political force intended to fight hard for the values to which it was committed and against the dangers it perceived.

Essential Principles

The Environmental Revolution has been based on a rich assortment of essential principles. The following discussion of these principles should not be taken to imply (a) that environmentalists originated them (since many of them have deeper or wider roots); (b) that they are the exclusive property of environmentalists (since they are shared by countless other people and other reform movements); or (c) that environmentalists are more principled than anyone else (that depends on who's judging).

The ideological drive behind the Environmental Revolution comes from three overriding goals that it embraces:

1. The safety and good health of individuals, including their psychological and physical well-being as affected by the natural environment.

2. The long-range survival and welfare of society, including the life-supporting environment on which these depend.

3. The achievement of a richer and fuller life, including desirable environmental characteristics.

The principles of the revolution derive from these goals and from the techniques used to achieve them.

In brief, environmentalism is based in a fundamental way on feelings that stress the importance of nature and all its diverse parts. This importance is expressed variously in terms of necessity, respect, reverence, or love. Together they add up to a strong negation of the long-accepted cultural machismo by which nature is fair game to be denigrated or destroyed in the pursuit of other goals.

Sociology professor Richard L. Means sees nature as "part of a system of human organization, a changing condition that interacts with man and culture." Thus, says Means, justification of a "technological arrogance" toward nature is "basically an immoral act."[6]

Far from being king of the jungle, man in the view of many is simply an integrated part of nature. His wisest course is to live in harmony with it and accommodate to it—whether this means protecting whales or avoiding settlement in a floodplain.

Man, with his awesome power to change and destroy, also is obligated to maintain careful stewardship of nature. (Most diametrically opposed to the customary view of man's superiority is the concept of humanity as a cancer on the planet. Thus, historian William H. McNeill says, "It is not absurd to class the ecological role of humankind in its relationship to other life forms . . . as an acute epidemic disease"— upsetting the balance of nature just as disease upsets the natural balance within a host's body.[7])

The Environmental Revolution also is based on an ethic that is humanistic. It believes in the sanctity of life. "The recognition of sanctity," says Henryk Skolimowski, professor of philosophy at the University of Michigan, "appears to be a necessary prerequisite for the preservation of life worth living in the long run."[8] The expression of such an ethic can be seen in efforts to protect people from chemical poisons, to preserve neighborhoods, or to provide rewarding recreational opportunities.

For all its imperfections, the Environmental Revolution can be credited with a social conscience. It believes in equal rights to a decent environment. It advocates public access to beaches and other coastal areas. It opposes the imposition of "externalities" such as pollution on people who receive no offsetting benefits or compensation—pollution without representation.

Indeed, it has been a cardinal tenet of the Environmental Revolution that the public's resources—air, water, land, health, money—shall not be casually sacrificed to promote or subsidize private interests. The plant that spews sulfur dioxide into the air, or the operator who ravages the land in stripping coal from it, imposes externalities on the public that must be reckoned with. Such subsidies, too numerous to list, include federal cleanups of oil spills and hazardous wastes; dredging of waterways and construction of water projects for the benefit of a particular industry; research and development; and federal assistance to victims of pollution.

If a company pollutes the air, it is likely to be subsidized by the health and medical costs of the people outside who breathe the pollutants or of the workers inside who suffer occupational disease (to the extent controls are not required), and by the taxpayers (to the extent federal tax or other policies relieve the company of control costs).

The environmental ethic also insists on a corollary maxim: Thou shalt not impose unreasonable burdens on future generations of people who are not here to defend themselves. Thus, environmentalists are dubious of irreversible effects and Faustian bargains. Said playright Henrik Ibsen, "I hold that man is in the right who is most clearly in league with the future."

Environmentalists seek to avoid diminishing the resources of the earth or ruining the environment so as to leave our successors bereft. Being ecologically conscious, says Skolimowski, means "taking a judicious stock of the existing resources and advocating stringent measures so that they last longer."[9]

Also, we are leaving our descendants a vast legacy of environmental damage that needs to be repaired (polluting plants, polluted rivers, unreclaimed strip-mined lands), of resources that are overexploited and depleted (fossil fuels, ground water, forests), of structures that are wearing out (bridges, highways, railroads, dams, urban water systems), and of dangerous wastes that require safe and costly disposal (nuclear wastes, nuclear plants to be decommissioned, toxic chemical wastes).

Actually, as the list makes clear, *we* are one of those future generations, already burdened with the need for subsidies to deal with problems created by our predecessors. Samuel Johnson, who said, "The future is purchased by the present," must fret in his grave.

Roger Starr, a former housing official now on the editorial board of the *New York Times*, sums it up this way:

> The conservationist movement set the value of what it sought to achieve in human terms. Its members measured their plans by asking what is good for a man in the broadest and longest sense; what raises him from present poverty without condemning him to future need; what raises his spirit by bringing him into touch with natural harmony; what teaches natural economics by preserving the resources to make life fuller.[10]

In various ways and to various degrees, environmentalists are further associated with life-styles that seek to minimize materialistic values, reliance on technology, and the waste of resources. They stress self-reliance, individual freedom, diversity, and the values of natural species. In general, environmentalists have a different mind-set from those who put their faith primarily in industrial and technological growth. Of course, there are exceptions, and some hypocrisy.

Arguments and Techniques

Aside from its ideological principles, the Environmental Revolution has achieved considerable success because it has utilized a remarkable assortment of arguments and techniques to achieve its goals. These fall into four critical categories: (1) skepticism and challenge, (2) new conceptual thinking, (3) identification of alternatives, and (4) political action.

1. The skepticism and distrust have been pervasive. Indeed, author

and lecturer Paul Shepard has said, "The ideological status of ecology is that of a resistance movement,"[11] As Skolimowski put it, the ecology movement "is not about small tactical gains here and there, but about remaking the unjust, parasitic, overexploited and shrinking world."[12]

Environmentalists have challenged cherished beliefs and goals, methods of evaluation and decision making, and means of achieving goals. They have at the same time distrusted the custodians of science, technology, industry, and government. They have disputed the credibility of pollution-control cost estimates; the claims of job losses; the results of chemical testing; the safety of nuclear power plants; the forecasts of electricity needs; the benefits of dam construction; the value of big cars.

These challenges bring to mind the works of people like Descartes, Milton, and Spinosa who, in author Max Lerner's words, "Applied to everything, including the powerful institutions of state and religion, the shattering method of critical inquiry."[13]

Caldwell says that the environmental (and consumer) movements have drawn heavily on the middle class for leadership and membership:

> These middle class activists command informational and organizational skills that can be employed to challenge official explanations and alibis. Among the citizens groups are accountants, lawyers, teachers, business executives, farmers, scientists, and engineers. They are quite capable of dissecting agency budgets, of uncovering the fallacies of cost-benefit ratios, and of pointing out alternatives that government officials failed to explore. For these activists, public office holds no mystique; and they have no patience with the proposition that government knows best, that government must act as it does on information that the public cannot have.[14]

Environmentalists have sought to hold agencies and other decision makers to higher standards of analysis, planning, and assessment—insisting on more comprehensive and interdisciplinary environmental assessments, energy assessments, and technology assessments in particular.

(Of course, environmental assessments were institutionalized across-the-board by the impact statement and other requirements of the National Environmental Policy Act of 1969.)

The Environmental Revolution has involved even more basic challenges to existing institutions. For example, in 1965, the U.S. Court of Appeals for the Second Circuit, after noting that the Federal Power Commission had often claimed to be the representative of the public interest, said:

> This role does not permit it to act as an umpire blandly calling balls and strikes for adversaries appearing before it; the right of the public must receive active and affirmative protection at the hands of the Commission.[15]

It has been a major premise of the Environmental Revolution that conflicts-of-interest—such as those that exist within an agency that both promotes and regulates any activity—be eliminated. This was the essential rationale behind creation of the Environmental Protection Agency (which, among other things, took over pesticides regulation from the chemicals-oriented Agriculture Department) and the Nuclear Regulatory Commission (which took its regulatory functions from the old Atomic Energy Commission, known for its avid promotion of nuclear power).

2. It is impossible to overemphasize the extent to which revisionist scientific, economic, and philosophical thinking has propelled the Environmental Revolution to its considerable political success. One single overriding concept—elaborated in various ways—has been that of inherent, unavoidable *limits*. Limits to population growth, limits to nonrenewable resources, limits to ecosystem carrying capacity, perhaps limits to economic growth.

Though the concept of limits sometimes has been shrilly expressed and derided for its doomsday pessimism, it has greatly elevated the level of futuristic thought and planning. While basically simple, in its more sophisticated elaborations (such as in "The Tragedy of the Commons" and the similarly influential book *The Limits to Growth*[16]), it has brought greater insight into mankind's predicaments. The idea of limits—and the potential for extending them through technological and other innovations—remains at the heart of debates over energy, resource use, and other social issues.

It also has contributed to the development of many derivative concepts—zero population growth, conservation and husbandry of resources, energy efficiency and end-use analysis, ecosystem and species protection, land use consonant with carrying capacity, and restraints on the use of private property endowed with a special public interest. All of these have been important components of the Environmental Revolution.

Worthy of special note is the concept of the ecological carrying capacity of a region or a piece of land. Many factors may limit this capacity: food, or arable land; ground and surface water; air canopy; weather and climate; soil characteristics; energy resources; topography; living space; waste disposal space; materials availability; and ecosystem maintenance.

Before an absolute limit on carrying capacity is reached, such as a finite land or water supply, overloading may cause unsafe, unhealthy, or unpleasant conditions. One can think in terms of a maximum carrying capacity, associated only with a subsistence level of existence, or an optimum density. "An area must be considered overpopulated if it can only be supported by the rapid consumption of nonrenewable resources," say Paul and Anne Ehrlich, of Stanford University. "It must also be considered overpopulated if the activities of the population are leading to a steady deterioration of the environment."[17]

Regions vary greatly in their vulnerability to excessive loading. Some soils absorb less rainfall than others; some vegetation is more susceptible to air-pollution damage; an aquifer recharge area might be judged out-of-bounds to development because of water needs. Because of its topography and weather, a floodplain could be assigned a human carrying capacity of zero.

Neil H. Jacoby, a UCLA economist, said years ago that the Los Angeles basin's capacity to disperse pollutants is already "intolerably overloaded," and added:

> After the design capacity of any facility has been reached, amenities diminish exponentially with arithmetic increases in the load. For example, when a twenty-first person enters an elevator designed to hold 20 persons, everyone in the elevator suffers loss of comfort; and when a twenty-second person enters, the percentage loss of amenity is much greater than the 4.8% increase in the number of passengers.[18]

California's Environmental Quality Study Council once concluded that the "continuing concentration of population in the most heavily urbanized regions of the state, and increasing production, consumption, and waste generation rates have, on occasion, combined to deplete and cause deterioration of vital resources beyond the capacity of natural processes to restore them." So long as technical methods to restore quality levels are unavailable, the Council said, public health standards must conform to these regions' "natural carrying capacities." The Council recommended that the legislature authorize a study of the carrying capacities of both the South Coast Air Basin and the nine-county San Francisco Bay region and come up with proposals for regulatory control of those factors which threaten to exceed the natural carrying capacities, as well as "maximum permissible population figures for each region. . . ."[19]

Planner Ian McHarg has said that "uncontrolled growth is inevitably destructive" and showed how a detailed analysis of water, soil, vegetation, topography, drainage, and other characteristics reveals that "certain lands are unsuitable for urbanization and others are intrinsically suitable." Thus, his path-breaking book *Design With Nature*[20] was a sophisticated discussion of alternative land-use choices within the limits imposed by nature.[21]

Yet, Malcolm F. Baldwin, now of the Council on Environmental Quality, warned in 1974 that "carrying capacity is a very dangerous concept. It's the antithesis of nondegradation." It invites what has been called "accommodation planning," under which growth is assumed and the only question becomes how to assimilate it. A related problem is that such ecological analysis does not take account of social or economic factors that may be extremely important.

Another important ecological concept of the Environmental Revolution is the need for a thoroughly comprehensive, interdisciplinary analysis of an issue. It is based on the notion that, as biologist Barry Commoner puts it, "Everything is connected to everything else."[22] This concept is embodied in a classic definition of ecology by Samuel T. Dana, former dean of the University of Michigan's School of Natural Resources:

> Ecology is the science that deals with the relations between all of the elements in an environment—the ecosystem. It rests upon all of the biological and physical sciences—botany, zoology, chemistry, physics, geology, soil science, meteorology, etc., with their innumerable ramifications—and when man is a part of the environment, the social sciences are also involved. Its distinguishing characteristic is that it uses these sciences in their relations to each other to determine what happens in a given environment, under both natural and modified conditions, and why it happens. In comprehensiveness and complexity, it is unique.[23]

Jay W. Forrester, of the Massachusetts Institute of Technology, has noted one of the ominous aspects of the interconnectedness of things: "The dominant characteristic of society is that its physical, social, and economic aspects all begin to interact. Solving one problem simply shifts the pressures elsewhere."[24]

One of Commoner's other terse laws of ecology is: "There's no such thing as a free lunch." In its traditional economic sense, this law simply means that every lunch must be paid for, one way or another. In an ecological sense, it might mean that if you build a dam or cut down a forest, it isn't just benefits in flood control or timber production that result, but countervailing environmental costs as well. (To which one might add the Second Law of Thermodynamics, as put by economist Nicholas Georgescu-Roegen: "The ecological predicament is harsher . . . in entropic terms; for every lunch, we pay more than the lunch represents."[25])

Various economic concepts—advanced by a phalanx of iconoclastic economists such as S.V. Ciriacy-Wantrap, Kenneth E. Boulding, Nicholas Georgescu-Roegen, E.J. Mishan, Herman E. Daly, E.F. Schumacher, and Hazel Henderson—also have been used by environmentalists to justify their goals.

The emphasis on accounting for environmental externalities such as pollution and other "spillover" effects already has been noted. In this connection, environmentalists have insisted on a wide range of remedial measures—from "best available" pollution-control technology (and even "technology forcing" requirements for future improvement) to wildlife mitigation measures, and from strip-mined land reclamation to oil-spill cleanup liability.

Environmentalists have firmly disputed charges that environmental regulation dampens economic growth. "The truth is 180 degrees in the opposite direction," says Russell E. Train, former head of EPA and now president of the World Wildlife Fund–U.S.:

> There can be bad regulations, bad statutes, and mistakes made. But overall, what will impede economic activity is environmental contamination—not its control. If it were not for environmental programs, it would be impossible to sustain our present growth level, let alone plan for the future.[26]

Environmentalists also have pointed out that regulatory controls and other changes have created many thousands of new jobs and new businesses, including pollution-control equipment manufacturers, research firms, consultants, and solar energy companies. The environmental movement is "a creative force in the nation's economy," asserts Byron Kennard, chairman of Earth Day '80.

Still more basic has been the idea that traditional notions of economic "progress" are myopic, and that the Gross National Product fails to give a reasonable measure of social well-being. (For example, the GNP is increased by countless socially and environmentally undesirable activities, from selling Saturday night specials to disposing of toxic wastes illegally.)

Ronald G. Ridker, an economist with Resources for the Future, has put the debate over economic growth into this perspective:

> The relevant question is not whether to grow or not to grow, but how to channel and redirect economic output, and whatever increases in it come along, in ways that will make it better serve humanity's needs.[27]

A similar point has been made in a study by SRI International, which says:

> Only now are we learning the central weakness of the market system: the market has no inherent direction, no internal goal other than to satisfy the forces of supply and demand.[28]

Herman Daly has decried society's preoccupation with allocating resources to achieve "intermediate" ends and means—without clearly postulating anything in the way of an "Ultimate End."[29]

Environmentalists have opposed the typical reliance of decision makers on those economic analyses which skirt over or ignore environmental costs or benefits that defy quantification—such as the value of a wetland being filled, or a year of human health, or a day of white-water canoeing.

Another economic concept stressed by environmentalists runs contrary to the frequent assumption that private enterprise has an obvious interest in extending the life of the natural resources it exploits. Economists have pointed out that, on the contrary, it may be in the economic interest of entrepreneurs to overexploit a resource even to the point of extermination—if competition induces such behavior, or if the short-term profits can be invested elsewhere at a rate more favorable than the return on prolonged resource exploitation.[30]

In the context of concern for the sanctity of human life and health, both now and among future generations, the Environmental Revolution has promoted a set of principles that stress, to put it simply, caution in the face of unknowns. The unknown ecological effects of damaging natural systems have had high priority, as have the unknown health effects of chemical pollution.

The latter concern has been reflected in warnings about the long latency period of the effects of some chemicals; the possibility that no threshold level of exposure exists at which all injury is absent; the relevance of animal tests; and the potential for unanticipated synergistic effects.

It has been further reflected in efforts to shift the burden of proof to manufacturers of chemicals, and to require more testing, more record keeping, and more information on products and marketing activities. For example, the Toxic Substances Control Act of 1976[31] requires that the Environmental Protection Agency (EPA) be given at least 90 days advance notice before the manufacture of any new chemical substance.

The principle of caution, which is associated with prevention rather than post-injury redress, has been adopted in many governmental decisions. For example, back in 1972, in his decision to ban general usage of DDT, EPA Administrator William D. Ruckelshaus cited the evidence as a "warning to the prudent" and spoke of the "unknown and possibly forever undeterminable long-range effects of DDT in man and the environment."[32]

Federal appellate Judge J. Skelly Wright, in a 1976 decision upholding EPA's regulation of gasoline lead additives to protect public health, wrote:

> Questions involving the environment are particularly prone to uncertainty. Undoubtedly, certainty is the scientific ideal. . . . But certainty in the complexities of environmental medicine may be achievable only after the fact. . . . Where a statute is precautionary in nature, the evidence difficult to come by, uncertain, or conflicting because it is on the frontiers of scientific knowledge, the regulations designed to protect the public health, and the decision that of an expert administrator, we will not demand rigorous step-by-step proof of cause and effect.[33]

3. The environmental revolutionaries cannot be accused of seeking to break down existing ideologies and systems without offering alternatives. One of the strongest thrusts of the environmental cause has been its development and advocacy of alternatives to environmentally destructive products and activities. Indeed, a key provision of the National Environmental Policy Act requires federal agencies to furnish a "detailed statement of alternatives to the proposed action." Often, so-called "nonstructural" alternatives are preferred, such as keeping development out of a floodplain rather than building a dam.

Environmentalists have championed the substitution of materials that are less polluting, less toxic, less energy intensive, more abundant, more renewable, and more biodegradable. Barry Commoner, in particular, has clarified the drawbacks of synthetic materials and chemicals.[34]

Commoner and physicist Amory B. Lovins, among others, have analyzed an assortment of alternative energy strategies—including solar technologies, a more efficient matching of energy sources to end uses, and conservation techniques.[35]

Many scientists and others have touted biological control methods in place of pesticides; land disposal of sewage sludge instead of expensive treatment; recycling instead of waste disposal; and so forth.

So thoroughgoing has been the emphasis on alternatives that "alternative life-styles" have become an entrenched social force.

4. A relentless wave of citizen protests and interventions has swept the Environmental Revolution along its path. Direct action has involved raw, physical—but nonviolent—opposition to private and governmental actions.

Much emphasis has been put on access to information—through open meetings (of advisory committees, and, since 1973, even of congressional committees' legislative markup sessions), through the Freedom of Information Act, the Securities and Exchange Commission reporting requirements, citizen workshops, whistle-blowing, court "discovery" procedures, product labeling, and statutory requirements making it more difficult for industry to withhold information from workers or the public by claiming "trade secrets."

Another critical form of citizen action has been participation in the decision-making process, through the formation of coalitions and lobbying, participation in election campaigns and referenda, testimony at hearings, and litigation. Of particular importance in court battles have been the often successful efforts of environmental groups to gain "standing" to sue.

Environmentalists also have been instrumental in forcing agencies to hold public hearings that provide for genuine consideration of public views, rather than the perfunctory shams that so often have passed for hearings in the past.

A classic example—which happened to take place in the pivotal year of 1969—involved air pollution in Pittsburgh. The Pennsylvania Air Pollution Commission proposed ambient air quality standards under federal law and scheduled a public hearing for September 9. The commission proposed an annual average level for particulates of 100 micrograms per cubic meter of air—despite evidence that fatalities among people over 50 increased markedly when 80 micrograms was exceeded in the presence of sulfur dioxide.

Public outrage spread rapidly. Opponents drawn into a "breather's lobby" included unions, women's organizations, cancer and tuberculosis groups, politicians, scientists, doctors, college students, professors, and conservationists.

The commission's action was of national importance, because it made Pennsylvania the first state to challenge or ignore the federal air-quality criteria. Should it succeed in holding firm, other states might feel encouraged to set less stringent standards.

The September 9 hearing was scheduled for a small state government office, but more than 450 people showed up and shaken officials moved the meeting to a church auditorium. Fifty witnesses testified against the proposed standards. Although earlier air-pollution hearings had been dominated by industry, not a single industry representative testified at the all-day meeting.

Citizen pressure continued after the hearing, and on October 20 the commission recommended a particulate standard of 65 micrograms, far below the earlier recommendation of 100, and a sulfur dioxide standard lowered by about the same percentage.[36]

Environmentalists have insisted on getting involved in early planning before decisions become set in bureaucratic concrete. One result of this insistence, for example, was a regulation adopted early in 1969 by the Federal Highway Administration. The regulation required states to hold at least two public hearings on any major federally aided highway project. In addition to the traditional hearing *after* a corridor, or general route, had been picked, the regulation required a hearing *before* a state highway department committed itself to a corridor.[37]

Environmentalists have insisted further that they be fully informed of changes in proposals, that they be given adequate notice of all proposals and hearings, and that they be provided sufficient time to prepare testimony in opposition. In the fall of 1969, for example, The Conservation Foundation charged in a letter to the federal air pollution control agency that the public had been given inadequate notice of hearings and was therefore deprived of meaningful participation. "The very nature of complex criteria and standards makes it essential that the concerned public have adequate time in which to digest this material," it said.[38]

An EPA pamphlet has summarized the beneficial role of public participation under the existing system:

> Citizen organizations are uniquely qualified. They are independent of both government and industry. They can objectively evaluate the performance of both government and industry. They can focus public attention on what is and what is not being done. They articulate the public's desire for a better environment, they attract press attention which, in turn, helps nurture the climate of public opinion necessary for action. They have power. . . . With their healthy skepticism, organized citizen groups have already demonstrated their great capacity to prod and stir government and industry to action.[39]

Measures of Success

What have been the results of all this political activity, this Jeffersonian ferment? To what extent have environmentalists realized their multifarious goals?

A true revolution must be a successful one—one that can boast considerable breadth and depth of achievement. Therefore, it is pertinent to evaluate what the Environmental Revolution has accomplished, where it has failed, and what remains to be done. But in making any such assessment, several points should be kept in mind:

• Achievements have been made in the face of great obstacles— including many powerful and recalcitrant industrial polluters; a devotion to the freewheeling consumption of resources, especially energy and especially to satisfy the passion for cars; and an unyielding zeal for private property rights.

Other obstacles have been the scientific complexity of many environmental problems, the pressures to subjugate environmental goals on grounds they would worsen already difficult economic conditions, and the need to counter a "backlash" movement against environmentalism.

• Some achievements are not easily perceived or measured. Many projects opposed by environmentalists have been approved—but only after design alterations or relocations to minimize environmental damage. And it is well known that many aspects of environmental quality cannot be quantified in any helpful way.

• Achievements should be evaluated in the context of what the situation would be without the pressures of the Environmental Revolution. Pollution controls may not have succeeded in eliminating all sulfur dioxide from the air, but how much worse would it be without controls? What kind of Alaska oil pipeline would have been built without environmental warnings? Or how much worse would the dangers of nuclear plant accidents and radiation be if environmentalists and others had not consistently demanded engineering and regulatory improvements over the years?

The great overall achievement of the Environmental Revolution lies in the general alarm it has sounded and the subsequent transformation of public thought and political activity to encompass a whole system of environmental values and goals. The evidence of this is everywhere. It is substantiated by public opinion polls that consistently show a high level of concern for environmental quality. These values and goals have seeped into all the crevices of government. They have become so embedded in public thought that often they are taken for granted. As Gladwin Hill puts it, "The enthusiasms of Earth Day 1970 have been 'institutionalized' in legislation, regulation, litigation, political dynamics and new personal values, and woven into the fabric of national life."[40]

One important manifestation of this new consciousness was the boom in membership of some traditional environmental organizations and the creation of countless new groups all over the country—local grass-root citizen organizations, public interest law firms, nonprofit foundations, lobbying groups, and coalitions.

In addition to alerting the public to various threats and advocating new goals, environmentalists helped draft and enact the legislation needed to achieve these goals, and then worked to develop the criteria and regulations necessary to implement the legislation.

In this respect, the Environmental Revolution can be said to have succeeded dramatically. The many new laws and regulations may not be worded just the way environmentalists would choose. But, as William K. Reilly, president of The Conservation Foundation, says:

> Every one of the major national environmental legislative objectives has been achieved, with one exception. We did not get a national land-use policy act. But we did get a Coastal Zone Management Act for one portion—in fact, the most heavily settled portion of the United States. That's an enormous accomplishment, that list of legislative victories.[41]

Beyond federal legislation, myriad state and local laws have been enacted, presidential Executive Orders have been issued, government agencies have been established and reorganized, appropriations for environmental programs have been boosted. Also noteworthy is the proliferation of research, monitoring, and education programs, including a tremendous increase in the number of environmental courses offered at all school levels.

Following is a more specific discussion of the Environmental Revolution's achievements in various fields, combined with comments (in italics) on unfinished business and the key issues that must be faced in the next decade. In addition to the referenced sources, the data were derived from a number of government reports, most notably *Environ-*

mental Conditions and Trends, a forthcoming Council on Environmental Quality (CEQ) study and *Environmental Statistics 1978*, also a CEQ report, issued in March 1979. Both contain plentiful valuable statistics and were compiled under the direction of Daniel Tunstall, a consultant to CEQ who says, "It's important to show that all the laws, and the money, and the haranguing have resulted in some positive achievements."

Air Pollution

The main thrust in the battle against air pollution has been passage of the Clean Air Act and a succession of amendments. Implementation has been extraordinarily difficult, involving as it has a wide range of technological, scientific, economic, and political problems linked to catalytic converters, scrubbers, auto inspection and maintenance programs, urban-transportation control plans, general high costs of controls, and the like.

In general terms, air quality in major metropolitan areas around the nation is improving, although many problem cities remain. According to the forthcoming CEQ study, between 1974 and 1977 there was a 17 percent drop in the average number of days in 25 metropolitan areas during which the air was unhealthful, very unhealthful, or hazardous. (The average declined from 87 to 72 days as measured by the Pollutant Standards Index, a health-related index that summarizes five major pollutants.) "More significantly," says the study, "the severity of pollution has declined. The number of days (when the air was very unhealthful of hazardous) decreased by 35 percent."

Of course, there is wide variation among areas and among pollutants. But on an overall national basis, between 1972 and 1977-78 the levels of sulfur dioxide are roughly estimated to have decreased 17 percent, with particulates down 8 percent, and carbon monoxide down 35 percent. On the other hand, nitrogen oxide pollution, while not as well monitored, is believed to have increased significantly. (Weather variations may distort trend measurements.)

By another measure, the CEQ study indicates that the amount of pollution from the average individual automobile has been reduced significantly, as the table shows:

Emissions in Grams per Mile

	All Autos			New Autos		
	Hydro-carbons	Carbon Monoxide	Nitrogen Oxides	Hydro-carbons	Carbon Monoxide	Nitrogen Oxides
1970	10.6	74.4	3.9	4.1	34	3.5
1978	6.4	55.6	3.0	1.5	15	2.0

The overall air pollution control achievements are notable, especially in the face of increased automobile ownership and travel, slow auto-fleet turnover, and increased combustion of coal by utilities. "As a holding action," says David Hawkins, an assistant administrator of EPA, "you could say [the Clean Air Act] has been successful. There are more cars and more industry, but the problem is not appreciably worse."[42]

Many problems remain for the 1980's, especially with the prospects of continued extensive driving, increased coal combustion, and new industries. The problems include: application of scrubber technologies (to control SO₂ from power plants); finding new industry sites under the controversial "offsets" policy or other techniques; protection of clean-air regions through regulations for the Prevention of Significant Deterioration; implementation of effective transportation control plans and auto inspection and maintenance programs; and research and regulation of various pollutants not well understood or controlled. There remains, in fact, a shortfall of good research on many pollutants (including the subtle effects of sulfates, acid rain, diesel exhausts, and the like on human health, plants, and wildlife), on unanticipated effects of interacting pollutants, and on chemical changes in the atmosphere.

Originally, it was planned to establish health criteria and then set national ambient air quality standards for three dozen pollutants—but only seven are now so regulated. (They are carbon monoxide, hydrocarbons, sulfur dioxide, suspended particulates, nitrogen dioxide, photochemical oxidants, and lead.) Some other hazardous pollutants are subject to control under national emission standards. But still others are essentially unregulated and await action. These "noncriteria" pollutants include sulfates, nitrates, trace metals, asbestos, and benzene. Of special concern are fine particulates, difficult to control and very hazardous to humans.[43]

The CEQ study points to another issue for the coming years: "There is growing evidence that the vast wilderness areas of the United States could be threatened with air pollution as people move to the South and West and industry and power plants locate away from major cities."

Water Pollution

Environmentalists helped ensure passage of the Federal Water Pollution Control Act, Clean Water Act, and Safe Drinking Water Act. Achievements under all three have been significant. Of course, much further progress is needed to achieve by 1983 a level of water quality compatible with fish, wildlife, and recreational uses and to eliminate the discharge of toxic substances in dangerous amounts.

Another major achievement of the environmentalists was the role they played in obtaining large appropriations from Congress for funding municipal waste treatment plants—for which the payoffs will be increasingly noticeable in coming years. As of March 1979, 5,276 out of 15,858 federally aided treatment plant projects had been completed, with the rest in progress. "As those plants come on line," says EPA Administrator Douglas M. Costle, "we will start to see a dramatic acceleration in the rate of clean-up."[44]

In dozens of specific cases, special efforts have turned or are turning once dirty rivers or lakes into environmental assets. These include Lake Washington, the Willamette River, the Red River, and many lesser-known waters. (Of course, there also have been major setbacks, such as Kepone contamination of the James River in Virginia.)

Various reports show improvement in water quality of the Great Lakes—targets of intensive pollution-control activity—although the picture is mixed. G. Keith Rogers, a scientist at the Canada Center for Inland Waters, says that, previously, people were asking, "How can we stop the lakes from getting worse?" Now, he says, "We are seriously talking about rehabilitating the lakes to their original state."[45]

Conditions around the country's lakes and streams vary enormously, but the CEQ study provides a general picture of the nationwide situation. In 1978, for example, 38 percent of monitored samples contained higher levels of fecal coliform bacteria (an indicator that infectious microorganisms may be present) than is recommended for swimming. The results were about the same as those in 1975.

On average in 1978, 6 percent of all samples violated levels for dissolved oxygen (a measure of quality for aquatic life), a figure a bit greater than 1975. Of 326 waterway units tested, 73 reported violations, but only 10 of these more than 20 percent of the time.

The 1978 annual average violation rate for phosphorus (excessive amounts of which cause eutrophication) was 47 percent—about the same as three years before. Between 1966 and 1977, phosphorus violations declined by 20 percent or more in nine of the 11 large rivers for which adequate information is available.

There also has been a general decline in the amounts of DDT, dieldrin, chlordane, and other pesticides in water samples.

An agenda for the '80's includes a number of problems that so far have defied solution. Of particular note are the "nonpoint" sources of water pollution such as animal feedlots, pesticides, fertilizers, soil erosion, mining, construction, detergents, urban runoff, and other ubiquitous contributors. These are chiefly responsible for high levels of phosphorus in many streams in the central regions of the country.

Among the pending issues are: What kinds of nonpoint source controls are available (whether they involve management and planning, regulation, technology, or economic disincentives)? Which are economically feasible? What political or institutional barriers block their implementation?

Other major problems are toxic substances in water, especially toxic metals, and preventing eutrophication of lakes (over 85 percent of U.S. lakes showed accelerated eutrophication in 1975).

Toxic Chemicals

The Environmental Revolution has helped spur research and disseminate warnings about many toxic substances suspected of causing cancer, birth deformities, and genetic changes. It has helped alert the public to a variety of dangers in the outdoors environment, the home, and the workplace. It lobbied for passage of the Toxic Substances Control Act of 1976, which requires pre-market testing of chemicals, and has supported control of workplace hazards through vigilant implementation of the Occupational Safety and Health Act.

But the production and use of chemicals continues at a fast pace, and it seems that while environmentalists work for bans or controls on some products (such as PCB's, asbestos, vinyl chloride, acrilonitrile, and benzene), this usually takes place after considerable damage has been done. Nor does it prevent the marketing of other dangerous formulations.

A host of difficulties still blocks effective implementation of the Toxic Substances Control Act. These difficulties involve the running problems of "trade secrets" and obtaining critical safety information from companies for the benefit of regulators and the public; of determining appropriate testing priorities and procedures; of developing techniques for risk and benefit assessment and determining what risks are acceptable to society; of devising ways to alleviate special burdens on small businesses and companies that must compete in export markets; and of developing and disseminating better scientific information on the health effects of chemicals, especially those related to low-level exposures and chronic effects.

Finally, and most fundamentally, environmentalists in the next decade could perhaps do much to induce the adoption of substitutes for the harmful chemicals and products that permeate the environment and endanger public health.

Pesticides

Environmentalists have supported enforcement of and amendments to the Federal Insecticide, Fungicide and Rodenticide Act. They succeeded in prying pesticides regulation away from the Department of Agriculture and placing it in the new Environmental Protection Agency. And they have successfully promoted a shift from the most persistent pesticides (such as chlorinated hydrocarbons) to those which break down more rapidly in the environment (organophosphates), although the latter may be more hazardous to workers and often kill wildlife unless handled carefully. Bans or severe restrictions have been imposed on DDT, aldrin, dieldrin, 2,4,5,-T, heptachlor, chlordane, Mirex, thallium sulfate, and organic mercury compounds.

It probably is still too early to assess the results in most cases, but the earliest prohibitions, on DDT and dieldrin, appear to have had significant effects. For example, Frederick W. Kutz, chief of the field studies branch of EPA's Office of Pesticides and Toxic Substances, reports that in 1971 the mean level of total DDT equivalent (including the breakdown product DDE) in human adipose tissue was 8.14 parts per million, whereas by 1977 this had dropped to only 3.25 parts per million. Similarly, says Kutz, in the same period the level of dieldrin in adipose tissue declined by about 50 percent. And where some 85 percent of air samples used to contain dieldrin, it is now unusual to find any.

Various other studies have shown reductions in DDT levels in mothers' milk, fish, birds, and soils. There also is evidence of more healthy populations of birds previously decimated because pesticide contamination made their egg shells too thin—brown pelicans, bald eagles, ospreys, and peregrine falcons.

Among the notable disappointments of the environmental movement so far has been the limited acceptance of nonchemical means of dealing with weeds and pests—the biological techniques used in "integrated pest management." There has been considerable scientific research in the field, and much publicity about successful tests, but the forces of tradition and the industrial profit motive have been major obstacles.

Meanwhile, the production of pesticides in the United States remains at a high level—though it has leveled off. Production almost doubled from 877 million pounds in 1965 to nearly 1.6 billion pounds in 1975, but by 1977 it had declined to below 1.4 billion. The herbicides component of the total jumped from 263 million pounds in 1965 to 788 million pounds in 1975, but two years later was down to 674 million. Closely related to production is another pending question: What exports should be permitted and under what conditions?

Also to be resolved is the dioxin issue (dioxin is a highly toxic contaminant in the herbicide 2,4,5,-T and was present in the defoliant Agent Orange used in Vietnam). EPA and the Veterans Administration have taken only limited action in the face of mounting claims of dioxin-

caused illness among veterans and people exposed during forest spraying operations.

Energy

Congress has passed a mishmash of energy legislation, though most people say not enough to deal adequately with the overall problem.

In any case, on the supply front, environmentalists can take credit for much of the new government enthusiasm—reflected in laws and appropriations—for energy conservation (including mandated fuel efficiency for cars, tax credits for buildings, and a standby gasoline rationing program), and for the development of solar and other renewable sources (tax credits, boosts in funding for research and development, information programs, etc.). Principally due to higher energy prices, industry already has conserved a great deal of energy.

On the environmental protection front, the Environmental Revolution has raised official concern about a variety of threats from energy production—nuclear radiation, safeguards, and waste management; coal strip-mining; water consumption; and oil spills (as well as air and water pollution). This concern has led to passage of the Nuclear Non-Proliferation Act, the Surface Mine and Reclamation Act, revisions of the Oil Pollution Act, and the Ports and Waterways Safety Act.

Other achievements include a more judicious oil and gas-leasing program and a more hard-boiled regulatory system for nuclear power activities. As it happens, nuclear-power plant construction is bogged down throughout the country. In mid-1975, 244 nuclear plants were built, being built, or planned. By mid-1979, the figure was down to 195. Most cancellations, however, were due to reduced demand for electricity and to financial constrictions.[46]

There have been failures, too, and they must be added to the long and difficult energy-environment agenda of the next decade. These are the most unsettling problems:

• Formidable obstacles—including political disruptions in the Middle East—have hindered effective implementation of the nuclear non-proliferation law.

• Congress, the states, and others must continue to wrestle with the critical problem of nuclear waste disposal, which won't go away.

• Environmentalists must seek ways to rescue the strip-mining control law and the regulations to implement it, which are under assault from every conceivable direction.

• Environmentalists must carefully monitor programs for "synfuels" development, which is fraught with environmental consequence. At the same time, they will have to deal with the proposed Energy Mobilization Board designed to speed up approval of priority energy projects.

  • *For years, Congress has fiddled with legislation to provide for effective liability and compensation for oil spills. A task for the coming years is passage of a strong law, coupled with effective enforcement. Also important is careful assessment of offshore oil development proposals and careful control of operations. The Bay of Campeche oil leak in Mexico was another dramatic reminder of what the consequences can be of failing to deal adequately with the problem.*

  • *Environmentalists and others must decide what to do about the threat of climate change due to the atmospheric accumulation of carbon dioxide from fossil fuel combustion.*

  • *Environmentalists must continue to help refine the system of grants, tax credits, loans, research and development programs, regulatory measures, and other strategies used to boost the contributions of energy conservation and solar, gasohol, geothermal, wood, wind, wave, and other renewable forms of energy. The proposal for a costly solar satellite also will undergo further analysis.*

Natural Areas Protection

Perhaps the greatest and most tangible accomplishment of the Environmental Revolution has been the accelerated protection of countless valuable land areas of every conceivable character. It would be impossible to state the full measure of this achievement, which includes everything from creation of the majestic Redwoods National Park to the installation of a "vest-pocket" park in New York City. Accompanying the drive for land protection has been an enormous increase in visits to parks and the public's blossoming participation in all sorts of outdoor activities.

Three types of natural areas have been of prime interest to environmentalists (with some overlapping):

1. *Scenic and recreational.* This includes the park, forest, and wilderness areas, wild and scenic rivers, shorelines and coastal zones, and historic sites.

2. *Ecologically critical.* Broadly defined, this category comprises prime agricultural lands, floodplains, estuaries, marine sanctuaries, barrier islands, wetlands, wildlife refuges, and endangered species habitats—all those areas that support natural life, including that making up the human food chain.

3. *Socially critical.* These are the human settlements and neighborhoods, the natural habitats of people.

There also are three general ways to protect such natural areas: (1) by acquisition, (2) by regulation and management, and (3) by preventing specific intrusions.

Within this framework, consider some of the Environmental Revolution's many major achievements:

Acquisition. Appropriations from the Land and Water Conservation Fund, which are used to acquire park lands, have increased sharply over the years—from $146 million in fiscal 1969 to $737 million in 1979. Between 1960 and 1978, the total acreage of federal and state parks jumped from 25 million acres to more than 75 million. By 1978, the National Park System included 88 natural areas, 53 recreational areas, and 181 historical areas.

Of particular interest—since 1980 was proclaimed the Year of the Coast—is the fact that many large national seashores and lakeshores have been established to protect highly valued coastal areas. They include park and recreation areas around New York City, San Francisco, Cape Cod, Assateague Island, Cape Hatteras, Cumberland Island, Gulf Islands, Padre Island, Cape Lookout, Apostle Islands, Pictured Rocks, Sleeping Bear Dunes, Indiana Dunes, Fire Island, and Point Reyes.

Also, there has been increased emphasis on urban parks and recreation, with Congress in 1978 setting up a special fund for them and voting $125 million in appropriations for fiscal 1980.

Stretches of 25 rivers, totaling 2,317 miles, have been designated part of the National Wild and Scenic Rivers System.

And by February 1979, there were 19.3 million acres of wilderness in 190 federally designated areas, with many millions of additional acres proposed, most notably 15.4 million acres recommended by the Carter Administration in 1979, including 5.5 million in Alaska.

Acquisitions also have focused on wildlife refuges and wetlands. Federal, state, and local government acquisitions have been supplemented by those of private organizations (the Nature Conservancy, Trust for Public Land, National Wildlife Federation, and National Audubon Society, for example).

One of the goals in the '80's will be establishment of new parks and ensuring an adequate flow of money to buy up those already authorized.

Environmentalists also will seek additional wilderness and river designations; a final resolution of the long and bitter dispute over how much of Alaska's incredible magnificence to protect; and the further use of mixed public and private ownership strategies such as those being tried in the New Jersey Pine Barrens area and California's Santa Monica Mountains.

Regulation. Many types of areas have been safeguarded by regulation. Wetlands can be protected against dredging and filling by the permit system under Section 404 of the Clean Water Act of 1977 and by the provisions of an Executive Order in May 1977. After an enormous loss of marshlands around San Francisco Bay, due to diking and filling, environmentalists forced area governments to set up a regulation and management system that brought these losses to a virtual halt.[47]

As a result of such measures, the widespread destruction of the nation's wetlands—the original total of 127 million acres in the lower 48 states has declined to roughly 70 million acres—undoubtedly has been checked to some extent.[48]

Coastal areas may be protected under the Coastal Zone Management Act of 1972, which set up a federal-state scheme designed to save critical areas from development. Several laws and an Executive Order, also in May 1977, are designed to close floodplains to dangerous and costly development. Marine sanctuaries can be designated under the Marine Protection, Research and Sanctuaries Act of 1972, and estuarine sanctuaries under the Coastal Zone Management Act. The "critical habitats" of endangered species can be protected under the Endangered Species Act of 1973.

Many states also have enacted land-use laws aimed at protecting scenic and ecologically important areas. Noteworthy examples are Oregon, Florida, Vermont, and Hawaii.

Many of the problems involved in protecting natural areas in the next decade stem from slow or ineffective implementation of existing laws, such as those covering floodplains, endangered species habitats, and marine and estuarine sanctuaries. Wetland destruction continues at an undesirable rate. Some states have been less than enthusiastic about coastal zone management programs, and coastal areas often are threatened by the impacts of energy as well as residential and other development.

Another major unresolved issue concerns what techniques or policies can and should be used to stem the loss of agricultural lands. "The national loss of prime farmland is currently estimated at about one million acres per year, a little over four square miles per day," says CEQ.[49] Most losses are due to urbanization and water projects.

Also on the agenda are land policies to prevent the revival of rural growth from gobbling up sensitive areas, and further consideration of various issues related to management of the nation's vast public lands, principally those of the Forest Service and the Bureau of Land Management. Does the "multiple-use" concept, as currently interpreted, provide the fairest system for allocating and managing forests and rangelands for often conflicting purposes—outdoor recreation, wilderness, grazing, logging, mining, watershed protection, and fish and wildlife conservation? As William E. Shands, a senior associate with The Conservation Foundation puts it, the allocation of national forest land uses "must be based on a careful assessment of land capabilities, natural characteristics, user demand, and opportunities elsewhere."[50]

Other issues are the amount of logging that should be permitted each year in particular forest locations and the proper harvesting techniques to be used.

Finally, of special interest to environmentalists are the types of control to be imposed on Alaska's vast and varied public lands.

Prevention of Intrusion. Environmentalists have specialized in the prevention of intrusions of every kind on natural areas. These intrusions include not only air pollution, water pollution, noise, hazardous chemicals, and solid wastes, but also the more physical intrusions of highways, dams, airports, industries, residential developments, energy facilities, power lines, and offroad vehicles. In many cases, projects have been stopped cold. In others, they have been stopped temporarily or redesigned to lessen the adverse impacts.

Among the major dams scuttled because of pressures to preserve scenic rivers and farmland have been Tocks Island, Salem Church, New River, Hell's Canyon, Red River Gorge, Spewrell Bluff, and Allerton Park. Also blocked was the Cross-Florida Barge Canal.

Of course, the list of projects that have plowed ahead despite adamant opposition is far longer. With help from the customary pork-barrel politics and economic sleight-of-hand, construction has continued on the Tennessee-Tombigbee Waterway, the Central Arizona Project, Tellico Dam, Garrison Diversion Project, and a host of others.

Energy facilities blocked by environmentalists include the Storm King pumped-storage power plant on the Hudson River, the Kaiparowits power plant in Utah, which would have degraded air quality in the region of many national parks, and a deep-water port and oil refinery on the coast of Maine. Environmental pressure also led to more careful design and construction of the trans-Alaska oil pipeline.

A number of interstate highway projects have succumbed to similar opposition because they would ruin urban neighborhoods or parks. The list includes Three Sisters Bridge (Washington, D.C.), Vieux Carre (New Orleans), Overton Park (Memphis), and the Crosstown Expressway (Chicago).

The environmental movement was instrumental in achieving passage of legislation requiring careful attention to environmental impact in planning highways. And it has partial success in diverting some Highway Trust Fund appropriations to other purposes such as mass transit and bicycle lanes. More generally, environmentalists have with some success challenged the validity of the total automotive life-style.

Environmental groups nixed plans for a huge airport in Big Cypress Swamp, six miles north of Everglades National Park. An Interior Department study said the airport "will inexorably destroy the south Florida ecosystem and thus [the park]."[51] A new runway for Kennedy International Airport was cancelled when opponents, concerned about destruction of valuable wetlands in Jamaica Bay, showed it was not necessary.[52]

Among the major achievements in the field of noise were halting the development of the commercial SST with its sonic boom threat and passage of the Noise Control Act of 1972 and Quiet Communities Act of 1978. Also, many airports have imposed curfews to alleviate neighborhood noise problems. And between 1972 and 1977, EPA reports, the number of municipalities with some type of noise ordinance increased from 59 to 1,607.[53]

In the 1980's, environmentalists will need to continue opposing dams, waterways, highways, airports, and energy facilities that threaten natural areas to an unnecessary or unacceptable degree. This will involve further attempts to reform water policies in ways suggested by the Carter Administration—with the intent of producing more honest economic appraisals of projects and increasing the adoption of nonstructural solutions to water problems. Such reforms have been vehemently resisted by Congress.

In the urban environment, important items still on the agenda are programs for neighborhood and historic preservation, increased open space and recreation, better forms of urban transportation, and more effective noise control. So far, only sluggish progress has been made in suppressing the noise of existing aircraft, machinery, appliances, and the like.

Wildlife Protection

Most of the Environmental Revolution's efforts on behalf of wildlife are well known and have helped sensitize the world public to the values of threatened species. The unrelenting international campaign to save whales can claim substantial success, as the International Whaling Commission has gradually scaled down allowable catches of these remarkable creatures.

Other efforts have been directed at preserving African, Asian, and South American wildlife through a series of international treaties to restrict hunting and trade involving endangered species.

On the domestic side, environmentalists have joined the fight for survival of such species as the whooping crane, California condor, grizzly bear, dolphin, and alligator. They helped enact the Endangered Species Act of 1973 and the Marine Mammal Protection Act of 1972, among other laws. As of mid-1979, the Fish and Wildlife Service listed 200 plant and animal species as endangered and another 39 as threatened. Many hundreds of others await needed designation.

Advances have come laboriously, and in the next decade much protection work remains to be done for both international and domestic species. The Endangered Species Act was weakened by Congress, and there is considerable opposition to effective implementation. Interna-

*tional traders and poachers continue to flout the law, thereby jeopardiz-
ing many populations of exotic species. Deforestation and other ecologically destructive activities threaten thousands of plants of possibly
unique value. Thus are the challenges ahead defined.*

*"The whales, the rhinos, the tigers, the elephants, these are the visible
tip of the iceberg," says Russell Train. "But what we're really talking
about is the biological impoverishment of this planet."*[54]

Water Resources

With their emphasis on resource limits, environmentalists have helped
alert the public and its representatives to the demands for water on
behalf of recreation, fish and wildlife, agriculture, and energy production—demands that often are in conflict.

Of 106 designated water regions in the United States, 16 are considered in an average year to have inadequate water to support instream
uses such as navigation, hydropower, recreation, fish, and wildlife. In
some areas of the South and West, ground-water aquifers are seriously
depleted or are rapidly becoming so.

*Among the major policy issues ahead are finding ways to allocate
water among farmers, energy producers, governments, environmental
interests, and Indian reservations, which have strong legal claims. More
basically, in some areas of water scarcity, it is a question of developing
better techniques of conservation and recycling, or of limiting some
kinds of growth.*

Waste Disposal

Environmentalists helped achieve passage of the Solid Waste Disposal
Act and then the Resource Conservation and Recovery Act of 1976.

There is evidence of some improvement in the more serious problems
of dealing with municipal solid waste—through better landfill siting
and management, better control of leaching, improved incineration,
and gradual restrictions on ocean dumping. There have been significant increases in the percentage of ferrous scrap metal and aluminum
recycled since 1971. However, the percentage of all municipal waste
recycled has remained quite constant; in 1976, it was 6.4 percent. Also
quite stable is the total amount of municipal waste discarded, which
was 144.7 million tons in 1976. (This includes municipal and commercial waste, such as sludge, building demolition residues, discarded
autos, and street sweepings.)

*But we have barely scratched the surface of the nation's potential for
materials conservation and recycling, which leaves a great task for the
next decade. Success in enacting "bottle bills" has been limited. Another
major activity will involve finding ways to burn more wastes for energy*

THE ENVIRONMENTAL REVOLUTION

production. Finally, and most importantly, is the newly recognized dilemma posed by hazardous waste sites of the past and future.

One key task is implementation of a regulatory scheme for hazardous waste disposal, as called for by the Resource Conservation and Recovery Act. The law was designed to eliminate "the last remaining loophole in environmental law"—the unregulated land disposal of wastes, particularly hazardous wastes.[55]

Also unanswered are some critical questions arising from hazardous waste damage to human health and the environment. How do you establish proof and liability for leakage from closed dump sites? What kinds of fees or taxes should be imposed on industries or chemical feedstocks to pay for past and future damage? Is the government obligated to help compensate victims, and under what circumstances?

These issues are now being debated in Congress, where the Carter Administration has proposed a $1.6 billion "superfund" to finance clean-up or containment of hazardous wastes as well as oil spills. In addition to a federal contribution, the fund would be financed by fees imposed on industries that use the kinds of chemical and petroleum feedstocks that typically cause the damage.

Meanwhile, the courts are busy with many government and private lawsuits for damages in cases such as the Love Canal disaster in Niagara Falls, N.Y.

These issues all have thorns, and industry has vehemently opposed most efforts to hold companies legally and financially responsible. The size of the problem is enormous: There are some 30,000 hazardous waste sites around the country, and a nationwide cleanup program could cost as much as $50 billion, according to Barbara Blum, deputy administrator of EPA.[56]

Population Growth

The environmental movement has played an important auxiliary role in the remarkable achievement of dramatically slowing population growth in the United States. In 1978, the growth rate was about 0.8 percent. Women in the United States now have 1.8 children on average, whereas in the late 1950's the figure was 3.6. If current trends continue, this country could reach zero population growth by the year 2025. Major factors in this momentous social change have been invention of the pill, greater education of women, and increased affluence.

There also are welcome signs that control programs and other factors are finally having an impact on global population growth, though overpopulation remains one of the world's most horrendous problems.

For the 1980's, continuing vigorous efforts on behalf of both birth-control and economic-development programs are imperative. In addi-

tion, the United States needs to work out a fair and coherent policy on refugees, particularly for the large number of illegal immigrants from Mexico.

Land Use

The Environmental Revolution has sharpened the public's awareness of the value of land and the urgency of using land in the wisest ways. At the local community level, this has led to greater attention to planning, zoning, growth controls, and other management techniques. The efforts of such cities as Ramapo, Boulder, and Petaluma to deal with growth problems have been of great interest, as have the dozens of court cases highlighting conflicts between real-estate developers, residents bent on preserving their own environmental values, and civil rights and other groups seeking better housing opportunities.

The conflicts are certain to continue into the foreseeable future because, as one observer puts it:

> So far, the legal battle has produced no clear winner. The various federal and state court decisions have left those on both sides of the issue somewhat confused as to the state of the law. Perhaps the only indisputable fact is that little housing for low- and moderate-income persons has been built as a direct result of the suits.[57]

A related issue—at a time of high energy and housing costs—is the need to develop new settlement patterns and possibly new policies to cope with the burning desire of so many people to live in single-family dwellings. "I believe we're going to see more than 40 million people enter the housing market in the 1980's," says Conservation Foundation President William K. Reilly:

> We will see, I think, 42 million people turn 30. That's 10 million more than turned 30 in the 1970's and 20 million more than in the 1960's. Thirty is the age at which Americans typically invest in a home.
>
> It's difficult to see how we can accommodate that. It does seem to me that it would put a heavy strain on many localities that receive these new people. Many of these localities are not prepared, psychologically or financially, for the growth that they are going to experience. There will be a need for a great deal of attention to problems of accommodating growth in environmentally sound ways.[58]

There has been a substantial migration to rural areas in recent years. The change in population patterns is shown by figures from Calvin Beale, an analyst with the Department of Agriculture:

	Average annual percentage rate of population growth, U.S.	
	1950-1960	1970-1978
Metropolitan counties	2.3	0.7
Nonmetropolitan counties	0.3	1.2

Communities in rural areas will face increasingly difficult land-use decisions of interest to environmentalists.

Ways and Means

The Environmental Revolution has taken advantage of a great variety of techniques and organizations to produce results. As already noted, there has been aggressive public participation and litigation. Also important was creation and vigorous use of the National Environmental Policy Act (NEPA), with its requirements that federal agencies evaluate adverse environmental impacts of projects and assess alternatives. (Many states have passed their own versions of NEPA.)

Environmentalists also succeeded in establishing important federal government agencies such as the Environmental Protection Agency, the Council on Environmental Quality, many state counterparts, and the United Nations Environment Programme.

In the coming years, environmentalists will need to advance the effectiveness of NEPA—by seeing that it induces better substantive decisions rather than just better procedures, by keeping Congress from mandating exemptions as it already has done a number of times, and by extending the reach of NEPA to more international activities.

Evidently, it also will be necessary to muster opposition to efforts in Congress and elsewhere to trim the sails of regulatory agencies that have mandates to protect public health and the environment. Regulatory "reform" is in the wind—including proposals to give Congress legislative veto power over regulatory decisions traditionally left to administrative agencies such as EPA.[59]

In the debates over regulation, the parties will continue to grapple with some fundamental sociopolitical questions: Should economic values be placed on human life and health? If so, how should the value be determined? And by whom?

Finally, the environmental movement faces a web of fundamental problems that have the potential of eroding its effectiveness, in spite of the general support of public opinion and the general health of environmental organizations. A diminishing interest in social causes has been noted in colleges. Public-interest law firms as well as environmental groups are having greater difficulty getting financial support from foundations, while at the same time the number of opposing industry-oriented groups has been increasing.

The Writing on the Wall

What do the coming years look like for the Environmental Revolution? Will it be able to retain its political momentum and clout in a world beset by a swarm of depressing problems? Can it avoid being overwhelmed by international chaos (as represented by recent events in Afghanistan, Iran, elsewhere in the Middle East, and Cambodia), by the pressures of economic distress, by energy scarcities and skyrocketing costs, and by national security imperatives?

Ecologist Kenneth E.F. Watt has quipped, "The future is not what it used to be." One can see from the past decade, however, that much of the writing is already on the wall. There remains most prominently that all-important knot of problems critical to the essential human needs of the Third World—intransigent problems of food production, population growth, water supply, deforestation, desertification, and malignant urbanization. The Environmental Revolution must apply itself to their solution.

In the United States, new environmental threats undoubtedly will raise their heads. But, to a great extent, it will be more of the same issues, though they will grip us more tightly. A major preoccupation will be energy—finding enough and mitigating the adverse environmental effects of energy production and use. It will be the major "burden" of the decade, say Juan Cameron and Richard I. Kirkland, Jr., writing in *Fortune*. "Costs will be increasing rapidly, and supplies will be precarious. . . . The transition to more efficient use of energy promises to be the dominant concern of the 1980's."[60] Other critical domestic problems will include dealing with hazardous wastes and protecting the public from toxic chemicals.

These and other environmental problems will have to be confronted under a new and more difficult set of circumstances, however. For one thing, with a more or less full set of laws in the books, most attention must focus on implementation and enforcement of regulations to carry them out. Scientific, economic, legal, and administrative complexities will grow, tending to make the issues more inscrutable.

"From now on, our movement will need fewer rabble-rousers like me, and more technicians," says Brock Evans, Sierra Club director in Washington, D.C. EPA's Costle concurs that there has been a shift "from the ragged squad of citizens' militia to the disciplined platoons of lawyers, scientists, and civil servants who know how to translate passion into the tedious but essential minutiae of the statute books. This transition . . . inevitably entails a drop in emotional temperature. Yet such a cooling-off is part of the natural maturing process of any successful public movement."[61]

For all the truth evident in Costle's appraisal, to remain effective the Environmental Revolution may also from time to time have to be able to regenerate the same kind of emotional and political heat as before. For one of the other factors in the coming decade is the vigorous campaign against environmental regulation.

In addition, the nation's technological and scientific capabilities—constantly expanding and enabling us to both create and discover more risks to health and environment—seem likely to further outdistance our more primitive abilities to evaluate and control. To the extent that we manage to deal with risks, will it be in a way that retains sufficient political power for the public? And in a way that does not engender the kind of centralization and authoritarian control that threatens a democratic system?

Finally, economic and energy pressures doubtless will tend to impede environmental protection efforts more and more.

Eugene Kennedy, author and professor of psychology at Loyola University of Chicago, writes that the so-called "Me Decade" can be understood as a time of people "struggling against recognizing the need of limitation and compromise, of people angry at the basic conditions of life imposed upon them by time and distance and human relationships, of people terminally out of sorts with the human condition." Among the basic constraining conditions are those related to economics, energy, and the environment. Kennedy adds that:

> America's gradual and grudging acceptance of a sense of national and individual limits during the '80's may arise not so much from a sense of renewed virtue as from exhaustion and desperation at discovering that, although learning to make sacrifices may be unpleasant, trying to be happy without giving something up for others is impossible.[62]

In the Stream of Human Progress

In a historical context, how should one appraise the great changes that have been brought about in the name of environmental protection and environmental quality? Does it all simply add up to a reaction to established interests and forces? Is it merely a cultural caprice, a temporary aberration in the stream of progress? Is it a reform movement, a crusade, a religion? Or a true revolution?

Herman Kahn, chairman of the Hudson Institute, says in a recent book that, "excluding great religious events, there are two great watersheds of civilized history"—the agricultural revolution that started thousands of years ago and the Industrial Revolution.[63] Like the labor and consumer movements, the Environmental Revolution can be viewed as a reaction to the excesses of the Industrial Revolution (including its pollution, its poisonous wastes, its workplace hazards, and its destruction of natural resources). It also can be viewed as a response to the threats of the scientific and technological revolution, and to individual materialism, extravagance, and waste.

But these and other reactions comprise a massive *new* revolution now taking place in America, in the opinion of Jean-Francois Revel,

French journalist and author. "It is absurd to regard the ecological battle as a mere skirmish or a spin-off from the main war," says Revel. "The ecological battle is one of the pieces of the revolutionary puzzle, and it is necessary to complete the picture."[64]

Revel says that a real revolution must be successful, and its successes must consist only of "those concerted and permanent transformations which mark the passage from one civilization to another." Aside from the revoluton that he sees now emergent in the United States, Revel says there has been only one other world revolution in modern history—the political transformations in England, the United States, and France in the latter part of the 18th century.

That political revolution was based on such concepts as authority in the hands of the governed; the power of the law; an egalitarian society; the separation of church and state; and the freedom of knowledge and culture from political and ecclesiastical control. "Even the retrogressions, the restorations, and the counterrevolutions took place within the framework provided by the new civilization which had been born of that first revolution."

Among the characteristics of this "revolutionary universe," says Revel, are "a determination that the natural environment is more important than commercial profit" and "a radical reappraisal of the goals of technology and its consequences." Revel says that a revolution "is not simply a transfer of power, but also a change in the goals for the sake of which power is exercised, and a new choice in the objects of love, hate, and respect." The ecological revolution is part of a "moral revolution."

In this and other respects, the Environmental Revolution can be seen as part of a long and organic process of social and political evolution, as one tributary in a great stream of human progress.

Chapter 1

HISTORICAL FAILURES

History is all explained by geography.

—Robert Penn Warren

The skeletons of many dead civilizations are strewn around the world. They are seen most clearly in harsh, sterile landscapes—the victims of deforestation, overuse, erosion, war, and neglect. They also are scattered in the mysterious underground strata of archaeology.

To what extent did these civilizations decay or die of environmental causes? Can their records teach us something about current environmental stresses? Do they indicate whether such stresses could cause or contribute to the demise of existing civilizations?

The skeletons of the past are found all around the Mediterranean, in the Near East and Middle East, in parts of Pakistan, India, and China, in Cambodia, Mexico, Peru. They represent the decline and fall of great civilizations developed by the Egyptians, Romans, Assyrians, Persians, Harappans, Hittites, Khmers, Incas, and Mayans, among others.

Conservationist Vernon Gill Carter and the late Tom Dale, of the Soil Conservation Service, said that with only a few exceptions in 6,000 years, civilized man has never been able to continue a progressive civilization in one locality for more than 30 to 70 generations—750 to 1,750 years.[1] Many societies, of course, have disintegrated more quickly. Why?

With much oversimplification, one can divide the causes of decline into two main categories: sociopolitical and environmental.

The sociopolitical category would encompass a range of problems derived from such human frailties as greed, selfishness, laziness, dishonesty, and poor leadership qualities. These can manifest themselves in a variety of ways (often associated with the fall of the Roman Empire)— moral decay, loss of will, political corruption, ineffectual governance, counterproductive taxation and economic policies, and military aggression.

37

In the environmental category, some problems were external to the society in question; man was the instrument creating others, but often the unwitting instrument, without an adequate understanding of causes, effects, or preventive measures:

1. *Pressures of depopulation or overpopulation.*

2. *Disease.*

3. *Climatic change (including short-term, long-term, natural, and man-induced regional changes).*

4. *Invasions (in the sense that an invasion from outside a society may have been triggered by environmental pressures such as drought, degradation of land, and such).*

5. *Deterioration of the resource base. (This would include the effects of deforestation, burning, overgrazing, soil erosion, siltation, loss of soil fertility, salinization, loss of water supply, fish and wildlife depletion, plant diseases, and pests.)*

These causes of decay frequently are interwoven. For example, the deterioration and abandonment of farmlands in North Africa and elsewhere toward the end of the Roman Empire is widely attributed to excessive taxation.[2]

Another analytical problem is distinguishing causes and effects. Even when experts agree that something happened, they may dispute whether it was a cause of collapse or a result. Thus, while some historians tend to portray disease epidemics as aftermaths of wars and disintegration, William H. McNeill, of the University of Chicago, makes a strong case that plagues, smallpox, malaria, and other diseases have been major factors in bringing down civilizations.[3]

Similarly, there has been disagreement over the events that led to a breakdown in the irrigation system critical to the agriculture of Mesopotamia: Was it wrecked by invaders from the east in the 13th century A.D., or did the system's decline so weaken the society that it became vulnerable to successful invasion?

According to Yale University's Paul B. Sears, "The immense piles of silt alongside the ditches show that the system was well on the way toward being choked out before it was destroyed."[4] And two other historians have concluded that by the middle of the 12th century "only a trickle of water passed down the upper section of the main canal to supply a few dying towns in the now hostile desert. Invading Mongol horsemen under Hulagu Khan, who first must have surveyed this devastated scene a century later, have been unjustly blamed for causing it ever since."[5]

In the analysis of such distant eras, small rocks of proof are washed over by sweeping waves of theory. Whatever the available evidence, it is apt to generate many opposing viewpoints. For example, while some scientists discount the effects of climate, others make it the preeminent explanation. Some historians credit warfare with the downhill slides of most civilizations, while others dismiss wars as mere symptoms of decline.

Among those who seek to explain the past, some virtually ignore environmental factors. At the other extreme are the scientists and historians who find environmental problems at the root of most decaying civilizations. In between are those who may feel that environmental factors have been slighted and should receive greater consideration, or who link them to a complex pattern of causes. Thus, J. Donald Hughes, associate professor of history at the University of Denver, wrote:

> The decline and fall of the Roman Empire evidently had an environmental dimension . . . . The Romans placed too great a demand upon the available natural resources . . . ecological failures interacted with social, political, and economic forces to assure that the vast entity called the Roman Empire would disappear or be changed beyond recognition.[6]

No special effort will be made here to untangle the diverse theories applied to particular civilizations, or to assess their relative validity. Instead, some environmental rationales will be presented and emphasized solely to illustrate possible dangers that may have relevance for present societies.

Environmental Threats

Climatic change is seen by some experts as a force to which civilizations adapt, to others as a major determinant of societal welfare. Barbara Bell, of Harvard University, has argued that the two dark ages and numerous natural disasters in Egypt and adjacent lands between 2200 B.C. and 900 B.C. "can be given coherence and can all be explained at once by a single primary cause—drought—widespread, severe, and prolonged." She added that "a climatic-economic deterioration of sufficient magnitude can set in motion forces beyond the strength of any society to withstand."[7]

French historian Fernand Braudel has written that the climate throughout the Mediterranean area in general is so disadvantageous— in great part because the substantial rainfall is out of phase with the warmth of summer—that the region "affords a precarious living" in spite of its "famous charm and beauty."[8]

The Harappan civilization in the Indus River valley of what is now eastern Pakistan and northwestern India may have suffered severely from drought on its way to oblivion. In any case, Reid A. Bryson and David A. Baerreis, of the University of Wisconsin, have concluded that the Rajputana desert in that part of India is largely man-made. They said the air canopy above the desert contains as much moisture as that above the Amazon Valley or the Congo. But as the Harappan population grew, as more intensive farming destroyed the grass cover, and as forests were cut and burned, huge clouds of dust formed. This greatly reduced surface heating of the earth and resultant rainfall, resulting in a drier climate and desertification. "As the climate gets drier," they said, "any people tries a little harder to grow enough food to supply the population if the population is dense and not very mobile. This means tearing up more of the surface and loosening more dust to blow into it."[9]

The ravages of deforestation make a recurring theme in the literature of departed civilizations. Regarding China, Georg Borgstrom, professor of geography and food science at Michigan State University, said:

> Already in the famous era of the bronze vases, when the water buffalo was domesticated, China in effect committed its great ecological blunder of cutting down the forest in order to gain agricultural land. The stage was then set for the catastrophic floods which in recurrent sequences wrought havoc upon the country for centuries to come. Heavy downpours were no longer caught and stored in the soil.[10]

Dozens of examples of the severe consequences of deforestation around the globe could be cited. They include Greece, Roman Italy, North Africa, Lebanon (the famous cedars of Lebanon), Spain, India, and Mexico.

Carter and Dale have reasoned that deforestation led to the collapse of the Singhalese civilization in Ceylon, one of the most advanced of its time. And they said that deforestation gradually forced the center of the amazing Inca empire of Peru to move into the higher valleys of the Andes. There, they were taking

> . . . heroic measures to save their soil, and had constructed bench terraces on nearly all the slopes where there was enough soil for cultivation, but they were fighting a losing battle with nature. It . . . seems fair to assume that the Incas had only a few more generations of wealth and power ahead of them, even if the Spaniards had not come.[11]

McNeill said that not long before Pizarro appeared, Mexico already had a serious erosion problem and salting of the soil in some irrigated coastal areas of Peru had led to population collapse. "Everything points to the conclusion that Amerindian populations were pressing hard against the limits set by available cultivable land in both Mexico and Peru when the Spaniards arrived."[12]

George Perkins Marsh cited many examples in his pioneering ecological treatise *Man and Nature*, first published in 1864, and noted that

> . . . clearing of woods has, in some cases, produced within two or three generations, effects as blasting as those generally ascribed to geological convulsions, and has laid waste the face of the earth more hopelessly than if it had been buried by a current of lava or a shower of volcanic sand.[13]

Walter Clay Lowdermilk, a longtime official of the Soil Conservation Service who studied foreign lands extensively, said, "Soil erosion, if not controlled, has demonstrated its ability to undermine nations and civilizations regardless of what may have been the social or economic conditions that set it going or stimulated its destructiveness."[14]

Many commentators also have linked the decline of the Roman Empire to overexploitation of the land and soil deterioration, and attributed this to various social, political, and economic factors. If there really were widespread exhaustion of the soil, was it caused by lax agricultural husbandry? By abandonment of the farms because the Roman military machine took too many farmers' sons, or because taxation was excessive? Was it because the fields came to be tended by slaves who cared less about fertility, or because they came to be concentrated in larger estates, the Latifundia, whose owners, "in their haste to get quick returns, starved the soil of manure"?[15]

These questions also take on a chicken-and-egg quality: Were farms abandoned because the soil had become exhausted, or did the soil deteriorate because the land was abandoned? Did lands concentrate in larger holdings because they were becoming economically less productive, or did they become less productive in the hands of those owners?

Perhaps Braudel offered the most clarification when he said the

> . . . Mediterranean soil too is responsible for the poverty it inflicts on its people . . . . The thin layers of topsoil . . . are enabled to survive only by man's constant effort. Given these conditions, if the peasants' vigilance should be distracted during long periods of unrest, not only the peasantry but also the productive soil will be destroyed . . . . In the Mediterranean the soil dies if it is not protected by crops: the desert lies in wait for arable land and never lets go.[16]

However one slices the causes and effects, it has been argued that "the progressive exhaustion of the soil was quite sufficient to doom Rome, as lack of oxygen in the air would doom the strongest living being."[17]

Similarly, Carter and Dale zeroed in on the environment: The fundamental cause for the decline of most civilizations in the past was "deterioration of the natural-resource base on which civilization rested."[18]

What of the barbarian invasions? The rationale, again, is that they gravitated to, and succeeded against, weakened societies. Speaking of the Roman Empire and civilizations in the Near East, Donald R. Coates, professor of geography at the State University of New York, Binghamton, says, "It's almost invariably the case that incursions by outsiders are the final straw."[19]

In fact, the invasions themselves sometimes are explained in environmental terms—with invaders pushing out of their territories in response to drought or other food and water supply failures.

Other environment-related disasters have reduced, though not necessarily wiped out, civilizations. Consider the Black Death and other plagues and epidemics. The devastation of locusts is legendary. So is the potato blight that destroyed half of Ireland's population of eight million around 1845. In other commentary on the dangers of monoculture, it has been suggested that the demise of the classic Mayan civilization could have been due to overemphasis on a single crop—such as maize or a root crop—with its vulnerability to diseases and pests.[20]

Early "Solutions"

How did ancient peoples respond to environmental threats, or cope with disaster as their societies began to crumble? And do their responses provide any insight to the present?

One answer, of course, is that they did *not* cope—that people simply perished by the millions and land became desolate. Another common reaction was to throw hordes of laborers—or slaves—at tasks such as flood control or removal of silt from irrigation canals. Karl A. Wittvogel, a professor of Chinese history, wrote at length about "hydraulic civilizations" and their "unending drudgery on a socially and culturally depressing level."[21]

Another response requiring masses of humans was the invasion of other regions in order to alleviate population, land, climate, and other pressures.

Such measures generally required an iron-fisted centralized authority to implement them effectively. Thus, for example, Wittvogel wrote of the "despotism" needed to maintain the hydraulic way of life in such nations as China.

Perhaps the most common response to environmental pressures was to move elsewhere, to find fresh land. These moves ranged in scale from the microcosmic level (including the slash-and-burn farmers who razed the trees in a small area, burned them, grew crops for a year or two until the soil's fertility was gone, and then moved on), to the settlement of America's West, to the mass migrations of millions in Asia and Europe.

The desperate exodus from Ireland in reaction to the potato famine is but one of many examples. Between 1814 and 1914, notes British biologist Harry Walters, some 55 million people departed Europe, a massive emigration which, together with industrial and commercial advances, made it possible for the progressing Western European civilization to survive a population explosion.[22]

Alas, all these "solutions" have one thing in common: They don't work anymore. By and large they are no longer realistic or acceptable in the world today. Slavery is taboo, and pressing mass, cheap, hard labor into service is generally not feasible, except perhaps in countries like China.

Lowdermilk pointed to the enormous cost in human labor required to level some terrace slopes in Lebanon, for example. "Such remarkable works demonstrate to what lengths a people will go to survive, as well as the necessity of maintaining the soil resources to support a population," he wrote. "Such examples warn us to find ways of saving good lands before necessity drives a people to such extremes in costs of human effort."[23]

Reprinted by permission of the Chicago Tribune–New York News Syndicate, Inc.

And what of migration? There isn't a great deal left in the way of new frontiers and virgin lands in which to resettle. Access is apt to be blocked by the firm national boundaries that have been established. "Partly through migration, the planet has been filled with people," said the *Population Bulletin*. "There are no longer unoccupied 'safety valves' available."[24]

When their civilizations collapsed, the peoples of the Euphrates River valley presumably moved, as best they could, to find new places of subsistence. Today, it seems there is no place for Palestinians in the region. When their great empire at Angkor fell, the Khmers moved elsewhere. Now, it seems, their descendants in Cambodia have nowhere to go.

When the Harappan civilization disintegrated—possibly due to drought and floods over a period of time—its people may have moved to new environments to create new societies. But now, by comparison, there is no practical way for millions of people to move from the Ganges River delta, where they squeeze out a living but face inevitable devastation from typhoon-generated floods. (Nine years ago, for example, some 300,000 people were killed.)

One of the few examples of a present-day escape hatch is the accessibility of the United States to immigrants from Mexico—facilitated by a common border almost 2,000 miles long. The socioeconomic and environmental impacts of this immigration are, of course, the subject of much debate.[25]

In any case, history suggests the need for an international migration policy—as proposed by Daniel Bell, professor of sociology at Harvard University[26]—as well as a need for all nations to take stock of their population growth and resources, and to plan their futures accordingly.

Possible Remedies Today

Most problems implicated in the demise of earlier civilizations are still very much with the world today—overpopulation, disease, drought, natural catastrophes, and the degradation of critical natural resources. And modern societies have added such latter-day environmental hazards as nuclear proliferation, chemical pollution, hazardous waste disposal, and carbon-dioxide-induced climate change. Such problems suggest, in fact, that there may be only *one* civilization today and that, unlike the past, we have the power to destroy *everything*.

Modern science and technology have come up with ways to guard against most of the ancient and modern threats mentioned above. As for the timeless dilemmas of overpopulation and land degradation, in general the remedies consist of reducing the birth rate, protecting lands from environmental damage, or increasing the carrying capacity of these lands.

Population growth is susceptible to a technical (and cultural) fix: Contraceptives may be mankind's most important technical advance. The history of agriculture is a long series of new techniques, some to protect soils, but most designed to increase yields per unit of land. Certainly, there is room for much improvement, though a tendency toward diminishing returns—which is inherent in the process of photosynthesis, and is evident in the increasing needs for water, energy, fertilizers, stabilization measures, and the like—suggests the existence of technological limits.

"It is not difficult to imagine a time when technology will no longer be able to offset the decreasing land under cultivation," says Thomas A. Sloan, assistant professor of political science at Kansas State University.[27]

There are even more obvious limits to the creation of new productive land. The days of filling wetlands and of slash-and-burn farming must end; the possible ecological side effects in places such as the Amazon River basin are a reminder that such remedies can create serious new problems. What, for example, will be the climatic effects of extensive tropical deforestation?

Significantly, there is a glaring exception to the general rule that man has the power to cope with the old environmental nemeses: There is no way to prevent natural disasters—such as a volcanic eruption, an earthquake, or a sharp climatic change that brings drought, flood, or severe temperature fluctuation, thereby ruining agricultural production.[28]

To be sure, there are ways to mitigate the effects of natural disasters. For example, to soften the impact of climate change, strategic reserves of grain can be stored in advance. They can be transported quickly to other parts of the world. More drought-resistant crops can be developed. Population levels can be stabilized. But these measures, even if politically and economically feasible, seem very inadequate in the face of the kind of dramatic change that previously has plagued various regions of the earth, and that, many experts feel, must inevitably recur.

Reversing the Trend

James R. Dunn, an environmental geologist and president of Dunn Geoscience Corp., Latham, N.Y., has visited many countries and studied with fascination the geological evidence of deforestation, soil erosion, salinization, desertification, and other causes of decline in past civilizations. But he believes that "in man's environmental history, depressing though it is, there may also be answers." He explained in an interview:

> I have long been impressed with the fact that it has only been within the past 100 years or so that any major civilization has been able to reverse a trend of environmental degradation. The industrial societies have done relatively well, not perfectly, of course, but better than anyone in the past.
>
> The manicured farmlands of central and northern Europe and the United States and Canada are evidence of this. In those areas, we find contour plowing, steep slopes left in woods or natural grasses, grassed waterways, and general soil improvements to be the prevalent situation. In addition, the forests of these areas have expanded for the past 100 years or so. In the eastern United States in particular, the forests in whole states have better than doubled in size.

Dunn notes that this became economically feasible in the East for a number of reasons, including the opening up of highly productive farmlands in the Midwest. "We had the good fortune to have large quantities of unused land and time to correct many of our mistakes," says Dunn. "The currently less-developed countries, to a large extent, have no such luxury."

The situation is entirely different in Africa, the Middle East, Southern Asia, South America, and Central America, Dunn says:

There, deadly and accelerating environmental degradation is the rule. But had we traveled in the United States and Europe 100 to 200 years ago, we would have seen similar signs of widespread degradation.

What does this tell us? First, it is apparent that virtually no poor society has ever been able to improve its environment. But it seems equally clear that wealth alone is not enough. Nor is understanding the problem enough.

The Spartan general, Pausanias, in the 5th century B.C., described the accelerated sedimentation by the Maeander River in western Turkey and accurately related it to deforestation and erosion of the local mountains. [A number of other observers in Greece and Rome were similarly perceptive.[29]]

Thus the knowledge of causes was not enough in the wealthy society of Greece to reverse their own environmental degradation. Other great and wealthy societies of the past could not solve such problems either. Consequently, in addition to wealth, it is clear that *technology* is needed to reverse the trend.

Historically, says Dunn, the processes of degradation "have proven virtually impossible to change without advanced technology in combination with major socioeconomic improvements in the lot of the populations which created the problems."

For the advanced nations to help, as they should and must, they will have to maintain their own economic strength—difficult in the face of soaring energy costs. (Dunn sounds an ominous domestic note when he says he is concerned that, as the U.S. becomes poorer and its socioeconomic conditions worsen, we will see an increase in the rate of soil erosion, a decrease in agricultural productivity, greater demands on our forests, and an increase in game poaching—all trends "probably now occurring in the United States.")

Even with economic strength, says Dunn, "the wealthy nations simply do not have enough money to help by redistributing their wealth. The answers lie in applied technology."

Hopes for Technology

The issue then becomes: What kinds of technology? Some have deleterious environmental side effects of their own—for example, herbicides and energy-consumptive tractors. Also, it generally is not feasible to simply transfer sophisticated farm and other machinery to less-developed countries. A tractor, notes Dunn, cannot be amortized in a society that doesn't have enough money to buy the food produced.

Yet many technological improvements could help stem environmental damage: Remote satellite sensing to assess problems of desertification and deforestation; reduced tillage; and the introduction of plants and trees that are not only productive but at the same time effective in stabilizing steep slopes, holding back advancing deserts, using less water, or alleviating other problems.

Of course, even the technology that exists may not be effectively transferred to, or utilized by, countries that sorely need it. But the technological means to make such transfers—communication, education, transportation—are infinitely greater than in the past.

Much evidence, both historical and current, suggests that the critical obstacles to environmental protection often are not technological, but economic, social, or political. For example, as mentioned earlier, some historians theorize that the chief factor in the disintegration of the remarkable Mesopotamian civilization in the "fertile crescent" of the Tigris and Euphrates river valleys was a failure to cope with increasing siltation of its elaborate networks of irrigation canals. Huge banks of silt piled up, stark evidence of the ultimate failure to maintain an adequate food production system.[30]

It was technologically, if not logistically or politically, feasible to prevent the population pressure, upland deforestation, overgrazing and resultant soil erosion that led to most of the damage. It may also have been possible—without modern mechanical dredges, but simply with the manual tools available—to prevent the damage or undo it and put the system back into effective operation.

Salinization also has been cited as a major contributor to the demise of the environment in Mesopotamia. McGuire Gibson, associate professor of archaeology and anthropology at the University of Chicago's Oriental Institute, says that the farmers lacked the technology to put in drains to prevent salinization, but they did have a system of fallow to slow the process. However, he says the system was violated, and this "led inevitably to the deterioration of the agricultural base through a combination of increased salinization, lowering of yields, consequent indebtedness of farmers, subsequent flight to the cities for work, resulting in both an abandonment of the countryside and the creation of an urban population that consumed rather than produced food." (He adds that drains are being installed in the region now thanks to increased revenues from the oil boom).[31]

Historians have suggested that various other problems, not inadequate technology, caused the abandonment of the Mesopotamian plain. These include inadequate manpower, because the citizenry was spending too much time in battle; lack of capital to invest in maintenance or reconstruction; the absence of necessary leadership; and a loss of public motivation.

Gibson has argued that "no bureaucracy could consistently, over several hundred years, carry out the enormous task of maintaining so large a system" as the Mesopotamian network of canals. He also says there is evidence that in the 18th century B.C. an economic crisis coincided with a natural disaster that affected the water supply.

Historian McNeill has said:

> In general, the more elaborate Mesopotamian water engineering became,
> the heavier became the tasks of maintenance and the greater the chance of
> sporadic breakdown. By a cruel irony, therefore, populations dependent
> on dikes and canals exposed themselves to periodic disaster just in propor-
> tion as they pushed technical mastery of their style of gravity-flow irriga-
> tion to its technical limits.[32]

Is there a disturbing similarity to the present United States domestic
water supply situation? Consider: Ground water resources in various
regions are seriously depleted; the decay and leakage of vast water
delivery and sewer pipe systems in many Northeast cities is growing into
an enormous problem of plant rehabilitation or replacement; large
dams in the West and elsewhere are subject to siltation and physical
obsolescence; pollution requires an untiring application of expensive
control measures, including measures to deal with previously unsuspected leakage of hazardous chemicals.

There is a hint of Mesopotamia in the words of Michigan's environmental enforcement chief, who says that "chemical contamination may
be so widespread and pervasive . . . that it's to the point where we may
find it cheaper to simply write off the ground water supplies of large
portions of southern Michigan."[33]

The next steps up the technological scale for water supply are desalinization and the recycling of wastewater. These are costly in terms of
both money and energy—and, as McNeill's comments suggest, they will
require attentive maintenance and be subject to breakdowns.

Dealing with the Modern Threats

The more modern environmental threats—nuclear proliferation and
waste management, chemical pollution, hazardous waste disposal, carbon dioxide accumulation in the atmosphere—can be ameliorated in
two ways. The first way is simply to cut back or eliminate the use of
offending substances or technologies, by changing life-styles and reducing dependence on them, or by using substitutes. The second way is to
prevent the release of the damaging substances into the environment.

With several important qualifications, one can say that both strategies are generally within mankind's technical capabilities. One qualification involves nuclear energy. Either by adjusting our life-style or by
using substitute sources of energy, we could at some point avoid relying
on nuclear power. But it is unclear at present whether we can completely
prevent the release of radioactive materials to the environment if we
choose to use nuclear energy. The problems of disposing of radioactive
wastes are obviously great, and a technological "fix" is not available.

Another qualification is that societies do not control unsuspected pollutants that only later are revealed to be dangerous. For example, the Romans, and many others, seem not to have realized the broad implications of lead poisoning, to which they exposed themselves in a number of ways.

Josef Eisinger, a research scientist at Bell Laboratories, believes that the most damaging way was the widespread Roman practice of cooking, in lead pots, a syrup used to preserve and enhance the taste of wine.[34] It has been argued that a major factor in the Roman Empire's decline was the death, sterility, and disease caused by lead poisoning.[35]

Eisinger adds that unrecognized lead poisoning was a major problem all over Europe for centuries, and many doctors even freely used lead as a medicine. He speaks of the "similarities between the problems posed by lead in the past and those confronting us today as a result of the proliferation of modern environmental poisons."

Similarly, James Dunn is convinced that nitrate contamination of drinking water contributed to the crumbling of Mesopotamian civilization. As distances for serving the urban population grew, it became necessary to bring cattle and goats into the city. "The meat products had to come in on the hoof," says Dunn. "They must have had feedyards for them, and these must have been enormous sources of nitrate." Nitrate must have got into the Mesopotamians' well water—as it has in the United States. "It may well have happened again and again," says Dunn. "They got weaker psychologically and physiologically. I think that's a logical reason their cities fell to more energetic peoples."

While this past may not be a prologue, it appears to have some relevance. The present use of chemicals is incredibly widespread, and some already have caused heavy damage which was unsuspected for many years—asbestos, PCB's, DDT, and the like.

Is any such chemical capable of bringing a society to its knees? Perhaps not, but who is to say that we are able to keep out of circulation substances that might turn out to induce far-reaching cancers and genetic mutations?

Constraints on Technology

Two other technological systems have shaped civilizations through the ages—transportation and energy. Both, of course, are used to facilitate the production and distribution of agricultural products. Dunn describes one historical connection between the two:

> Depletion of soil nutrients, erosion, and salination caused by poor agricultural practices made it more difficult for the ancient civilizations to produce sufficient food nearby. This, coupled with expanding populations and extended primitive transportation lines, must have created

enormous logistic problems and must have contributed significantly to the demise of the cultures.

Present transportation systems certainly are not primitive from a technological standpoint. But they may be subject to the same kinds of economic and institutional constraints as in the distant past. Whether or not the atrophy of the famous Roman systems of roads was a cause or effect of the empire's decline, it brings to mind such current transportation problems as deteriorating railroad tracks, escalating costs of replacing bridges and maintaining interstate highways, fuel shortages, and the trucking industry's vulnerability to strikes.

Did the Romans have a Highway Trust Fund as richly endowed as our own? Perhaps the Roman Empire had simply advanced farther down a path of economic constraints that the United States now appears to be traveling.

Likewise, are there similarities between the Roman lifeline for grain shipments from northern Africa and the United States' pipeline for oil shipments from the Middle East? It is tempting to say that the grain was more critical to Rome than oil is to the U.S. But an abrupt cutback of oil could trigger economic havoc and, with it, agricultural ruin. In any case, the problems were not, and are not, wholly technological.

In addition to the economic vulnerability of increasingly large and complex transportation and energy technologies, they have their own adverse environmental impacts, they tend to require more centralized and authoritarian governance (as attested by the autocratic regimes of early civilizations, which frequently mobilized slaves or enforced laborers to build and maintain irrigation and other systems), and they are susceptible to setbacks and failures on a large scale.

There is considerable evidence that this sort of breakdown was characteristic of some early civilizations with elaborate food, water, and transportation systems.

Yet advanced technology always remains a legitimate source of hope. There is serious talk about the technical feasibility of a car that gets 80 miles per gallon.[36] The "microelectronics revolution," by which people can be plugged into offices, supermarkets, newspapers, etc.—may have enormous effects on transportation and energy use.[37] An energy consortium is testing a means of exploiting oil shale deposits by using radio-frequency electric fields to heat them to gaseous or liquid forms in place—thereby avoiding the extensive environmental problems associated with mining, retorting, and waste disposal.[38]

For every sign of technological improvement, there are words of caution. One might say, for example, that the oil shale resource will only buy time, and not much of that in the long-range perspective of a civilization.

Robert Strausz-Hupe, a consultant to the Foreign Policy Research Institute at the University of Pennsylvania, has written of the Romans' "technological backwardness." He says that, more likely than not, "Roman imagination stopped short at the threshold of machine technology because cheap and abundant slave labor supplied the 'machines' of production." Thus there is a great gap between ancient Rome and modern America.

> Yet notwithstanding this, we must ask whether our machine technology makes us proof against all those destructive forces which plagued Roman society and ultimately wrecked Roman civilization. Our reliance—an almost religious reliance—upon the power of science and technology to forever ensure the progress of our society, might blind us to some very real problems which cannot be solved by science and technology.[39]

Others have offered similar warnings. Historian Arnold J. Toynbee wrote, "The most important questions that Man must answer are questions on which Science has nothing to say."[40] And Denis Goulet, a senior fellow at the Overseas Development Council, put it this way:

> Given that any human group's psychic energy is limited, if it channels most of it to solve technological problems, little is left for truly civilizational creativity in esthetic and spiritual domains. The price paid for success in science and technology is often regression on more important fronts, a societal analogue of the tragic persona familiar to our age: the brilliant scientist or industrialist who is emotionally a child and politically an idiot.[41]

At the same time, one must keep in mind the recognizably great benefits of technology in the past and, presumably, in the future. The future seems sure to confront existing civilizations with some problems that can be solved *only* with technology—for example, as the population problem perhaps can be solved only with contraceptives.

In sum, societies will be obliged to assess technologies wisely and use them judiciously. They also will have to overcome—or accommodate to—the many nonengineering constraints.

Not long ago, a scientific magazine, referring to a prospective source of energy, said, "The technology is now available. The only barriers are political, social, and economic."[42] To which the *New Yorker* commented: "It could be our collective epitaph."[43]

Chapter 2

FOOD

In simplest terms, agriculture is an effort
by man to move beyond the limits set by
nature.
—Lester R. Brown and Gail W. Finsterbusch

Some said there could never be another year like 1972-73. Others were
sure it was just a taste of much worse to come. But there it was, for all the
world to see: the unthinkable menace of global food shortages, a fleeting
but ominous glimpse on the horizon of that horseman of the Apoca-
lypse, Famine.

Of course, the vision was nothing new to the many millions who live
always with hunger, malnutrition, or starvation. But the rest of mankind, comfortably insulated from those poor, was jolted out of its
complacency. It could imagine, perhaps for the first time, a world
pressed to its ecological limits and embroiled in a bitter struggle for
food.

The signs of trouble were everywhere—an abrupt decrease in food
supplies at a time of relentless growth in demand; a scramble for grain
on world markets, particularly the Soviet Union's surprising and enormous purchase of wheat from the United States; rapidly rising prices
around the world (as well as in America's supermarkets); the hasty
imposition of some export controls; an overall depletion of grain
reserves; and, most visibly, starvation among the inhabitants of sub-
Saharan Africa. Senator George McGovern of South Dakota, former
director of the Food for Peace Program, expressed the view, held by
many, that 1972-73 "was not an aberration but the sharp warning of a
deeply troubling new trend."[1] It seems clear, in any case, that the world
was forced to ask itself two questions: How did the crisis arise? And what
lies ahead?

A seemingly impossible chain of events thrust food problems into the
world's consciousness. Highly capricious weather brought widespread
and severe droughts, frosts, and floods, particularly in Asia. It desiccated

53

sub-Saharan Africa. It cut heavily into the Soviet grain harvest, and prompted the Soviet Union to barge into the world market, instead of letting its citizens go a little hungrier, or slaughtering livestock to fill the gap, as they have during past crop shortages.

North American grain reserves, long the world's shock absorber, already had been gradually reduced to meet growing demand. (Two devaluations of the dollar also stimulated other nations to buy more U.S. food). The problem of supply was further exacerbated by an overall decline in the world's fish catch. The most dramatic aspect of this was the sudden depletion of an important source of fishmeal, the anchovies off the Peruvian coast, because of overfishing and an inauspicious shift in the Humboldt Current. The yield, which hit a peak in 1970 of 12.3 million tons—almost 20 percent of total world fish production—was down to little more than 2 million tons in 1973.

Two long-term factors also were adding to the pressure on supplies. One was world population growth of about 2 percent per year. The other was a general demand for more food of higher quality, principally animal protein. People with rising incomes—particularly in Japan and Europe—are turning away from the old staples of rice and wheat in favor of beef and other animal products. This emulates affluent U.S. consumers, whose strong demand for meat drains the available grain supply. (As a rule, it takes seven pounds of grain to produce one pound of beef, four pounds of pork, or three of poultry.) One food expert with the Overseas Development Council has pointed out that "as incomes in the U.S. have risen, per capita beef consumption has climbed from 55 pounds in 1940 to 117 pounds in 1972; combined with population growth this has tripled total beef consumption in the U.S."[2] Louis Thompson of Iowa State University has noted that the number of cattle in the world rose close to 10 percent from 1970 to 1973, and that hog production was growing by more than 5 percent a year.[3]

That is a nutshell summary of how the situation became critical. Says Professor Willard Cochrane of the University of Minnesota: "The world, and more particularly the U.S., moved from a grain surplus condition to a shortage condition in one peacetime year."[4] Norman Borlaug, the Nobel Prize-winning agriculture expert, notes similarly that the crisis was precipitated by a seemingly small reduction in world food production—less than 4 percent.[5]

Short-Term Variables

As for the future, it is most uncertain. It depends on some important variables that are impossible to predict. And the farther ahead one seeks to prophesy, the more numerous the variables and the cloudier the crystal ball. The following are key factors in the supply-demand equation:

• Weather is the most critcal factor. Continued good weather could provide a string of abundant crops. But the world's heavy reliance on favorable weather is highlighted by this comment from Borlaug: "It is my fundamental belief that [in 1973] the ice was so thin that only because of favorable summer monsoon rains in Asia was a serious famine prevented. Fifty to 100 million people could have perished."[6] Weather is by nature freakish, or at least not inclined to be consistently favorable over a period of time. More bad weather could upset the world food cart. Still more foreboding are the possibilities of unfavorable climatic change.

• Much depends on whether or not the Soviet Union—and to a lesser extent China—decides to improve its national diet by importing grain and soybeans to feed more animals. Lester R. Brown, president of Worldwatch Institute, said that, although bad weather was the principal reason why the Soviet Union purchased nearly half a year's U.S. wheat crop in 1972, "it's possible the huge Russian grain order may represent a more fundamental decision to turn to cereal imports on a continuing basis in an effort to alleviate the chronic shortage of animal protein in that country."[7] In any case, bad weather caused the Soviet Union to resort to heavy purchases of U.S. grain again in 1979.

• Other nations—in Asia, Africa, and Latin America—may or may not be able to increase their grain production significantly. The results will depend on successful application of green revolution techniques; on the size and nature of international aid programs; and on the emphasis that those nations place on agriculture. If the past is any indication, much needs to be done. An analysis of agricultural progress in developing countries "reveals some extremely disquieting facts," said Addeke H. Boerma, former director-general of FAO. From 1961-71, the 92 developing countries as a whole raised their production at an average rate of 2.8 percent per year—barely faster than their population growth of 2.6 percent per year.[8] FAO figures indicate that for the period 1970-76, the average annual increase in developing countries' food production per capita was 0.3 percent—so food barely moved ahead of population growth in those years.[9] The FAO said that in 1970-76 food production failed to match population growth in no less than 50 of the individual countries for which it calculates production indices. And it noted that "the recurrence of widespread unfavorable weather could quickly reverse the present improved situation." It said further that 1977 figures showed the developing countries actually lost ground—with aggregate food production up 1.5 to 2 percent from 1976, while total population, according to Census Bureau figures, grew more than 2 percent.

• Complicating the picture is the chicken-and-egg relationship between food supplies and population growth. It is a common oversimplification to conclude that any world food problem can be directly alleviated by strict control of population growth. There is a converse, however: More abundant food supplies and improved diets will induce voluntary population control, as has apparently been the case in developed countries. "As health conditions improve," according to Edgar Owens of the Agency for International Development, "parents understand that they do not need to have 10 babies in order to have five adolescent children . . . [and] that endless numbers of children limit their ability to share in the benefits of development."[10] Alan Berg, a nutrition expert at the World Bank, points to a study showing that a couple in India must bear 6.3 children to be 95 percent certain that one son will still be alive at the father's 65th birthday, and that the average number of births in India per couple is 6.5. "The combined desire for adult sons and recognition of high child mortality are among the contributors to the population dilemma," Berg writes. "This suggests paradoxically that keeping more children alive, although it inevitably will increase the population in the short run, may be a powerful contribution toward lowering the population growth rate in the long run."[11]

Over the longer time span, other variables also are critical. Will the rate of population growth increase or decline? How much higher quality food will be demanded by the newly affluent and other consumers? What are the ecological constraints on greater production?

No one knows what combination of the above variables will occur. Moreover, trends may be "either sharp and precipitous or long-run and sustained," says Cochrane. "In short, we cannot predict with any degree of certainty whether the world grain supply situation is going to become tighter, hence more critical, over the next few years, or will ease and possibly move into a surplus situation."[12]

The most obvious way to deal with these uncertainties, to head off the possibility of food shortages, is to provide a safety margin by setting up grain reserves that can be drawn upon in times of scarcity—to meet emergency human needs, as well as to forestall wild price fluctuations. Says Georg Borgstrom of Michigan State University: "Every civilization has safeguarded the human element with food storage—the Chinese, Aztecs, Incas, everyone."[13] Establishing food reserves in the modern age has got much more complicated, however—with conflicts among the various multinational corporations that control most of the grain trade, and between the foreign and domestic policies of food exporting and food importing nations.

Borlaug says that reserve stocks should be strategically located in different parts of the world, where they are not likely to be immobilized in time of need by strikes, shipping shortages, or other problems. He adds that such reserves should not reduce the responsibility that importing nations have to maintain their own stocks.

It should not be forgotten that U.S. agricultural policies—as well as those of other nations—are framed by officials and legislators charting a perilous political course between the Scylla of consumer complaints about high supermarket prices and the Charybdis of farmer complaints about low farm prices. In a time of tight supplies, of course, there is a basic conflict between lowering domestic prices and providing more concessional or humanitarian aid. The *Washington Post*, after remarking how relatively easy it is for the United States to be benevolent when its grainaries are bulging with surpluses, said that "the real test of this country's conscience and responsible world leadership comes now that American resources no longer appear unlimited."[14]

There appear to be many reasons for the United States' earlier frostiness toward most commodity reserve proposals. The high cost was often cited. Reserves were also viewed as a constant Damoclean threat to farmers because they hang over the market and thus tend to depress prices. There was a feeling, based on past experience, that the U.S. and other exporting nations can meet demand. There was a hint of peevishness over the fact that, during the past, the U.S. couldn't get others to share much of the burden of maintaining stockpiles. And there was a suspicion that, even under any international reserve plan, the U.S. will be paying the bills as before while surrendering most of the control.

"It's related to that spirit, at the top, of big-power dealing among the grain exporting countries," says one international official. "If the exporters are getting together, why bring in the enemy that needs the food? They prefer to deal among friends and not with people who are hungry . . . when they can sell it and get a quid pro quo."[15] In a similar vein, Borgstrom suggested that the U.S. is not enthusiastic because "we like to play poker with the great power of the Soviet Union . . . . The more they can keep it within the family, the more secure they feel and the greater the profits."[16] Lester Brown had a concurring opinion: "There is little doubt that the shots in the [Agriculture] Department are being called by a small handful of major grain trading companies." He suggested that the Department may be cool to certain reserves proposals "because the grain companies thrive in situations of maximum uncertainty—because they usually know more about what's happening than others do. Establishment of a reserve would take much of the uncertainty out of it. If they're holding all the stocks they're in control." Others feel, however, that the grain companies have an interest in stability.[17]

Despite the benefits of world grain reserves, in the long run it is probably far more important to foster greater agricultural development in the poorer countries. The world has had large grain stocks in the past, but this has not put a stop to hunger, malnutrition, and starvation. The problem of increasing agricultural development, however, is inextricably bound up with the limits of food production inherent in the earth's ecosystem.

How Far Can Man Push Nature in Search of Food?

With an ever-expanding population, and hundreds of millions already underfed, the pressures have grown enormous to wrest more food from the earth by stretching nature's capacity. Thus, food experts Lester Brown and Gail W. Finsterbusch observe: "The relevant question in any effort to project the food situation into the future is no longer simply: Can we produce enough food? What are the environmental consequences of attempting to do so?"[18]

The expansion of agriculture too far beyond natural constraints becomes self-defeating, resulting in soil erosion, soil deterioration, water pollution, flood hazards, pest depredations, depletion of resources and, of course, decreased yields. Yet the world's population of four billion is expected to reach more than six billion by the year 2000, and this could well represent a staggering strain on the earth's ecosystem and the food it can supply. Furthermore, even a doubling of food production in the next three decades would only maintain the world's population at present dietary levels. What of the seemingly countless malnourished citizens of the globe? Are they to be condemned to continued hunger and nutritionally induced disease? Are their numbers to continue increasing?

Climatologists, agriculturalists, nutritionists, ecologists—nearly all stress the need for stringent birth-control measures. But putting their urgent warnings aside for the moment, one can ask how much agricultural production, and hence how large a population the earth can sustain. There are many variables that make it difficult even to approach an estimate—for example, what per-capita calorie and protein consumption is to be assumed? What kind of food are we willing to eat? How much is society willing or able to pay to put another acre of marginal land into production.

There are two basic limitations on production: the amount of potentially arable land, and the yields that can be achieved on it. Historically, man has taken the easiest available alternative and simply taken over more land. In recent decades, with the best farmland put to the plow, the emphasis has been on increasing the yields from cultivated land.

It is estimated that, of the globe's 32.5 billion acres of plains, valleys, deserts, mountains and tundra, about 8 billion acres are susceptible to crop production. Some 3.5 billion of these acres already are under cultivation (though much of this total is not actually planted in a given year because it is kept fallow or temporarily in pastures). An additional 8 billion acres have some potential for grazing, and roughly 5 billion of these already are so used.[19]

The total amount of cropland, then, could be more than doubled. However, as a National Academy of Sciences committee put it, "The best lands have long been preempted."[20]

A presidential study[21] in 1967 gave the following breakdown for the *percentage* of potentially arable land that was cultivated:

Asia	83%	North America	51%
Europe	88%	U.S.S.R.	64%
South America	11%	Australasia	21%
	Africa	22%	

Worldwide, 56 percent of the potentially arable land is *not* being used for crops. However, there are serious limitations on much of the land in South America, Africa, and Australasia, because it is either desert or tropical.

The largest areas of uncultivated land are south of the Sahara in Africa and east of the Andes Mountains in South America. But they present problems, because the seemingly lush tropics generally have soils that are deficient in nutrients. In some areas they become exceedingly hard after deforestation, a process called "laterization."[22]

"When the forest cover is removed," says a Food and Agriculture Organization study, "the soils are subject to extremely rapid decomposition of the organic matter that exists because of the high temperatures, and to extremely rapid leaching of the mineral matter because of the heavy rainfall. These processes are accelerated by plowing, especially if the soil is left without a crop cover for even a limited time."[23]

Nevertheless, some experts are quite sanguine about the production potential of the tropics, deserts, and other marginal lands. Charles E. Kellogg, a retired U.S. Department of Agriculture scientist, has said that "on the whole, the long-time potentialities in the tropics can be regarded as enormous, with the application of a symmetrical agriculture science."[24]

To be sure, if soil, disease, and other problems can be solved, the rainfall and temperature of the tropics could become an advantage, permitting three and more crops a year. But the costs of converting and protecting such land could be high.

Boerma says it has been estimated that "an investment of $1.5 billion for the elimination of the tsetse fly in infested areas of tropical Africa could open up 4.5 million square miles (2.9 billion acres) to livestock and crop production."[25] The FAO study further suggests that a lot of arid and semiarid land could be brought into production through irrigation.

But these possibilities do not seem to warrant any relaxation of concern over a food-population squeeze in the future.

United States Potential

In the United States, too, much land is marginal or worse. Some of it is considered unsuitable for agriculture—it may be too steep, too eroded, or too susceptible to wind or water erosion, too stony, too shallow for rooting, too wet, too quick to lose moisture, too saline or alkaline, or too prone to an adverse climate. These drawbacks are sometimes subject to mitigation or correction, sometimes not.

According to a 1967 national inventory of land by the USDA's Soil Conservation Service (SCS),[26] there were 1,438 million acres of nonfederal rural land in the nation. This land is broken into eight basic classifications according to its suitability for cultivation. This is a summary of the SCS findings:

At the time of the survey 438 million acres were in cropland, 482 million acres of pasture and rangeland, and 462 million acres of forest land. Of more relevance to the future, 631 million acres are considered suitable for regular cultivation (Classes I, II, and III). Another 180 million acres are characterized as marginal (Class IV), because the choice of plants is restricted or because very careful management is required, or both. The remaining non-federal rural 627 million acres (Classes V through VIII) are considered unsuitable and generally limited to pasture, range, forest, or wildlife areas, although a small percentage is cultivated.

Assuming that all acreage both suitable and marginal were put into cultivation, the total would increase from 438 million acres to 811 million acres. That is a measure of the U.S. potential, but there would be some trade-offs. Most of the additional acreage would have to come at the expense of grazing or forest lands. Also, of all the land suitable for cultivation, only 47 million acres are considered Class I or without limitations. Of these, 36 million acres are in cropland. All other land has a "dominant soil limitation or conservation problem," the SCS said.

With the pressing into service of millions of acres of marginal lands comes the danger of a new "Dust Bowl." Expanding agriculture to lands that are particularly prone to wind or water erosion may actually decrease agriculture efficiency and possibly result in those lands becoming unfit for other uses, such as grazing or forestry.

An additional problem is that some farmland is being converted to other uses. The Urban Land Institute has estimated that the land area of urban regions will increase from 196,958 square miles in 1960 to 486,902 square miles in 2000, or from 6.6 percent of the U.S. land area (excluding Alaska and Hawaii) to 16.4 percent.[27] James I. Middleswart, an Iowa farmer and member of the state legislature, said, "There are 500 to 600 little towns spotted all over the state, and 75 percent of them set on prime, Grade-A food producing land." So a new house or new industry is apt to encroach on such land, and the farmers frequently find it advantageous to sell to developers.[28] Harry M. Caudill, strip-mining foe and author of *Night Comes to the Cumberland*, has described the great pressures to provide energy by stripping land in 13 western states for coal—land that is otherwise important for food production. "Half of Iowa is underlain by strippable coal, as is 40 percent of Illinois," says Caudill. "This is the nation's breadbasket."[29]

The Limits to Production

How much can the world expect to increase yields on those acres suitable for cultivation? At what point do the environmental—and economic—costs go beyond the pale?

Certainly there is still considerable room for raising yields per acre—through development and greater use of new genetic plant varieties, through increased use of fertilizers, through better cultivation and pesticide management techniques, through extension of irrigation, perhaps through increased rainfall via weather modification, and through increased mechanization. But it is impossible to gauge with any certainty how large an agricultural buffer the world has.

There are quite a few potential constraints on the future of any worldwide green revolution. Generally they are not quantifiable, but the following sampling of cautionary comments serves to put the overall food production problem into perspective:

• The basic limitations on production are imposed by temperature, available moisture (from the sky, from aquifers, from rivers and irrigation works), amount of sunshine, and soil properties. Of course, the serious ups and downs of weather and climate have enormous impacts on agriculture. But potential productivity is governed by the normal parameters of climate and the amount of sunlight that plants are able to use in photosynthesis.

This has been discussed in detail by David M. Gates, professor of botany at the University of Michigan. He cites the work of Jen-Hu Chang, of the University of Hawaii, who based his estimates on photosynthesis on intensity and duration of sunshine and mean monthly temperatures. Gates notes that all the developed countries have a four-month potential photosysthesis of more than 27.5 grams per square meter per day, while all the underdeveloped countries have much lower potentials. "What the difference means is that countries such as the Philippines can expect to increase their yields by 30 percent through improved agricultural methods," says Gates, "but no matter what they do they cannot improve 500 percent or more in order to reach the yields of such countries as Spain. In other words, the underdeveloped countries are climatically limited . . . . [T]hey are the climatically deprived countries."[30]

• A chief constraint, certainly, is money. "Any land, even a mountaintop, can be brought into cultivation if enough money and labor are put into it," authors William and Paul Paddock say.[31] But poor countries may have a hard time finding the funds to employ improved techniques, and farmers—small farmers, in particular—are thwarted by the lack of money or credit.

• Roy W. Simonson, an international soils expert with the SCS, sees one of the major obstacles as educating farmers in new practices and getting them to change their habits. The soil resources and technology are often available, he says, "but you have to be able to manage a more complex type of knowledge. All the elements of management become critical."[32]

• Fertilizers—for all their chemical uplift—must have a point of diminishing return. Simonson points out, for example, that some farmers in Illinois figure they have reached a point of no additional return in the application of nitrogen fertilizers. Other complications include water pollution and eutrophication from run-off of fertilizer chemicals, and worldwide scarcities and high prices of fertilizers. There also is a shortage of natural gas, the principal component of nitrogen fertilizers.

• Water could be a greater restraint on production than land. "Competition among nations for the limited supply of fresh water is legendary in such overpopulated areas as the Middle East," says Brown. "Competition for irrigated water among states with low rainfall in the southwestern part of the United States can only be described as bitter."[33] Darnell M. Whitt, a deputy administrator of SCS, points out that in some western parts of the country, the amount of snowpack determines the water that will be available for irrigation, and this in turn is used to gauge the amount of acreage planted.[34]

Most of the rivers that lend themselves to damming and to irrigation have already been developed, says Brown. Water resource projects, in addition, are apt to be very mixed blessings, as the Aswan Dam project in Egypt and many others have dramatically illustrated.[35] "It's much cheaper to store food than store water," says Borgstrom.[36] Robert S. McNamara, president of the World Bank, has estimated that the more than 300 million acres irrigated in the developing world could be about doubled. "But the additional cost would be high: over $130 billion."[37]

• There have been many warnings about the dangers of pests and diseases that come with widespread monoculture.[38] The literature is similarly abundant on the health and pollution problems associated with the use of various pesticides.

• The energy crisis has brought forth a fuller realization that the "miracle" of U.S. farming is heavily dependent on energy and the mechanization that feeds on it. "If we should decide to measure efficiency in terms of the conservation of energy, then American agriculture comes out very poorly," says Michael J. Perelman, assistant professor of economics at California State University at Chico.[39]

Quentin M. West, Administrator of USDA's Economic Research Service, said in 1973 that "while we have about doubled our farm output in the last 30 years, we have more than quadrupled our fuel consumption so that farm output per gallon of fuel has declined by half." West said that fuel consumption by U.S. agriculture has increased to eight billion gallons a year. "Counting the whole process of growing, processing, transporting, wholesaling, retailing, refrigerating, and cooking, food probably accounts for 12 to 13 percent of the U.S. total energy requirement."[40]

Clearly, if developing nations are to follow U.S. footsteps in agriculture, energy needs will be very large.

Brown and Finsterbusch have given one prognosis for future world productivity: "In the future, man's ability to match crops to land rationally and his ability to breed more efficient and productive plant varieties suited to particular soils and climates will greatly determine the land's productive capacity." They suggested that present yields are "a long way from physiological limits," but that "ultimately, the rate of increase for man's major food crops will begin to slow."[41]

Taking into account likely increases in both available land and per acre yields, what are the prospects for man's future?

Simonson estimates that the U.S. could more than double its food production by "better use of soils in cultivation and making use of some land not in cultivation." He notes the climatic constraints and the fact that the use of fertilizer is not unlimited.

On a worldwide basis, Simonson guesses that production could be doubled "without too much trouble," and perhaps doubled again but with much more difficulty. His estimate does not assume great breakthroughs in new plant varieties; it assumes some but not a great deal of additional irrigation ("it becomes very expensive"); and it assumes substantial use of tropical lands ("the technology to manage some of these soils doesn't exist, but I think it could be developed").[42]

The National Academy of Sciences committee said the facts warrant neither optimism nor pessimism. The population factor aside, the committee said it

... adhered to a "rule of two" for food increases in the world: twofold by new lands, twofold by increased productivity, and twofold by innovation. The new lands will be of lower quality than those now used, which will make it difficult to double their productivity. . . . Productivity can be increased almost everywhere, however, by better use of fertilizers. The final twofold factor of innovation would be impressed on the other two—a doubling from four to eight. This would have to come in part from great changes in food habits toward use of the primary grains for human consumption.

The commitee added: "While the total factor of eight is possible for the United States, it would impose severe demands on rational use of water. Other nations will have to struggle to obtain even a twofold increase, being limited by fertilizer supply in inadequate economies."[43]

One major hope for the future would seem to be the widespread application of *labor-intensive* farming practices—particularly on small holdings in the poorer nations. It has been demonstrated in Japan, Taiwan, and other nations that plots so farmed can be highly productive. They do not require as many expensive capital inputs as some large-scale green revolution techniques. And they can utilize the great abundance of unemployed labor while distributing income benefits more equitably.[44]

The Protein Dilemma

Unfortunately for a world increasingly fond of meat and other high-protein luxuries, there are additional built-in constraints on *protein* production. Brown says that "the grazing capacity of much of the world's pastureland is now almost fully utilized." He also notes that a cow can have only one calf per year, so that "for every animal that goes into the beef production process, one adult must be fed and otherwise maintained for a full year."[45]

Another major source of quality protein is soybeans, which are fed to livestock and poultry as well as eaten directly by more than a billion people. Yet, says Brown, soybean yields per acre in the United States have increased by only about one percent per year since 1950. One reason is that soybeans have a built-in nitrogen supply and are thus not very responsive to nitrogen fertilizer.

One way to increase protein availability would be to persuade Americans and others to forswear their gluttonous consumption of meat, which is so inefficient to produce. Frances Moore Lappe, in *Diet for a Small Planet*, offered these statistics on the effects of America's heavy emphasis on meat consumption: One-third to one-half of the total U.S. continental land surface is used for grazing. One-half of the harvested agricultural land is planted with feed crops, and 78 percent of all grain is fed to animals. In 1968, U.S. livestock (not counting dairy cows) were fed 20 million tons of protein "primarily from sources that could be eaten directly by man." Yet only two million tons of protein were retrieved in human consumption of the meat. Finally, "an acre of cereals can produce five times more protein than an acre devoted to meat production; legumes (peas, beans, lentils) can product 10 times more; and leafy vegetables 15 times more." Borgstrom says that Americans are up to an average animal protein intake of more than 70 grams a day—three-and-a-half times the minimum requirement.[46] Many Americans have already discovered that vegetarian and other non-meat dishes can be highly varied and tasty. (At the same time, research is advancing on substitute meat products, including vegetable-based creations that taste like meat.)

More importantly, a shift from meat to vegetable protein would reduce cholesterol intake and be a great boon to health, according to many doctors. It would relieve some of the strain on the consumer's pocketbook. And it would release large amounts of edible protein for direct consumption by those endless, forgotten millions suffering from protein malnutrition. Of course, it cannot be assumed that the quality of protein in an acre of crops would be as high as that derived from the meat. Also, livestock consume and convert much feed that is not digestible by humans, and they utilize much grazing land that doesn't lend itself to crop production.

Special fortified food mixtures and protein supplements have become important components of the world protein supply. There also is considerable research on genetic breeding to improve protein quality and quantity, and on alternative sources, such as synthetic nutrients, algae, leaf protein concentrates, and "single cell proteins" derived from yeast and bacteria grown on such abundant and inexpensive culture mediums as oil and papermill wastes.

At the same time, there has been a steady loss in an important source of nutrition—human breast milk—as more and more mothers abandon the practice of breast feeding. "As increasing numbers of people settle in urban communities, so the trend from breast to the bottle grows," says an FAO booklet. "Mothers have access to paid jobs and they adopt urban ways which make suckling seem a backward custom."[47] Alan Berg has noted that breast feeding is the ideal form of infant nutrition, and that breast feeding can also be a major factor in birth control because of the contraceptive effect of lactation.[48]

Yet protein malnutrition, especially among children, is rampant. "At present over 300 million children suffer grossly retarded physical growth and development," says the FAO, "and many of these have an additional burden of impaired mental development."[49] Berg also decries the situation: "There is little dispute that malnutrition is the biggest single contributor to child mortality in the developing countries." He adds that more than two-thirds of the 800 million children now growing up in these countries "are expected to encounter sickness or disabling diseases either brought on or aggravated by protein-calorie malnutrition."[50]

Looking to the Seas

And what of the oceans, long viewed by man as a virtually inexhaustible tank of protein?

The ocean fisheries catch increased a hefty 280 percent from 1948 to 1970, says Borgstrom.[51] Much of the increase was due to the expansion of ultramodern, far-ranging fishing fleets. But the 1970's have seen several years of no growth in world fish production. "The press of man on the world's fishing grounds," write Brown and Finsterbusch, "is one of the less-visible but increasingly important dramas of modern times."[52] Writer Robert H. Boyle says that "in just a few years of intense fishing the once enormous stocks of sea herring have been diminished by 90 percent, and haddock have been reduced to such low numbers that the species may become almost nonexistent in East Coast waters."[53] The abrupt disappearance of the anchovies off Peru in 1972 already has been noted.

Although there are widely divergent opinions about the seas' potential, Berg says that "most marine biologists agree that for traditional table fish, the maximum level of sustainable catch has almost been reached."[54] And what are the prospects for the oceans' unused resources? The FAO estimates that taking fishing to the limit—by extending fishing to areas at present unexploited or underexploited, by recovering discarded by-catches, and by initiating fishing of previously neglected species—could increase world fish production by slightly more than half. This is certainly not a comforting total.[55]

An expansion of aquaculture holds some promise. Even the squid and octopus are cited as potentially highly productive. Man also could harvest some species farther down the oceanic food chain, such as krill. But it is difficult to imagine that all of these expedients combined could provide more than a partial answer to the food-protein-population dilemma.

The Distribution of Human Degradation

Unfortunately, providing an adequate over *supply* of protein—and other food—is by no means the end of the global problem. The unconscionable starvation and malnutrition in the world is in great degree a problem of maldistribution.

The United Nations' Protein Advisory Group has said that "foods containing high-quality protein are inequitably distributed between the developed and developing regions of the world, between high and low socioeconomic groups within countries, and within households where the vulnerable members rarely receive a share of the available protein foods commensurate of their needs."[56]

Raw assessments of food production, demand, and reserves overlook other serious dimensions of the problem. Poor nations often cannot afford to buy enough food, particularly at recent prices. Indeed, their inability to import more food is one reason why many observers conclude that reserve stocks of wheat, for example, are sufficiently large. Says Boerma: "It is a bitterly ironic commentary on the present situation that prospects of a world balance in the supply and demand of wheat should partly depend on prospects of deprivation for a very large part of humanity."[57]

For years, Borgstrom has acidly condemned the inequities and anomalies. Modern agriculture and fishing both involve capital-intensive processes which are "beyond the reach of the hungry world." Countries like Peru and Chile, which together produce some three-fifths of the world's fishmeal, export this protein to feed American and European hogs and chickens. Borgstrom calls it "preposterous" that the two most protein-needy continents, South America and Africa, are the main suppliers of animal protein feed in world trade.[58] Says Borgstrom: "Agriculture has never been adjusted to nutrition considerations. It's based on what is profitable."[59]

The food distribution dilemma is enormous. Per capita food consumption figures, given as an *average* for the world or for particular nations, obscure the critical fact that millions of individuals below the average are in trouble. Average per capita consumption of food in developing countries has remained quite stable for a decade or so, as noted earlier, but since some people in those countries are earning more and improving their diets, others must be correspondingly worse off.

Food imbalances result not only from environmental factors but a range of economic, political, and educational barriers. The situation was stated succinctly by Paul and Arthur Simon:

> The problem is not so much an inability to produce food as it is an inability of the poor to purchase it. This, in turn, points to the need for major social and economic reforms within underdeveloped countries, as well as for reforms in the way that rich and poor countries deal with each other.[60]

Chapter 3

WATER

Water is the best of all things.

—Pindar

Seemingly, we rock from one resource crisis to another. From 1972 to 1973 we were shaken by the abrupt disappearance of food reserves and the potential for widespread famine. In 1973 it was the energy crisis—which does not go away. And in 1977 it was water.

Those three resources are intimately related, of course. But the shattering impacts of the 1977 drought—one of the worst in the nation's history, and *the* worst in some areas—focused our attention on water. We were reminded most forcefully that water, like air and sunlight, is indispensable to mankind for a number of reasons, including the production of food and energy.

Nature furnishes, overall, a superabundance of water. As with energy and food, however, it frequently is not available at the right place, the right time, or the right cost. Drought, of course, is a familiar and expected fact of life in arid and semiarid regions. It is a question of degree, and the extent to which man's incursions magnify water shortages, as in America's Southwest, or in Africa's Sahel in recent years.

We are not confronted with anything so dramatic as an "immediately threatening global thirst," says Gilbert F. White, a noted water expert at the University of Colorado. Rather, he says, there is a "more subtle and complex situation in which welfare in many regions will be degraded unless effective use is made of existing technology and managerial skills. . . . This is a more difficult message to communicate."[1]

What are the longer-range prospects for U.S. river basins? It is inappropriate to generalize, but perhaps this assessment of the Yellowstone River by a staff member of the Montana Department of Fish and Game is typical:

Is there enough water? Yes and no. The Yellowstone drainage *does* have enough water to satisfy predictable agricultural and industrial needs if Montanans are willing to pay the high environmental and financial costs of storage development. The Yellowstone River as it flows today (without that development) *does not* have enough water to satisfy all future demands if they are developed anywhere near the maximum proposed.[2]

Three basic questions serve to define the problem of water supply at a particular location for a particular use:

1. *How much total water is available?*
2. *How shall the available water be allocated?*
3. *How can the supply of water be increased or the demand reduced?*

Generally, these determinations are made for each river basin, within which water flows are most conveniently measured and water management most effectively carried out. Each basin must be self-reliant, unless there are interbasin diversions of water.

The amounts of ground water and surface runoff are governed by a variety of factors such as the weather, soil and rock types, vegetation, and geological and other characteristics. These determine the rates of seepage, evaporation, and transpiration from plants. The capability to actually use all the available water may be constrained for technological or economic reasons, or because its quality is deficient.

Water Outlook as Uncertain as the Weather

Weather is the most critical factor in the water equation. It also is the most unfathomable (as climatologists cheerfully concede), the most variable, and the most uncontrollable. The extreme unpredictability of rainfall (or snowmelt) in many regions makes it necessary for water planners to cope with the extra dimension of timing, or reliability of supply.

Richard Deidleman, an ecologist at Colorado College, says that based on past cycles revealed by tree-ring studies, and barring a major climatic change, we can expect a continuation of "patterns of boom and bust in the West." The average annual flow of the Colorado River at Lee Ferry, Arizona, is believed to be about 13.5 million acre-feet (An acre-foot covers one acre to a depth of one foot.) But in 1917, there was a flow of 24 million acre-feet (maf). And in 1934, the flow fell to 5.6 maf.

John F. Griffiths, a meteorologist at Texas A. & M. University, says that "an increase in variability is serious anywhere, but it is extremely serious in marginal areas such as arid and semiarid lands."[3] Also, a single major rainstorm may bring such a region a major portion of its annual rainfall. One deluge kept the Great Plains from being labeled a drought area in 1974.

The weather's capriciousness is not limited to the short term. The potential for long-term, adverse climatic change is similarly ominous. It already has led to some serious miscalculations. Historians have noted that people gradually ceased to be intimidated by what had been called the "Great American Desert." One of the great tragedies in U.S. history occurred in the 1870's when settlers, encouraged by a period of plentiful rain, rushed to homesteads in the West. But a prolonged drought started in 1884. It ended a dozen years later after complete crop failure, great suffering, and widespread emigration. The "Dust Bowl"period in the 1930's is well-known.[4]

In another example of miscalculation, the states served by the Colorado River apparently have been apportioned a good deal more water than the river provides. The Colorado once poured water into the Gulf of California; but now it is dry by the time it reaches that point, 1,450 miles from its origins. Man has consumed, diverted, and stored its flow. A division of the river's water between upper and lower basin states was agreed to in the Colorado River Compact of 1922. Because the previous 30-year period had been extremely wet (and perhaps because measurements were faulty), the average annual flow at Lee Ferry was calculated to be about 18 million acre-feet. But historical records now indicate the true annual, long-term flow is far less, only 13.5 maf by one estimate.[5] The implications of this miscalculation are enormous. The 1922 Compact allocated 7.5 maf per year to the Upper Basin, 8.5 maf to the lower Basin, and 1.5 maf to Mexico. It also specified that the Lower Basin receive its share over the long run (75 maf in any consecutive 10-year period) even if the river's flows are far below average. If the virgin flow actually averages 13.5 maf, says one study, "the total projected demand will exceed the surface water supply in little more than a decade."[6] California, which has been granted 4.4 maf of Colorado River water per year, in 1977 was using more than 5 maf.

Stephen H. Schneider, deputy head of the Climate Project at the National Center for Atmospheric Research in Boulder, Colorado, says that the historical record of Colorado River runoffs shows that "significant drought periods have lasted anywhere from a few years to a few decades." Some of these apparently decreased runoff by 20 percent.[7] There is no reason to assume such droughts will not recur. Indeed, there is even a chance of climatic change broader than the variations revealed in the historical record. Such change could either increase or reduce rainfall.[8]

Schneider assessed the situation thus: "We have reached the stage where, today, we have a high dependence upon the long-term stability of Colorado River stream flow, and much of the concern with the [1977] drought in the West centers on the economic importance of maintaining adequate water supplies from sources such as the Colorado River." With the prospects of dry periods, but no definitive way to predict the climate, Schneider said a difficult political decision emerges: "How to decide just how much water should be retained in the reservoir system now merely to hedge against the *possibility* that this drought period could last many more years."[9]

There is similar anxiety over the possibility of extended drought in the High Plains area. Schneider said that over the last 160 years, the region has been subjected to droughts that last from 3 to 10 years. "They move around regionally, and their intensity varies," he said.

Potentially more significant, they have been spaced roughly 20 to 22 years apart, and we have been at a drought point in the cycle.

The worst scenario, said Schneider, would be simultaneous droughts in the Soviet Union, India, and the U.S., big grain producers. (The Soviet drought of 1972 is well known, as are recurrent monsoon failures in the Indian subcontinent. The summer of 1976 parched much of Europe, and China was reported as undergoing a severe drought.)

Residents of the eastern United States who viewed the 1977 western

WHEAT BELT CLIMATE

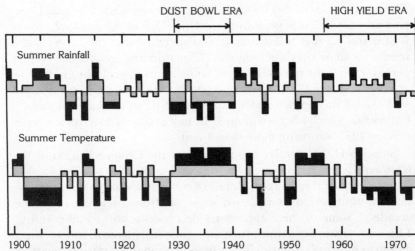

A 75-year record of weather in the High Plains is shown in the graph. It covers the five major wheat-producing states of Kansas, Nebraska, Oklahoma, South Dakota, and North Dakota. Drought correlates with low summer rainfall and high summer temperatures. Years in the normal range are shown in gray, those outside the normal range in black. A drought cycle of about 22 years is reflected, most dramatically by the "Dust Bowl" period in the 1930's. The data was compiled by Donald Gilman, of NOAA.

Climatologist Stephen Schneider notes that we recently have enjoyed a lengthy "high yield era" during which the weather was "extremely cooperative"—with plentiful rainfall and below-normal temperatures. During this time, major grain crop production in the plains region roughly doubled, due to the favorable weather as well as use of fertilizers and improved grain varieties. But, warns Schneider, "The chances for another 15 years of comparable good weather are rather remote."

water problems with some detachment should have remembered that they rely on food produced in the West, and that the waters in many of their own rivers are fully utilized or even oversubscribed, suggesting constraints on growth. More importantly, the East also is subject to drought. Most people no doubt have forgotten the drought of 1962-66 which brought severe water shortages to cities such as New York, Philadelphia, and Washington.[10]

The Uses and Abuses of Water

Available water may be sought for a number of purposes—sometimes conflicting, sometimes not. The chief uses can be classed as domestic, agricultural, industrial (including energy development), and environmental. Environmental purposes are achieved for the most part by maintaining the minimum stream flows for fish and wildlife, recreational use, pollution dilution, and estuary replenishment. But most claims on water are made by farmers, corporations, municipalities, Indian tribes, states, and federal agencies.

It is important to distinguish between *consumptive* uses of water, which more or less permanently remove it from the regional hydrological cycle, and *nonconsumptive* uses, which do not withdraw the water, or withdraw it but return it for possible further use.

A large percentage of irrigation water is consumed—much of it through evaporation—and agricultural use accounts for about 83 percent of nationwide consumptive use. In some areas the share goes up to about 95 percent. Even more water is *withdrawn* for steam electric power plants, but almost all is returned (although evaporation losses increase because the water is heated). The following figures for 1970 illustrate types of uses.[11]

	Withdrawals	Consumptive Use
	(billions of gallons per day)	
Irrigation	130.0	73.0
Public water supply	27.0	5.9
Rural domestic	4.5	3.4
Industrial and miscellaneous	47.0	5.3
Steam electric power	170.0	1.0
Total	370.0	88.0

When water is stored in a reservoir—whether for timely irrigation, municipal supply, flood control, or hydroelectric power generation—evaporation losses magnify. Also, any export of water to another region must, of course, be counted as a consumptive loss in the exporting basin.

Many uses of water are classified as *instream* uses. Natural stream flows are utilized for environmental, navigation, hydroelectric-power, and other purposes. For the most part they are nonconsumptive in nature.

It is also important to keep in mind that the problem of water supply cannot be divorced from that of water quality. If water is too contaminated for drinking, irrigation, or industrial use, it cannot be considered available for these purposes. Furthermore, reduced flows increase pollutant concentrations. A major problem in the Colorado River Basin is the concentration of dissolved solids, or salinity. Much of the basin's water dissolves salts from natural deposits and irrigation, rendering the water too saline to be very useful. Other causes of degradation may be mine drainage, feedlot runoff, heated power plant discharges, and the like.

Water Rights and Use Conflicts

Decisions on how to divvy up available water usually emerge from a maze of state laws, regional and interstate compacts, international treaties, and simple power politics. Typically, decisions are fragmented, not linked to an overall plan that sets priorities or is based on a river basin's carrying capacity. Since the situation varies greatly from place to place, like the weather, and since the laws are continually modified, some generalized observations must suffice.

In western states, for the most part, water rights are obtained pretty much on a first-come-first-served basis. (In the East, water rights usually are tied to the land.) Unfortunately, present water users and those waiting in line with conditional rights have greatly oversubscribed the amount of water that river basins like the Colorado can provide.[12] Thus any new applicant, like an energy company, must obtain someone else's water. Energy developers have, of course, been buying up rights in many places.

In some states, it is relatively easy to transfer water rights; in others, it is difficult. Also, in Colorado, for example, the right to water can be lost if, over a period of time, the holder cannot show "due diligence" in utilizing or storing the water. Hundreds of lawsuits currently seek to abrogate rights for the benefit of the next in line.

Certain types of water-use conflict can be expected to recur, or persist, in various river basins around the country. Many already have been triggered by proposed energy developments. The impact of an energy project is linked to the local or regional water supply and the competing demands on it. But it also depends on how water-intensive the project is.

In general, Colorado officials are far less concerned about the prospect of coal mining (which requires only 0.25 to 0.61 million gallons per BTU of energy) than of coal gasification or fossil fuel power plants (estimated at 72 to 158 million gallons per BTU, and 120 million gallons per BTU, respectively).[13]

To be sure, Colorado also wants to avoid becoming "a smokestack for the rest of the nation," as one official puts it.

Energy development is only one of many demands on Colorado River Basin water. "It simply happens to be the most prominent, rapidly changing, nonagricultural variable at this point in the history of water demand in the basin," says one report. Any of the various demands, including energy, could precipitate a crunch, and the Bureau of Reclamation estimates that by the end of the century in the Upper Basin some 874,000 acre-feet more water than is now used would be needed each year to supply coal-fired steam plants, coal gasification facilities, and oil shale development.[13a]

On the other hand, Waren Viessman, Jr., a senior specialist at the Congressional Research Service, says that in the Missouri River Basin, for example, the amount of water needed for energy is very small in terms of total basin water supply. He personally feels it could be made up easily through better irrigation practices.

In Colorado, water-use conflicts have centered around the controversial dams and water projects that President Carter has attempted several times and with only limited success to kill, much to the dismay of the pork-barrel-oriented Congress. Colorado officials worry that if the dams are not built, the rights to too much available water will end up in the hands of environmentally undesirable energy developers—at the expense of a stable, diversified, agricultural economy that is compatible with the environment and life-style of the region. "We don't want to see rural decay," said Harris D. Sherman, director of the Colorado Department of Natural Resources. The situation is complex, but Sherman explained that if storage projects are not built to help farmers utilize water to which they are entitled, then the energy companies have the rights that follow, or they will try to purchase conservation district rights.

Critics of the dams, like the Environmental Defense Fund, argued that they are financially unsound; that they would help only a small number of marginal farmers in mountainous areas who grow forage for cattle; and that despite legal safeguards, energy companies will be able to get access to the water.[14] Sherman replied that Colorado has insisted that the repayment contracts for several of the projects forbid any transfer of water rights from agricultural to other uses without the written consent of the farmer, the conservation district, the Secretary of Interior, and the governor of Colorado. He also argued that, even if energy companies obtained such water rights, they would face many economic, political, and physical obstacles to their use.

In assessing a region's water supplies, it should be kept in mind that in some areas ground water is more significant than surface water— either on a regular basis or in getting through a dry period. Generally, too, it is more expensive to obtain. Surface runoff may or may not be inextricably linked to an underground aquifer. If it is, ground-water withdrawals can deplete the surface water supply, just as withdrawal of surface water can prevent recharge of an aquifer. In other areas, the aquifer may be impervious to recharge. Since each region's geology is different, generalizations are meaningless. Ground water supplies in such regions as central Arizona and the high plains of Texas have been massively overdrawn, with water tables dropping more than 200 feet. In Texas, the aquifer is very slow to recharge. In Arizona, much of the water derived from the huge and controversial Central Arizona Project would be used to restore underground supplies. The law provides that a farmer using Project water must reduce his use of ground water by the same amount.[15] But there's no good way to tell how much ground water most Arizonans use. Anyway, no one pretends the Project is much of an answer to the ground water depletion problem. According to two investigators with the Lake Powell Research Project, "Arizona is already in a water-deficit position and only continued mining of ground water will sustain the current level of use even when the state's full allotment of Colorado River water is used."[16]

Environmentalists and others have lambasted the irresponsible and wasteful use of water in regions such as central Arizona. They have called attention to the fact that land developers, energy companies, and agribusiness conglomerates sometimes can squeeze out small farmers. They can afford to develop their own water storage facilities while others must rely on a federal reclamation project for financing, and they can afford the expense of drilling deep to tap ground water when shallower supplies are gone.

Criticism does not spare the ordinary residents who feel they must have the kinds of lawns, golf courses, and swimming pools they left behind on Long Island. "People have brought their old environments with them here and they resent being told they're in the middle of the desert," says former Tucson City Council member Barbara L. Weymann.

Three Claims on River Water

For many rivers, all conflicting water uses by farmers, energy industries, and municipalities may be as drops in a bucket compared to three other claims that loom larger and larger.

1. The maintenance of "instream flows" at minimum levels is designed to preserve the stream's biological and recreational values. Estimates of flow requirements for fisheries, in particular, are crude, but it is clear that substantial amounts of water are at stake. Paul Wehr, of the University of Colorado's Institute of Behavioral Science, says: "One of the sharpest environmental conflicts of the future will involve the *maximum beneficial use* doctrine supported by water law, and the *minimum stream flow* demand powered by the conservation ethic."

The Congressional Research Service (CRS) staff has estimated that, in general, the amount of water available for storage or for new use at a particular location would be reduced by 30 to 60 percent if the designated instream flow needs are met. A CRS study of the Missouri River Basin says that if minimum flows are required, all eight subbasins will be water deficient in the year 2000. "Tradeoffs with other uses will be required, particularly during periods of low flow."[17]

On some rivers, minimum flow needs, combined with other uses, already exceed the water supply. State laws vary. Some give minimum flows a high priority, others put them into the pot with competing claims. One might expect that unless instream flow needs are agreed upon or embodied in law, they may be forced to retreat when energy, argiculture, or other demands become more pressing.[18]

2. There is a doctrine of "federal reservation" under which the government has an implied right to reserve enough water in national parks, national forests, and other lands to serve the purposes for which these areas were established. These water needs also can be substantial, and in conflict with other uses.

Maintaining fishing and other recreation in a national park might require a minimum flow, with the impacts felt mainly by upstream users. On the other hand, mining leases on other public lands could involve a heavy consumption of water.

The Supreme Court appears to have given the government a solid claim to water for these purposes.[19] The government insists its rights date back to the time the lands were withdrawn from the public domain, and are superior to all other rights in a stream. However, many court suits on the issue are pending, and quantification of such rights will be difficult.

3. Last and far from least, in many parts of the West considerable water is needed by Indian tribes. And the Supreme Court has made it clear that Indian water rights are independent of any state water laws. They date back either to aboriginal use or to the time the reservation was established, and thus usually have priority over all non-Indian uses.[20]

The Court reasoned that the government would not have set up reservations without at the same time implying the right to sufficient water for a meaningful existence on them. Most of the arid western lands would be nearly worthless without irrigation water.

The Court later defined sufficiency as the amount needed for all "practicably irrigable acreage" on a reservation.[21] But many questions remain, and many lawsuits to resolve them. How much acreage is "practicably" irrigable, and how much water is needed per acre? Are not the tribes also entitled to water for energy development? (Many western reservations are underlain with rich deposits of coal, for example.) And for recreation?

Indian claims on water have proliferated only in recent years, and the potential demand is largely unknown. But it may be very large. The tribes are particularly concerned that their rights and their opportunities for further development will suffer as competing users capture more water.

However, their strong legal position suggests that Indian tribes may be able to obtain the water they need, even if it means preempting water already apportioned to others. This poses a major threat to billions of dollars worth of investment in non-Indian water projects.

Until tribal rights are fully resolved and tribal needs clearly quantified, the water situation in many river basins will remain very clouded.[22]

Get It While You Can

The essential fact of life is that almost everyone is determined to appropriate and use as much water as he can, and in many cases to press for the construction of water storage projects. The reiterated demands are not confined to meeting current needs, but to accommodate future development as well. For example, the city manager of Tucson, Joel D. Valdez, in 1977 asked the Arizona Water Commission to recommend (to the Interior Department) an increase in Tucson's share of Central Arizona Project water. He said the city by the late 1980's will have 100,000 more people than the commission calculated, and the City Council hopes the commission will allocate enough water to sustain anticipated growth through the year 2034.[23]

Upper Colorado River Basin states have similar feelings. Indeed, no state wants to relinquish any of its water to another. One reason Colorado is so anxious to build its dams is so it can capture and utilize water to which it is entitled (as spelled out in the Colorado River Compact of 1922 and the Upper Colorado River Basin Compact of 1948) rather than continue letting it flow downstream to where other users, including the Central Arizona Project, can lap it up.

Another manifestation of the every-state-for-itself doctrine is the strong antagonism in the Pacific Northwest to several elaborate and costly proposals for diverting large amounts of water from the Columbia River and other basins to areas of shortage. Even though water in the area seemed plentiful at the time to many, a moratorium on any Interior Department reconnaissance studies of such transfer projects was enacted in 1968.[24] Then, as an Oregon newspaper has bluntly put it, "Agreement soon developed in this region that the best way to fend off the Southwest when the moratorium ran out was to establish uses in the Northwest for all the water in the Northwest."[25]

Unfortunately, as the paper added, no one knew that a condition of scarcity would arrive as early as 1976. A Corps of Engineers official recently observed: "Any expansion of use of the Columbia River, whether that be instream or out-of-bank use, will involve costs and tradeoffs to other river uses."[26]

As John Wesley Powell told a convention on irrigation in 1893, "I wish to make it clear to you, there is not sufficient water to irrigate all the lands which could be irrigated, and only a small portion can be irrigated. . . . I tell you, gentlemen, you are piling up a heritage of conflict!"

Ounces of Prevention or Pounds of Cure?

Will concern over the nation's water shortages drift from the public consciousness—to be revived only by the next crisis? One can hope, at least, that those people professionally responsible for coping with water resource problems will press hard for solutions. For it is a safe bet that the weather will deal many more bad hands over the years. We also can count on people and industries remaining greedy and wasteful, and continuing to impose their demands on relatively arid lands despite those land's limited carrying capacity.

Fortunately, water shortages can be prevented or alleviated in many ways. Unfortunately, each remedy involves some degree of financial, social, or environmental pain. Each, therefore, is certain to generate political opposition.

Figures for the amount of water available vary according to measurement methodologies, the historical periods used to find averages, various assumptions that must be made, and the confounding weather itself.[27]

As for measuring usage, a 1977 General Accounting Office (GAO) report[28] illustrates the difficulties. It says that regional officials, in estimating water use in part of the Texas-Gulf Region, found water withdrawals for manufacturing to be 26 percent less than the federal Water Resources Council (WRC) figure, and found water consumed for manufacturing to be 65 percent more. For the Missouri River Basin, regional estimates of consumptive use by irrigation in the 11 subareas of the region differed from WRC estimates by 22 to 177 percent.

The GAO report pointed to a further problem with the 1975 National Water Assessment under which WRC is collecting data from 106 subareas making up the nation's 21 water resource regions.[29] It noted a consensus among western regional officials that

> . . . simple comparisons of total water supplies and requirements at the aggregated subarea level do not reveal water shortages within such an area due to geographical distribution and institutional restrictions, such as state water rights. These officials believe that the subareas used in the assessment are so extremely large that critical water shortages in particular portions of a subarea are lost in the total figures.

Projections of future use enter the realm of speculation. They depend on the extent of energy and other development, the amounts of water needed or to be appropriated to maintain stream flows for environmental purposes (fish, wildlife, recreation, and ecosystem protection), the amounts demanded and received by Indian tribes, and many other factors.[30] It is interesting to note, for example, that some states refuse to use any population projections other than those developed by their own state agencies, despite the fact that the Water Resources Council has comprehensive projections covering the entire U.S.[31]

It is clear that decision making and problem solving would be aided by further basic research on historical stream flows, climatology, instream flow needs, and Indian tribal requirements.

Solutions to Water Problems

Solutions to water problems fall into three general categories: (1) increasing supplies (which may include improving water quality to the point of usefulness), (2) reducing demand, and (3) shifting demand from one place to another or shifting allocations from one user to another. (Another category might be drought aid and other relief measures, but that's locking the barn door afterwards.)[32]

©Copyright 1977 James Stevenson.

Historically, water resource managers have leapt at concrete methods to provide additional water, principally with dams and diversion canals. Certainly many benefits can derive from impoundment and regulated releases of water from a reservoir, particularly during a drought. But such projects increasingly have become part of the problem.

They induce further development, so that additional supplies are claimed even as the projects are built. "In the long run," says climatologist Schneider, "the problem is to make sure that any additional reservoir capacity added to the [Colorado River] system is maintained as precisely that: reservoir capacity . . . to hedge against the kinds of weather fluctuations that have occurred in the past."[33]

Specific water development projects make sense if they enable a river basin to achieve its desired goals, says Helen Ingram, associate professor of political science at the University of Arizona. However, she says that

... in the politics of federal water development, the focus from the very beginning is upon specific local projects, shortcutting a general discussion of where the basin should or could be going . . . . The need to prove favorable benefit-cost ratios has tempered questions and suppressed debate on larger questions of basin development.[34]

Future water projects appear to be dubious for more clearly pragmatic reasons. The amount of water available for storage or diversion is diminished. Prime sites for effective impoundment are scarcer. Reservoirs increase evaporation and seepage losses. The economic and environmental costs of projects weigh heavily.

"Water projects don't create water," says Interior Secretary Cecil D. Andrus, "they move it around, and sometimes lose some in the process. We are coming to the end of the dam-building era in America."[35] The Carter Administration made it clear that it views water projects with what might be called—in a phrase literary critic Frank Turaj applied to H.L. Mencken—"zero-based skepticism."

Many proposals have been made to transfer water from one region to another. In the multibillion-dollar category are the elaborate pump and pipe projects to bring huge quantities of water from the Yukon or the Columbia River to the arid Southwest,[36] from the Mississippi or its tributaries to the high plains of western Texas,[37] and from the Hudson River above the point of salinity to New York City—the last a $4.6 billion proposal by the Corps of Engineers.[38]

Such diversions do not appear to have a bright future, however, since they do not increase the overall supply of water and since someone must be willing to give up water for export.

In many parts of the country, according to the U.S. Geological Survey, large supplies of ground water are available for tapping. In other areas, efforts to increase the use of ground water are likely to be costly, to cause land subsidence, or to result in serious depletion (including loss of surface water when it recharges the aquifers). The quality of ground water also can be degraded.[39]

An Infinite Supply of Water

Theoretically, the usable water supply can be enlarged almost infinitely in two ways: recycling and desalting. In both cases, the technologies, while difficult, are pretty well advanced. But major obstacles, such as high costs, remain.

"Desalinization is still extremely expensive, and extremely energy intensive," says Aaron Weiner, central director of Water Planning for Israel, Ltd. Israel has several plants in operation and is building a large new facility in conjunction with a nuclear power plant. "It promises to become substantially cheaper."[40]

Israel, an arid land needing a high degree of self-sufficiency, has a major program for recycling sewage and industrial wastes. A number of recycling facilities also are being tested in the United States.[41]

The costs of recycling are intimidating, but industrial recycling systems can significantly facilitate pollution control and reduce water expenses. To put it another way, a plant that has to meet effluent discharge standards in any case may find that, with relatively little additional expense, it could produce water clean enough for recycling.[42]

The 1977 drought kindled growing interest in weather modification to increase rainfall or snowpack. Colorado and California resorted to emergency cloud-seeding. But many serious questions about atmospheric rape remain unresolved—efficacy, environmental effects, disruption of weather patterns, legal rights to cloud moisture, and so forth.[43]

Jerome W. Kirby, a Texas attorney specializing in the field, has warned of "mountains of sorrowful litigation" over weather modification disputes.[44] The dilemma could be funny if it weren't so serious, as this editorial comment shows:

> The Attorney General of Idaho has accused the neighboring state of Washington of "cloud rustling," and announced plans to file suit in federal court to stop its rainmaking activities. Idaho's governor, however, objects, in part because he foresees the possibility that drought-stricken Idaho may soon want to try its own luck at rainmaking.[45]

Still farther out on the fringe are a number of schemes that keep resurfacing—removing water-consumptive vegetation; reversing the flow of rivers that empty into the Arctic Ocean; melting icepacks by darkening them; and towing icebergs to an arid land where the water from melting would be siphoned off. A French engineering firm is studying the feasibility of this for Saudi Arabia. Preliminary estimates indicate a cost of water far less than desalinization.[46]

Conservation Is the Best New Source of Water

Because of their increasing disenchantment with technological fixes, many water resource experts have been stressing better management of existing supplies—by such techniques as shifting usage patterns, water rights reform, greater reuse of water, and reducing waste.

The parallels with energy are striking: Waste of both energy and water is enormous. It is cheaper to save a barrel of oil or an acre-foot of water than to create a new one. And the techniques for conservation are plentiful.

The chief problem is overcoming the traditions and habits of farmers, industries, and homeowners whose lives and livelihoods long have been tied to the profligate use of cheap water. Any restrictions are apt to trigger violent opposition. In the summer of 1976, for example, the City

Council of Tucson voted a sharp increase in water rates when it was faced with excessive ground-water pumping and an outmoded distribution system. The reaction was so vehement that one of the four Council members who voted for the increases resigned and the other three were recalled by large margins in an election in January 1977.[47]

Proposals to meter water use bring similar responses. Many cities—like New York and Denver, for example—do not have metering. Nor do irrigation pumps in some areas of the Southwest where ground-water levels have dropped sharply.

Farmers are apt to resist new, water-saving methods of irrigation, and even if they didn't, a vast effort to acquaint them with available modern techniques would be necessary.

There is an overriding need to reform the institutional incentives to waste water. In some places, for example, farmers pay for water according to the number of acres farmed rather than the amount of water used, so they have no incentive to cut consumption. Generally, a farmer's water rights are tied to the land, and he may be unable to use or profit from water he saves. To put it another way, an irrigator with a right to divert a certain amount of water must use it or lose it.[48]

Says Thomas Barlow, of the Natural Resources Defense Council:

In California, the irrigation districts make little effort to resell the water draining out of their areas even though much of the water is suitable in quality for further irrigating use. The reason for the district's lethargy is that they would have to pay all proceeds from such resales to the Bureau of Reclamation rather than retain any part of the income for their own operations.[49]

The options for reform under such circumstances are obvious. For example, the National Water Commission has recommended that "rights should be created in salvaged water, and the rights should be freely transferable to other uses and users, subject only to the limitation that rights of others should not be injured."[50]

The Commission also suggested that before Congress authorize a project, it evaluate the efficiency of present water use and the prospects for alleviating shortages through water-saving practices instead. The allocation of water could be conditioned on the application of conservation measures. Within the next 10 to 20 years, many of the Bureau of Reclamation's water contracts will expire, possibly offering opportunities to reform water allocations and require conservation practices.

A more direct approach has been taken by New Mexico. In eastern parts of the state, all wells must be metered. Also, in some areas such as Pecos Valley, irrigation use has been limited to three acre-feet of water per year. (In a dry year, farmers can use part of their total from other years in a five-year period.) Such restrictions do not necessarily reduce yields.[51] Generally, allotments in the state are made according to the amount of water currently stored in the reservoirs.

Farms, Factories, and Flush Toilets

In short, there are many ways to achieve more efficient use of water. They include metering, rationing, mandated conservation practices, water rights reform, and pricing strategies. (Pricing can be aimed at eliminating subsidies or recovering full costs, and discouraging the use of water through high rates or a rate structure that progressively penalizes increased consumption, similar to those now commonly urged for electricity rate-setting.)

Because agriculture accounts for such a large share of national water consumption (about 83 percent), the potential for conservation in that area is great. "If you cut agricultural use 10 percent, you're talking about enormous quantities of water," says Viessman, of the Congressional Research Service.

Such a reduction seems quite feasible. "Irrigation is a relatively inefficient water use, since under present practices less than half of the water delivered is actually consumed by the crops," says a General Accounting Office report.[52] A Bureau of Reclamation study put average irrigation efficiency at 44 percent. It said this could be increased to 55 percent with minor changes in water management, and up to 70 percent and 90 percent with more elaborate techniques and improved facilities.[53]

How can such savings be achieved? One way is lining irrigation ditches with concrete, plastic membranes, or other materials to reduce seepage. In some fields, tiles or sheets of plastic have been buried just below the crop's root zone for better conservation or drainage.

Farmers frequently irrigate too often, too much, or at the wrong time. Better scheduling of irrigation deliveries could provide major savings, water experts say. There are automated systems that "respond to soil moisture rather than when the Bureau of Reclamation says the water is available," says Viessman. Computerized irrigation scheduling systems and consulting services are available.

The irrigation system itself often is very wasteful. Sprinkler methods can be far more efficient than border or furrow irrigation, and drip or trickle techniques add still another dimension to water conservation. With trickle irrigation, water is slowly dripped at the base of individual plants, through a network of very small plastic tubes. Automated controls release only as much water as the plants need. Israel, which originated the system, says water savings for some crops can reach almost 40 percent, with yields also increased.[54]

Other argicultural options are shifting to crops that require less water, or genetic development of plants that are drought-tolerant. This by no means exhausts the list of possible conservation measures.

On the industrial and municipal side, the potential for conservation also is enormous. "An effort should be made to arrange a sequence of uses and reuses [of water] where possible," said the National Water Commission.[55] For example, waste treatment plant effluent can be used to water parks and golf courses, or for some industrial purposes. Land can be zoned for activities that require relatively little water, such as light industry.

Detection and control programs can correct the many leaks, defective connections, and "conveyance losses" that make some municipal distribution systems extremely wasteful. "Leakage and other losses may account for 35 percent of the total supply," says a Water Resources Council report.[56]

At the domestic level, the opportunities are similarly numerous and varied. They range from the social in nature (abstaining from lawn watering, sharing showers, and skipping flushes) to the technological and economic. In addition to metering, rationing, and pricing policies, municipalities can adopt plumbing code amendments and otherwise promote the installation of water-saving fixtures and appliances.

Toilets are available that save water or do not use water at all. Automatic flow regulators can reduce consumption for shower, kitchen sink, and other uses, as can foot pedals for faucets. And so forth.[57]

Adjusting to Finite Water Supplies

In a complex and strange way, water supplies are finite like those of energy. One can at least theorize a situation in which almost unlimited amounts of ocean water are desalted and piped as far inland as necessary. One also can theorize a river basin in which water is recycled but there *still* isn't enough to meet increasing demands.

However, the financial and environmental costs of continually expanding water supplies can be exorbitant. Presumably the many taxpayer and environmental subsidies already built into water programs in the West cannot be continued and inflated indefinitely. Robert D. Miewald, a professor of political science at the University of Nebraska, describes one of many examples:

> Unfortunately, since disaster relief in the United States is a strange combination of humanitarian impulses and political machinations, all within an unwieldy administrative structure, there has been no comprehensive evaluation of the total cost of such an approach. For example, some South Dakota counties have been declared disaster areas for four years in a row. When can taxpayers in the rest of the country indicate to these people that perhaps Mother Nature is trying to tell them something?[58]

Even assuming normal weather, there are limits to every area's hydrological carrying capacity—limits which may be ignored at great costs.[59]

Speaking of California and its Marin County, planning consultant Ted Kreines says that no agency has "confronted the fundamental questions of why transfers [of water from one region to another] are imperative in the first place and what would happen if regions had to be self-sufficient in water."[60]

The California Water Plan, says Kreines, used self-serving population projections, assumed growth would occur and water would be available, and then "set out to make the water available." The plan is "based on the concept of maldistribution: that is that water is not readily available where it is wanted . . . . Nowhere did it deal with what would happen if the water were not available in the future."

Instead of a simple demand-responsive model, Kreines argues, states need a comprehensive allocative planning process. The truly basic question in a region is whether the amount of water is used to guide or limit growth, or the amount of in-migration is used to justify increasing the water supply.

This triggers the next question: Is it feasible or desirable to steer migration and development away from places where water shortages are prevalent or imminent? Presumably so, in the same manner that local governments have sought to control growth for other reasons.

Yet most regions remain hospitable, despite the resource constraint. Says Arizona Congressman John J. Rhodes: "People from the congested East and elsewhere are attracted to Arizona. There is no way that Arizona could keep them out, even if it wanted to. Americans have a right to live wherever they want. They have a right to seek a better way of life."[61]

"We get seven inches of rain in a whole year," says former Arizona Governor Raul Castro. "But the people still keep coming in. We don't have to ask them to come here. We do have a dilemma."[62]

If people are at liberty to migrate to dry sunbelt areas, are they also entitled to watered lawns, golf courses, and swimming pools? Ten years ago, Frank Quinn wrote that "neither nature nor morality" dictates that people adjust their living habits to a paucity of water:

> If this kind of living reflects the popular preference, it will hardly be thwarted by the jealous designs of better-watered but less-developed regions to divert population growth in their direction. But although people may continue to live where they want, they must pay a price for their choice. In other parts of the country this price may be expressed in higher bills for fuel or in the cost of winter clothing; in the drylands it is the cost of water.[63]

It's not quite that simple, of course, since the costs of water include environmental costs that are regional and national in impact; since undesirable marketplace inequities are difficult to avoid; and since various subsidies are not easily removed. Still, by default, marketplace costs ultimately may become the most effective limits to further growth in arid regions.

The recognition of a region's carrying capacity implies a readiness to consider limitations on growth and the allocation of water according to an overall plan. A study of the Missouri River Basin by the Congressional Research Service says that decisions could be facilitated by displaying alternative futures—for example, futures that emphasize either irrigation development, energy developments, instream flow needs, or Indian water use. "For each alternative the impacts of several levels of water used by specific water users could also be presented."

The study illustrates the approach:

> Assume that one alternative is to provide an optimal level of instream flows for fish and wildlife preservation, navigation, and hydroelectric power generation. Within this constraint, the remaining flows could then be apportioned in several alternative ways to satisfy the other major uses—namely irrigation, energy, resource development, and municipal and industrial water supply. The analysis would show the impact of the various trade-offs by each sector and would provide the basis for a reasonable compromise. In like manner, the instream flow optimizing alternative could be compared with those stressing irrigation, Indian water use, and energy resource development.
>
> The selection of a policy for future water resources development should be made less difficult in this manner and the implications of that choice explicit.[64]

If future policies and use priorities can be firmly established—no mean task—another tough problem remains. Since climate and river flows can fluctuate so widely, responsible officials must develop a clear and legally sound formula for sharing scarcity when cutbacks are forced by drought.

In sum, as Gilbert White puts it, there is a need to "sort out and apply an immense number of water management techniques to local and national conditions."[65]

Chapter 4

POPULATION

One of the best things people could do for
their descendants would be to sharply limit
the number of them.

—Olin Miller

If the Earth is viewed as a physiological entity—a single, massive, living creature—then people are its cells, and population growth is its cancer. A new diagnosis says that the *rate* at which people-cells are proliferating has shifted downward, that the cancer is being slowly arrested. Yet the condition of the Earth as a whole can be said to deteriorate still, since population is increasing rapidly even if less rapidly. In other words, the pain continues, and will do so for many years.

This population cancer does not really attack the Earth as a whole. It attacks many of the limbs and vital organs that make up the global creature—the 200 different countries that function in their own ways. These parts of the Earth are in different stages of illness and treatment. Some have little or no population growth, or they are applying effective control measures. A few have considerable growth, but are able to accommodate it so it is benign. Many others suffer from obviously malignant population growth.

To be sure, each of the 200 countries is linked somehow to the others—economically, environmentally, socially. In some cases, population growth cancers can spread from one part of the world to another, for example through emigration. (These shifts do not necessarily decrease the overall well-being of the Earth.) In other ways, cancerous growth in one country can cause problems elsewhere: through conflicting claims on limited international resources, through pressures on global commons, through political instability and terrorism, and through the creation of moral dilemmas.

Since circumstances in the 200 countries are so different, aggregate population figures do not greatly aid in diagnosis. They obscure the regional, national, and urban—not to mention individual—problems

89

of population growth. These involve starvation and malnutrition, disease, severe unemployment, dreadful housing, crime, and other forms of human degradation. These are problems the world will have to deal with for years and years to come, even if the recent trend toward a declining population growth rate continues.

Recent attention has focused on the welcome news in several population reports. One contained the U.S. Census Bureau's demographic estimates for 1977. "In sum," said the bureau, "throughout the world a perceptible decline in population growth rates has begun to emerge, with the persistent exception of Africa. In some areas the decrease is substantial, in others incipient; in general the decrease is no longer questionable."[1] More specifically, the report showed a decline in the estimate for the average annual world growth rate from 1.98 percent of the 1965-70 period to 1.88 percent in 1975-77.

The estimate for the decline would have been greater except that the bureau's figures for China's growth rate were above earlier estimates and also substantially higher than those made by others. Its median estimate for the 1978 growth rate was a robust 2 percent. Other estimates range down to almost 1 percent, an enormous difference. While noting the dearth of solid information on China, the bureau said, "Nevertheless, despite considerable doubt as to the actual level and pace of change, there is little question that the growth rate is also declining in China."

Of the 50 most populous countries containing 90 percent of the world's people, 24 experienced a reduced growth rate in the last decade, the Census Bureau said. Most importantly, the global decline is reflected not only in a lower growth rate in the more developed countries—a well-known phenomenon that has been taking place for 15 or more years—but also in the less-developed countries as a whole. These, of course, contain the bulk of the world's population, crowding, resource constraints, and economic problems. Thus:

	More developed countries	Less developed countries
Mid-1977 population (millions)	1,154	3,103
Average annual growth rate (%), 1965-70	1.0	2.4
Average annual growth rate (%), 1975-77	0.7	2.3

The growth rate has declined in some of the less-developed countries with the largest populations—including China, the Philippines, Indonesia, Thailand, and Turkey.

"I think it is an undeniable fact that fertility rates have fallen appreciably in a number of developing countries," says W. Parker Mauldin, a senior fellow at the Population Council. He has noted that, of the 13 largest developing countries, 10 showed a significant decline in crude birth rate in the period 1965-75. The overall average decline was 13 percent.[2]

Another optimistic report, from the Population Reference Bureau, estimated that the world fertility rate in the period 1968-75 dropped from 4.6 births per woman to 4.1. It notes that declines occurred in a number of less-developed countries "formerly viewed as potential seedbeds for population-related catastrophes."[3] The report, written by two experts at the University of Chicago's Community and Family Center, Amy Ong Tsui and Donald J. Bogue, said, "The turning point seems to have occurred between 1970 and 1975, and appears to be progressing at an accelerating pace."

BIRTH AND DEATH RATES: DEVELOPED AND DEVELOPING COUNTRIES, 1775 TO 1977

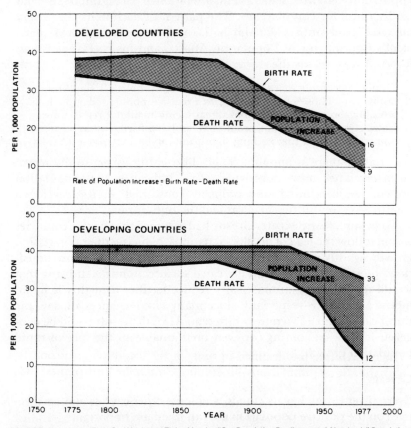

SOURCE: Jean van der Trak, Carl Haub, and Elaine Murphy, "Our Population Predicament: A New Look," *Population Bulletin*, Vol. 34, No. 5 (Population Reference Bureau, Inc., Washington, D.C., 1979), Figure 3.

Most reactions to the worldwide decline in the population growth rate have been enthusiastic but guarded. Samuel Baum, assistant chief of the Census Bureau for international demographic statistics, commented, "This is really a major turning point in world history." Ansley J. Coale, professor and associate director of the Office of Population Research at Princeton University, concurred that the growth rate has peaked. "This is a turning point," he said. "I don't think it is going back up."[4]

The Census Bureau report provides "a glimmer of light," according to Lester R. Brown, head of the Worldwatch Institute. The decline, editorialized the *Washington Post*, "conveys an unmistakable sense of a shift of immense forces. At least, it suggests the world is not fated to be overwhelmed by a rising tide of people."[5] Said the *New York Times*: "The demographic sky may be overcast, but it is not falling."[6]

Rafael M. Salas, executive director of the United Nations Fund for Population Activities, stated, "This alteration of pace is impressive, but hardly cause for complacency. The pattern of decline has been very uneven."[7] And Ambassador Marshall Green, formerly the State Department's Coordinator of Population Affairs, and his special assistant, Robert A. Fearey, say the slower rate of growth

> . . . does not imply that the world population problem is significantly easing . . . . Those of us who regard excessive population growth as probably the most fundamental threat facing mankind regret unwarranted suggestions that the problem is resolving itself, just as we reject counsels of despair that nothing significant can be done about it.[8]

Certainly there is one undeniably heartening aspect to the recent estimates: They seem to provide a firm indication that population growth *can* be slowed, and probably controlled, in less-developed countries—given sufficient effort and the right inputs.

To be sure, many experts already had assumed that poorer countries would follow the lead of developed nations, reducing their population growth steadily if they could pass through the "demographic transition" process and achieve an increased socioeconomic well-being that would more or less automatically reduce fertility. But this is by no means a certainty—especially since many circumstances in, say, the European countries were very different. Also, the result could be dangerously slow in coming, or even unattainable in the face of rapid population growth.

Caveats

Every silver lining has its clouds, and some other caveats and perspectives on the positive population growth trend are important:

- Of particular significance is the fact that the growth rates of many countries are still extremely high and, like a supertanker, their population has enormous momentum. Every second, the world gains two and a half humans. Every day, some 215,000. Every year, about 78 million.[9]

The momentum of currently high rates of fertility will be greatly increased by the high ratio of children in many countries. In Mexico, for example, nearly half the population is 15 years old or less.

Even if the world as a whole could attain a zero growth rate, the population would continue to grow for five decades or more afterwards. The eventual size would depend upon when the growth stopped and the age composition of the population. Thomas Frejka, of the Population Council, has estimated that results of the built-in momentum under several scenarios.

In one, stabilization would be achieved quite rapidly between the years 2000 and 2005, and the world population would finally level off in the year 2100 at about 8.4 billion, roughly twice its present size. With a slower decline to a stabilized level between 2040 and 2045, the population in 2100 would peak at a staggering 15.1 billion.[10]

(Stabilization here was defined as a "net reproduction rate" of 1— meaning that a generation of mothers has just enough daughters to replace itself. This involves an average family size of 2.1 to 2.5 children, depending on mortality condition.)

Of course, there will be great disparities in the growth of various countries' populations, and that is where the rubs will be. Even assuming rapid stabilization, Frejka obtained estimates such as these:

	1970 (millions)	2100 (millions)	% increase
United States	205.7	314.0	53
Mexico	50.7	173.5	242
India	534.3	1,407.0	163

• A similar way of stating the problem is to note that fertility levels in many countries are high and have a long way to go down before population stops growing. "The fertility transition is, at best, only in the beginning stages for many countries," say Tsui and Bogue.[11]

They noted that the estimated average rate of childbearing worldwide in 1975, 4.1 per woman, is nearly double that needed to reach the replacement level. There is another way of putting it, in terms of the less-developed countries: The Census Bureau report estimates that their overall rate of birth per 1,000 population in 1976 was in the 36-39 range.[12] Population Reference Bureau figures show the rates in 1978 were 46 for Africa, 30 for Asia, and 36 for Latin America. Even in Asia, 24 countries still have birth rates over 40 per 1,000.[13] (Since China and

India have lower rates, their large populations reduce the overall Asia and world averages for less-developed countries.)

In contrast, population stabilization requires birth rates of roughly 10-15 per 1,000, again depending on mortality conditions. It seems obvious, then, that complacency would be dangerous, and that strenuous efforts in family planning and development programs will be needed to continue pressing growth rates downward.

• Producing statistics and estimates on population is a slippery business—particularly so for China, but for most other countries as well. Few if any experts consider the estimates highly reliable. In China, for instance, the government itself may have little more than a rough idea, considering the enormous task of estimating such a huge and scattered population. Of questionable reliability are the data collected by local political cadres—the same people who report to higher-ups also are responsible for meeting quotas for the number of births or sterilizations in an area. "There are only two ways for them to meet quotas," says John S. Aird, the China expert at the Census Bureau. "They can falsify the data, or then can use coercion." Some experts feel the Chinese frequently use two types of figures, one for exhortatory purposes (and foreign consumption) and another for actual planning.

• Many uncertainties about future trends remain: "A diminishing but still significant number of governments remain opposed to or ambivalent about population programs," says a State Department report.[14] Mauldin and Bernard Berelson, of the Population Council, also caution that "several large countries have had hardly any change and still have high fertility—Bangladesh, Pakistan, Nigeria—and the changes in Mexico and Brazil are quite recent and still rather small."[15]

Most experts feel, however, that once a population growth rate decline sets in, it will continue. Mauldin notes that, in the opinion of demographer Dudley Kirk, once the birth rate gets below 35 per 1,000, the chance of it going back up is very small indeed.

Yet, there apparently is at least one example of regression: Egypt. Mauldin says the evidence indicates that Egypt's birth rate declined 20 percent between 1963 and 1972, from 43 per 1,000 to 34.4—but that since then it has risen again to 37.7 and remains more or less constant.

In some situations, family planning programs may have an accelerating effect, if the word spreads and cultural barriers weaken. However, the opposite could more often be the case, at least in the absence of considerable economic and social development, if the first millions are much more easily enlisted in programs than those that follow. R.T. Ravenholt, director of AID's Office of Population, stated during an interview that it is relatively easy, with a strong program, to reduce birth rates from the 40's per 1,000 to the 20's, but to go from 20 to 10 requires an additional dimension, a "powerful political will which then has to be implemented."

Another future uncertainty involves changes in death rates. The chief reason for the explosion of population growth rates in developing countries has been the precipitous decline in death rates due to progress in medical care and prevention. But when a certain point is reached, further improvements become more difficult.

According to Davidson Gwatkin, a visiting fellow at the Overseas Development Council, earlier optimistic forecasts of continuing sharp declines in death rates "failed to foresee the declining power of communicable-disease programs or the economic difficulties that would continue to affect the poor majority in the developing world."[16]

Tsui and Bogue put it another way: "Death rates have sunk to such a low level in many developing areas that further decline can only come from a slower and gradual improvement in nutrition and environmental conditions and treatment of chronic and degenerative diseases."[17]

A leveling off in the sharp decline in death rates has the effect of reducing the population growth rate, of course, and Tsui and Bogue note that this is an important factor in the recent decline in that rate.

However, this is not a desirable way to achieve population stability, especially since about 40 percent of the deaths in less-developed countries are of infants or children under five. Gwatkin deplores the fact that the current slowdown in population growth can be partly attributed to a greater number of infant and child deaths than anticipated. (Specifically, in 1975 there were 15.1 million such deaths in the developing world, he says. If the developed countries' rates had been achieved, the total would have been only 2.6 million. If present trends continue, it is estimated that in the year 2000, there will be 11 to 12 million infant and child deaths in developing countries—an improvement but far above earlier assumptions of 5 to 7 million per year.[18])

• Finally, population statistics, however favorable, tend to distract attention from the present, very real, and very dire situation in many countries around the world. In commenting on the Population Reference Bureau study which discussed the welcome news that the world fertility rate is declining, a *Wall Street Journal* editorial writer said, "It seems to be getting harder and harder to keep a crisis going, even when a lot of people have a vested interest in stirring up public fears. The latest crisis to face the risk of public boredom is the population crisis . . . ." The writer then added that

> . . . we would not want to make light of the earlier fears, since no one could be certain they were exaggerated . . . . If you credit birth control, you are saying that the earlier fears were not wasted. That may well be true, but it is not pleasant to think that crisis-mongering has become a

necessary adjunct to the making of public policy. We would prefer to think that less fear and more rationality would serve better, and there might be fewer vested interests to support after the "crisis" has been downgraded to a mere problem.[19]

Two days after these squeamish thoughts appeared, John J. Gilligan, then Chief of AID, replied in a speech:

The World Bank . . . concludes that even with recent encouraging economic trends in the developing world, 600 million people would live in

THE PLIGHT OF THE 13 MOST POPULOUS DEVELOPING COUNTRIES

	Population (millions)	Population growth rate (annual, %)	Crude birth rate decline, 1965-75 (%)	Family planning effort score	Population under 15 (%)	Death rate (annual, per 1,000 pop.)	Population density per square km
China	930.0	1.4	24	25	33	8	96.9
India	634.7	2.0	16	19	40	14	193.5
Indonesia	140.2	2.4	13	14	44	14	73.6
Brazil	115.4	2.8	10	0	42	8	13.6
Bangladesh	85.0	2.7	2	3	43	20	590.3
Pakistan	76.8	3.0	1	8	46	14	95.5
Nigeria	68.4	2.8	1	2	45	21	74.0
Mexico	66.9	3.4	9	4	46	8	33.1
Vietnam	49.2	2.2	11	10	41	19	147.7
Philippines	46.3	2.5	19	16	43	10	154.3
Thailand	45.1	2.3	23	11	45	10	87.7
Turkey	42.2	2.3	16	6	40	11	54.0
Egypt	39.6	2.5	17	8	41	12	39.5
World	4,219.0	1.7	—	—	36	12	31.5
United States	218.4	0.6	—	—	24	9	23.3

NOTES: Many of the figures, of course, are subject to reporting deficiencies and differences in definitions. Several of the figures for Vietnam are unweighted averages of those for North and South Vietnam.

Figures for population, population growth rates, and population under 15 are estimates for 1978. The family planning effort score was developed by Mauldin and Berelson, of the Population Council, using 15 program criteria, with a maximum possible score of 30.

Death rates, estimated from United Nations data, generally are for 1976. If the high death rate in, say, Bangladesh is lowered significantly, the population will grow accordingly, whatever the results of birth control. Conversely, a low death rate like China's is not likely to go down much further.

Figures for population density per square kilometer used 1974 data for the total area of a country. (A hectare is almost 2.5 acres.)

Figures on arable land per capita are necessarily rough and, even more importantly, do not begin to assess actual or potential food production because they do not account for different soil conditions, rainfall, insolation, use of fertilizers, harvesting of more than one crop, etc. Some efforts are being made to relate the number of hectare growing data to abject poverty by the year 2000. Abject poverty means that they will be hungry, sick, ill-clothed, illiterate, unemployed, and without hope. I, for one, do not wish to be the person who tells these millions that they have a problem and not a crisis.[20]

Special Circumstances

It should be kept in mind that every country has an altogether different mix of population pressures, impacts, attitudes, and feasible solutions. Author John Passmore has written:

	Percent population in cities	Hectares of arable land per capita	Agric. pop. per sq. km arable land	Indices of change in food prod. per capita, 1972 to 1976	Energy consumption per capita	Physical quality of life index	Per capita GNP ($)
China	24	.14	—	110-116	567	71	410
India	21	.26	96	95-97	186	41	150
Indonesia	18	.13	158	106-114	133	48	240
Brazil	60	.31	40	116-128	532	66	1,140
Bangladesh	9	.11	227	84-90	32	32	110
Pakistan	26	.25	57	116-116	158	36	170
Nigeria	18	.37	60	83-80	66	27	380
Mexico	64	.41	25	106-103	1,318	75	1,090
Vietnam	22	.11	—	94-89	213	52	160
Philippines	32	.22	99	96-120	311	71	410
Thailand	13	.31	90	99-112	305	71	380
Turkey	45	.66	37	110-121	564	56	990
Egypt	44	.07	192	105-105	324	44	280
World	39	.36	—	104-109	1,984	65	1,628
United States	74	.95	—	111-124	11,611	95	7,890

population. In general, it is estimated to require roughly .40 hectares per person to provide a minimally adequate diet. Figures above combine 1978 population and 1974 land estimates.

Figures for "economically active agricultural population" per unit of arable land are for 1975.

The per capita food production figures are based on an index in which 1961-65=100. Thus, to take Thailand as an example, the 1972 figure of 99 shows that per capita production that year was still a shade below the average for the 1961-65 period; in 1976, production was 12% higher.

Energy consumption per capita is in kilograms of coal equivalent, 1972 estimates.

The Physical Quality of Life Index, developed by the Overseas Development Council, is based on an average of life expectancy at age one, infant mortality, and literacy rates.

Per capita GNP figures are preliminary, for 1976.

SOURCES: "1978 World Population Data Sheet." Population Reference Bureau; *The United States and World Development Agenda 1979.* Overseas Development Council (Praeger, 1979); *Studies in Family Planning,* May 1978; *World Bank Atlas,* 1977; *The State of Food and Agriculture 1977,* Food and Agriculture Organization, 1978; International Food Policy Research Institute; *Production Yearbook 1975,* FAO; and *Ecoscience,* by Paul R. Ehrlich, et al., (W.H. Freeman, 1977).

The distribution of the population, the size of the country it inhabits, the degree and kind of its industrialization, the flexibility of the ecological systems in which it lives and works, the nature of its social traditions and attitudes, all of these play a notable part in determining its degree of ecological destructiveness.[21]

One might add some other factors: the amount of arable land, the age structure of the population, the distribution of income, the way a country is situated geographically or with respect to its neighbors, the religious and political sensitivity of population control measures and different degrees of coercion, and the type of government and its population policies.

For example, in many developing countries, a heavy demand for contraceptives and sterilization exceeds what is being supplied. In contrast, other populations—conservative Catholic and Moslem societies, for instance—tend to be hostile to family planning programs. Columnist Joseph Kraft, writing about the political strengths and limitations of the Moslem populations, which make up more than a sixth of the world, says:

Effective economic development requires a modern outlook on many aspects of society—education, property rights, interest rates, the rights of women, and population control. But Islam has not yet come to terms with those requirements.[22]

Countries also differ greatly in their opportunity to alleviate population pressure through emigration. Geographical islands (like Japan, Indonesia, and Sri Lanka) and political islands (like China) tend to be forced to control their populations internally. On the other hand, Mexico, whatever its internal policies, has the "safety valve" of both legal and illegal movement into the United States.

The situation in China could change substantially with continued liberalization. It does not seem too far-fetched to imagine a time when hundreds of thousands of Chinese are leaving their country, either illegally or with the concurrence of the Peking regime. It is not an idle thought for a country of about a billion people, where a political upheaval or natural disaster could trigger a mass exodus.

In the case of the world's developed countries, most now appear to be approaching zero population growth, according to Charles F. Westoff, of Princeton University's Office of Population Research. Some European countries have already reached stabilization, and most of the others should reach it by 1990, if current trends continue. Westoff estimates that, because of the post-World War II bulge of births, the United States will reach zero population growth "somewhat farther down the road than most European countries." Specifically, he notes the Census Bureau's "low" projection which envisions a halt to growth in the year

2015 at a level of 253 million people—compared to the present population of about 220 million. The estimate includes legal immigration and
assumes "an ultimate level of completed cohort fertility of 1.7 births per
woman," compared to the present rate of about 1.8. Westoff says that
"even if fertility should climb back to the replacement level of 2.1, the
population would be only . . . . 283 million in 2015"—considerably
below forecasts of a few years ago. It is a sign of the success of controlling
population growth that Americans have been able to focus more of their
concern on some controversial subsidiary population issues—abortion
law; teenage pregnancy; the economic and social effects of the population's changing age structure; migration patterns and their effects on
cities, rural areas, the Sunbelt, etc.; illegal immigration; and the social
implications of a stabilized population.[23]

Immigration, it should be noted, accounts for a substantial portion of
U.S. population growth each year, and the share has become increasingly significant with the lowering of the nation's birth rate. The
Census Bureau estimates that net *legal* immigration has been ranging
between 325,000 and 425,000 per year. While the figures for legal immigration are still considered unreliable, those for *illegal* immigration are
practically nonexistent. One can only guess at the number of illegal
entrants to the U.S., just as no one knows how many of them stay only
temporarily. In any case, most estimates of net illegal immigration
range between 500,000 and one million per year. The House Select
Committee on Population says, "The best guess is that legal and illegal
immigration combined probably account for somewhere between 30
percent and 50 percent of current population growth in the United
States."[24]

Implications of Growth

It is not the number of people itself, but the effects on the human
environment and human condition in a country that define the problem. These effects, most of which are interrelated, involve income, food
and nutrition, employment, land and housing, urbanization, political
stability, education, and various other components of human rights and
well-being. Here are some observations on what seem to be the most
critical dimensions of population growth:

• *Children.* The plight of millions of children is of particular concern, says Ambassador Green. "Do you realize there are 17 million
effectively abandoned children in Brazil?" he asked intensely in an
interview.

They are condemned to lives of drudgery, wasted health, and early death.
The children have no prospects. It's bad enough to abandon a dog. It gets
taken to a kennel and put to death. The procedure for children is just more

drawn-out. Sometimes they prolong their existence through lives of crime . . . . Why do we ignore the greatest denial of human rights in the world today? It's time people spoke up very strongly about this.

• *Unemployment.* Growing unemployment can be expected to produce frustration, alienation, and possible political instability of staggering proportions. It is clear enough that there is no way for employment opportunities to be created fast enough to cope with population growth—especially with so many millions already unemployed or underemployed, and with the 15- to 24-year-old age group projected to to grow so rapidly.

"The birth rates in the 1960's were terribly high and now they're coming onto the job market," says Green. "Nothing can be done to stop it." Lester Brown says, "In many poor countries, entrants into the job market outnumber new jobs by two to one."[25] A typical country is Egypt, where Green says a greatly concerned government official has estimated that 350,000 to 400,000 males enter the work force *every year.*

It takes about $10,000 to create one job, Green adds. "The costs are astronomical," he says. He suggests that the high costs of job creation through industrialization, and the increasingly limited potential for increasing agricultural production in job-creating ways, require the development of new techniques. There is much discussion of labor-intensive development.

• *Urbanization.* Urbanization is another by-product of the population crisis. It has been estimated that at the end of the century, almost 41 percent of the total less-developed countries' population will be urban.[26] Here are some examples of projected growth in Third World urban agglomerations, based on United Nations estimates and median projections, the figures representing millions:

	1960	1975	2000
Calcutta	5.5	8.1	19.7
Mexico City	4.9	10.9	31.6
Greater Bombay	4.1	7.1	19.1
Greater Cairo	3.7	6.9	16.4
Jakarta	2.7	5.6	16.9
Seoul	2.4	7.3	18.7
Delhi	2.3	4.5	13.2
Manila	2.2	4.4	12.7
Tehran	1.9	4.4	13.8
Lagos	0.8	2.1	9.4

• *Environment.* The population pressures on ecosystems are well-known. They result in the serious depletion of such natural resources as forests, agricultural land, wetlands, wildlife habitat, water, and energy.

• *Food.* How much is there to say about food and population when even now hundreds of millions of people around the world are either hungry, malnourished, or starving? Or when there is such great disparity in the distribution of food and income—between countries and within countries? Or when the costs of inputs needed to boost agricultural production are so high? Or when natural disasters and severe weather fluctuations are a constant threat?

• *Freedom.* "China is the world's foremost example of what happens with the population explosion," says AID's R.T. Ravenholt. It is true, he says, that with enormous effort it is producing enough food for all those people on only 12 percent of the land mass. "But this has taken a very large toll. It has wiped out obesity, household pets, birds, private ownership of automobiles . . . and most importantly, freedom. It is a sheer fact that the Chinese had to choose between starvation and regimentation. They chose regimentation."

Searching for a Magic Formula

How can the Third World countries pull themselves out of the quicksand of population growth? How can they raise their poor to higher levels of socioeconomic well-being? Thousands of experts and officials are devoted to discovering some magic formula guaranteed to achieve these goals in underdeveloped nations. But, after decades of study and debate, they still disagree sharply about such basic concepts as the relative importance of family planning programs and economic development.

Some insist that the most effective strategy is to flood a country with contraceptives. The theory is that plenty of people want them and will use them, or can be persuaded to, and that the resulting decline in population growth will ipso facto pave the way for greater economic growth. At the other end of the spectrum are those who belittle family planning efforts and swear instead by economic development or other forms of modernization. In this sequence, when standards of living rise, families as a matter of course will adopt birth-control measures.

It is reminiscent of the argument over whether the chicken or egg comes first. And each side can produce evidence to support its thesis, and to show that alternative approaches have failed. One reason for this is that countries are so culturally, politically, and economically diverse. Their people and organizations respond differently to the same techniques. A single formula for success is not in the cards.

The fundamentally different population and development priorities are at the heart of political battles waged in Congress, the Agency for International Development, the international community, and elsewhere. At stake are political power, bureaucratic fiefdom, appropriations allocations, and personal prestige and gain.

For example, a major component of the running "North-South" hemispheric debate is the antipathy that many undeveloped country officials have to family planning programs, which they see as demeaning and interfering with the sovereign conduct of their own affairs. These officials frequently put a much higher value on development aid, which certainly is more immediate and tangible. A slogan at the World Population Conference in Bucharest in 1974 was, "Development is the best contraceptive." (Some Third World officials undoubtedly represent, directly or indirectly, the urban-industrial elites of their countries—those who benefit disproportionately from development aid.)

A large body of expertise makes a strong case for pursuing *both* family planning and development. In other words, why argue over whether it's the piston or the gasoline that makes a truck go? Family planning and development projects can be operated independently or, better yet, integrated so as to boost the effectiveness of both.

There is a further position held by many professionals in the field: Family planning and development projects are essentially a waste of time in the absence of a third component—a broader distribution of land, income, or both. It is argued that redistribution is an indispensable prerequisite to progress of any kind.

Finally, some feel that emigration is the only effective short-term solution to population pressures—as it so often has been in the past.

The arguments for a three-pronged program of family planning, development, and redistribution—with many possible variations—is buttressed by the fact that economic development and redistribution are desirable in their own right, whether or not they also contribute to birth control; the former because it improves overall well-being, and the latter because it alleviates extreme inequities.

Of course, problems arise when money and staff are too limited to fully support all three types of effort, or when political and bureaucratic disagreements thwart or distort programs. An associated problem is the lack of knowledge about which development factors contribute to lowered fertility. Is it economic development as measured by GNP? Lowered infant mortality? Increased percentage of homes with electricity? Better transportation? Raised educational levels? Also missing is real insight into the ways in which birth-control and development techniques interact or can be integrated. Illustrative is the testimony of Alexander Shakow, assistant administrator of AID for the Bureau of Program and Policy Coordination:

> While we are confident of development's general influences on fertility, we are hard-pressed to go beyond, to give recipes for project development in particular conditions. Our shortage of precise information on how development influences fertility has inhibited project development.[27]

He added that some officials remain skeptical about the value of coordinating the two types of programs and are "reluctant to devote scarce staff time to a field where success seems difficult to predict." The House Select Committee on Population said it is not surprised at the skepticism, but indicated its displeasure that a specific, congressionally mandated policy to link population and development projects "should be the subject of such deep controversy within AID more than one year after its promulgation."[28]

The policy, contained in Section 104(d) of the foreign assistance act, was initiated by AID. It states that development assistance shall

> . . . be administered so as to give particular attention to the interrelationship between (a) population growth and (b) development and overall improvement in living standards in developing countries and to the impact of all programs, projects, and activities on population growth. All appropriate activities proposed for financing under this chapter shall be designed to build motivation for smaller families in programs such as education in and out of school, nutrition, disease control, maternal and child health services, agricultural production, rural development, and assistance to the urban poor.

The provision, passed in 1977, also authorized AID to study "the complex factors" affecting population growth and identify those which might motivate people to plan family size or space their children.

AID does not require "population impact statements" for development projects, although such a requirement has been discussed and sometimes utilized. For example, a population officer with the AID mission in Pakistan prepared population impact assessments for all projects there.[29]

The section 104(d) policy is somewhat in contrast to prior AID population policy, which concentrated chiefly on straightforward provision of family planning information and services.

The House committee said in a recent report that it "rejects the notion that family planning programs and development activities are competing claimants for U.S. development assistance. Both are needed, they are mutually reinforcing, and both should continue to receive high priority and adequate funding."[30]

AID's Ravenholt is more than skeptical of activities under section 104(d). "That's essentially the mining of low-grade ore," he says. Ravenholt, of course, is concerned about dilution of the "sharply focused" birth-control projects he has single-mindedly and forcefully pushed for many years. If appropriations for section 104(d) activities are additional, he's all in favor, but if money is shifted from the distribution of contraceptives and other family planning efforts, he feels this will divert attention and energies from the highest-priority activities.

Formulas for Success

"Organized family planning efforts have been a major contributing factor in the fertility decline now evident in much of the developing world," according to the study by Tsui and Bogue. They concluded that the "massive effort" for family planning is "paying off" in fertility reduction more rapidly than otherwise might occur via economic and social development.[31] A prime example cited by family planning adherents is Indonesia, where a strong national commitment to birth control has reduced fertility considerably despite the absence of much economic improvement.[32]

A pair of investigators at the Carolina Population Center have concluded that, in countries with high birth rates—those over 30 per 1,000, which is the case for nearly all Third World countries—development without family planning is not likely to reduce fertility much, if at all, in a reasonable period of time.[33]

Mauldin and Berelson did an elaborate analysis of crude birth rate declines in developing countries in the period 1965-75:

> We found that the level of "modernization" as reflected in our seven socioeconomic factors has a substantial relationship to fertility decline: The better-off countries, particularly those near the top, do better than the less well-off. That was to be expected in sociodemographic theory. But we also find, as a less-expectable finding, that on balance family planning programs have a significant, independent effect over and above the effect of socioeconomic factors.[34]

They said that weak family planning programs are of virtually no use:

> The key finding probably is that the two—social setting and program effort—go together most effectively.
> The policy implications are that, if a country wants to reduce its fertility, it should seek a high degree of modernization (which of course all do, and find costly and difficult) and it should adopt a substantial family planning program; for countries at or near the bottom of the socioeconomic scale, however, the results would probably be slight and the administrative implementation very difficult. In such settings it requires a special kind of determination—as found in India, Indonesia, and China in the early to mid-1970's—to implement a strong program effort in a deprived setting.

Sometimes the debate boils down to the simple question of what families really want. Family planning proponents feel there is a large existing demand for contraceptives and services. Development proponents, on the other hand, stress that millions want large families for reasons of prestige or because their children often begin to contribute to the family's economic welfare in only four or five years. They argue that only socioeconomic improvements can change that motivation. Undoubtedly, both arguments are correct.[35]

Closely related is the widely endorsed theory that reduced infant mortality is an inducement to have fewer children, if only because more of them survive. But reduced infant mortality is in turn dependent on such development inputs as improved health services and increased food production. And, say three analysts at the University of Southern California's Center for Future Research:

> [S]ignificant reduction in birth rates as a result of improved food consumption can only occur after a 10- to 20-year time delay. Meanwhile, a successfully managed food program will actually increase the rate of population growth by decreasing death rates in the poorest regions. The task of maintaining adequate food supplies will grow more difficult before it gets easier.[36]

To simplify the point: the development process usually lowers the death rate more quickly than the birth rate.

Emilio Casetti, professor of geography of Ohio State University, did a simulation study and concluded that the current prevalent 5 percent or greater annual growth rate of the GNP in developing countries "is enough to bring the rate of population growth down from explosive levels. . . ." However, he warned that while this process is taking place, populations may grow too large to be accommodated.[37]

In another study of India, Casetti estimated that "accelerated economic progress" will have a small impact on India's population levels 50 and 100 years from now. "A good economic performance capable of raising GNP per capita to very high levels is not sufficient per se to prevent reaching high levels of population density."[38]

The importance of the *kind* of development should not be overlooked. Is it capital- rather than labor-intensive? Does it promote the interests of exporters, bankers, and the like, rather than domestic agricultural enterprise? Political scientist William Pfaff says that Iran has been "a model of how a developing country goes into shock as a result of economic development, social change, and the resulting attack upon its traditional culture."[39]

Marshall Green is impatient with the "idle and empty controversy" over whether family planning or development programs work best. "It's boring and senseless to argue one against the other. Both are needed." He has summed up the gist of the arguments:

> The discouraging cycle of development handicapped by excessive population growth, and of such growth continuing because of stalled development, can be overcome only through a variety of carefully formulated, vigorously pursued measures adapted to each country's needs.[40]

The Need for Reform

Many experts, as noted, put little faith in any programs unless those programs are accompanied by more equitable distribution of income, of land, of water, of the economic benefits of development, of foreign aid, or of domestic program funds. The University of Southern California investigators make this point:

> Incumbent governments in developing nations are typically supported by urban industrial interests. A shift in resource allocations toward agriculture would be viewed as a threat to those interests. Very few governments of developing nations enjoy sufficient support to introduce changes that are likely to antagonize their urban constituency.[41]

Even when a country adopts land reform, it can fail if skimpy or corrupt agricultural programs or seemingly unfair income distribution keep many farmers economically depressed. A prime example is Iran.[42] To the extent that foreign aid favors the already well-to-do, or promotes capital-intensive, technologically advanced industrial enterprises, the effects are likely to be the same. A lottery ticket seller in Brazil told one reporter: "For the people, nothing has changed. Tell them to stop developing and maybe the cost of living will improve."[43]

"The important thing to realize," says Lawrence C. Stedman, a development specialist, "is that hunger is not caused by population pressure. Rather, both hunger and population growth are *symptoms* of the failure of a political and economic system to meet human needs. The redistribution of wealth *does* eliminate hunger and control population growth."[44]

Stedman argues that 30-year data on the Philippines, Taiwan, Korea, Mexico, and Brazil reveal that land reform and income redistribution are the keys to lowering birth rates. Taiwan and Korea have implemented both and seen their birth rates drop substantially. "The other three countries, which have relied upon the traditional approach to economic growth, have experienced little change in their birth rates."

Robert Repetto, associate professor of population and economics at the Harvard School of Public Health, believes that "there is a consistently close relationship between more equitable income distribution and lower fertility."[45]

He reasons that in order to benefit from modernization and changed attitudes, people must "have the means to partake of a variety of consumption activities, to invest in themselves and their children, to be concerned with more than day-by-day subsistence, to come in contact with a broader range of experience."

Repetto says that, typically, at least half of any addition to national income in a country accrues to the upper 15 percent of households, and this income may be irrelevant as far as reduced fertility is concerned:

Disillusionment with conventional family planning programs as the main policy instrument with which to induce fertility declines is already widespread. At the same time, especially in the poorest and most populous countries, the prospects for rapid increases in the level of living are not bright . . . . Redistributive measures and a selective strategy of growth designed to raise the incomes of the relatively poor would be more successful in lowering the rate of population growth than the present mix of development policies in most less-developed countries.

Repetto adds that the "positive feedback" from reduced fertility to greater equality in income distribution "would tend to sustain and accelerate the process, producing further increases in the rate of growth of income per capita."

World Bank President Robert McNamara has cited a study of 40 developing countries which revealed that a $10 increase in the income of the lower 60 percent of the population was associated with a decline in the crude birth rate of 0.7 per 1,000, whereas a $10 increase in the overall average income of everyone was associated with a decline of only 0.3 per 1,000.[46]

Also of concern is the mounting potential for unemployment in poor countries. "Actual deterioration in the employment situation would act to deepen the maldistribution of wealth," notes one report.[47]

In the holistic view, says Kariba J.C. Munio, a Kenyan scientist, population control can succeed only with the sincere implementation of such measures as "land reforms, both political and economic changes to allow more balanced distribution of resources, reliance by industrialized countries on Third World countries for finished natural-material products, and establishment of ecologically sound, labor-intensive technologies in the Third World."[48]

All of which is easier said than done, of course, given the realpolitik of development.

Elements of Success in Population Control

What does it take to make family planning programs themselves successful? One of the truly essential ingredients, says Marshall Green, is the strong commitment of a country's leadership. A good example is the firm family planning policy of President Suharto, which permeates Indonesian life down to the village level. "He put his heart into it," Green says of Suharto.

Green has spearheaded an effort to use top-level diplomacy to persuade other governments' leaders to give the utmost attention to food and population problems, without causing resentment over a frequently sensitive subject.

"Our diplomats are not being involved," Green commented. "It's usually left to the AID people, the doctors, and demographers. But you have to get to the leaders. We have an immediate responsibility to bring it to their attention."

There appears to be general agreement that a highly effective way to reduce fertility is to provide more education for girls and women, and to expand the roles of women in work and public life. "It's terribly important that the status of women be improved," according to Green. "It should be done anyway."

Green says that "men are quite hopeless when it comes to the whole field, what with their machismo, ingrained attitudes, and so forth . . . . Where the women are slaves of their husbands, there is very little chance of a successful program." Thus women need an enhanced status and a greater voice in family decisions.

Green also stresses that too little attention is paid to treating family planning customers with dignity and understanding. He cites a Presbyterian mobile hospital team in northern Thailand whose motto is "Every patient is a VIP." The previous average of 6.6 children per women in the area has been reduced to 2.3.

A good reputation does much to increase effectiveness. "If people are handled the right way, the satisfied customers will go out and tell everyone," says Green. "The rumor of the marketplace is far more powerful in developing countries than all the newspapers and radio and TV."

Family planning programs in countries like Indonesia and Thailand, while strongly pushed on the populace, have been voluntary, even amiable, in nature (although Indonesia reportedly has adopted some penalties[49]). In Thailand, one reporter wrote:

> The Thais shun a direct monetary payment for the farmer who gets a vasectomy (as was the case in the disastrous, involuntary program tried by . . . Prime Minister Indira Gandhi in India). Instead, the cows of the Thai farmer who has had a vasectomy get the lifetime services of what is amusingly called "the family-planning bull". . . . There are some good-natured titters—but that's all—when the "family-planning bull" shows up.[50]

In Green's view, programs are best when rooted in village life, with word-of-mouth and peer pressure functioning effectively. In wives' clubs and other groups committed to family planning in Indonesia, members who do not adhere to the commitment may be criticized or embarrassed by the others, "but they do it in a very humorous way." Village commitment and participation in Indonesian family planning usually begins with the wife of the village leader heading up the program—that way most everyone wants to be in the club.

Unfortunately, says Green, the Indonesian village system is unique, and therefore not necessarily a model that can be imitated by other countries—except for the factor of national leadership. In Pakistan, for example, a contraceptives program was a disaster, because it completely overlooked the question of the women's motivation.

The bitter reaction to India's involuntary sterilization program is well known. Green adds that India had a good loop program, but forgot to warn about possible side effects. "When they occurred, rumors spread, and the program collapsed overnight.

China apparently uses the full range of techniques to limit births, including the familiar contraceptives (and a chemically treated contraceptive paper wafer that is easy to swallow), abortion, sterilization (including injectable sterilants), and hormone pills for males. "The side effects don't worry the Chinese as much," according to Aird, of the Census Bureau. "They accept as safe things other countries never would."

Other methods include policies calling for late marriages, spacing of children at five-year intervals, setting of local quotas, and use of incentives and disincentives such as granting or withholding food rations, water, or work opportunities. Aird notes that a radio broadcast in Hunan Province included a statement by a provincial official that "such social and economic questions as the distribution of rations in rural areas and of housing in urban areas, and other regulations, must benefit the extension of the work on planned parenthood."

Leo A. Orleans, a Library of Congress specialist, has commented:

China is attempting to motivate smaller families not simply by focusing all the available resources and means of persuasion on the women in the reproductive ages, but, in a sense, by "going over their heads" and making the planning of births the responsibility of local governments, productive units, residential communities, birth control committees, public health personnel, and almost every other segment of the society.[51]

Birth-control efforts in China undoubtedly are enhanced by a number of socioeconomic factors—a certain sexual puritanism, the extensive emancipation of Chinese women, widespread education, and improved sanitary conditions and health services. Coercion is ostensibly against official policy, says Aird. But there have been scattered indications of it—and of resistance to it. Aird says a Canton broadcast complained of births far in excess of a provincial goal, and of leaders with five, six, and even seven children setting terrible examples. An article from a major Peking newspaper discussed an apparently burning issue: When it comes to birth-control measures, what constitutes the law? When a cadre issues orders, do they become law? Orleans cautions against assuming that coercion is common, and notes that in Chinese terms, some pressures may seem mild, such as not getting a promotion or the kind of housing you want. No one can guess what may happen to the birth-control programs and policies if liberalization and democratization take firm root in China. A Peking wall poster reportedly scored the government for its insistence on late marriages and abstinence from premarital sex, calling it "a cruel crime that destroys young hearts and bodies."[52]

The fact remains that uncontrolled population growth has the potential to destroy hearts and bodies indiscriminately, not simply the young ones. And there is no room for complacency, even though the world's population growth rate has edged downward. Population growth remains at a high level and has considerable built-in momentum. And until mankind manages to cope with the population-related problems of food, employment, urbanization, and environmental degradation, hearts and bodies all over the world will suffer as a result of population pressures.

Chapter 5

CLIMATE MODIFICATION

Some say the world will end in fire,
Some say in ice.
From what I've tasted of desire
I hold with those who favor fire.

—Robert Frost, *Fire and Ice*

From outer space, the sunlit earth shows no sign of human life. The scene is dominated by massive geological features: turquoise oceans, brown and tan land masses, white polar ice caps—all encased in a swirling, milky sea of clouds. Except perhaps for a glimpse of the Great Wall of China, mankind and its civilization are simply not visible.

But journey halfway around the planet, toward the night, and a different scene unfolds. Across the dark continents, cities blaze with light, a galaxy of man-made stars. And in the Persian Gulf, in Mexico, Russia, and other parts of the world, huge orange flares mark the underground reservoirs of oil and natural gas.

This view of the earth—the night view—offers graphic evidence of man's recent emergence as a "major geological and geophysical agent in his own right," says ecologist Charles F. Cooper, of San Diego State University.[1] Cooper adds that man can now influence the "physical and biological conditions of the future, deliberately or inadvertently, in a way not open to our ancestors."

And mankind is using that capacity—deliberately, in order to modify the short-term weather (to calm down hurricanes, to induce precipitation, and so forth), and inadvertently, to affect the climate of the whole planet. This is quite aside from the natural changes in climate inherent in atmospheric and other fluctuations—critical changes that are discussed in the chapters on Food and Water.

Jim Norwine, a professor of geography and climatology at Texas A & I University offers a clear distinction between weather and climate:

The section on carbon dioxide in this chapter was written by David D. Sleeper, an associate of The Conservation Foundation.

Climate refers to the state of the atmosphere at any place or area, as measured by such factors as mean temperature, rainfall, and solar radiation, over a long time span—years, decades, centuries, millennia, and so on. Weather, by contrast, delineates variables or events, like storms, occurring at any given instant or over a very brief period of time (meaning a few days to a few months).[2]

We may already be influencing the climate of the entire planet, chiefly in a way aptly symbolized by the gas flares: the exploitation of fossil fuels for energy. By burning coal, oil, and natural gas, mankind has been releasing from sedimentary rocks large amounts of concen-

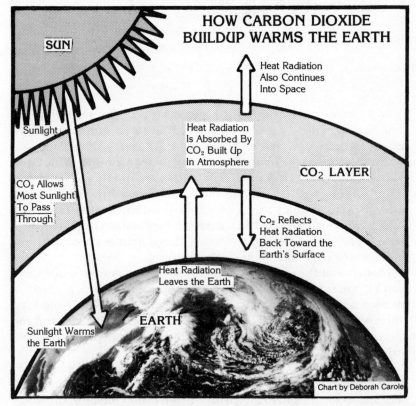

HOW CARBON DIOXIDE BUILDUP WARMS THE EARTH

SUN

Heat Radiation Also Continues Into Space

Sunlight

Heat Radiation Is Absorbed By CO_2 Built Up In Atmosphere

CO_2 LAYER

CO_2 Allows Most Sunlight To Pass Through

Co_2 Reflects Heat Radiation Back Toward the Earth's Surface

Heat Radiation Leaves the Earth

EARTH

Sunlight Warms the Earth

Chart by Deborah Carole

trated organic carbon, a good portion of which returns through combustion to the atmosphere as carbon dioxide—and stays there, perhaps for as long as 1,000 years.

The amount of atmospheric CO_2 has been increasing rapidly since the onset of the Industrial Revolution. And in the past 20 years, the annual rate of increase has grown sharply.

All this has caused a mild panic in the scientific community, primarily because of the so-called "greenhouse effect." It seems that the carbon dioxide—a colorless, odorless gas which constitutes only .03 percent of the atmosphere and is known best for its essential function in plant photosynthesis—plays a disproportionately large role in regulating the flow of heat energy from the planet.

Carbon dioxide molecules allow sunlight to pass through and strike the earth, but they absorb energy returning as infrared heat. Thus a process occurs somewhat similar to what happens in a greenhouse, with heat becoming trapped in the atmosphere instead of radiating into space.

The point is that if average temperatures rise more than a few degrees, climate could be affected, perhaps with disastrous results.

For the past decade, debate in the scientific community has been sharply divided between those who thought the earth was heading into a cooling period—perhaps even a new ice age—and those who forecast a global warming. This "fire and ice" controversy still continues, but recently the weight of scientific opinion has shifted toward the warming thesis. The current belief is that rising levels of carbon dioxide will simply overwhelm any cooling brought on by sunspot activity, increases in air-borne particles, or other phenomena that might cause long-term cyclic changes.[3] Global temperature has yet to rise, however, and probably won't until the 1990's.

Expressions of Concern

Concern about anthropogenic (man-caused) carbon dioxide is not new. In 1938, a British scientist pointed out that burning fossil fuels was changing the composition of the atmosphere, and he unearthed several theories from the turn of the century suggesting that higher CO_2 levels would lead to higher temperatures.[4]

In 1957, Roger Revelle and Hans E. Suess, both with the Scripps Institution of Oceanography, warned about possible climatic changes if the rate of worldwide fossil fuel consumption continued unabated and urged that accurate measurements of CO_2 be kept.[5] The following year, Charles D. Keeling, also of Scripps, began monitoring CO_2 from the Mauna Loa Observatory, perched high on a volcano in Hawaii. (In 1974, the National Oceanic and Atmospheric Administration [NOAA] took over the job of running the observatory.)

Since the Mauna Loa measurements began, CO_2 levels have increased from 314 parts per million to 335 parts per million.[6] Similar rises have been recorded in Alaska, the South Pole, and Sweden. Further, it is now believed that levels have grown by as much as 18 percent since 1850, roughly the beginning of the Industrial Revolution.[7] And unless the world sharply curtails its use of fossil fuels, atmospheric CO_2 may double in the next 60 years.

The ever-rising curve from Mauna Loa has taken on the characteristics of a cobra poised to strike. The "uncontrolled experiment,"[8] as some researchers put it, leads to one perplexing question after another. How has the combustion of fossil fuels contributed to the rise? At what point will the climate change? Are there technological solutions to the problem? How would societies be affected?

An interdisciplinary army of climatologists, oceanographers, chemists, biologists, political scientists, agronomists, economists, and others is trying to answer these questions. Lester Machta, director of NOAA's

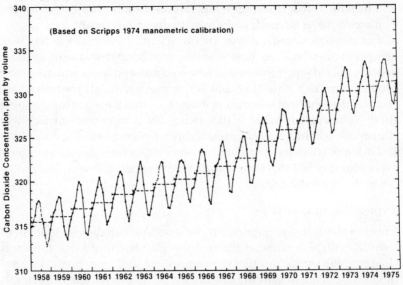

This shows the concentration of carbon dioxide in the atmosphere as recorded at Mauna Loa Observatory in Hawaii, beginning in 1958. The oscillations reflect the normal growth process of plants in the northern hemisphere. Since plants absorb CO_2, the atmospheric concentrations are highest in April just before plants begin to grow; concentrations are lowest in the fall when the year's intake of CO_2 has stopped.

SOURCE: Charles D. Keeling, 1976, in "Summary of the Carbon Dioxide Effects Research and Assessment Program," Department of Energy, April 2, 1979.

Air Resources Laboratory, estimates that 100 researchers are currently working on the carbon dioxide problem in the United States, with perhaps 1,000 more doing related research on the carbon cycle, agriculture, and other issues. The corresponding numbers outside the U.S., says Machta, are 100 full-time researchers and 10,000 ancillary ones.[9]

The names of the institutions currently working on the CO_2 problem suggest how seriously it is taken. In the U.S., they include the National Center for Atmospheric Research, the Marine Biological Laboratory at Woods Hole, the MITRE Corporation, SRI International, the National Academy of Sciences, the Oak Ridge National Laboratory, and at least two dozen universities. Most of the government work is being handled by NOAA and the Department of Energy's Carbon Dioxide and Climate Research Program, set up in 1977. (Until recently, the Council on Environmental Quality and Environmental Protection Agency have not paid much attention to CO_2. Among private environmental groups, only Friends of the Earth seems to have followed the issue.)

Two United Nations units, the World Meteorological Organization and the U.N. Environment Programme, have been spearheading international action.

A report released in 1979 by the Department of Energy (DOE) says: "It is the sense of the scientific community that carbon dioxide from unrestrained combustion of fossil fuels potentially is the most important environmental issue facing mankind."[10]

Despite this impressive scientific concern, major pitfalls to a speedy resolution of the problem remain. These include:

• *Scientific uncertainty.* Although more than 500 scientific papers have been published about anthropogenic carbon dioxide,[11] scientists understand little more today than they did 20 years ago. According to marine biologist George M. Woodwell, "The greatest puzzle is the basic stability of the global carbon budget."[12]

Only about half of the carbon dioxide coming from the burning of fossil fuels remains in the atmosphere. Until recently, most scientists thought that the other half either dissolved in the oceans or was absorbed by plant life during photosynthesis. Woodwell and others now contend that because of widespread deforestation, especially of tropical rain forests, the biosphere (which is composed of the earth's biological matter) may actually be a significant *source* of atmospheric carbon dioxide. These biogeochemical cycles must be better understood before any long-term strategies can be devised.

• *Energy crunch.* At a time when scientists finally seem to be reaching agreement that a global warming is in the cards, the world's energy planners are calling for greatly increased use of coal and coal-based synthetic fuels—the two worst contributors to carbon dioxide pollution.

• *International cooperation.* Carbon dioxide is perhaps the world's most vexing global environmental problem. Even if the U.S.—which contributes 25 percent of the world's carbon dioxide loading—cuts back consumption of fossil fuels, other countries may not be so inclined, especially considering that some countries may *benefit* from climatic change.

• *Public apathy.* Carbon dioxide represents an enormous problem of public education. Not only are the figures too large to grasp (that the atmosphere now contains 700 trillion tons of carbon, which is increasing at a rate of 1.5 percent per year, is meaningless to most people), but the time of real impact is too far in the future. Even the most pessimistic scientists say the earth really won't start warming up until the 1990's.

Considering the complex uncertainties about biogeochemical cycles, future energy demands, and effects of man-induced climate changes, some people may incline to a laissez-faire attitude. According to a report of the National Academy of Sciences, this could prove disastrous: "Unfortunately, it will take a millennium for the effects of a century of use of fossil fuels to dissipate. If the decision is postponed until the impact of man-made climate changes has been felt, then, for all practical purposes, the die will already have been cast."[13]

Possible Scenarios

What exactly would happen if the climate changes? Some of the answers are a doomsayer's delight.

Think of snow-bound Boston during the winter of 1978 and the heat wave that hit Washington the following summer. Then consider more serious events: The "Dust Bowl" years during the Depression; the Sahelian drought that began in 1968; the failure of Russia's winter wheat crop in 1972. All had serious social and economic repercussions. All were caused by short-term climatic variations.

Climatic changes due to increased carbon dioxide could be much more severe, causing widespread social strife. A report by SRI International lists mass migrations, political changes, economic chaos, and agricultural disruptions, among other effects of climate change. "You can see why people are not totally able to emotionally accept this," says David Slade, manager of DOE's carbon dioxide program.[14]

According to a group of researchers at the Oak Ridge National Laboratory, "Any rapid change in a regional climate is more likely to produce detrimental effects that far outweigh the beneficial ones."[15]

The "unhappy truth," according to Jim Norwine, is that "world society seems to have become increasingly dependent on climatic stability, because our world food reserve is nearly nonexistent and because the human population continues to grow."

Temperature represents only one aspect of climate, albeit an important one, and scientists have focused on that in constructing theoretical models to predict the effects of a heavier carbon dioxide load. Several models have been developed in the past few years. Using an arbitrary point of time when atmospheric carbon dioxide doubles (depending on future energy use, this could occur between 2025 and 2075), the models predict a rise in average temperature of between 2.7 and 5.4 degrees F.[16] Because of global circulation patterns, temperature increases at the poles would be two to three times greater than at lower latitudes.

With these temperature estimates in hand, some disturbing scenarios become possible:

• Precipitation and warm temperatures might shift northward in the U.S., returning Kansas, Oklahoma, and surrounding states to the drought conditions of the 1930's and seriously diminishing the corn, wheat, and soybean crops of the central part of the country.[17] According to Earthscan, a U.N. supported group that provides information on global environmental issues, "The U.S. would then be the potentially hungry but militarily powerful country which might be tempted to use force to control the situation."[18]

• The major Atlantic fisheries, already heavily overfished, might be further weakened by shifting ocean currents and decreased nutrient replenishment. Fisheries off Georges Bank might move to Greenland.[19]

• Because of higher temperatures, inland lakes and waterways might dry up, causing severe transportation and water-supply problems. Among the hardest hit might be the Colorado River system.

• Warming might even lead to melting of glacial ice at the poles. Although the melting processes are not fully understood, and most scientists believe a total melting and subsequent raising of the sea level by 18 feet would take 300 years, some feel the Antarctic ice cliffs might fall into the sea after only a short period of higher temperatures.[20] This in itself might raise the sea level enough to inundate many coastal population centers and agricultural lands.

A temperature change of only 3-5 degrees F. may not seem like much, but consider what happened to Europe in 1816-1819, when the temperature dropped by only 2 degrees F. According to political scientist John Dexter Post in *The Last Great Subsistence Crisis in the Western World*, famine conditions occurred in large areas of Switzerland, Italy, and the Hapsburg and Ottoman Empires.[21] The entire Western economy was "shaken by violent price fluctuations." Hundreds of thousands of people depended on public charity and thousands more migrated to the U.S. or Russia. (The cause of the climatic variation is thought to have been violent volcanic activity which spewed large amounts of dust into the atmosphere. The dust reflected incoming sunlight, thereby causing worldwide cooling.)

Many scientists have looked to the past for lessons concerning carbon dioxide and rapid climatic change. Wallace C. Broecker, of Columbia University's Lamont Doherty Geological Observatory, analyzed ice cores from Antarctica and Greenland and sediment cores from the oceans. He found that the temperature difference between the last glacial age about 20,000 years ago and the last warm-up period about 6,000 years ago amounted to only 4 degrees F. If anthropogenic carbon dioxide warms the earth by the same amount, according to Broecker, "We will have succeeded in making a change about half as large as that which occurred when the great ice sheets which covered virtually all of Scandinavia and Canada shrank to oblivion."[22]

Dewey M. McLean, a geologist at Virginia Polytechnic Institute and State University, has looked back still further—to the end of the Mesozoic Era, 65-70 million years ago, or the so-called "time of great dying" when many species of dinosaurs became extinct. After examining oxygen isotope data from marine microfossils, McLean theorized that natural geologic processes caused the destruction of coccolithophorids, a small planktonic organism which thrived in the shallow Mesozoic seas. This released large amounts of carbon dioxide into the atmosphere which in turn "triggered" a process of oceanic warming which released much greater amounts of CO_2. According to McLean, many animals, especially the larger dinosaurs, were ill-equipped to deal with rapid climatic warming and thus became extinct.

McLean believes that the burning of fossil fuels and clearing of forests may be altering the carbon cycle in ways disturbingly similar to what happened millions of years ago:

> A critical problem for humans is to avoid arriving inadvertently at a critical threshold that might trigger an abrupt accelerated warming of the climate. . . . Animals today are generally adapted to relatively cool conditions, as were faunas prior to the terminal Mesozoic extinctions. A sudden climatic warming could potentially impose on us conditions comparable to those that terminated a geologic age.[23]

Complicating the carbon dioxide picture is the fact that some areas would benefit from global warming. The Saint Lawrence Seaway would remain open all year. Soviet Union and Canadian wheat production would increase, with the Soviet benefiting more because of better soils. Regions of northern and eastern Africa now suffering from drought would become major grain producers. China's rice yield would improve significantly.[24]

William W. Kellogg, of the National Center for Atmospheric Research in Boulder, believes that "some will fare better, some worse, but on the whole the earth will have a climate more favorable for feeding the increasing population." But he adds: "That is some slight consolation to a society that is obviously going to have to face a difficult transition."[25]

The Energy Culprit

Leaving aside the unresolved question of deforestation, the heart of the carbon dioxide dilemma involves energy. In the 1970's, the world's industrialized countries finally accepted the fact that oil is running out, but instead of stressing conservation or rapid development of renewable solar resources, they are looking eagerly for new fossil fuels to burn. The recent multibillion-dollar proposal to create a synthetic fuel industry exemplifies this attitude perfectly—new and increased production will provide the solution to the energy shortage.

We may not have that option. The National Academy of Sciences study concludes that "the primary limiting factor on energy production from fossil fuels over the next few centuries may turn out to be climatic effects of the release of carbon dioxide."[26]

This has obvious implications for coal, the linchpin of President Carter's National Energy Plan and synthetic fuel proposals. Experts believe that the U.S. has a 300- to 400-year supply of coal. A report from the Office of Technology Assessment (OTA) says the U.S. could easily triple its coal production by 2000.[27] The International Energy Agency is calling for a seven-fold increase in international coal trade.[28]

But disregarding the major environmental drawbacks of increased traditional coal usage—such as air and water pollution, strip mining, and occupational safety—there remains the greenhouse gas problem. For every ton of coal burned, *three tons* of CO_2 are released into the atmosphere. In producing the same amount of energy, coal generates 70 percent more carbon dioxide than natural gas and 20 percent more than oil.[29]

The conclusion of the OTA report says: "With the possible exception of carbon dioxide pollution, all the significant problems associated with substantially increased coal use appear to be solvable." That exception could rule the day.

According to a report released in 1979 by JASON, a group of concerned scientists, development of synthetic fuels would greatly accelerate the CO_2 buildup. Synfuels produce 1.4 times as much CO_2 as coal and a whopping 2.3 times as much as natural gas.[30]

This knowledge comes at a time when a "synthetic fuel fever" has stricken the President and a majority of congressmen, who seem to agree with Senator Dale Bumpers of Arkansas that it is better to do something big, "even if it is the wrong thing."[31]

In an editorial entitled, "The Carbon Dioxide Gamble," the *New York Times* warns energy planners to resist

> . . .irrevocable commitments to the dirtiest fossil fuels. Other things being equal investing in solar power or in conservation is far less apt to disrupt the world's climate than investing in fossil fuels. . . . The nation may come to decide, carbon dioxide notwithstanding, that it must bet on coal and synthetic fuels, but it should do so in full recognition of the gamble.[32]

In 1979, Gordon J.F. MacDonald, a geophysicist and head of the JASON team, and three other CO_2 experts recommended to the Council on Environmental Quality that synfuels should not be developed without first seriously considering the effects on CO_2 buildup.[33]

Solar advocates have been following the carbon dioxide issue with keen interest, because energy from biomass, wind, hydroelectricity, photovoltaic cells, and direct solar heating do not contribute to the greenhouse effect. Even biomass—the burning of methane, wood, or other biologically derived fuels—is environmentally benign. According to solar expert Denis Hayes, CO_2 emitted by biomass energy systems in equilibrium will make "no net contribution to atmospheric concentrations, since green plants will capture carbon dioxide at the same rate that it is being produced."[34]

The handy sword provided to solar advocates by the carbon dioxide issue has a second, equally sharp edge. Nuclear power, also, does not produce carbon dioxide.

Coming to Grips

The problem facing us today is this: When should the studying stop and political action begin?

Stephen Schneider, a climatologist at the National Center for Atmospheric Research, puts it this way:

> The dilemma rests, metaphorically, in our need to gaze into a very dirty crystal ball; but the tough judgment to be made here is precisely how long we should clean the glass before acting on what we believe we see inside.[35]

The decision to act will undoubtedly be hampered by problems involving the interaction between scientists and policymakers. Scientists may prove adept at complex formulas regarding deep ocean currents, shifting precipitation, cloud patterns, and so forth, but this information must be put into forms accessible to politicians and the public.

"In my opinion, gentlemen, what we have here is a rather extraordinary example of the greenhouse effect.

Says DOE's Slade: "There is a tremendous amount of information already. But the point is how to choose from this vast bank. You can't just jimmy something up on a computer."[36]

It then becomes a Catch-22 situation: With many scientists unable to agree on basic facts—for instance, the role of the biosphere in the carbon cycle—policymakers may decline to act.

David Gushee of the Congressional Research Service says: "Congress wants judgment based only on the facts. . . . And if it takes more than a page to give your assessment, you don't know your subject. The only way to get their attention . . . is to lay one page on their desk."[37]

Where does this leave us? At least three types of action seem warranted:

• *Research.* Scientists must determine what specific research areas to focus on and avoid preoccupation with subjects not important to crucial policy decisions.

The JASON team identified seven priority research areas, of which the three most important are improved estimates of the contribution of the biosphere, a detailed oceanographic survey to determine the transfer rates of carbon from the surface water to deeper waters, and development of more sophisticated statistical models of climate.

According to a comprehensive research plan proposed by the Department of Energy (some portions of which were severely criticized by the JASON study), reports representing "an international consensus of the perceived costs or benefits" of the carbon dioxide problem will be issued in 1983 and 1988.[38]

Research should also examine possible technological ways of solving the carbon dioxide problem. Cesare Marchetti, of the International Institute for Applied Systems Analysis, has proposed collecting CO_2 from the exhaust of power plants, and injecting it into "sinking thermohaline currents" off the Straits of Gibraltar.[39] The Soviet climatologist M.I. Budyko has suggested increasing the earth's albedo, or reflectivity, by artificially maintaining certain levels of aerosols in the stratosphere. This would be done by using planes or rockets to spread 600,000 tons of aerosol particles consisting of sulphuric acid.[40] Both schemes would be extremely expensive, and perhaps environmentally disastrous.

• *Government awareness.* Congress and other governmental agencies must keep abreast of the carbon dioxide issue, and perhaps should factor it into policy decisions about future energy use. Agencies preparing environmental impact statements should consider including the effects of carbon dioxide. And Congress should thoroughly explore the issue before allocating massive sums to the development of synthetic fuels.

• *Global concern.* Every effort should be made through the World Meteorological Organization (WMO) and other U.N. organizations to keep the carbon dioxide issue before the world community. A beginning has been made. In February 1979, WMO sponsored a World Climate Conference in Geneva and CO_2 was widely discussed.

If carbon dioxide does prove as serious a problem for the global commons as some people predict, an unprecedented amount of international cooperation will be needed. A world summit of major industrial nations might become necessary.

The greatest danger would be if people were caught unprepared. Charles Cooper feels, in fact, that nothing can be done to stop global warming and so every effort should be made to adapt to the coming change. "The only practical strategy is adjustment," he says. "Technology will help to ease that adjustment but the institutional rigidities of our advanced societies may correspondingly make the response to the changed climate stickier than in early simpler ages."[41]

Kellogg views the "adjustment" with a stark fatalism: "The famines ahead, wherever and whenever they occur, will assure that millions in the poorer, less developed countries will not survive to witness a 'warmer earth.' "[42]

This argues strongly for current research efforts to concentrate on plans to cope with the coming lean years. In Schneider's words, we need a "Genesis strategy," an idea taken from the Biblical story in Genesis when Joseph correctly predicted that seven years of famine would follow seven years of feast. Joseph had enough sense and political moxie to convince Pharoah to store food for the future.

A major recommendation of a 1979 conference held in Annapolis on the societal consequences of CO_2 buildup was that policymakers should learn to manage the problem as a "trend crisis" rather than as an immediate threat. According to some conference participants, "adaptability" and "decentralized decisions based on understanding of details" will suffice.[43]

Unfortunately, as the current energy situation attests, societies have proved marvelously ill-equipped to deal with crises that lurk just around the corner.

Weather Modification

Meanwhile, man's efforts to control and shape short-term weather are gaining momentum.

Most people probably are not aware of the extent to which scientists and commercial interests are changing and planning to change the weather more to their liking. As Stephen Schneider has put it: "Nowadays, everybody is doing something about the weather but nobody is talking about it." Certainly there is little public appreciation of the widespread ramifications of manipulating such a critical component of man's complex environment.

The prospect of extensive weather modification—involving rainfall, snowfall, hail, fog, cloud cover, lightning, and severe storms—raises myriad questions of public policy that will not be easy to resolve. But the sooner they are dealt with, the more likely is society to make choices based on sound scientific information and sound political decision making.

The following discussion of weather modification is based on three premises:

1. At some point in the future, man will have the expertise and technology to exert an extensive mastery over the weather.

2. The pressures to take advantage of this power—chiefly in the name of economic benefits, as usual—will be great.

3. Full and objective evaluations of modification programs—in terms of their social, environmental, and economic consequences—are not likely. Technology also can be expected to outdistance an appropriate system of regulation (to control modification) and law (to deal with conflicts that arise).

Weather-control programs have ranged from a private firm spraying silver iodide from a six-foot pole to induce more snowfall on a ski slope in Sun Valley, to a large government program seeking to suppress hurricanes. (Also noteworthy was the Defense Department's extensive cloud seeding in Vietnam between 1967 and 1972, for the purpose of increasing rainfall and hampering the movement of enemy troops and supplies.[44]) Most weather modification work is done in the Midwest and West and is designed to aid agriculture. Most large programs are government-sponsored and consist of both laboratory and field operations research. Following is a brief description of some major federal projects and the benefits sought:

• Project Stormfury is designed to reduce the destructive, maximum winds of hurricanes by seeding clouds around their eye walls. Noteworthy success was claimed for Hurricane Debbie of 1969, in particular. Hurricanes, of course, are responsible for lost lives and enormous property damage. Hurricane Camille killed more than 300 people in 1969; Hurricane Agnes in 1972 caused some 120 deaths and property damage estimated at $2 billion to $3 billion. A significant portion of the damage, say some experts, could be avoided with even moderate seeding success.

• Estimates of hail damage to crops in the U.S. run up to $300 million a year. A good deal of it takes place in "Hail Alley," where Colorado, Wyoming, and Nebraska meet. This was the locus of the National Science Foundation's National Hail Research Experiment. It sought to suppress hail or reduce the size of the stones, which can be large enough to strip a cornfield bare. Data from the experiment are still under study.

• The Interior Department's Bureau of Reclamation operates a program called Project Skywater. One pilot cloud-seeding project, now completed, sought to demonstrate that snowpack in the San Juan Mountains could be built up to provide greater spring runoff in the Colorado River Basin—for the benefit of irrigation, hydroelectric power generation, and urban water supply. A similar snowpack augmentation experiment is currently under way in the American River basin area of the Sierras. The Bureau also is conducting field experiments, in a program called Hiplex, to augment summer rainfall in the High Plains.

• The alleviation of drought is another goal of some modification activities. NOAA has been conducting a cumulus cloud-seeding project in Florida. Techniques have been used there and in several other states to increase rainfall in dry periods.

Other federal projects of note have involved seeding and other techniques to dissipate or improve visibility in warm and cold fogs, which hamper airport, highways, and harbor traffic (Federal Aviation Agency, among others); suppressing the biggest lightning strokes to avert forest fires (Forest Service); and redistributing snowfall in Great Lakes coastal areas so it doesn't smother cities like Buffalo and cost so much for snow removal and other inconveniences (NOAA).

In addition to the federal efforts, dozens of private firm's activities range from sophisticated research and experimentation under federal contracts to fly-by-night seeders trying to stir up some rainfall for local farmers. Among the notable commercial enterprises have been two seeding programs to increase snowpack, and hence runoff for hydroelectric power, in the Sierra Nevadas. One project for Southern California Edison is aimed at the upper San Joaquin River Basin; another for Pacific Gas & Electric is for Lake Almanor. (The latter, for example, used eight ground-based, high elevation, radio-controlled silver iodide and sodium iodide generators.)

Dozens of foreign nations also are carrying out weather modification programs. The Soviets, for example, have been operating an extensive hail suppression program in the Caucasus wheat belt for years. They seed with rockets and artillery fire from the ground. "Every time a cloud comes over a hill they fire away," says Louis J. Battan, of the University of Arizona.

This brief survey only hits some high points of the current extensive worldwide modification activity.

It should also be noted that we are modifying the weather inadvertently in a number of ways—through urbanization, agricultural activities, and deforestation, for example. "These unintentional effects on local and regional weather can be quite dramatic," says Richard A. Frank, administrator of NOAA. "For example, the Metropolitical Meteorological Experiment, a major field investigation carried out at St. Louis in the early 1970's, showed that the St. Louis urban-industrial complex influences convective storm behavior in such a way as to increase cloudiness by 10 percent, in a localized area within 20 miles of the city center."[45]

Pressures to Act

One obvious question is whether the deliberate programs are successful enough to presage a glowing future for weather modification. No attempt will be made here to evaluate individual program results. But some general observations are appropriate:

Atmospheric scientists are not necessarily hesitant to acknowledge how little they know about the earth's incredibly complex weather systems, about the mysterious physics of individual clouds, and about techniques to control. At the same time, there may be an irrepressible tendency by some of those in charge of modification programs to inflate their claims of success—whether it be a federal agency concerned with justifying its work and appropriations, or a private operator whose livelihood is at stake. Unquestionably, also, one of the great difficulties in evaluating results is differentiating between the rain or snow generated by man's seeding and that which would have fallen anyway.

But there are a number of factors that suggest man is well on his way to managing the weather and climate. In the first place, despite setbacks and doubtful experiments, many of the programs have produced solid evidence of effectiveness. Weather experts seem to have moved from a period of self-doubt and uncertainty to one of confidence. The Interdepartmental Committee for Atmospheric Sciences, which coordinates federal programs, has said indications are that "technology now available is nearly ready for regular application."[46] Similarly, the National Advisory Committee on Oceans and Atmosphere said it is persuaded that "we stand on the threshold of a new era of environmental control."[47]

Of great import for the future is the fact that, although the science of weather modification is still in its infancy, it is growing rapidly. It is being fed a rich diet of information that will get progressively richer in the coming years. One type of information relates to modification itself, and includes results from research and experimentation programs, more sophisticated monitoring and measuring devices, better understanding of clouds, and better delivery systems for seeding agents and the like.

A second type of information is more basic: an enormous amount of data that is being sent back from satellites, balloons, ships, and other observation posts, and that provides an increasingly detailed and complete picture of the earth's atmospheric process. Mathematical models of cloud and atmospheric processes are already widely used, but scientists happily anticipate the use of computers so powerful that they can handle the intricate and voluminous numerical information needed to plot the complex workings of the global atmosphere. The implications for weather and climate control are clear.

If the knowledge is there, will it be used? The pressures to change weather will be enormous. One need only consider the inducements—cheap water in the dry West; the possibility of raising crops in poor, arid regions of the world; protection of crops from hail damage and the burden of hail insurance; safety from hurricane, flood, tornado, and other damage; cheap dependable hydroelectric power; elimination of many travel inconveniences and hazards; comfort and health; and so forth.

"Weather modification is one of the most important scientific developments now visible on the horizon," said Gordon MacDonald. "If research and applications in this field are properly encouraged and managed, man may soon free himself from stoic acceptance of capricious weather and thereby reap a bountiful harvest of additional crops, new water resources, and a safer environment."[48]

Some years ago, Walter Orr Roberts, president of University Corporation for Atmospheric Research in Boulder, spoke of the great promise of weather modification for the "benefit of mankind" and the need to attain the "maximum possible mastery of our atmospheric environment."[49] "The enemy is hail, blizzards, floods, droughts, hurricanes," he has also said. "The enemy is the innate intransigence and inscrutability of nature."[50]

In addition to the rather tangible benefits of weather control, not to be dismissed lightly is the bureaucratic and scientific momentum of a technology on the move.

Finally, evidence shows that most types of weather modification—when they are at all successful—are likely to produce benefits far in excess of costs incurred. For costs are usually very low, and it is agreed that many clouds have been seeded because farmers felt they had so little to lose and so much to gain. The Interdepartmental Committee for Atmospheric Sciences (ILAS) noted, for example, that "where rainfall is marginal, an increase of only 5 percent rainfall at the right time of the year may mean the difference between crop failure and a bountiful harvest."[51]

Dangers and Drawbacks

Nevertheless, as in any activity of such scope and complexity, hazards exist and miscalculations can occur. And it can be expected that if and when they do, the ill effects will be irreversible.

There is concern that errors of knowledge or judgment could lead, for example, to a hurricane changing course toward a more populated area, or moving forward with greater vigor even if seeding reduced maximum wind velocity. A cloud-seeding experiment was taking place at the time and general location of the storm that caused the disastrous Rapid City, S.D., flood in 1972. Though scientists associated with cloud seeding insist the project did not affect the storm, others believe it greatly magnified the torrential rainfall.[52]

In any case, weather modification projects that benefit some are likely to harm others in the area or downwind. (Scientists recognize a dearth of knowledge on downwind effects.) The farmers may want rain, but not the resort owner or the outdoor concert promoter. Hurricane rains that cause flood damage in the Southeast may bring badly needed water storage to the Northeast or to Mexico.

Contrary claims on the weather lead to legal disputes. But most law cases on weather modification have floundered for lack of decisive evidence—not to mention such thornier questions as who owns the rain in a cloud, under what circumstances is there liability for damage, what constitutes negligence, and so forth. As noted before, it is most difficult to prove a cause and effect relationship. Most frequently cited are two cases that were resolved, and that illustrate some of these problems:

1. In Jeff Davis County, Texas, ranchers sought and obtained a temporary injunction against cloud seeding contracted for by nearby farmers seeking suppression of hail. The ranchers claimed, and the judge agreed, that the seeding would retard rainfall on the ranchers' properties. In upholding the decision on appeal, the court said a landowner has the right to "such rainfall as may come from clouds over his own property that Nature, in her caprice, may provide."[53]

2. Rather than granting the existence of such vested property rights in clouds or their moisture, the New York Supreme Court applied the principle of balancing interests. New York City was suffering from a serious water shortage and decided on some cloud seeding. The owners of a Catskill resort sought an injunction. But the court said that even if they could show impending damage, the water supply needs of New York City were much more important.[54]

Howard J. Taubenfeld, a law professor at Southern Methodist University, suggested in a speech to the American Association for the Advancement of Science (AAAS) that weather modification will be used extensively, with a balancing of interests and payment of compensation to injured parties. "Insofar as it can intervene with nature to do so," he said, "society is likely to attempt to seek the greatest good for the greatest number from its weather, at least in such cases of clearcut majority need, even if this injures the status quo rights or property values of some minority."[55]

Modification programs can be expected to produce all kinds of rami-fications and side effects—social, economic and environmental. Are they likely to be fully evaluated beforehand? Certainly a conscientious application of the requirements for the National Environmental Policy Act would help. But there is still room for grave doubt, because of the complexities involved, the insufficiency of knowledge, and the political realities. It is instructive to consider some of the variables and uncertainties.

Schneider noted at the 1972 AAAS meeting that "the elements of the climatic system are tightly coupled and the system is nonlinear (i.e., a small stimulus could cause a large response). Slight changes in one area can set off feedback mechanisms that could cause an entirely unexpected result." He recognized that much work is being done to identify such mechanisms, but suggested also that "a great difficulty is presented by the role of oceans, which are strongly coupled to atmospheric conditions."

Ecological uncertainties abound. What are the effects of silver and other residues from seeding agents? What changes might occur in soils, and in watershed hydrology, erosion, sedimentation, and the like? What instabilities and imbalances might be caused in plant and animal com-munities? These are only some of the questions that are easier to ask than answer.

According to a National Science Foundation study, "Major weather modifications may alter the balance among species of plants and animals—with sharp declines in the number of some, and inordinate growth in the abundance of others. In particular, major weather changes may result in the rapid spread of certain weeds, pests, and vector-borne diseases."[56]

There also are countervailing economic considerations not confined to areas where modification takes place. One region's agricultural benefits may adversely affect markets in another. And can one expect the political process to come to grips with the fact that, while rainfall is increased for irrigation, there is already an overcapacity to produce crops? At the same time, there may be more efficient ways to attain the same benefits sought through weather control.

A thorough evaluation, of course, must assess feasible alternatives to modification programs. There are many possibilities, among them better weather predictions and warnings, better ways to make people pay attention, better insurance coverage, better building protection, zoning for floodplains and other hazardous areas, and development and substitution of hail-resistant or drought-resistant crops.

Finally, what of the effects on man's psychological and spiritual well-being? There are many reasons to believe that the weather may have a mysterious, unquantifiable, therapeutic effect on man. A few scientists have discussed the values inherent in its aesthetics, its diversity, its uncertainty, its ethnological or cultural roles, and even its stresses. Robert L. Hendrick, a research meteorologist at the Agricultural Research Service, has spoken of the "wilderness of weather," and asked: "How can proper account be taken of natural weather scenery, the stimulation, the unique experience of living with weather in its more robust forms?"[57] Similarly, Adrian Chamberlain, president of Colorado State University, said, "It seems clear that the power and motion of severe storms provide some of the most exhilarating opportunities that the human mind experiences."[58]

Increasing weather modification calls for further scientific exploration of the psychic values of weather variations. In the meantime, there will be plenty of gut reactions. To the environmentalist, for example, it's "a problem of increasing social control or regimentation. Weather is one of the few things left in this world more or less completely free." Another environmentalist, asked why he opposed weather modification, said: "It's just a general feeling we've fouled up everything else, why the weather?"

Chapter 6

CHEMICALS
AND PUBLIC HEALTH

The health of the people is really the foundation upon which all their happiness and
their powers as a state depend.

—Benjamin Disraeli

One of the persistent malignancies attacking our society is the steady
penetration of the environment and of people by poisonous chemicals.
Yet protection of the public's health—including protection from such
environmental pollutants—is indisputably a backbone of public policy
in the United States.

Of course, this policy frequently conflicts with other government
policies; with the pursuit of profits by industry; with the pursuit of work
by labor; with the pursuit of cheaper products by consumers; and with
the pursuit of more energy across the board.

The result has been a series of protacted battles over radiation,
drinking-water supplies, pesticides, air pollution, chemicals in food
and in factories, and a variety of other problems. These battles feature
efforts to weaken environmental protection legislation and administrative regulations, disputes over the import of scientific findings on
health effects, and disagreements over the feasibility of pollution control technology.

Where does all this leave us? What do we *know* about environmental
pollutants and health? Equally important, what do we *not* yet know?
And what is being done about the various threats? Following is a series
of postulates designed to facilitate an assessment of environmental
health problems and possible responses to them:

**We are exposed regularly to a fearful assortment of known and
suspected pollutants.**

**Environmental pollutants are having serious adverse effects on
health.**

**It is a myth to think that only a small, idiosyncratic fraction of the
population is in danger from pollution.**

Chemical pollution may be doing far more damage than we realize, for we are still alarmingly ignorant about its effects.

It is extremely difficult—many experts say impossible—to establish a pollutant exposure level or threshold below which adverse health effects are absent.

Animal tests generally are relevant to assessments of human risks.

Chemical reactions caused by mixing pollutants often are far more pernicious than those pollutants acting alone.

The regulatory picture is not bright.

More effective regulation in the name of public health has been thwarted by public apathy and by industry opposition.

Individuals have a right to know about exposures and risks.

In the final analysis, the government may wind up putting a price on people's heads.

A dollar of prevention is far more effective than a dollar of cure.

The following discussion elaborates on each of these twelve points.

1. We are exposed regularly to a fearful assortment of known and suspected pollutants. These include substances that have long been part of the natural environment (lead, sulfur, mercury, etc.), but in forms and doses not experienced by humans before. They also include a barrage of modern toxic substances and synthetic compounds.

It has been estimated that 70,000 chemicals are in common use and that 2,000 new chemicals enter the environment "to a significant extent" each year.[1] Just before the onset of World War II, U.S. production of synthetic organic chemicals totaled less than one billion pounds per year. By 1976, the total had rocketed to 162.9 billion pounds.[2] From 1960 to 1970, manufacture of polychlorinated biphenyls (PCB's) rose from 40 million pounds to 86 million pounds per year. Production of vinyl chloride in 1952 was 321 million pounds, but by 1973 the total had jumped to 5.3 billon pounds.[3]

Some 46,000 pesticide products currently infest the marketplace. They contain roughly 1,400 active ingredients, some of which are under particular suspicion of being hazardous. Agricultural usage accounts for about 60 percent of the U.S. pesticides total, but pesticides are also used promiscuously in homes, businesses, cities, and parks, as well as farms and forests.

The herbicide business, in particular, is flourishing. "Over the past decade," says a National Academy of Sciences study, "the most startling and dramatic change has been the continued rise in the use of herbicides compared to other pesticides. Herbicides have largely substituted for hand labor and machine cultivation in a large number of crops."[4] Another report estimates that two-thirds of all the feed and food crop acreage in the U.S. is treated.[5] Herbicides now account for an estimated 45 percent of all domestic pesticide use of some one billion pounds a year.[6]

Even after enormous amounts of publicity, it is impossible for the mind to grasp the full extent to which our industrialized society has come to depend on chemicals and to take them for granted. They are released in the manufacture and use of plastics, paints, cleaners, water disinfectants, construction materials, pesticides, fertilizers, dyes, preservatives, fire retardants, batteries, brake linings, fabrics, food additives, cigarettes, drugs, and many other products. Other widespread technological activities also have serious implications for chemically induced cancer, heart and respiratory diseases. They include copper and lead smelting, coke oven emissions, radiation, and combustion of fossil fuels in automobiles, power plants, and the like. Finally, and of particular concern, there are the thousands of hazardous waste disposal sites—such as Love Canal in New York—that leak carelessly handled chemicals into the environment.

In short, we have rather abruptly fashioned a society seemingly dependent on a staggering variety and quantity of chemicals, and an environment suffused with harmful chemical agents. It is an environment totally unlike any other in human history.

Exposures to chemicals are acute, chronic, short-term, and long-term. Some are knowing and intentional (the coal miner who exposes himself to black lung disease because he needs the job, or the cigarette smoker to whom the weeds seem essential). Other exposures are unwitting (the worker who for decades handles materials such as asbestos or vinyl chloride, unaware that he is getting cancer as a result); or unavoidable (the urban dweller who inhales carbon monoxide spewed into the ambient air by automobiles); or accidental (the farmer who dies because he misuses the pesticide parathion, or because he eats bread accidentally made from seed wheat treated with a methylmercury fungicide).

As a result of the myriad exposures, the throat, the lungs, intestines, kidney, liver, heart, blood, and genes are all subject to excessive stress, infection, poisoning, cancers, genetic mutations, and birth defects. True, the body puts up a good fight. But is the body a match for present pollution loads?

2. Environmental pollutants are having serious adverse effects on health. The damning evidence against various pollutants—detailed in many studies[7]—ranges from clear-cut cause and effect to suspicious.

It is ominously suggestive that: an estimated 370,000 people in the U.S. alone die of cancer each year and almost one out of every four Americans now living is expected to contract some form of cancer; there

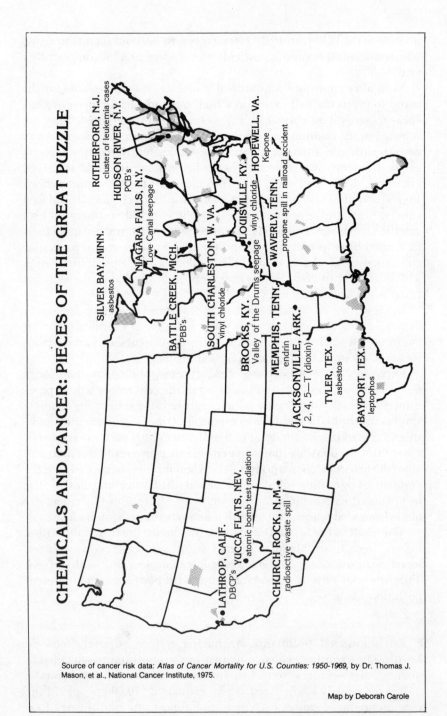

CHEMICALS AND CANCER: PIECES OF THE GREAT PUZZLE

RUTHERFORD, N.J.
cluster of leukemia cases

HUDSON RIVER, N.Y.
PCB's

HOPEWELL, VA.
Kepone

SILVER BAY, MINN.
asbestos

NIAGARA FALLS, N.Y.
Love Canal seepage

BATTLE CREEK, MICH.
PBB's

SOUTH CHARLESTON, W. VA.
vinyl chloride

LOUISVILLE, KY.
vinyl chloride

WAVERLY, TENN.
propane spill in railroad accident

BROOKS, KY.
Valley of the Drums seepage

MEMPHIS, TENN.
endrin

JACKSONVILLE, ARK.
2, 4, 5—T (dioxin)

TYLER, TEX.
asbestos

BAYPORT, TEX.
leptophos

LATHROP, CALIF.
DBCP's

YUCCA FLATS, NEV.
atomic bomb test radiation

CHURCH ROCK, N.M.
radioactive waste spill

Source of cancer risk data: *Atlas of Cancer Mortality for U.S. Counties: 1950-1969,* by Dr. Thomas J. Mason, et al., National Cancer Institute, 1975.

Map by Deborah Carole

are about a million heart attacks each year, half of them fatal; and additional millions of Americans suffer from emphysema, asthma, and chronic bronchitis.

An Environmental Protection Agency official summarized the situation in this way:

> We have a considerable body of evidence showing a relationship between air pollutants and acute respiratory illness, aggravation of chronic heart and lung disease, and development of chronic respiratory disease. Cancer, heart disease and congenital malformations cannot as yet be causally associated with air pollutants, although substances which are known carcinogens, mutagens and cardiovascular irritants can be found in ambient air.

He added that, until we understand the causes of the latter three problems, "we are more likely to understate greatly the true impact of pollutant exposure on human health than we are to attribute erroneously many health effects to air pollution."[8]

A 1973 government report noted that, of the eight causes of death with the biggest rates of increase in the 1960's, five are known to be heavily related to cigarette smoke and other air pollutants. "It may be supposed that major changes in smoking and other air pollution are responsible for a substantial part of the rise in death rates" for lung cancer, bronchitis, and other bronchopulmonic diseases, and associated "to a lesser degree" with other cancers and other circulatory diseases.[9]

("In large urban areas," says Carl M. Shy, director of EPA's Human Studies Laboratory, "the effect of air pollution was comparable to the effect of moderate smoking."[10])

Other illnesses, of course, are caused by toxic substances, dusts, radiation, and noise. These references merely scratch the surface; there is

---

To sort out the relationships between chemicals and cancer and other diseases requires a painstaking analysis of basic research, test data, epidemiological studies, and disease occurrences themselves. The map on the facing page shows two kinds of more or less unrelated information. The shaded areas are counties in which the cancer death rates for white males is "significantly higher" than the nationwide average.

Investigators are seeking to follow up this epidemiological data to pinpoint causes. For example, they are probing in New Jersey, where 18 of the state's 21 counties have bladder cancer rates in the highest decile of all U.S. counties, and in Louisiana, where male lung cancer rates are extremely high. In Louisiana, interviews are being conducted with an eye to sorting out petrochemical plant factors, smoking habits, drinking water supplies, and the like.

In a counterpoint to the long-term exposures generally reflected by the epidemiological information are the periodic eruptions that gain public attention, generate political concern, and highlight the many dangers latent in the modern environment.

In the sampling of places around the nation, hazardous or potentially hazardous chemicals have been much in the news because of serious occupational exposures, accidental releases, and other episodes. The dangers from these chemicals are not necessarily confined to such locations—for example, problems with asbestos, vinyl chloride, PCB's, and dioxin have been widespread.

even a growing body of work dealing with pollution-produced stress and mental problems.[11] For example, Leroy Schieler, of South Seattle Community College, says there is a correlation between levels of hydrogen sulfide pollution and the incidence of mental depression and suicide.[12]

The World Health Organization has estimated that there are 500,000 pesticide poisoning cases worldwide each year, and that about 5,000 of them are fatal.[13] Equivalent figures for the U.S. have been estimated at 15,000 to 20,000 illnesses and 150-200 deaths.[14] Pesticide applicators and children—who are exposed around the home to countless chemical products—are the most common victims. Many additional cases may be unreported or undiagnosed.

3. It is a myth to think that only a small, idiosyncratic fraction of the population is in danger from pollution. An American Public Health Association (APHA) study in the mid-1970's estimated that the number of people in the U.S. "at risk" from pollution was 21 million.[15]

Urban dwellers and industrial workers generally encounter the most pollution. But there are many categories of people who are particularly susceptible to environmental stresses. Major factors that decrease resistance, the APHA study noted, include:

• Genetic defects (such as asthma, sickle cell anemia, atrial or ventricular wall defects.

• Developmental defects (including coronary insufficiency, rheumatic heart disease, chronic bronchitis, and emphysema)

• Cigarette smoking or exposure to cigarette smoke

• Aging or debilitation

• Preschool age (when detoxifying enzyme mechanisms have not yet matured)

• Overcrowded living conditions

• Malnutrition

Other suspected causes of increased susceptibility are childhood infections, heavy physical exertion, and obesity.

The U.S. Public Health Service has figured conservatively that long-term exposure to occupational hazards results in 100,000 worker deaths and 390,000 disabling diseases each year.[16] *Business Week* magazine has said:

> After three decades of unprecedented and virtually unregulated proliferation of new chemical products, American industry now confronts a frightening fact. . . . Long-term exposure to an unknown number of chemicals can produce irreparable damage to the organs of employes who work with them—and chemicals are used in every nook and cranny of U.S. industry, not just the $70 billion, 1-million-worker chemical industry.[17]

4. Chemical pollution may be doing far more damage than we realize, for we are still alarmingly ignorant about its effects. The evidence incriminating many chemical agents has accumulated only slowly and laboriously. Tests are typically expensive and time-consuming. They may be inconclusive. Testing techniques sometimes are not sophisticated enough to detect minute amounts of poison.

What we already know about the effects of chemicals is disturbing enough;[18] what we don't yet know, but can reasonably expect, is perhaps more disturbing still. Probably less than 10 percent of the chemicals in commerce have been tested for carcinogenicity. Our ignorance can be illustrated in many ways:

• It is very difficult to ascertain the effects of prolonged low-dose exposure to chemicals. Part of the problem is sorting out the many personal and environmental factors that simultaneously contribute to ill health and death. Chronic bronchitis is a good example, said former Surgeon General Luther L. Terry: "It develops over a long period of time and can become crippling through a combination of many factors—air pollution, smoking, repeated and recurring bouts with infectious agents, occupational exposure—all affected, perhaps, by a hereditary predisposition."[19]

• The APHA study points to research findings that 80 percent of known clinical congenital malformations and spontaneous abortions are of unknown origin, while at the same time "a very broad range of chemical agents have been shown in the laboratory to produce teratogenic effects (birth defects, etc.) under certain conditions."

• Long periods between cause and effect do much to compound our ignorance. It wasn't until 1974 that vinyl chloride, a gas widely used since World War II as an aerosol propellant and component of plastic products, was identified as the culprit in angiosarcoma, a usually fatal liver cancer. Thus, cases of angiosarcoma are attributable to an agent that apparently started taking effect 15 to 35 years before.[20] It is now also clear that thousands of cancer deaths and other illnesses are linked to asbestos exposures dating back a similar period of time.[21] Such discoveries should be enough to make anyone uneasy about the proliferation of other unevaluated substances in the environment.

• Pollution could be causing genetic mutations that will not be apparent for decades, or generations. Some have surmised that we may be instigating genetic changes with the potential for the destruction of mankind itself.

• Many avenues of chemical investigation are in their infancy. These involve the prevalence and nature not only of mutagens, but teratogens, cardiotoxins, and neurotoxins which cause nervous system degeneration. They also include the role of nutrition, the effects of various stresses, the nature of genetic susceptibility, the workings of immuno-logical systems, and the effects of aging in general.[22]

• Many mysteries of cancer remain—though there has been much enlightening research (as will be noted below). It has become clear, in any case, that the problem of cancer—as well as of the two other chief health scourges in the United States, heart and respiratory disease—involves a complex maze of interacting chemicals, other environmental and life-style factors, exposures, and susceptibilities.

5. It is extremely difficult—many experts say impossible—to establish a pollutant exposure level or threshold below which adverse health effects are absent. "At every level of stress," says the APHA study, "some die, some fall ill, and some suffer minor insults, depending on their individual adaptive capacity."[23]

In the view of Gregory J. Ahart, director of the General Accounting Office's Human Resources Division, "Most scientists agree with the director of the National Cancer Institute that 'there is no practical scientific method to prove experimentally the safety of any level of exposure to a carcinogen.' "[24] Similarly, medical writer Harold M. Schmeck, Jr., says, "The current view is that there is probably no threshold below which a radiation dose can be presumed entirely safe."[25]

Charles F. Wurster, of the State University of New York at Stony Brook, decries the agrument that a person can be exposed to small amounts of a carcinogen without danger. "Carcinogens do not become safe in low concentrations," he says. "They merely cause cancer in fewer individuals."[26] Thus unless a huge number of animals are used in a test, "weak" carcinogens may not reveal cancers if used in low dosages. "The argument that anything can cause cancer if administered in large enough doses is false," adds Wurster. "High dosages do not convert innocuous substances into carcinogens."

The controversy over thresholds has been enduring. The Clean Air Act, in mandating air quality standards for various pollutants, seems to endorse the feasibility of setting threshold limits, if only for reasons of practicality. At the same time, however, the law makes clear that all persons, not just those who are normal and healthy, must be protected, and with an adequate margin of safety.

John T. Middleton, formerly the top federal air pollution control official, commented in an interview: "In the history of the biological sciences, we find that with increasing knowledge, we discover effects that occur at lower and lower doses." This results from better under-standing of the life system and from the fine tuning of research technologies.

6. Animal tests generally are relevant to assessments of human risks.
There is now far less resistance than before to the concept that animal
tests for carcinogenicity provide reliable warnings against human exposure. For example, tests on rats first revealed that vinyl chloride was
causing liver cancer in humans. "Most scientists agree that a chemical
that causes cancer in animals is a potential cancer hazard for humans,"
says Gregory Ahart.[27]

The Council on Environmental Quality (CEQ) sums up the empiri-
cal evidence that animal tests can be validly applied to humans: "Not
only have rodent experiments given positive carcinogenic tests results
for compounds known to cause cancer in man, but also—in every case
except arsenic—each chemical known to cause cancer in man has been
found to do so in animal species."[28]

In fact, the chemical companies that commonly denigrate unfavorable animal tests as having no relevance to humans are silent on the
possibility that a chemical might be hazardous to humans even though
it does *not* test unfavorably on animals. Indeed, former Environmental
Protection Agency (EPA) Administrator William D. Ruckelshaus, after
noting that dioxin is "one of the most teratogenic chemicals known,"
has said: "As with another well-known teratogen, thalidomide, the
possibility exists that dioxin may be many times more potent in humans
than in test animals (thalidomide was 60 times more dangerous to
humans than to mice, and 700 times more dangerous than to
hamsters)."[29]

The evidence on inorganic arsenic seems to show that human carcinogens can invade the environment even after passing animal tests. David
P. Rall, director of the National Institute of Environmental Health
Science, has said that humans may have more types of cells susceptible
to cancer than lower animals.[30]

The possibility that testing may not detect many potential hazards
has boosted interest in epidemiology as a supplementary technique for
spotting culprits. "Although it is crucial that laboratory testing be
carried out on all chemicals in the environment," says Joseph F.
Fraumeni, Jr., associate chief, Epidemiology Branch, National Cancer
Institute, "it should be noted that the identification of all human
carcinogens to date has come first from observation on man. These
observations have been made primarily on occupational groups with
heavy exposure to chemical agents."[31]

Of course, epidemiology studies can only be done long after the
chemicals have been introduced. They do not solve one of the great
obstacles to detection—the fact that carcinogens, mutagens, and teratogens typically do not tip off their dangers for decades or even a generation or more.

Full tests for carcinogenicity can take up to four years and obviously are expensive. Happily, a rather simple test introduced in the mid-1970's offers promise for a quick screening process to spot suspect chemicals that should be tested more elaborately. Called the Ames Test after Bruce Ames of the University of California at Berkeley, it is based on the apparently solid premise that there is a high correlation between carcinogens and mutagens. Chemicals are tested for their capacity to cause mutations in bacteria—which requires only about 48 hours and roughly $500—and the results used to single out those likely to be carcinogenic.[32]

7. Chemical reactions caused by mixing pollutants often are far more pernicious than those pollutants acting alone. This conclusion underscores the fact that there are great gaps in scientific understanding of the chemical processes at work. This ignorance not only compounds the difficulty of assessing health effects; it also hampers pollution control efforts.

A National Academy of Sciences conference of experts in Washington, D.C., in 1973 concluded that new research "suggests that observed adverse health effects may arise in considerable part not only from interactions of body tissues with the primary pollutants but with unidentified reaction products generated by complex chemical events in the atmosphere or indeed within the lung."[33] We only know the "bare details" of these reactions, Jack G. Calvert, of Ohio State University's Department of Chemistry, told the conference.

A prime example is the rather recent realization that sulfur dioxide is a far less insidious enemy than the sulfuric acid mists and sulfate salts derived from it as it goes through successive states of oxidization. This occurs through photochemical and catalytic processes. For example, manganese, iron, and other metallic substances in fuels, in fuel additives, or in the air from other sources, may act as oxidizing catalysts. It also is felt that sulfuric acid formation is enhanced when more moisture is in the air.[34]

The problem is exacerbated because the acids and sulfates are very fine particulates. Thus, they can penetrate the respiratory tract deeply, and can be dispersed over a wide geographic area. (One result of this may be the "acid rainfall" which does not respect state or national boundaries.) John F. Finklea, director of EPA's National Environmental Research Center, says we may be seeing "the exposure of a large region of the United States to levels of finely divided particulate sulfates which exceed our current best judgment estimate for an adverse effect threshold." He says the area in question extends from Indiana to the Atlantic seaboard and from Rhode Island to Virginia.[35]

EPA says that sulfate levels in urban areas are high enough to aggravate existing respiratory illnesses and to increase mortality on the worst fews days each year.[36] Sulfuric acid mists and sulfates seem to be "one or two orders of magnitude" more harmful to the respiratory tract than sulfur dioxides.[37] The problem might be "severely aggravated" by increasing the use of high-sulfur fuels, Finklea says.

John B. Moran, an official of EPA's National Environmental Research Center, has drawn attention to another matter of concern with pollutant interactions: many metals, in trace quantities, are associated with automobile exhaust particulates. Of the possible metallic compounds, says Moran, the "greatest uncertainty" surrounds the toxicity and possible long-term health effects of the noble metal compounds (including platinum, palladium, and rethenium) resulting from catalytic reactor attrition and from their interactions with other pollutants. Moran says the noble metals are of special concern because:

> They are novel pollutants in the general environment with which mankind has had limited biological experience; they are likely to be persistent; they may be metabolically transformed to more toxic products; exposures will involve the general population, including especially vulnerable subgroups; and exposures may affect the frequency of serious disorders like lung cancer and the severity of common disorders like asthma.[38]

These uncertainties—and many others that could be cited—are reminiscent of some suprises from the past, such as the unnerving discovery in 1969 that supposedly inert mercury in the water can be transformed by sediment microorganisms into dangerous toxic compounds. (The results ranged from many deaths and severe illness in Japan to the virtual disappearance of swordfish from American tables.)[39]

In a similar vein, Nicholas A. Ashford, associate professor at the Massachusetts Institute of Technology, says:

> Chemical, physical, biological, and stress hazards are often found in combination, and their effects can be not merely additive but intensified (synergistic). Carbon monoxide and heat, amphetamines and overcrowding, asbestos and smoking, and promoters of cancer are all examples of agents whose effects can be synergistic. Most such combination effects are probably still to be recognized. . . .[40]

Sir Richard Doll, professor of medicine at Oxford University, and others have noted that it is well established that both asbestos and ionizing radiation interact with cigarette smoking to produce lung cancer. Doll says further that men who drink 81 or more grams of ethyl alcohol (equivalent to seven whiskeys) and smoke 20 or more cigarettes daily have a 45 times greater risk of getting cancer of the esophagus than men who drink and smoke half as much or less.[41]

8. The regulatory picture is not bright. A case in point is the 1976 Toxic Substances Control Act. On one hand, the Act is an environmental milestone, a comprehensive and progressive law to protect the public from dangerous chemicals. On the other hand, the Act also is a compromise and an administrative nightmare unlikely to result in thorough protection from the proliferation of dangerous chemicals.

"Ladies, have you anything to declare besides eye of newt and toe of frog?"
Michael Rawson, The Conservation Foundation

How can this be so, this Jékyll and Hyde situation? Briefly, the law is very carefully worded. It aims to block off all the escapes. And it is designed to spot dangerous chemicals *before* they go on the market. The law has enormous potential.

But the law also has several basic weaknesses. It is so complex and expansive, the Environmental Protection Agency may simply choke on it. Effective implementation of the act will require aggressive administration in the public interest, adequate scientific data, plentiful money and manpower, and attentive oversight from the outside—altogether a long-shot parlay.

Endless examples of scientific, management, and political problems with implementation of the Toxic Substances Control Act—as well as other laws regulating food, pesticides, workplaces, and consumer products—could be cited. Opposition to regulation by industry and the public is discussed below. To illustrate the type of scientific problems involved, consider this comment of Herman S. Bloch, chairman of the board of directors of the American Chemical Society:

> Since a material which is essentially innocuous in one form may be hazardous in other forms and under other conditions, each new form in which a product is introduced should be examined for possible changes in

hazards. . . . Many substances undergo transformations upon introduction into the environment. . . . Also, the toxicity of a substance may be
due to impurities or byproducts associated with a given process or method
of manufacture. Therefore it is important that, within the limits of
detection, the true levels of exposure be ascertained. . . .[42]

Or consider an added dimension to the problem of particulates. The
APHA study put it this way: "It might be argued that containment of
large particles is at least a step in the right direction, but we could
deceive ourselves if we assume it is safe to increase fuel combustion
because of our increasing the concentrations of the fine particles, presumably the most harmful."[43] Middleton says, "We're taking out a
helluva lot of tonnage. But a few tons of very finely divided stuff may be
more important."

Speaking of various pollutants, Middleton says, "My guess is that it's
not so much different techniques of control as much higher levels of
control that will be necessary." But he is concerned that there is a
tapering off on control technology research and development. "Is there
an adequate pressure system to force development of improved technology?" he asks. "There has to be some driving mechanism. It doesn't just
come along by itself."

**9. More effective regulation in the name of public health has been
thwarted by public apathy and by industry opposition.** Most of us tend
to have a rather casual attitude toward health—until it slips away. "The
feeling of health can only be gained by sickness," said G.C. Lichtenbert.
More directly, one senses that many people are becoming irritated by the
endless stream of alarms about exposure to carcinogens in everything
from asbestos to saccharin and from bacon to drinking water. This
irritation can give way to disbelief and disregard, or even antagonism.

Such reactions—sometimes encouraged by scientists, journalists,
politicians, members of the medical establishment, and representatives
of affected industries—are oddly perverse: They suggest that the greater
the evidence or suspicion of danger from environmental contamination, the more we should belittle the problem. But without a bedrock of
public concern and support, efforts to cope with chemical pollution, or
even gain greater understanding of it, are likely to be seriously
undermined.

As to business opposition to regulation, former Congressman Paul
G. Rogers of Florida has charged that American industry has

. . . fought every inch of the way against every environmental health requirement. Every dollar invested to reduce deadly coke oven emissions, to
control arsenic and lead from copper smelters, to block unnecessary
radiation exposures, to capture chemical plants' carcinogenic discharges,

to curb toxic sulfates and nitrate particles from coal combustion, has come only after protracted political and legal struggles.[44]

Donald Kennedy, when he was commissioner of the Food and Drug Administration noted that, while the "size, complexity, and power of regulated enterprise" have grown, the public is being persuaded that government agencies are trying to gain more control over their lives. "This piece of deliberate nonsense has a clear purpose," he said. "It is to make regulators and other government officials more cautious than their duty requires."[45]

Various colorful arguments and ploys have been used in the fight against control of chemical pollution. For example, following the announcement that mutagens had been found in charcoal-broiled hamburgers,[46] commentator David Brinkley said, ". . . if all these foods and drinks we've been swallowing for centuries were as dangerous as they say, we'd all be dead, but we're not."[47] (Maybe *we're* not, but many people are.) Another variation of the same theme is this comment from William Tucker, a contributing editor of *Harper's* magazine: ". . . there seems to be no limit to what the federal government is willing to do to indulge the fanatical concerns about what we eat, drink, and breathe."[48]

One might think that the public—if not those who speak for it and to it—would be grateful to be alerted not only to proved health dangers but also to suspected dangers in the absence of substantial proof. This at least would permit people to make a more informed choice about whether to smoke, whether to work in an asbestos plant, whether to live near a smelter, and so forth.

Liebe F. Cavalien, a professor at the Sloan-Kettering Institute for Cancer Research, comments, "It is illogical to conclude that, since we are already subjected to many risks, a few more will not matter. It would seem to me that the public should be encouraged by scientists to consider carefully what they put into their bodies, intentionally or otherwise."[49]

Several techniques for belittling the proliferation of warnings about environmental hazards have become popular. One is to suggest that everything we do or touch must be carcinogenic or otherwise dangerous, so there isn't much use getting too concerned. (This dovetails nicely with the human tendency to feel that it-won't-happen-to-me.)

Gus Speth, a member of the Council on Environmental Quality, says, "The ridicule arising from the saccharin episode may stimulate contempt about our regulation of other widely used but potentially hazardous chemicals—and we may find ourselves, some years from now, laughing all the way to the hospital."[50]

Cousin to this adverse public reaction is a slightly more scientific, albeit fraudulent, formulation of the concept—namely, that just about every substance can cause cancer if given in sufficiently heavy dosages to experimental animals.

Actually, a relatively small number of tested chemicals—an estimated 10 to 15 percent—show some evidence of animal carcinogenicity. The percentage for all chemicals in use is most likely considerably smaller, since tests usually are run on compounds already under suspicion.[51]

A corollary argument is that so many carcinogens are about, we would have to shut down almost everything to avoid exposure. "Admit-

"We're not dumping it anywhere, Ma'am. We're just going to keep driving it around."

Drawing by Dana Fradon; © 1979 The New Yorker Magazine, Inc.

tedly, we may be living in a sea of carcinogens," states Daniel S. Martin, of the Institute of Cancer Research at Columbia University, in arguing for more research on therapeutic cures. He contends, however, that

> . . . the goal of eliminating all cancer-inducing agents from the environ-
> ment remains an obscure illusion . . . [and] would require the continu-
> ous redesign of our whole industrial sector. To shunt cancer research
> funds heavily into such a prevention effort is to fund a bottomless pit.[52]

As to the need for redesigning the whole industrial system, Cavalieri says he is distressed by the often-heard argument that

> . . . society is dependent on industrial chemicals, including carcinogens,
> for progress and prosperity. The assumption that these and a great many
> other technological innovations are required for "progress" is too often
> made without any real justification. . . . It is paradoxical that those who
> talk most about progress are in fact almost always the enemies of change.[53]

Another popular argument against regulation runs like this: Chemicals are not necessarily bad. The world is suffused with natural chemi-

cals, some of which are toxic or carcinogenic. They are in the air, water, food, soils, everywhere.

"Almost everything in nature involves chemicals," says John F. Schmutz, assistant general counsel of Du Pont:

> Food is as much an organic chemical as a plastic sheet or a solvent . . . . Chemical carcinogens and other chemical chronic health hazards are not necessarily man-made. Asbestos . . . is a chemical and a naturally occurring carcinogen. . . . Charbroiled steaks contain benzopyrene, a carcinogen.[54]

(To be sure, asbestos is a form of natural fibrous mineral. Tobacco is natural, too. But as used by man, both are deadly. Steaks don't contain benzopyrene; it is formed during the pyrolysis in cooking the beef.[55])

Schmutz says that many chemicals are essential for health in small quantities but highly toxic in large quantities. He cited zinc, manganese, copper, selenium, chromium, silicon, nickel, potassium, and others. (He does not mention such hazardous chemicals as mercury, lead, and cadmium, which are not necessary to the body at all.)

But these comments miss the essential point: We are, in this chemical era, subject to greater exposures—not to mention new compounds, new combinations, and new processes, under new conditions.

The implications of these new dimensions have been discussed by many scientists. Speaking of a wide variety of major changes in society, David A. Hamburg, president, and Sarah Spaght Brown, a division director, respectively, at the Institute of Medicine, National Academy of Sciences, said, "Natural selection over millions of years shaped our ancestors in ways that suited earlier environments. We do not know how well we are now suited biologically and behaviorally to the world our species has so rapidly made."[56]

Industry has adopted a variety of positions on the health effects of its effluents. They include genuine concern, studied silence (evident in the massive advertising campaigns on behalf of energy production), and glib counterattacks on research findings and control measures (reminiscent of the cigarette companies stance on cancer and that of the auto manufacturers on safety). All of this has brought health issues out of the laboratory into the political arena.

The question of what constitutes proof is at the heart of most chemical controversies. Many scientists, including experts not readily identified with industry, insist on more-or-less ironclad proof of human hazards before accepting regulatory action. They dismiss circumstantial evidence as beneath their dignity. They tend to see chemicals as innocent until proved guilty, a more than dubious approach to health problems since it turns people involuntarily into guinea pigs.

It is easy to challenge research and standards based on it, as industry has often demonstrated. One need only insist on a greater degree of proof; claim that the test sample was not large enough; that excessively large doses were used to demonstrate ill effects; that test results on animals have no relevance to human health; and so forth. But the scientists conducting these studies generally are careful to acknowledge their limitations and the fact that further research is necessary. In any case, endless calls for more research are a poor substitute for regulatory action based on current knowledge.

Some industries challenge the adequacy of the research on which federal standards are based, while others oppose legislation requiring more pre-market testing of the chemicals they produce. And in a case involving a group of manufacturers who challenged EPA guidelines for pesticide discharges in water effluents, the First Circuit U.S. Court of Appeals chided industry for its practice of withholding information on the effectiveness of pollution control technology (on grounds of confidential trade secrets) and then turning around and claiming that EPA's guidelines are based on insufficient information.[57]

Many of these advocates also do not shrink from applying a double standard of proof when it suits their purposes. Thus, when a company seeks to *register* a pesticide, it will not want to be held to a strict standard of proof that the product is harmless. But when a company is faced with EPA *suspension or cancellation* of a registration, it will want full proof that the product is hazardous. Thus, in congressional hearings in 1975, the National Agricultural Chemicals Association objected to EPA's "regulatory philosophy that total knowledge must be accumulated in response to any and every question that might be raised. . . ." The same day, the National Pest Control Association asked the Committee to tell EPA to stop suspending and cancelling pesticides without "absolutely indisputable proof."[58]

By the same token, those who belittle animal tests with ominous results when there is an issue of safety do not hesitate to proffer favorable animal tests when they are seeking EPA approval of a new pesticide product. This does not even reach the serious question of the trustworthiness of industry tests, on which EPA is forced to place much reliance. Unfortunately, there have been cases in which companies have withheld from the agency test results that indicated a product might be hazardous.[59]

10. Individuals have a right to know about exposures and risks.
Individual choices and actions should be based on adequate knowledge of causes, effects, and risks. This knowledge all too often is sorely lacking. In some cases, science has not yet discovered it. In many others,

however, the knowledge is available but has not been effectively imparted to those at risk. This, in turn, can be due to a number of factors:

• Failure on the part of many doctors and health officials to concern themselves with providing adequate advice to patients. "Preventive counselling" as practiced by physicians has been "a weak tool," says Ernest Saward and Andrew Sorenson, of the University of Rochester School of Medicine and Dentistry.[60]

William H. Glazier, of the Albert Einstein College of Medicine, Yeshiva University, speaks of the "complexity of the medical task" in dealing with modern diseases, multiple causes, social and behavioral factors, and "long-term, sophisticated, and expensive" treatment. "The answer," he says, "is for medicine to orient itself toward a more interventionist approach, by which I mean that the physician and the medical system should be prepared to take the initiative in delivering medical care, rather than leaving the initiative to the patient."[61]

• Failure of both formal and informal education programs to provide appropriate information to the public. Environmental scientist Merril Eisenbud, criticizing priorities, says that "above all, we could spend money on health education that could achieve dramatic results in the next generation."[62]

• Resistance by industry and other opponents of regulation to the release of information on chemicals and hazardous products, and of other health data. (It is strange that some of those who like to stress the individual's freedom of choice in risk assumption seem to fight tooth-and-nail to suppress the kind of information that makes such choices meaningful.)

Adequate understanding is an essential ingredient for both individual and political action or choice. One would think that citizens have an essential right to know what they are being exposed to—whether in the workplace, through consumer products, or in the air and water. People also need this information to participate in political discussions on what risks are permissible and what regulations must be imposed.

But the "right to know" is poorly recognized in current laws and regulations. In addition, because of the highly complex nature of chemical hazards, it is difficult to provide the general public with an adequate understanding of risks that may even perplex the scientists. For these and other reasons, most individual "choices" about risk assumption—even many choices normally thought to be voluntary in nature—are in reality quite involuntary.

Can a teenager be brought to a realistic appreciation of the mortality and morbidity rate of various diseases associated with cigarette smoking? Do the casual warnings about dangers to health, coupled with the insistent appeals of cigarette advertising, add up to a voluntary choice? Can the person who has decided to avoid nitrite or saccharin know what he's getting at a restaurant? Does the factory worker anxious to retain his job really have a voluntary option of quitting to avoid chemical exposure? What of the rights of fetuses whose mothers expose them voluntarily or involuntarily to dangerous chemicals?[63]

11. In the final analysis, the government may wind up putting a price on people's heads. As the costs of pollution control climb, there is a growing tendency to weigh the public's health against these costs. Despite the inherent logic in cost-effectiveness analysis, it is difficult to imagine a more Orwellian intrusion on individual freedom than for a government to set a dollar value on someone's life or good health. There may be something basically wrong with a society so locked into an industrial-technological-political system that it forces itself to make such tradeoffs in the name of material welfare and progress.

On the other hand, it can be and is argued that the costs of pollution control designed to be almost 100 percent safe, and to protect the most sensitive, vulnerable members of the population, are so exorbitant that some cut-off point is mandatory.

"A strict application of cost-benefit analysis is simply not relevant," says Douglas E. Costle, head of the Environmental Protection Agency.[64] In the view of Nicholas Ashford:

> Environmental legislation is not an instrument of economic policy, although economic consequences result from its implementation. [It] is an instrument of *social* policy with its main emphasis directed towards protection of workers, consumers, and other victims of pollution.[65]

And Ralph Nader says:

> It seems anomalous that institutions bent on private greed need not apologize for their polluting activities, whereas agencies that are devoted to the protection of public health, under due process of law, must apologize in terms that it's good for the economy.[66]

Sometimes, corporate philosophers seem to tell the public: If you can't stand the pollution, get out of the environment. One idea floated recently was that it might be more economic to install air-cleaning systems in the homes of the most sensitive people.[67] Presumably they would then be confined indoors when necessary. Another idea is to have susceptible people move to less polluted parts of the country. But such advice doesn't sit too well with many patients. "Somehow they don't understand that," says one doctor. "They don't have the flexibility to move whenever they want. And they've lived in the communities all their lives."

To be sure, dollar values have been placed on human lives, injuries, or illnesses, most frequently in courtrooms for automobile and other liability cases. One government report has estimated the average cost of a traffic fatality at $140,000.[68] Ralph Nader has retorted that this calculation "ignored the radiating costs of family disruptions, personal suffering, reduction in standard of living, bypassed educational opportunities, economic dislocations, and other less quantifiable factors."[69] Another report put the "quantifiable losses" of an individual death at $200,000, but was quick to emphasize that the value an individual places on his or her own life "is probably infinite and constrained only by the amount of money a person could beg, borrow, steal, or earn."[70] As for illness, courts also have put dollar values on a day of suffering but, as a congressional staffer has observed, "When someone is chronically ill, the cost of pollution to him is almost infinite."

12. A dollar of prevention is far more effective than a dollar of cure.
When one considers the costs of health care, it seems clear that effective regulation to *prevent* pollution-induced disease would be highly cost-effective. Paul Rogers has pointed out how ironic it is that inflation fighters, while professing concern over hospital and medical costs, support more lax policies on regulation that will increase the costs of treating preventable diseases.[71]

"I suspect," said Rogers, "that our efforts and success in controlling radiation, safeguarding drinking water, and limiting air pollution from coal combustion will do more to determine the demand for and the cost of health care over the next generation than all the direct regulation of health care combined."[72]

Certainly an enormous amount of money already is being spent after the fact to compensate for damages caused by chemical pollutants or for diseases linked to them. Payments are made through damage recovery suits, insurance payments, federal subsidies and indemnification, workmen's compensation, and Social Security disability payments.

Sheldon W. Samuels, of the AFL-CIO's Industrial Union Department, says that from 1972 to 1977 Social Security disability benefits (for loss of income and not including medical costs, loss of productivity, or pain and suffering) jumped from $4,475 million to $11,465 million. "If that isn't inflationary, I don't know what the hell is," says Samuels. Among the major components of the total, payments for cancer disability rocketed from $430 million to $1,150 million; for respiratory illnesses, $330 million to $760 million; for muscular and skeletal system diseases (such as arthritis), $750 million to $2,140 million; and for circulatory system ailments, $1,140 million to $3,440 million.

Many medical experts are sorely disenchanted with the way billions of dollars have been poured into largely unsuccessful effort to find cancer cures, while the great potential for preventive measures has been barely explored.[73] John Cairns of the Mill Hill Laboratories in London, argues:

> Because there is no sign that we are about to discover the cure for any of the common forms of cancer (and here I mean cure in the sense that the antibiotics are cures for most bacterial infections), we are forced to concentrate on prevention as the only plausible route open to us at present for the conquest of cancer.[74]

Faced with the increasingly disturbing evidence about environmental health hazards—with environmental defined broadly to include smoking, eating, exercise, and other personal habits as well as communal pollution—and faced also with ominous shadows of scientific ignorance, what is society to do?

The most obvious remedy is to find out more about the causes of disease, the interaction of chemicals, and so forth, through greater public and financial support for research aimed at prevention. There are signs, indeed, that the scientific sleuths seeking to solve the great mysteries of cancer are beginning to close in on the culprits. Says Cairns: "The detective work needed to discover exactly which variables are contributing to the incidence of each of the major cancers seems to me to be within our present capabilities; that is to say, no additional discoveries in the basic sciences are needed."[75]

Some research findings illustrate the kinds of detective work than can be highly useful. For example, some researchers have reported that they have found serious defects in the immunological cells of people who ate food contaminated with polybrominated biphenyls (PBB's) as a result of the disastrous incident in Michigan in which a fire retardant containing PBB's was accidentally added to cattle feed.[76] Other researchers have shown links or suspected links between cancer and various food substances or between cancer and a diet heavy in fat, calories, meat that is broiled or fried, alcohol, and natural chemicals such as aflatoxin.[77]

Cairns points to the discovery that many carcinogens have to be converted to reactive, unstable intermediates before they produce their effects:

> We now would say that the susceptibility of a tissue to any carcinogen is determined partly by whether the carcinogen reaches it and, if so, in what form; partly by exactly which carcinogen-metabolizing enzymes it happens to contain; and partly by its ability to repair damaged DNA.[78]

For example, benzidine is not considered carcinogenic until after it has been metabolized to an active form in the liver, after which it is concentreated in the bladder, its chief target. Thus some carcinogens are tissue- or organ-specific and are converted to an active form near their target, while others, such as vinyl chloride, induce malignancies at various locations in the body.[79]

Also ripe for further research are the interactions between chemicals and between chemicals and other environmental factors. This is a particularly important field because of the fact that some agents act synergistically with each other (only in combination do they have adverse effects, or effects more potent than separately) and because of the relatively recent realization that many cancers have multiple causes.

There is much discussion of "cocarcinogens," "tumor promoters," and other triggering or exacerbating agents. Thus Ernest Wynder, president of the American Health Foundation, says that components of the diet generally do not cause cancer directly but induce its development by modifying or promoting other factors.[80]

According to a report in *Science*, cancer can be produced by "combining a single exposure to a known carcinogen, but in a dose so low that it would not normally cause cancer, with prolonged exposure to very small quantities of an agent—the tumor promoter—that is not carcinogenic by itself."[81] The report notes that carcinogenic chemicals can cause cancer by themselves and may also act as tumor promoters. It says that cigarette smoke contains not only a number of known carcinogens but also several promoters.

R. Saracci and J. Cooper II, of the International Agency for Research on Cancer, Lyon, France, say it is a

> . . . biological truism (sometimes neglected) that for the development of any disease, including cancer, both genetic and environmental components are necessary. In this general sense it is legitimate to say that as many as 100 percent of cancers are "environmentally related," the concrete challenge for environmental research being to find out what the relevant environmental components are.[82]

As increased evidence is proffered, it should be treated with respect as well as healthy scientific skepticism. Nor can society put up with more of those episodes in which test data showing chemicals to be dangerous have been swept under the rug by industry or ignored by government agencies.[83]

At the same time, it is appropriate to ask that someone make clear what the benefits of a chemical are (in terms of health, safety, economics, or convenience), what its costs are (in terms of disease), and what substitutes might be feasible or desirable.

Regulation should be tuned to fit the evidence as closely as possible. But this seems certain to involve *more* rather than less regulation, despite the current antipathy to government interference. That is because so many new and old chemicals remain to be tested, so many interactions remain to be investigated, so many theories and techniques remain to be explored. It is also because of current weaknesses in the language and implementation of laws covering toxic chemicals.

Many expert observers have called for basic reforms in the health industry and a redirection of efforts from medical treatment to preventive measures.[84] Some have at the same time stressed the individual's responsibility for his or her own health. The late John H. Knowles, president of the Rockefeller Foundation, said that an individual should be willing to follow "reasonable rules for healthy living." If not, he should "stop complaining about the rising costs of medical care. . . ."[85]

It seems quite likely that much of the significant—and heartening— decrease in the incidence of heart disease since 1968 is due to changes in individual habits related to diet, smoking, and exercise.[86] Yet there are major limitations to individual action—what Knowles called "barriers to the assumption of responsibility for one's own health." Many environmental hazards are beyond the direct reach of the individual—air pollution from a power plant, contaminated dust in a factory, the cigarette smoke that is reported to have significant ill effects on nonsmokers.[87] Also, those who choose to take risks indirectly impose larger insurance premiums and medical costs on those who don't. "The prudent and dutiful are paying heavily for the irresponsible," says columnist George F. Will.[88]

Thus, community-initiated regulatory programs are important in any scheme of prevention. In sum, say Saward and Sorenson:

> The responsibility for the prevention of disease and disability through health education, improved life-style, and environmental control permeates all aspects of society: the individual, the family, the school, the workplace, and every voluntary agency and level of government.[89]

Chapter 7

ENERGY RESOURCES

> I have no doubt that we will be successful
> in harnessing the sun's energy. If sun-
> beams were weapons of war, we would
> have had solar energy centuries ago.
>
> —Sir George Potter

Implementation of an effective, responsible national program to extri-
cate the United States from its energy predicament borders on a hopeless
task. So many complex and interacting economic and political variables
are at work. And there is so much unreliable information.

One wonders if we have the intellectual capacity or political ability to
establish and manage a comprehensive, coherent energy strategy. The
politicians and experts are up to their ears in scenarios. But each
scenario is a linear patchwork of assumptions and guesses. Any final
decision to produce or consume energy is based on a sequence of intermediate conditions or decisions, and unanticipated changes within the
sequence can skew the end result substantially.

There is another problem: Many of the key decisions are made in
corporate board rooms—or in OPEC countries—on the basis of narrow
economic considerations. As Lee C. White, former Federal Power
Commissioner, notes, "There are some national objectives that are not
necessarily the same as, or may even be antithetical to, the profit
motive." In cases of conflict with other goals involving the well-being
or safety of the public, for example, White says the government has a
responsibility to make the appropriate decisions.

Some factors in the energy equation are subject to a degree of
government control—through conservation requirements, strip-mining
regulation, oil and gas price controls, or air pollution control requirements, for example. Other steps can be taken to shape energy demand
and the mix of fuels used to meet it. But the consistent set of tools needed
to mastermind an effective, responsible energy program seems not to be
politically feasible. These tools might include forced conservation
measures, rationing, allocation of fuels, manipulation of oil and natu-

ral gas prices, promotion of synthetic fuels, creation of a federal energy corporation, and so forth.

Overall, we remain quite at the mercy of volatile economic and political factors, relying on a series of halfway measures. One suspects that no recognizable energy program will emerge unless the country is pressed very hard indeed. Until then, it seems likely to evolve only through the economic pushing and shoving characteristic of our system.

Any formulation of a comprehensive energy strategy has to begin with an assessment of the opportunities for conservation and the fuel supplies available.

Conservation has been called "the best new source of energy." In recent years, the public has become especially conscious of three things about energy conservation: It is greatly needed, it has enormous advantages, and there are countless ways to achieve it. Robert Stobaugh, professor at the Harvard Business School, and Daniel Yergin, lecturer at the Kennedy School at Harvard, in their book *Energy Future*, summarized the potential of energy conservation this way:

> If the United States were to make a serious commitment to conservation, it might well consume 30 to 40 percent less energy than it now does, and still enjoy the same or an even higher standard of living. That saving would not hinge on a major technological breakthrough, and it would require only modest adjustments in the way people live. Moreover, the cost of conservation energy is very competitive with other energy sources.[1]

These points, concurred in by most experts, are further developed in Chapter 10.

The major targets of conservation efforts are industry, buildings, and transportation. For all three, dramatic savings have been demonstrated. They have involved a staggering variety of techniques, including use of better construction materials, insulation, cogeneration, heat pumps, burning of urban and agricultural wastes, product redesign, and so forth. Of particular interest is transportation—because it involves almost all Americans in a direct way, because automobiles make a ravenous demand on oil supplies, because Americans are in bondage to their cars, and because there are so many ways to release them from this bondage.

As to the availability of fuel supplies, one can begin with an appraisal of the global oil situation, since oil is the world's primary fuel. An accurate picture of oil reserves and production, so hard to come by in the welter of estimates and guesstimates—as well as the political and economic uncertainties—can help crystallize the supply and demand policy choices. An energy resource assessment also must deal with this country's buried energy treasure—coal. The economic, ecological, and social costs of fully exploiting coal reserves cannot be overlooked. And finally, prospects for the various forms of solar energy are important considerations.

These three factors, then—the supply of oil, the potential of coal, and the feasibility of solar—are the foci of the energy resource assessment that follows. (Nuclear power, which currently supplies less than 3 percent of total U.S. energy demand—and some 13 percent of its electricity—is discussed in the next chapter, in the context of the many problems associated with it.)

I. THE SUPPLY OF OIL

Oil, shipped and burned in countless tanks, pipes, and machines, is the blood that pumps life and strength into the world economy. But how pinched are world supplies?

It is critically important to assess oil reserves in the United States and the rest of the world, so political leaders and the public can evaluate the prospects for developing alternative supplies of energy, and can plan the kind of life they will lead in the future.

The oil supply picture can be viewed from two differing time perspectives:

1. How much oil is likely to be produced—and exported and refined—in the next decade or so, and to what extent will it meet demand?

2. What is the long-term potential of the petroleum resource itself?

The short-term question is fraught with variables. How much oil will key countries like Saudi Arabia and Mexico decide to produce? Will there be any politically motivated embargoes, or revolutions, strikes, accidents, and other disruptions? Will production be curtailed to boost prices? Will refinery capacity be limited by environmental constraints? Will there be transportation or distribution bottlenecks?[2]

In some ominous respects, the world oil problem reminds one of the world food problem. Oil, like food, may be producible in large quantity. But it also must be refined, distributed, and marketed effectively so that it reaches all those in need. The world's politicians have failed tragically to achieve this with food. Similar shortcomings have occurred and can be foreseen in the distribution of oil.

Geoffrey Kemp, associate professor at Tufts University's Fletcher School of Law and Diplomacy, writes that "national perceptions of 'scarcity' are likely to derive much less from the existence of an absolute situation of shortage, or even the prospect of one, than from difficulties of access in terms of economic and political factors. This is most notably true in the case of oil." And he adds, "Conflict over food supplies

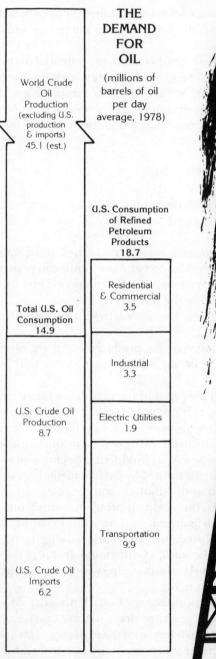

THE DEMAND FOR OIL

(millions of barrels of oil per day average, 1978)

World Crude Oil Production (excluding U.S. production & imports) 45.1 (est.)

U.S. Consumption of Refined Petroleum Products 18.7

Total U.S. Oil Consumption 14.9

Residential & Commercial 3.5

Industrial 3.3

U.S. Crude Oil Production 8.7

Electric Utilities 1.9

Transportation 9.9

U.S. Crude Oil Imports 6.2

Chart by Deborah Carole

SOURCE: Monthly Energy Review, DOE, April 1979

usually arises because of asymmetries in demand and distribution rather than because of shortages in total supply."[3]

There are other analogies. Just as the United States has provided large grain shipments to the Soviet Union to offset the shortfall caused by its deficient harvest, so Saudi Arabia boosted its oil production to offset some of the shortage caused by the Iranian revolution.

"Clearly, America is critically sensitive to even minor dislocations in foreign oil supply," says Harold D. Hoopman, president of Marathon Oil Co.[4] So, too, some countries are critically sensitive to small food supply deficiencies.

"In both the food and energy sectors, efforts to rapidly expand output appear to be facing rather steeply rising cost curves," says Lester R. Brown, president of the Worldwatch Institute.[5] Also, an all-out food production effort in the U.S. would depress prices and cause economic havoc in agriculture, somewhat the way an all-out oil production push by OPEC countries could exhaust the resource prematurely and also cause social and economic distress.

The long-term question of supply is subject to additional important variables. Will geologists discover any more "giant fields"—perhaps the only kind that would extend the life of the resource in a major way? How much exploration can be expected from Third World countries with reserve potential? How much will new recovery technology add to reserves? (How much has the green revolution been increasing food supplies?)

American Oil

Estimating petroleum reserves is a bit like guessing how many herring are in the sea. Still, the geological numbers game seems a necessary attempt to bring the fuzzy energy future into better focus.

Futurists should be cautioned that past estimates of U.S. reserves have fluctuated wildly, and may have gravely distorted policy. For example, the late economist John M. Blair recalled that for a long time, starting in the late 1950's, the U.S. Geological Survey (USGS) and others produced some enormous estimates of U.S. oil reserves, three and four times higher than previous estimates. Blair pointed out that these estimates— revised sharply downward in a USGS study in 1975—encouraged a heavy reliance on oil in general, accelerated the depletion of limited domestic reserves, and provided a rationale for the import quota on foreign oil.[6] (Blair added that a possible explanation for the changed 1975 estimate is that the inflated one had served its purpose. "Since the import quota had been terminated in 1973, the need for excessive estimates had ceased to exist.")

Following are the U.S. crude oil resource estimates used in 1979 by the federal government[7] in billions of barrels:

Proved reserves (as of January 1978)	29.5
Indicated and inferred reserves	27.6
Undiscovered recoverable resources	85.4
Total	142.5

A "recoverable" resource generally is defined as that which can be produced with known technology at current prices.

Estimating methodologies are varied and incredibly complex.[8] So the degree of uncertainty is great, and estimates usually are couched in broad ranges. For example, the 1975 USGS study offered a range of undiscovered recoverable resources from 50-127 billion barrels.[9] (It figured there is a 95 percent probability that such reserves will be at least 50 billion barrels, but only a 5 percent probability they will amount to as much as 127 billion barrels.) The statistical mean is about the same as the Administration's current figure of 85.4 billion.

Some prognoses of recoverable oil are higher, some lower. At the lower end of the scale—of interest to those of the better-safe-than-sorry persuasion—the highly respected petroleum geologist M. King Hubbert has estimated that proved and probable reserves are 47 billion barrels and ultimately recoverable reserves are about 28 billion, for a total potential of 75 billion, little more than half the government total figure of 142.5 billion.[10]

The more bullish estimates for undiscovered reserves generally range from 85 billion barrels up to about 130 billion. There are a few hopeful signs in the U.S., aside from the drilling disappointments off the Atlantic Coast. Optimism in the Gulf Coast area is having a revival of sorts, and estimates of recoverable reserves in the "overthrust belt" in the West's Green River Basin have been rising sharply. This is a major reason why geologists, including those at USGS, recently raised their low estimate of undiscovered reserves—which is particularly significant—from 50 to 60 billion barrels.[11]

Such changes amount to buying a few years more leeway. To put the figures into a time perspective, the U.S. last year produced some 3.2 billion barrels of oil. Assuming a static situation—with no increased demand and the same level of imports—the proved and indicated reserves (Administration figures totaling 57.1 billion barrels) would last about 18 years. Adding undiscovered reserves would stretch this to more than 44 years. If Hubbert is right, as he has been in the past, the total would last only 23 plus years—again not taking increased demand into account. Also not accounted for are the escalating costs and difficulties of finding and tapping the undiscovered oil.

In any case, the rate of additions to proved reserves will be the chief limiting factor in the next 30 to 50 years, in the view of Charles D. Masters, of USGS.[12] These additions have been trailing off—with the notable exception of the important Prudhoe Bay find in Alaska. (Of the government figures cited above, Alaska accounts for 9.6 billion barrels of proved reserves, 6.4 billion of indicated reserves, and 27 billion of undiscovered resources—or altogether 43 billion of the 142.5 billion total for the nation.[13])

Since Prudhoe Bay was added to reserves in 1970, new discoveries have fallen significantly below the historical trend. Proved reserves have dropped from 39 billion barrels in 1970 to an estimated 28 billion or so today.

The American Petroleum Institute reported that additions to proved reserves in 1978—through the discovery of new fields, the extension and development of known reservoirs, and the revision of earlier estimates—was only a little more than 1.3 billion barrels. Since withdrawals for production totaled more than 3 billion, there was a net reduction in reserves of some 1.7 billion barrels.[14]

The reasons for the drop in new discoveries are a matter of dispute. Efforts have been made to reverse the trend through increased exploration and drilling. But these have become increasingly costly and difficult, as the growing emphasis on offshore areas and Alaska suggests. A Resources for the Future study notes: "It does appear unlikely that there are a number of Prudhoe Bays cleverly hidden by nature along the Gulf Coast or in the Rocky Mountains."[15]

Masters calculates that domestic production is now at a "reasonable maximum"—which does not augur well for accommodating any increased demand or for decreasing reliance on imports. Masters reasons that the size and physical constraints of existing reservoirs effectively limit the average "production-to-reserve" ratio of 1-to-10—which corresponds to the current production of about 3 billion barrels a year and the current proved reserves of roughly 30 billion barrels.[16]

Maintaining the current ratio and level of production would require additional reserves of 3 billion barrels per year. But in the past seven years, since the "unique and seldom equalled" Prudhoe Bay find, the rate of additions to reserves has been only about 1.75 billion barrels. So to reach 3 billion would require an increase of more than 50 percent—a "prodigious task," says Masters.

Just to increase production from 3 billion to 4 billion barrels per year over the next decade would require a doubling of the rate of additions to reserves. There's little chance of that, says Masters. "We will be fortunate indeed to maintain our present rate of production."[17]

Stobaugh and Yergin make the point in similar fashion. Taking both newly found oil and enhanced recovery into account, they judge that total domestic output in the late 1980's will be about the same as now:

> But even this is quite speculative and perhaps on the optimistic side. To maintain that production level would require the finding of almost 4 billion barrels annually; but there has been only one year in the last 30 in which more than 3 billion barrels of reserves have been found.[18]

They conclude that there is no domestic oil solution to the problem of increasing imports—the multimillion-barrel-per-day gap between U.S. production and consumption. "In fact, higher oil prices will be required to maintain production at current levels."

Counting both crude oil and refined petroleum products, the gap last year was 8.2 million barrels per day (mbd) average in imports needed to meet total domestic demand of 18.7 mbd. After sharp rises for several years, crude oil imports in 1978 declined 6 percent from 1977—but only because of a drawdown of domestic inventories and the one-time build-up of Alaskan production. These more than offset the 1.6 percent rise in domestic demand and the 4 percent decline in non-Alaskan domestic production.[19]

Imports were expected to continue rising over the next few years, but at the meeting of industrialized nations in Tokyo in June 1979, President Carter committed the United States to a goal of holding imports through 1985 to 8.5 mbd, about the same as the level in the first quarter of the year.

Oil of the World

If there is wide agreement that the United States is approaching the end of its petroleum rope, the global supply situation is far from clear. Blair put it this way:

> In contrast to the grim picture presented for the United States of falling production, declining proved reserves, and a limited ultimate recoverable supply, the prospects for the world as a whole are decidedly more favorable.[20]

He estimated that total resources should be adequate for at least a generation, adding that if a shortage develops before then, it is most likely to result not from the "niggardliness of nature" but from man's "commercial or political restrictions."

Whether a generation is a comfortable margin depends on one's point of view. A few experts, such as Bernardo F. Grossling, of the Geological Survey, believe that enormous reserves await discovery. He estimates that undiscovered recoverable reserves could be as much as 4.8 trillion barrels, as the World Oil Reserves table shows. Others, however, are far less sanguine.

WORLD OIL RESERVE (In billions of barrels)				
	Proved and probable		Undis-covered	Recoverable
	(Moody)	(Grossling)	(Moody)	(Grossling)
United States	51	*77*	76	*
Canada	7	*16*	71	*
Latin America	39	*65*	91	*224-848*
Middle East	430	*562*	131	*352 or more*
Africa...............	61	*107*	86	*223-873*
West Europe	21	*63*	45	*
Asia and Pacific	27	*38*	93	*181-597*
Communist countries. . . .	104	*231*	350	*
TOTAL..........	740	*1,158*	963	*1,353-4,813*

*Figures for these regions were aggregated by Grossling and contribute to the total at the bottom of the column.

The table illustrates the highly discrepant methodologies and judgments used to arrive at estimates—one could almost say speculations—about the unseen reserves of oil that lie hidden in their complex, mysterious geological formations. The two left-hand columns show 1974 estimates by John D. Moody, then a Mobil Oil executive.[21] These figures closely resemble a number of other estimates, and can be considered representative of a fairly conservative, general view bordering on consensus. However, some analysts have strong convictions that these greatly understate reserves. The Grossling figures in italics represent the most optimistic end of the spectrum.[22]

Moody himself allowed that his estimates may be greatly understated if deep ocean drilling turns out to be rewarding. Grossling feels that *he* is being conservative and argues that "the petroleum potential of about half of the world's prospective area has been grossly underestimated by the current conventional wisdom." He refers principally to the non-communist, non-OPEC developing nations of Latin America, Africa, and Asia. The rationale underlying his elaborate calculations is that a "vast drilling gap" exists in the developing countries, which account for about half of the world's prospective petroleum area, because only about 4.3 percent of the exploratory drilling has taken place in them.[23]

There are moves afoot to find and tap this oil. The World Bank has launched a $3 billion, five-year program of loans to accelerate oil development in non-OPEC developing countries. The aim is to help them cope with painful oil import costs as well as increase petroleum supplies generally.[24] A dearth of capital and management skills, the previous availability of cheap oil, and other factors have discouraged such activity. The World Bank staff has estimated that more than 70 countries could become oil producers within a decade, and that production in non-OPEC developing nations, which now totals some 4.8 million barrels per day, could reach 10 million barrels by then.[25]

Many U.S. officials also are interested in an "oil proliferation" policy.[26] And Senator Henry Jackson's catchall energy bill, introduced June 11, 1979, would require the Department of Energy to evaluate the potential for increasing exploration and production of oil in non-OPEC countries, and to assess the costs and benefits of initiatives to encourage petroleum development "such as loan guarantees or tax incentives to domestic or foreign corporations, joint ventures or other arrangements with foreign governments by the United States, and initiatives through multilateral organizations."[27] Already there are signs of the inevitable disputes over the roles, if any, to be played by the oil companies.[28]

How Many More Years?

Although the world's petroleum reserves are more plentiful than those of the United States, world reserves, too, apparently are shrinking because additions to them have now fallen below consumption. For several decades, such additions, boosted by the discovery of vast oil fields in the Middle East, ran comfortably ahead of demand. But in 1978, global oil production (excluding communist countries) totaled almost 16.9 billion barrels, while for almost a decade additions to reserves have averaged less than 15 billion barrels per year.[29]

"Most geologists believe that Middle East-type reservoirs are so unique, that one cannot expect to find similar geological conditions elsewhere in the free world," says one congressional report.[30] There may be occasional finds such as those in Mexico and the North Sea, but they will generally be smaller than the large Middle East fields and in "more remote and hostile physical environments." (It adds that much of the Soviet and Chinese oil potential is located in such Arctic and offshore areas.)

Yet the Mexican discoveries alone give the credence to the kind of optimistic estimates made by Grossling, Dutch economist Peter Odell, and others. Estimates of Mexican reserves have been climbing dramatically in the last couple of years. In January 1979, PEMEX, the Mexican national oil company, estimated 61 billion barrels of proved and probable reserves plus 150 billion barrels of potential recoverable reserves.[31] Mexican President J. Lopez Portillo has said that estimates of the potential reserves "will surely increase,"[32] and some outside experts think the true figure could be as high as 225 billion barrels. (That is the equivalent of more than 10 years of current total world oil production.)

There are skeptics who feel the Mexican estimates are unrealistic.

Another pessimistic perspective is that the Mexican discovery has been the only major oil find in the 1970's.

Some analysts stress what they see as a bright oil future for China, Egypt, India, and Argentina, as well as Mexico, while others emphasize the fact that some major producing countries such as Venezuela and Libya already have peaked or soon will begin to decline. Some 34 billion barrels of oil have been taken from Venezuelan oil fields, leaving proved reserves of only 18 billion barrels and leading to a sharp decline in exports.[33]

Prospects for the so-called enhanced recovery techniques add to future uncertainty. "Today the average world recovery rate is probably about 30 percent," says Andrew R. Flower, a policy analyst with the British Petroleum Co. If this were eventually raised to 40 percent, as some experts judge feasible, it could mean "an addition of 250 billion barrels to reserves in currently known fields."[34] (This would be a significant increase in current world proved and probable reserves, estimated conservatively at 740 billion barrels.)

Another open question is how much oil can be technologically and economically coaxed out of the huge resources of heavy oil in Venezuela, of oil shale in the U.S., and of tar sands in Canada. For example, the Orinoco Oil Belt in Venezuela could alter the world oil outlook, though recovery obstacles could be very difficult. Combining the lowest estimates of both the amount of heavy oil in place and the percent that can be recovered from the Orinoco area gives a total reserve of 70 billion barrels. But combining the highest estimates for the resource and the recovery rate raises the potential to a staggering 1,050 billion barrels.[35]

These various possibilities for increasing reserves could add a number of years to their lifespan. But most experts would agree with consultant Walter J. Levy when he says that "nothing now in sight changes the basic prognosis of declining physical availability of oil."[36] Levy adds that, in formulating an energy policy, "we must assume that the period available to use for transition from an oil-based economy to one founded substantially on new energy resources will probably not exceed 20 to 25 years."

Current Production

The prospects for oil reserves should not be confused with the outlook for actual *production* of oil and whether or not it will be adequate to meet current demand. In mid-1979, according to prevailing estimates, the world supply of crude was some 1.5 million to 2 million barrels per day short of demand. Most experts warn of serious shortages in the near future.

Most importantly, for various political and economic reasons, many key nations plan to restrict production. Some clearly see the limits of their petroleum resources and want to stretch out the benefits.

"Venezuela," says Alberto Quiros Corradi, an oil official in that country, "is the classic case of an oil-producing country in which increased wealth led to development programs and social spending that could only be maintained by high and sustained oil revenues, leading in turn to a rate of production exceeding the long-term capacity of its conventional oil resources."[37]

With inflation eating at their dollar investments, many OPEC countries see their oil as more valuable in the ground. Some were sobered by the Iranian revolution and other evidence that sudden infusions of capital and rapid development can be socially destructive. Another factor in some cases may be disenchantment with the results of Middle Eastern peace negotiations.

The Oil Production table shows the leading oil producing countries as of 1978. Other countries that contributed to total 1978 production of 60 million barrels per day—to the tune of 160,000 to 490,000 barrels each—were, in descending order: Egypt, Qatar, Argentina, Australia, Norway, Oman, Trinidad and Tobago, India, Brunei, Malaysia, Ecuador, Syria, Gabon, and Brazil.[38]

OIL PRODUCTION, 1978
(millions of barrels per day, average, estimated)
OPEC and communist countries in italics

Soviet Union	*11.5*	*United Arab Emirates*	*1.9*
United States	8.8	*Kuwait*	*1.8*
Saudi Arabia	*7.9*	*Nigeria*	*1.8*
Iran	*5.1*	*Indonesia*	*1.7*
Iraq	*2.3*	Canada	1.2
Venezuela	*2.2*	Mexico	1.2
China	*2.1*	*Algeria*	*1.1*
Libya	*2.0*	United Kingdom	0.9

SOURCE: *World Oil*, February 15, 1979.

There is a distortion in the table: Iran's production the year before the revolution was 5.7 mbd. Shut down at that time, it rose back to 3.5 mbd. The outlook for the future there is cloudy at best, and some believe production won't go any higher.[39] At the same time, Saudi Arabia boosted its output to 10.4 million barrels, later reduced to 9.5 million. And Kuwait increased its yields to 2.6 mbd, then slacked off to 2 million.

Because of its market clout, Saudi Arabia's intentions are of the greatest importance. The government has indicated a firm intention to increase production gradually over the next few years to a permanent ceiling of 12 million barrels per day.[40] But it is generally agreed that this will be at least 4 million barrels less than needed to meet demand in the

1980's—barring a debilitated world economy. Conflicting signals from Saudi Arabia are the norm, however, and other reports indicate plans to hold production far below 12 million.[41]

The only other OPEC country believed capable of sustaining increased production without drawing too quickly on reserves is Iraq. Petroleum Economics, Ltd. estimates that its production will be lifted to 4.5 mbd in 1990.[42] It was reported in mid-1979 that Iraq already had boosted its production to 3.5 mbd.[43] There also were indications of an increase in Libya's production, which totaled almost 3.9 mbd a decade ago.[44]

Mexican officials also have announced they intend to produce their oil at a moderate pace consistent with their own country's economic development rather than the exigencies of foreign demand. Most U.S. analysts believe, however, that production will reach about 4 mbd in 1985, of which some 2.5 mbd will be exported.[45] The figures could go higher, and in any case would rank Mexico among the world's largest producers. However, the prognosis does not add up to a solution for the global oil dilemma.

In 1977, the CIA forecast that by 1985 the Soviet Union and its bloc would turn from an oil exporter to an importer of 3.5 to 4.5 mbd.[46] The suggestion was ridiculed in many quarters and bluntly denied by a Soviet official.[47] In 1979, the CIA made a similarly skeptical appraisal of the Soviet Union's petroleum prospects.[48] It has again been disputed.[49] Nevertheless, the USSR, while it may have very large reserves, surely has production problems, so doubts about its future posture remain— including the unnerving possibility that it will compete for large amounts of OPEC and other world oil supplies.[50]

Stobaugh and Yergin estimate that by 1985, China's oil exports will not exceed 1 to 2 mbd.[51] And they figure that the combined North Sea production of Britain and Norway could rise to 4 mbd in the next five years or so, but then would start to decline soon afterwards.

Some anticipate that U.S. production will increase only by 1 mbd or more between now and 1985.

In sum, the figures suggest a tight situation at best, with no dramatic difference if projections are extended to 1990. Some experts believe, furthermore, that a serious constraint will be refinery capacity.

If world petroleum supplies are impossible to pin down, so is future petroleum demand. Among the major factors influencing that demand are the degree of health and growth in the world's economies, the amount of conservation or of energy used per unit of productivity (a ratio that has been declining in the U.S., for instance), and the amount of demand that is satisfied by shifting to fuels other than oil.

The Tough Questions

What options should the United States—and the rest of the world—contemplate? The suggestions range from tightening belts (through conservation, higher prices, or rationing) to "breaking up OPEC" (for example, through a massive push to synthetics) and to negotiating an agreement between the consuming and producing nations that will calm the stormy and uncertain relationships between them.

Quiros Corradi asks:

> How can we move from an excessive preoccupation with short-term advantage to a longer term view of the problem that both balances the power factors and takes into account the needs of the world as a whole?[52]

He says the world must understand that at present there is no balance between the requirements of developed nations for energy and undeveloped nations for social and economic benefits.

> If the industrialized world were to reduce consumption of natural resources in order to keep pace with the long-term resource extraction policies by the underdeveloped producer nations, then world growth would come to a standstill and stagnation would result. If the underdeveloped world were to produce its resources at the rate required by the developed nations, it would exhaust its one element of power, natural resources, and would still sit at the tail end of the growth line in the future.

James E. Akins, a consultant and former ambassador to Saudi Arabia, argues that the OPEC countries are concerned about the strength and stability of western economies. He feels that a "broad agreement" between oil producing and consuming countries "seems more necessary now that ever" and that it "has a good chance of success."[53] The components of such an agreement?

> It would cover oil supply, with exports increased marginally for a few years by OPEC, and with stringent conservation measures in the consuming countries. It would freeze the price of oil, fixed in constant dollars, for several years to be followed by a gradual rise in real terms in price to the cost of producing alternatives.

Akins concedes that the U.S. would experience considerable anguish over OPEC nations' insistence that their investments be protected from continued depreciation of U.S. dollars.

> They insist that if we want their oil, we must take actions to protect their investments. If we could bring inflation under control, the problem would be solved. But our record has been sorry. Pending that happy day, OPEC will demand that its dollar investments be pegged to the inflation rate, that the principal amount of their treasury bonds rise with our inflation. We have never sold such bonds in this country although other countries have. It is something we will be forced to consider quite soon.

Pending such an agreement, whatever its terms might be, the United States is faced with a series of tough questions. How do you slow oil consumption without unacceptable social and economic consequences? Is the oil prognosis favorable enough to avoid major reliance on nuclear plants and synthetic fuels (whose environmental and economic drawbacks are not pleasant to contemplate)? And how do you open the door to renewable energy sources of the solar variety?

It is an unfortunate paradox that dire warnings about imminent oil shortages *may* be somewhat overstated—but that without an urgent concern, the world will lock itself into greater dependence on oil, will fail to take the necessary remedial steps, and will thereby add greatly to the rudeness of the awakening.

Whether the U.S. and the rest of the world have 10, 25, 50, or even 100 years of oil left, the main question remains: Will the time be used wisely, to minimize economic dislocations caused by high energy prices, to maximize environmental protection, and to make the least painful shift to renewable energy sources?

II. THE POTENTIAL OF COAL

The problems associated with energy policy formulation are fully illustrated by the coal situation. Everyone knows that we have coal to burn. U.S. coal reserves contain three times as much energy as the oil reserves in the Middle East, or enough to last hundreds of years.

Why, then, can we not devise a program to use enough coal to remove the risks of dependence on foreign oil, obviate the need for unbridled growth in nuclear power and offshore oil drilling, and so forth? Basically, it is because we cannot predict or control enough of the myriad factors that determine the production, transportation, and utilization of coal.

Now consider the many contingency factors involved, some of them relating to coal production, some to consumption, and some to both:

1. Obviously, there must be a market. "Coal production is very strongly demand-oriented," says Duane Thompson, a specialist with the Library of Congress's Congressional Research Service. "The utilities have to come on stream to create the demand." Electric utilities now use more than two-thirds of the coal produced. They also offer the major potential for increasing coal consumption and substituting coal for oil and gas.[54]

Therefore, future coal consumption is very sensitive to the electricity growth rate. But as the Council on Wage and Price Stability pointed out some years ago, "current estimates of annual growth in electricity output range all the way from 3 percent to 7.2 percent, a difference which could mean as much as 600 million tons more or less of coal consumption in 1985."[55] Or to put it another way, each percentage point change in the compound rate of growth would change utility coal demand by about 150 million tons in 1985.

Electricity growth, in turn, depends on other factors such as the general health of the economy, the success of conservation efforts, the rate of home building, and consumer life-style choices.

2. The market for coal depends on its price and competitiveness with other fuels. The cost of *producing* coal hinges on a host of factors: severance taxes, the cost of reclaiming strip-mined land and the extent to which reclamation is required, mining equipment technology and productivity, union wage demands, mine safety costs, black lung disease payment requirements, and coal-leasing policies for federal lands. Other possible constraints include the availability of investment capital, government subsidies, and trained miners, and the occurrence of strikes.

The cost of *using* coal is dependent on the availability and cost of transportation. This may be insignificant if the power plant is located at the mine mouth, but can be stiff if western coal is shipped to the East. Railroads, barge lines, and coal slurry pipeline companies are all anxious to cash in on this traffic. But some experts doubt their capability to meet a very large demand.

The cost of using coal also depends on existing federal and state limitations on sulfur dioxide emissions from power plants and the expense of meeting them.

Utilities have three main control techniques: burning low-sulfur coal, installing stack gas scrubbers, or cleaning the coal. They may use a combination of the three. Uncertain about changes in the Clean Air Act and the Environmental Protection Agency's enforcement, utilities have been reluctant to install the expensive scrubbers that would allow them to burn the more readily available and cheaper medium- and high-sulfur coal.

There have been short-term scarcities of low-sulfur coal to meet emission standards, says the Council on Wage and Price Stability,[56] and it was estimated in 1975 that of the roughly 400 million tons of coal burned annually by utilities, more than 100 million tons are used in violation of sulfur dioxide limitations.[57]

For a time it seemed clear that these limitations—the subject of intense controversy—would preclude the use of substantial amounts of high-sulfur coal in the East. Now, Douglas M. Costle, administrator of the Environmental Protection Agency (EPA), claims that under the New Source Performance Standards for coal-fired power plants promulgated in June 1979[58] "virtually all coal reserves can be used" and still meet emission requirements.[59] However, this view is sharply disputed by many.[60]

3. Coal consumption by utilities is highly sensitive to the price of oil, a major alternative fuel. Thus the coal picture is closely related to the international price-fixing actions of OPEC, as well as domestic oil price controls and any restraints on market pricing that might develop within U.S. industry.

Already there is considerable skepticism about whether present arrangements permit fully free market competition: There is a clash of views on whether or not that competition is being inhibited by concentration in the coal industry and by the oil and gas companies' expanding control of coal production (it is now 26 percent of the total.) A Council on Wage and Price Stability (CWPS) report found the market to be normally competitive. A different viewpoint was offered by Arnold Miller, president of the United Mine Workers:

> The bigger companies, with effective control of their market, have no incentive to expand except when they are absolutely certain in advance of selling every ton of coal at acceptable prices. . . . The biggest oil-coal combines are sitting on vast reserves of readily recoverable coal. But that coal will come out of the ground only when the men who own it can be sure of the price they will get for it.[61]

The Federal Energy Administration (FEA) predicted in 1976 that coal prices, in the long run, will *not* rise to the levels of oil or gas prices: "Coal reserves are vast and reserve ownership is generally widespread enough that long-term contract coal prices are and will be cost-based."[62] The CWPS saw a good chance of stable coal prices in the next decade.

This view was contradicted by Matthew J. Kerbec, president of Output Systems Corp., who argued that we can expect coal prices to make a steady march upward, in keeping with the fact that a ton of coal has the Btu equivalent of roughly four times a barrel of oil. "Logical profit concerns on the part of coal producers will dictate that they increase their prices to the precise point that will keep power companies from switching to oil or other substitute fuels," Kerbec said.[63]

Other doubts about competition are raised by the fact that utilities, through fuel adjustment clauses, have been allowed to shift the increasing costs of coal and oil directly to their customers. Some experts feel that this removes the incentives for companies to seek the cheapest ways of generating power. The problem is compounded by increasing utility company ownership or control of coal supplies, which offers opportunities for intra-company manipulation of prices. In any case, there is evidence of many abuses under the adjustment clause system, with consumers paying artificially inflated prices for fuels.[64]

4. The unknown extent to which nuclear power plants will be brought on line—in the face of public opposition, uncertainties about their economic advantages and reliability, and construction delays—contributes further to the difficulty in predicting or influencing coal

utilization. FEA estimated that for each 10 percent change in the nuclear plant capacity in 1985, coal consumption would change by about 40 million tons.[65]

5. In the longer run, the demand for coal could be greatly increased by progress in producing synthetic fuels through coal gasification and coal liquefaction. But the economic and environmental feasibility of these processes remains uncertain.[66]

6. In recent years, approximately 10 percent of U.S. coal production has been exported. If exports increased, or if the government required that this coal be used to meet domestic needs as some have urged, the coal picture would change accordingly. (Most exported coal is of the high-priced coking variety used by the steel industry. Much of this is eastern low-sulfur coal, but a substantial percentage is not suitable for utility boilers.)

7. There is some potential for increasing electrification and expanding coal markets, even in the field of transportation, where almost no coal is now used. Development of better electric vehicles is one way. Barry Commoner, professor of environmental science at Washington University in St. Louis, says that electricity can be converted to the motion of a train with almost 100 percent efficiency. "A large power network receiving electricity from a number of coal-fired plants. . . that is employed to run electrified railroads, would be an ideal way to make thermodynamically efficient use of coal," he says.[67]

8. Under federal law[68] there is a concerted program to require oil and gas-burning plants to shift to coal—provided that the Environmental Protection Agency finds such conversions do not violate clean air standards. EPA has identified a dozen states whose emission requirements were stricter than necessary to meet national primary ambient air standards. Many of them have been revising their air quality implementation plans, and EPA estimates that 110 million tons of coal could be freed for use.

Meanwhile, the Department of Energy is moving on its program to convert existing oil and gas-fired power plants to coal, to require that new power plants have the capability to burn coal, and to convert "major fuel burning installations" (MFBI's) from oil and gas to coal.[69]

9. Last but not least, coal development will be constrained to the extent that environmentalists and other opponents are able to delay or halt mining operations or power plants they find objectionable. Certainly there are numerous adverse environmental effects from coal production and use, and opponents have included some western governors as well as a wide range of other citizens bent on preserving the western life-style.[70]

If one cranks in all the variables, only one thing seems certain—that the coal is there. The rest is uncertainty, and industry bemoans the difficulty of planning and attracting capital in the face of so many unknowns. Of course, industry does not wish the kind of certainty embodied in a stringent federal strip-mine law, in an unequivocal commitment to strict clean air standards, or in government intervention to stabilize prices.

East Versus West

Aside from the difficulty of implementing national coal policies, there is the highly controversial issue of how much coal should be mined in the relatively unscathed West rather than in the heavily mined East. (The East is defined broadly to include not only Appalachia but the Midwest east of the Mississippi River as well.)

Because of the complexities in the choice, a good deal of oversimplification is unavoidable. However, it seems clear that a number of industries find the economic lure of western coal irresistible. On the other side, a phalanx of environmentalists seeks to prevent what they see as an unnecessary invasion and disfigurement of the West—unnecessary because, they reason, the East can provide the needed coal.

Western coal has several very alluring attributes. Most of it lies in very thick deposits close to the surface, where it can be strip-mined in large quantities and at low cost. In addition to the economic advantages, surface mining has lower accident and disease rates than underground operations. Also, says one congressional staffer, "The companies are trying to get out from underneath the power of the United Mine Workers union." Another says that western mining enables the companies to "reduce their manpower needs, in addition to avoiding payments for the UMW miner's welfare fund, for underground health and safety equipment, and for black lung benefits."

A second great advantage of the West is the fact that some 84 percent of its coal resources contain less than 1 percent sulfur. Therefore, the West is greatly valued by utilities anxious to meet clean air requirements without installation of the more expensive stack-gas scrubbers.

A third advantage is that ownership of western coal is more easily obtained. Much of it is public, and has been leased by companies from the federal government on shamefully permissive terms with little or no obligation to mine the lands except when the companies wish.[71]

While these advantages are substantial, so are the arguments against western coal development:

Since most of the coal would be strip-mined, large areas would need to be rehabilitated. Yet a much-cited National Academy of Sciences (NAS) study has warned that such rehabilitation in the West, because of the minimal rainfall and other factors, would be far more difficult than east of the Mississippi. It says that revegetation of the drier areas, those receiving less than 10 inches of rainfall a year, "can probably be accomp-

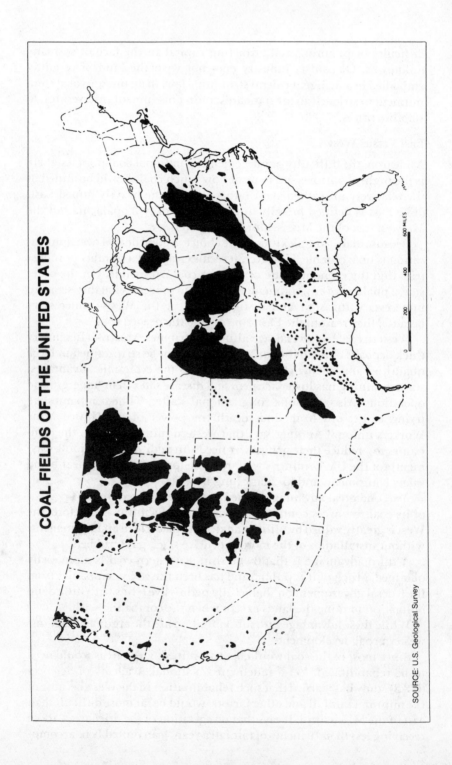

COAL FIELDS OF THE UNITED STATES

SOURCE: U.S. Geological Survey

lished only with major, sustained inputs of water, fertilizer, and management."[72]

Even assuming decent reclamation potential, there must be laws requiring it, and they must be effectively enforced, which is problematic.

How much land would be disturbed by coal development in the West? NAS estimates 300 square miles by the year 2000 (compared to nearly 2,000 square miles strip-mined in the East so far). But in reviewing the study, John V. Krutilla, of Resources for the Future, Inc., says the figures seem "somewhat conservative." He notes that they do not include projections for synthetic fuel production. "If we take a somewhat more expansive view of the competitive possibilities of the low-sulfur, strippable coal," says Krutilla, "it is possible to conceive of an area equivalent to several thousand square miles eventually disturbed. . . . "[73]

The undeniable economic and safety advantages of western coal are diminished by several factors. To the extent that less manpower is required, fewer jobs will materialize in the East. As presidential candidate Jimmy Carter said in a 1976 position paper:

> A change in the geography of energy production—for example an emphasis on expanding coal production in the Rocky Mountains and northern plains instead of in the Midwest and Appalachia—could cause a massive shift in the distribution of capital, tax revenues, and job opportunities away from the industrial East and Midwest to the agricultural regions of the West. We must question whether that is in the best interests of this country.

Safety and health conditions in underground eastern mines could be greatly improved—though this would require money and political will. A Library of Congress study gives these figures on the situation:

> The fatality rate in 1973 for underground and surface coal mines was 0.51 and 0.36 per million man hours respectively; and the nonfatal injury rates in 1970 were 53.80 and 32.66 for underground and surface mines, respectively; although those numbers may seem excessive, since 1948 the fatality rate has decreased by 62% and 12%, and nonfatal injuries by 14% and 13% in underground and surface mines respectively.[74]

In many cases, western coal would be mined far from its point of use, and transportation costs are substantial. In 1972, comparative costs were estimated at 1.1 cents per ton mile for western coal and 1.4 cents for eastern. Some unit-train shipments apparently were costing only about half a cent per ton mile.[75] Since then, costs have increased sharply.

Many tend to overlook the fact that the economic and safety advantages of surface mining also are available in the East—though the degraded land is likely to be more valuable and mining conditions are likely to be more difficult. In 1975, in the four largest coal-producing eastern states (Kentucky, West Virginia, Pennsylvania, and Illinois), 42 percent of total bituminous coal production was surface-mined.[76]

Another problem is that, on the average, western coal has a significantly lower heating value. Typically, the sub-bituminous and lignite deposits have a heat content ranging from 7,000 to 9,000 Btu per pound, while the bituminous and anthracite coals more common in the East contain from 10,000 to 15,000 Btu per pound.[77] Obviously, then, more western tonnage must be mined and burned to get the same energy.

Many studies comparing eastern and western production, prices, accident rates, and the like, have not properly factored in this major difference in heat content, or the greater moisture and ash content of western coal. The difference is particularly important when it comes to air pollution control.

Thus, even though the western coal is low in sulfur, more of it has to be burned to generate an equal amount of power, with the result that more sulfur is emitted. Therefore, coal with a low sulfur content may not be able to meet sulfur dioxide emission standards, without more costly controls, because its heat content also is low. For best comparison of coals, both factors should be assessed by measuring the amount of sulfur per Btu rather than per pound.[78] But when figures are used for political purposes, it can be convenient to give an incomplete picture.

The main argument by opponents of western coal exploitation is that there is plenty of low-sulfur coal in the East—particularly West Virginia—to satisfy the nation's needs for a long time. The U.S. Bureau of Mines estimates that the East harbors about 33 billion tons of bituminous and anthracite coal reserves containing less than 1 percent sulfur. It says about 14 billion tons of that lie in West Virginia.[79]

Even that figure could be a considerable understatement. Some observers suspect a deliberate shrinkage of the estimates which, combined with large estimates of strippable reserves in the West, is calculated to encourage western development as desired by industry.

There are many other environmental impacts from mining western coal—preemption of farm and grazing land; consumption of valuable water and damage to aquifers, many of which lie in coal beds; loss of scenic, historical and archeological values; erosion, sedimentation, and water pollution; the intrusion of transmission line corridors; and the noise and other impacts of railroads with unit trains of coal.[80]

Of great importance is the social impact of bringing intensive development to areas highly valued for a different, unfrenzied way of life. A Bureau of Land Management study has referred to the region's atmosphere of "isolation, solitude, and inspiration."

Surveys and other evidence indicate that most westerners do not wish

**DEMONSTRATED COAL RESERVES
BY SULFUR CONTENT**
(billions of tons)

	Underground	Strippable
East of Mississippi		
1% or less sulfur	27	5
1-3% sulfur	49	7
3% or more sulfur	67	15
West of Mississippi		
1% or less sulfur	99	68
1-3% sulfur	10	27
3% or more sulfur	8	4

Note: There are some additional reserves of unknown sulfur content.

SOURCE: Bureau of Mines, 1975.

to be overtaken by the kind of social and environmental exploitation for which Appalachia is so renowned. "There is widespread anxiety among landowners and their employees about what will happen to the character of the area, to patterns of neighboring, to the quality of life and the like," says University of Montana Professor Raymond Gold, in a research study on coal development in a southeast Montana region.[81]

The Northern Plains Resource Council has asked:

> Will we have at the end [of 35 years] a series of dying and ghostly towns spread across the prairie, an Indian community submerged in a white mining culture, and a marginally productive agricultural community?[82]

Some might argue that the U.S. should minimize coal production regardless of region—by substituting energy conservation, by restraining energy-consumptive growth, or by turning more to nuclear power or, somewhat later, to solar energy. Aside from that, no two people are likely to resolve the East vs. West tradeoffs in exactly the same way. One observation may be pertinent: In general, the ill effects of mining in the East seem more susceptible to control or elimination than those in the West—though certainly the costs could be substantial.

Surface mining can bring environmental and social havoc wherever it takes place. But health and safety in underground eastern mines can be greatly improved. So can control of sulfur dioxide pollution. On the other hand, in the West it is hard to avoid disruption of water supplies and the long-term or permanent removal of farming, grazing, and recreational lands. And the social and aesthetic transformation of rural areas of the West is quite irreversible.

III. THE FEASIBILITY OF SOLAR ENERGY

Energy from the sun may be the closest thing to a free lunch available. And a hearty lunch it is. Three days of global sunshine is the energy equivalent of all known world fossil fuel reserves.[83]

Solar energy is free in the economic sense (as a fuel it costs nothing), and relatively free in the ecological sense (it does not cause the pollution, safety, or waste-disposal problems that plague coal, oil, and nuclear technologies). "Solar energy," says William E. Heronemus, a professor at the University of Massachusetts, "could perhaps do more to improve the material well-being of mankind without increasing his tensions than any other good available to man."[84]

To be sure, significant obstacles impede the widespread exploitation of the sun's bounty. But the effective utilization of solar energy seems as certain as the rising of the sun itself. The question is not *whether* the various technological and economic problems will be resolved, but *when* and at what costs to *whom*.

Solar development is at an early stage, but it is coming on so strong, and is so logical, it could emerge as a true technological and social revolution—ranking in importance with the earlier shifts from wood to coal and then to oil and gas, or in some respects even with the Industrial Revolution.

After one assumes broad technological and economic feasibility of solar development, four essential issues remain: (1) to what extent, and when, can the nation rely on the sun's rays to bring relief from its energy and associated economic headaches; (2) what social and environmental impacts are involved; (3) given the need for solar energy and its favorable characteristics, how should it be advanced; and (4) how should the costs and benefits be distributed.

Broadly defined, solar energy encompasses not only the sun's radiation itself but all forms of renewable energy derived from the sun—most notably the wind (as captured by windmills), the rain (as captured in reservoirs for hydroelectric power), the ocean (using temperature differentials to generate electricity), and the plant kingdom (deriving energy from firewood, "energy crops," and organic wastes through bioconversion to methane gas and other processes).[85]

Though these sources of energy all have great potential, this discussion is largely confined to direct solar input.

The sun has certain inherent attributes that distinguish it greatly from other forms of energy. As noted, it provides the fuel free. No drilling, no extraction necessary. Putting that fuel to use, however, requires substantial investment. Yet once the front-end expenses are met, operation and maintenance costs are minimal. Solar energy is abundant, reliable, endlessly renewable, and totally ubiquitous. Nor can it be held hostage by foreign nations or domestic oil companies. On the other hand, it varies by region and by season, and it's not available on cloudy days or at night. It is diffuse and rather weak when it reaches the earth. Thus it does not lend itself readily—without expensive concentration, storage, or conversion—to certain end uses such as generating electricity.

However, says Theodore B. Taylor, a prominent energy expert and professor at Princeton University, "I have a strong conviction now that its diffuseness—the difficulty there is in collecting enough energy to really damage something—may, in fact, be its main blessing."[86] Which makes the point that the use of solar energy is remarkably free of adverse environmental impacts.

There are two basic, very different ways of using solar energy. One is largely for *buildings*—space heating, air-conditioning, and hot-water heating. The other is converting the sunshine to *electricity*.

To heat a building with solar energy, one can rely on "active" systems, "passive" systems, building design, or some combination. Solar experts generally insist that, to benefit truly from a solar system, a house should be tightly constructed and well insulated. In addition, a new house can be designed with a large window area facing south, with a proper overhang to shield it from the overhead summer sun, and with earth berms and minimal window surface facing other directions.

"It is readily possible," says physicist Raymond W. Bliss, "to design and build a house just as large as conventional construction, and keep it just as warm, but which requires only half as much heating fuel as current construction." He notes that one even must be careful to avoid a design that overheats on clear winter days.[87]

Passive and active solar systems, which can be built into new homes or retrofitted, include various combinations of roof collectors, circulation systems, and heat retention and storage (including concrete walls, drums or plastic bags of water, rock beds, etc.). Among the many decisions required is the number of square feet of collectors necessary; whether to use air or water circulation; the amount of storage needed; the extent to which a back-up system is required; and whether to combine the solar system with other equipment such as a heat pump.

Such systems also are used or being developed for industrial purposes, for drying crops, for heating swimming pools, and so forth.

Two principal technologies for converting solar energy to electricity are being pursued: First, photovoltaic cells, usually made from commonplace silicon, generate electricity directly from sunlight, no strings attached. Though their efficiency is low (at most about 20 percent), they can be easily massed together. They are the chief source of power in spacecraft.[88]

Second, a field of mirrors that track the angle of the sun can be used to heat fluid in a piping system and generate steam to run a turbine or can be used to focus sunshine on a boiler—located high on a so-called "power tower"—which also produces steam for a turbine.[89] (A more futuristic notion is to use a satellite to collect and focus the energy.[90])

The essential feasibility of all these technologies has been demonstrated. There are no outstanding mysteries. However, a number of engineering breakthroughs are needed to bring some systems into economic line or make them competitive enough for widespread use.

Space heating and hot-water systems are being installed around the country, and a number of studies report them to be economical under many conditions.[91] It is generally considered easier to fit a new home with solar than to retrofit an old one, and retrofitting, with its huge, immediate potential (some 60 million homes), is a field ripe for innovations.

"Theoretically, you could unroll a whole system on the roof," says one government official. "Installation costs now are very high—more than half the total using local plumbers and electricians. But maybe you could have gigantic, prefabricated roll-on sections. That's the kind of breakthrough needed."

Other technologies are still a good distance removed from commercial feasibility. These include space cooling, electricity generation (though photovoltaic cells already are used economically in some remote locations), and electric storage (as in batteries). A sharp reduction in the cost of photovoltaic cells would permit their use not only for a central electric utility system but also for on-site power in individual homes and other buildings. Auxiliary electricity might be required unless and until electric storage becomes feasible.

These developments seem inevitable, considering the healthy ferment in the industry, the technological competition, and the opportunities for improved design and mass-production economies with solar collectors, photovoltaic cells, and other components.

With hundreds and hundreds of entrepreneurs, from large corporations to closet inventors, already seeking to cash in on the potentially gargantuan solar market ($10 billion in the year 2000 by one estimate), improvements will come rapidly.[92]

Solar Forecasts

What is the prognosis for a major solar energy contribution to the U.S. energy budget? How soon could solar energy substantially reduce the need for natural gas, for oil, for coal, or for nuclear power?

Any forecast must be derived from many assumptions. Since these can be molded to fit a desired result, most forecasts must be viewed with suspicion. The results depend heavily, for example, on the assumed regulatory treatment and future prices of alternative fuels; the extent to which external costs or benefits are reflected (for instance, what value if any is attached to a solar plant that obviates the need for radioactive waste disposal, or for medical treatment of 500 people with bronchial problems from coal combustion); the extent to which government research efforts, subsidies, tax credits, loans, and other aids are used to promote the development and adoption of solar technologies; and the degree to which government and industry devotion to other energy sources weakens their commitment to solar.

For what it's worth, then, with so many major variables and slightly different definitions of "solar" (and overlooking the fact that the Paley Commission 25 years ago said solar energy could contribute 10 percent of the nation's energy supply as early as 1975), here is a sampling of some projections for the year 2000.[93]

	Solar percentage of total U.S. energy supply in the year 2000
Joint Committee on Atomic Energy (1973)	1.2
Mitre Corp. (accelerated program) (1973)	20–35
Project Independence (1974)	15–30
ERDA (1975)	7
ERDA solar official (1975)	20–25
ERDA (1976, 1977)	3–8
Stanford Research Institute (1977)	7–13
Council on Environmental Quality (1978)	23

Many experts, however, are not at all sanguine about the prospects for solar energy in this century and beyond. A number of critics have accused federal agencies of downplaying the solar potential and foot-dragging on solar programs. Other charges include: excessive emphasis on expensive, fancy solar electric-generating systems rather than simpler, more quickly available home heating and cooling techniques; a penchant for putting projects in the hands of big corporations while rebuffing solar pioneers and other small businesses; and lethargic implementation of the Solar Heating and Cooling Demonstration Act passed by Congress in 1974.[94]

Some observers feel strongly that the vigorous pursuit of nuclear and other "hard" technologies is wholly inconsistent with a simultaneous commitment to "soft" technologies such as solar. In short, there isn't enough time, money, skill, political energy, and cultural versatility to go around. Physicist Amory B. Lovins has written:

> Any demanding high technology tends to develop influential and dedicated constituencies of those who link its commercial success with both

the public welfare and their own. Such sincerely held beliefs, peer pressures, and the harsh demands that the work itself places on time and energy all tend to discourage such people from acquiring a similarly thorough knowledge of alternative policies and the need to discuss them.[95]

Biologist Barry Commoner, in an article sharply critical of President Carter's 1977 National Energy Plan, said that research on any kind of nuclear breeder reactor "would be so expensive as to preclude all but minor research on other energy systems."[96] Commoner also argued that the plan anticipated greatly increased penetration of the residential-commercial sector by electricity, and that this would "effectively block solar energy from the one market that is presently open to it," namely, space heating, hot water, and (shortly) space air-conditioning.

Solar and the Corporations

Private industry is potentially a far greater obstacle to solar energy utilization than any government agency, however. Of chief concern are the roles to be played by the electric and gas utilities and the oil and other energy giants that have staked out their own claims on solar development.[97] Paradoxically, these same companies also have the means to push solar energy fastest and most widely.

Some oil company advertising has given the impression of minimizing the role of solar energy for the next few decades, and this has brought charges of deliberately misleading the public in order to maintain profits from oil, gas, coal, and nuclear power.[98] One official of a small solar company has accused Mobil Oil of not only using deceptive advertising but engaging in research on an "irrelevant," or obviously uneconomical, technology.[99] Mobil and Exxon have sought to refute charges that they don't have their hearts in solar.[100]

In 1974, General Electric and Westinghouse, which manufacture nuclear plants, estimated that the solar share of just heating and cooling needs in the year 2000 would be only 1.6 percent and 3.04 percent, respectively.[101] This prompted Senator Gaylord Nelson of Wisconsin to say:

> The suspicion is unavoidable that these and other absurdly low estimates of the solar contribution during the next 25 years are not of what the estimaters think the country *could* do . . . but rather what they hope the country *will* do. Not because doing so little is in the best interests of the great majority of Americans and other people of the world, but because doing so could possibly threaten existing investment in other technologies.[102]

Certainly the potential for conflicts of interest and suppressed competition is clear enough.[103] "The bulk of the manufacturers are small, privately-held companies," one magazine noted, "but major corporations now dabbling with solar will have capabilities ready if the market mushrooms."[104]

The large oil companies' moves into the solar field doubtless have increased current interest in legislation to require their horizontal divestitures as a means of maximizing competition and protecting the market for small manufacturers, distributors, and installers of solar equipment.[105] Yet government leaders and the federal antitrust bureaucracy have been strangely complaisant as the oil companies have invaded coal, uranium, and other energy markets.[106]

Solar Economics

"The assessment of solar-energy utilization," says John B. Goodenough, of Oxford University, "becomes largely a cost analysis of schemes for its collection, conversion, and storage."[107]

To put it another way, an almost endless assortment of economic issues surrounds solar energy. They range from whether the small homeowner in Blue Earth, Minnesota, can save $5 a month on his heating bill to the economic future of the nuclear power industry. Some issues relate to the economic feasibility of the solar systems themselves, while others relate to how profits derived from the sun are to be distributed.

It must suffice here to indicate briefly how complex the evaluation of a solar system can be, and to indicate some relevant factors.

1. Obviously, a lot depends upon how much the sun shines at the place in question. This governs the size of the collector surface needed for a building. A relatively straightforward calculation may suffice, but not necessarily. Homes in the sunbelt obviously enjoy more sun. But a home in the north needs the heating for more months each year and so to that extent is able to derive greater economic benefits from the same investment in a solar system.

2. Solar systems become more economic as prices for alternative fuels climb, and recently escalating prices have done much to spur their adoption. The uncertainty of future prices, of course, makes it more difficult to assess solar options. It is unfortunate that solar energy—so desirable for environmental and other reasons—becomes more feasible as consumers are faced with higher oil and natural gas prices. (Also, existing high fuel prices in the Northeast add to solar's feasibility in that region.)

A related question is whether comparisons with other fuels include their external costs (such as oil spills, air pollution, and radioactive waste disposal). Or whether some value is attached to positive solar factors such as avoidance of coal mining accidents, decreasing reliance on foreign oil, increased employment, and the like.

3. An overriding fact of solar life is high front-end system costs. Even though followed by low operating and maintenance costs, they can be intimidating. Still, as *Engineering News Record* has noted, "A heating system can look attractive despite a higher first cost when it draws on a clean energy source that will provide free power for the next five billion years."[108]

A high initial investment means that economic feasibility may depend heavily on the interest rate obtainable and the cost of alternative investment opportunities foregone, and on life-cycle costing analysis so the long-term fuel savings are factored in. "The feasibility of solar energy can be determined almost solely by interest rates," says one congressional study.[109]

At present, aside from available tax credits, homeowners must bear the initial cost, whereas a utility can obtain cheaper money to build a power plant and average in the lower, embedded costs of older plants. Thus, economic feasibility also depends on the accounting methods used—whether or not the lower average costs for which consumers can obtain alternative energy are compared with the high marginal costs of solar.

As a practical matter, much depends on the extent of government incentives and commercial policies that can be used to facilitate solar equipment purchases.

4. Solar economics depend further on the equipment or combinations of equipment used. Is it efficient? Is it reliable? There is a general recognition of the need for industry performance standards. But inevitably there will be some incompetence, defective components, and faulty installation. In addition, warnings are out to watch for consumer fraud and an invasion of the market by charlatans.[110]

The economic analysis of a solar installation also must ask whether the building has been designed to take advantage of the sun and is well insulated—and thus whether the incremental savings of solar equipment is worth the incremental cost.

The potential complexity of such a question is illustrated by a congressional report that indicates retrofitting can have advantages over new-home systems. Analyzing houses in the Southwest, it said:

> The large fixed cost of installation assures that the total cost per square foot decreases with system size. Thus, poorly insulated older homes with flat roofs and large glass areas (the cardboard castles associated with cheap energy supplies), are hard to retrofit with insulation but are ideal candidates for retrofitting solar space heat. In fact, the cost per Btu will be lower than for a new installation with the ideal mix of thermal insulation and solar energy.[111]

The economics also will depend on whether heating and hot-water components are combined, and whether a heat pump—which can be very attractive when coupled with a solar system—is used. When economical *cooling* systems are developed, overall efficiencies could improve dramatically because the solar collectors will see more months of usage.[112]

5. Since the sun shines intermittently and not at night, a building owner must make an important economic choice on what kind of storage system, back-up source of conventional energy, or combination of both, to hook up. This decision, too, will depend on variables such as climate, the amount of heating needed, and fuel or utility rates for supplementary energy.

When a solar system produces the most energy on a hot summer day, it is likely to lower the utility company's need for expensive *peak* power. Sometimes, however, it may only reduce the load during the *base* period, when more power already is available and cheaply produced. The relevant question, therefore, is: If the homeowner must obtain back-up power from the utility, will this demand require the utility to increase its base, peak, or intermediate load? And either way, will the utility seek to charge rates that unfairly burden the solar homeowner? (It might do this to increase its profits, or to protect its investment in conventional power.)[113]

"If electricity rates are scheduled to decline with increasing use or otherwise penalize the consumer of relatively small amounts, solar users may find that their electricity bills are reduced much less than expected," notes Alan S. Miller, a staff attorney with the Environmental Law Institute.[114]

Various helpful economic interfaces with utilities could be adopted. For example, as an Environmental Law Institute study notes, a homeowner with a good energy storage system could buy back-up energy during off-peak periods and then use it to provide heat during peak periods.[115]

An electric heat pump can draw heat efficiently from water in a solar storage tank that is only lukewarm, so the solar collection system need not be so large and expensive. During cloudy or very cold days, the water in the storage tank can be heated as much as desired by the pump, using off-peak-load electricity.

6. Closely related to these economic issues is the question of who will control what part of the solar market. The battle between small and large manufacturers and distributors has been discussed. But what about financing, installation, and operation?

Will conventional utilities seek, and be allowed, to own and lease solar systems, maintaining them and billing monthly as they generally do with telephones, for example? There are efforts to move in that direction.[116] Alternatively, utilities might be allowed to finance home-owner purchases of equipment—or be given no role at all. Current utility company entries into the home insulation business may be a precedent.[117]

Many strong and complex reasons can be given for and against utility involvement. To scratch the surface, it seems clear, for instance, that utilities, with their huge infrastructures, could provide a large market sooner, thereby stimulating solar development across-the-board; could increase system reliability; and could lower financing and other costs.

Some contrary arguments are provided by Roger Noll, a utility specialist:

> A regulated utility has an incentive to invest in solar technology that is too durable, that is excessively efficient (because it is guaranteed a return on all investment in its rate base) . . . . If permitted this would lead to exces-sive costs and prices for solar energy, and inefficiently slow adoption of the technology.

Also, Noll says, regulated utilities "can use solar technology strategi-cally to recapture some of the monopoly profits that regulation takes away and to foreclose competition in the solar energy business."[118]

Ecological and Social Issues

The environmental impacts of solar energy development are relatively mild, but not without significance. Earlier claims that solar electric generating plants would devour impossibly large chunks of land appear exaggerated. The acreage required depends chiefly on the solar input and the efficiency of the cells or collectors. Estimates of the land needed for a 1,000-megawatt solar generating facility range roughly from 2 to 20 square miles and more.[119] Though this is substantially more than the space used by traditional plants, greater efficiency may reduce the solar requirements. One also must consider that solar plants need no support from land-intensive mining operations.

Obtaining the large tracts of land needed for solar plants may be difficult, especially east of the Mississippi River, considering the com-petition from other uses. But Richard S. Caputo, a mechanical engineer at the Jet Propulsion Laboratory in Pasadena, says that low-cost land in the eight southwest states would suffice. "Of the one million square miles of land in the Sun Bowl," he maintains, "about 2 to 16 percent is potentially available and suitable for use as a solar power plant. This is 4 to 32 times larger than the area needed to generate the current national electricity requirements."[120]

According to a Stanford Research Institute study, "Decentralized systems can mitigate the problem of large collection areas inherent in solar systems by permitting the use of small, unused spaces such as rooftops, parking lots, mass transit corridors, and utility easements."[121] Many observers also have noted that the land around and beneath solar plants may be available for other uses—grazing, for example.

The problem of providing cooling water for solar electric facilities— especially in the arid Southwest—is formidable. However, there exists the possibility of employing somewhat more expensive dry cooling methods.[122]

Some experts feel that the main rationale for solar energy is that it lessens the potential threat from excess carbon dioxide and adds little or nothing to the world's thermal load.[123] "For the most part, the solar plant is using energy that would have been absorbed by the soil and local atmosphere anyway," Caputo indicates.[124]

As for individual solar buildings, there is environmental concern about the aesthetics of building design and location, and about the fact that access to sunlight often may be incompatible with shading trees. Much legal activity involving control of foliage, building heights, zoning, and other restrictions can be expected.[125]

On a larger scale, there is anxiety that property owners will rush to build and claim solar rights. In at least one state, New Mexico, a 1977 law adopts the prior appropriation, or first-come-first-served, philosophy common to western water law.[126] This approach could be another inducement to wasteful, leapfrog growth. In any case, the dispersed or decentralized nature of solar energy development could make it far more difficult to manage growth in otherwise desirable patterns.

The control of solar technology raises broader social issues, particularly when it comes to solar generation of electricity. Essentially these issues hinge on whether energy is to be provided by traditional central power stations or by decentralized, on-site units.

Commoner, Lovins, and others have stressed the democratic, nonbureaucratic, flexible nature of decentralization. In arguing the advantages of choosing a soft-technology path, Lovins says:

> Its technical diversity, adaptability, and geographic dispersion make it resilient and offer a good prospect of stability under a wide range of conditions, foreseen or not. The hard path, however, is brittle, it must fail, with widespread and serious disruption, if any of its exacting technical and social conditions is not satisfied continuously and indefinitely.[127]

Environmentalists For Full Employment points out that solar-cell arrays can be expanded in small units as needed. Thus, energy planners "can avoid having to predict years in advance what the specific energy demand of a region will be."[128]

Andrew Tobias has sung the praises of autonomy:

When you install some kind of solar heater, you are actually buying your own small utility company. Not just 10 shares—the whole thing. You are the chairman of the board and sole stockholder, and you receive monthly dividend checks in the form of savings on your *other* utility bill. These "dividends" are recession-proof, inflation-proof, strike-proof, pollution-proof, terrorism-proof, computer-error-proof . . . and, most important, *tax free.*[129]

Chapter 8

ENERGY PROBLEMS

> Energy organizes society. With too little
> energy, man is a slave to its production;
> with too much, he is a slave to its consump-
> tion. These two conditions summarize the
> history of social evolution.
>
> —Charles J. Ryan

An effective, responsible energy strategy will not emerge from a resource assessment alone. Also to be considered fully are the various problems—environmental, social, economic—caused by using each of our energy sources, especially nuclear, coal, and oil.

The principal problems associated with oil are pollution by oil spills and national security and economic weaknesses inherent in massive reliance on high-cost imported oil.

Coal presents a host of problems: worker safety and black lung disease; economic and logistical problems (discussed in chapter 8); strip-mining (also discussed in chapter 8); carbon dioxide loading of the atmosphere (a subject of chapter 5); and the public health hazards of sulfur dioxide pollution.

Nuclear energy also involves a troublesome series of problems: high costs, waste disposal, plant safety, theft of weapons material, and terrorism. Also, nuclear power is limited—for example, it won't run gasoline-powered vehicles.

Even conservation of energy—at least in its more demanding prescriptions—raises problems: It is criticized as being incompatible with vigorous economic growth. (The problem of reconciling reduced energy consumption with economic growth is discussed in the next chapter.)

This chapter focuses on two critical drawbacks to expanded energy supplies: the various hazards of nuclear power, and the sulfur dioxide problem of coal.

I. NUCLEAR POWER HAZARDS

A minefield of ominous problems awaits the further expansion and international proliferation of nuclear power. These problems—environ-

189

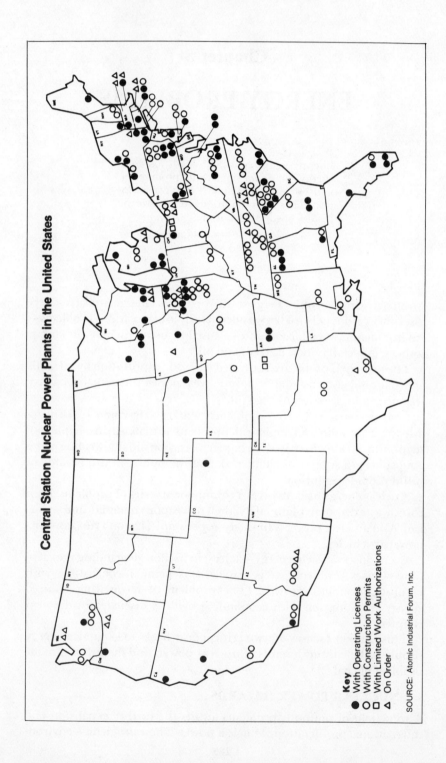

Central Station Nuclear Power Plants in the United States

Key
With Operating Licenses
With Construction Permits
With Limited Work Authorizations
On Order

SOURCE: Atomic Industrial Forum, Inc.

mental, social, economic, managerial, and regulatory—are at the heart of the nation's gigantic political tug-of-war over the future of nuclear energy.

The battle can be expected to endure for years, though it may now be at a peak of intensity and criticality. It is one of the most dramatic and important confrontations since man first raised a skeptical eyebrow on continuing technological "progress." For nuclear spread, with all its attendant dangers, could be the ultimate environmental pollutant.

There are three essential problems with nuclear power: (1) *safety*, or protection against excessive releases of radioactivity and other mishaps associated with nuclear reactors and related facilities; (2) *safeguards*, or the prevention of accidents, theft, hijacking, sabotage, blackmail, and other terrorist activities; and (3) *waste management*, or the safe disposal of radioactive materials for hundreds or thousands of years.

There also are two prerequisites to a satisfactory solution of *each* of these three basic problems:

• Adequate *technology* must be available, be it a back-up system to prevent a reactor core meltdown, an alarm system to spot intruders, or a container in which to store wastes.

• Even if all necessary technology is at hand, there must be *management and regulatory procedures* that assure its proper application. For there is an ever-present potential for relaxed enforcement, unforeseen dangers, negligence, and other human errors.

Even if the technologies and regulatory systems are judged adequate, nuclear power should pass other tests of public acceptability. It should be the most attractive alternative source of energy; and the economic costs, environmental effects, and social consequences should be politically tolerable.

A series of events over the past few years has cast much suspicion on nuclear power. To cite a few of the more visible occurrences:

The major scare was at the Three Mile Island nuclear plant close to Harrisburg, Pennsylvania, which left the plant completely disabled with a clean-up job estimated to cost $400 million. Repercussions included a moratorium on nuclear plant licensing by the Nuclear Regulatory Commission and a presidential commission investigation which blamed the accident on the NRC, the utility that owned Three Mile Island, and the technicians inside the plant.

Earlier, there was the embarrassing fire at the Brown's Ferry power plant in Alabama. Three veteran General Electric engineers resigned because of concern over the dangers of nuclear development, as did a safety engineer with the Nuclear Regulatory Commission. Power plants have been shut down because of possibly serious design defects. Leakages and careless handling of radioactive wastes have been reported at a number of facilities and storage sites. Terrorist activities in general have increased in sophistication and intensity. India exploded a nuclear "device" it made from plutonium derived from a research reactor imported from Canada. And, to counter India, Pakistan began developing what it called the "Islamic Bomb," using materials from a reprocessing plant it bought from France.

The simplified diagram of the nuclear "fuel cycle" for light-water reactors shows there are actual or potential problems throughout the elaborate, sensitive system. Safety questions aside, there are problems of isolating radioactive wastes all along the line. These range from "high-level" wastes that are directly and intensely hazardous, or that can be used to make bombs, to "other" wastes of varying degrees of harmfulness, including those that give out low-level radiation over long periods of time.

The diagram also shows that at many points safeguards are critical to prevent diversion of dangerous uranium or plutonium, or to prevent outright attack or sabotage.

1. The first steps are mining and milling uranium ore. They generate large quantities of low-level waste called uranium tailings.

2. The milling operation produces "yellowcake," which is then processed and enriched so it can be used as fuel in a reactor. The hazards at this point tend to be ignored because, as one observer says: "Plutonium, however, is not without attractiveness to a nation which requires military weapons because of its low cost, low critical mass, and ease of production." (A bomb can be fashioned from a few pounds of plutonium and, according to many experts, without great difficulty.) "Uranium, however, is not without attractiveness to a nation which requires but a few bombs for purposes of diplomatic leverage or nuclear blackmail."[1] The depleted uranium must be stored or disposed of. The industry hopes to make future use of it in breeder reactors.

3. In "fuel fabrication," the enriched uranium is fashioned into pellets which are packed into fuel rod assemblies for placement in the reactor core.

4. After several years in the reactor, the fuel rods are replaced and the "spent fuel" removed. It now contains potentially lethal plutonium, which was produced in the reactor. The spent fuel is stored, at least temporarily, in large water basins at power plants.

It has been accumulating relentlessly. However, it can be removed from storage and reprocessed to recover uranium and plutonium—both of which can be used, in turn, as reactor fuel. Thus the nuclear establishment is most anxious to relieve the waste glut *and* the expensive uranium fuel supply problem of creating sufficient reprocessing capability. Without such capability, the choice becomes essentially one of

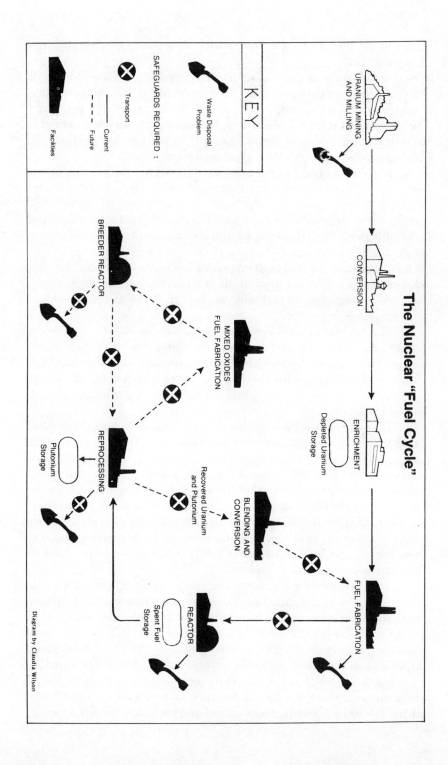

The Nuclear "Fuel Cycle"

Diagram by Claudia Wilson

either providing large-scale spent fuel storage capacity or shutting down reactors.

To some, such as Cornell University physics professor Robert O. Pohl, reprocessing, despite all its own problems, is "our moral obligation toward future generations" because "by recovering 99 percent of the plutonium from the spent fuel during the reprocessing, which is technically feasible, and then burning it in reactors, we decrease the nuclear waste's toxicity about a hundred times."[2]

5. The reprocessing plant must have its highly radioactive pollutants carefully controlled. And its superhot and dangerous liquid wastes must be isolated from the environment for thousands of years. These eventually must be solidified to reduce the risks of accidental release and allow for permanent disposal, and this is one of the more forbidding problems of the nuclear cycle.

6. Uranium recovered at the reprocessing plant is enriched for subsequent use in reactors. The plutonium also is adapted for use as reactor fuel, in a "mixed oxides fuel fabrication plant." It also can be sold, or used in a breeder reactor.

7. The breeder reactor itself, should it be successfully developed, would have the major advantage of producing more fuel than it consumes. So the mining, enriching, and conversion processes could be dispensed with. But with the greater use of plutonium, the safety, safeguard, and waste disposal problems, while not yet fully understood, would be considerable.

8. Throughout the cycle there is a need to transport fuel, wastes, and other radioactive materials from one facility to another. Some of these cargoes are not likely to be targets of mischief makers; others are highly sensitive. The facilities generally are far apart, thus increasing the shipments' vulnerability to theft or accident. In many cases they are located in different countries, and one story described an ordinary shipment of spent fuel from an Italian reactor to a Belgian reprocessing plant, whence the resultant plutonium oxide powder was shipped to New Jersey and then Pennsylvania, where it was to be converted to fuel and returned to the Italian reactor.[3]

9. Throughout the cycle, there is radioactive contamination of everything from gloves and instruments to piping systems and whole plants. After outliving their usefulness, all these must be either decontaminated or disposed of safely. "To date little attention has been paid to the total decontamination of reactor primary systems," say the three General Electric engineers who resigned. They note that the normal expected life of a reactor is 30-40 years, but that licenses generally allow for no permanent on-site waste burial. So, they say, the entire system "must ultimately be cleaned up, disassembled and packaged to meet necessary

shipment regulations, and hauled to permanent waste burial grounds for long-term storage."[4]

It should be noted that a "heavy water" or deuterium oxide reactor, such as that marketed by Canada under the name CANDU, is fueled by natural uranium and thus no enrichment plant is required. Significantly from a safeguards standpoint, it also produces about twice as much plutonium as a light-water reactor—and with far *less* of the attendant plutonium-240, which is so dangerous to handle it tends to deter thieves or would-be bomb makers. The breeder reactor would have the same two undesirable characteristics.[5]

Nuclear advocates insist there are no causes for alarm. Yet the situation is unsettling, because we are poised for a great leap forward in nuclear development. (That is not the editorial "we," unfortunately, but the international "we.")

In the first place, we are shifting fitfully, but perhaps inexorably, from uranium to the more efficient plutonium as a fuel base. And plutonium, produced by man not nature, is diabolically toxic. (The most frequently cited measure of its toxicity is that one twenty-eight-millionth of an ounce can produce cancer in animals. Roughly one twenty-eight-thousandth of an ounce, inhaled, is "enough to kill a person within hours by massive fibrosis of the lungs," says George Wald, Nobel Laureate biology professor at Harvard University.[6])

Plutonium-239, the principal isotope, has a half-life of 24,400 years and therefore does not disintegrate to a radioactively benign state for some 250,000 years. Finally, plutonium is the stuff of nuclear bombs, and a few handfuls are enough to make one.

The other reason we are at a nuclear threshold is that the world is plunging toward nuclear proliferation. Nuclear materials and facilities are being marketed at an increasingly furious pace, and precautions taken in the U.S. may soon become academic.

Technology and Regulation

With plutonium and proliferation staring us in the face, and requiring new magnitudes of care and management, it is important to consider what capabilities we have to cope with the dangers. Nuclear advocates seldom deviate from the position that there is a technological and regulatory fix for everything. Others have challenged many of the claims about nuclear *safety*, and those disputes continue unabated.

Even when technological and management solutions are still wanting—admittedly the case with some *safeguard* and *waste management* requirements—nuclear proponents assure the public that such solutions will be forthcoming, and that it is therfore safe to continue down the nuclear path. At a hearing on waste disposal, Congressman John

Young of Texas commented: "The fact is that there are problems that haven't been solved that we don't even know about yet. So, we just have to crawl before we walk and walk before we run."[7]

The disputes over technology and regulation are shaped by philosophical predilections. Nuclear proponents are confident in science and technology. They cite the lack of catastrophe in decades of nuclear development. They emphasize the benefits of adequate energy supplies in terms of economic growth, quality of life, jobs, and national security. They are willing to accept some human deaths and injuries if the greater good seems to justify them, as society does with many other endeavors.[8] A number of experts feel that at some point terrorists will steal enough plutonium and fashion a nuclear bomb—but that "civilization won't collapse" as a result.[9] And finally, there is that stubborn complacency in human nature which keeps whispering that if something goes wrong, it will be in someone else's back yard.

Nuclear opponents, on the other hand, are apt to be highly skeptical of the infallibility of technocrats, bureaucrats, regulatory bodies, and private industry. They cite a variety of fluke incidents in the past,[10] as well as the obvious bewilderment and incapacity of the nuclear technicians at Three Mile Island. They want much greater concentration on more benign energy alternatives, such as conservation and solar energy—and an altered life-style. And they worry that these alternatives will suffer if a self-indulgent public expects to be bailed out by plentiful nuclear power.

These opponents are asking: How can we proceed when we don't yet know the full extent of the risks involved? How can we bequeath to future generations such heavy economic and environmental legacies? And do we really want to live this way anyhow?

The flavor of their skepticism is captured in some comments from both sides of the nuclear fence. Alvin M. Weinberg, former director of the Oak Ridge National Laboratory and now director of the Institute of Energy Analysis at Oak Ridge, is basically a nuclear proponent, but he has asked:

> Can we expect these plants and their systems, including chemical plants and waste disposal, to work as planned? This . . . requires a social commitment, and perhaps even a stability of the society, over very long times to maintain the expertise, the quality assurance, the vigilance that will keep us out of trouble. Most of us in the nuclear business believe such commitment is realistic because there are at least partial precedents for such technological demands: for example, the dikes of Holland require a very long social commitment if they are to be kept in proper repair. Yet this is a debatable point. . . .[11]

A Natural Resources Defense Council booklet says:

Our experience indicates that rather than sustaining a high degree of esprit, vigilance, and meticulous attention to detail, our governmental bureaucracies instead become careless, rigid, defensive and, less frequently, corrupt. A basic question, then, is whether we want to entrust so demanding and unrelenting a technology as plutonium recycle to institutions which are negligent of their own responsibilities and insensitive to the rights of others, and to technical fixes which are untried and unproven.[12]

Henry Kendall, an MIT physics professor and antinuclear activist, says that the "uniquely unforgiving" nuclear technology was "designed by geniuses and is being run by idiots."[13]

"Technological fixes cannot run ahead of the human capacity to plan, construct, fund, and man them," says author and political commentator William Ophuls:

Delays or failures of planning or implementation abound, even today. . . .
Because of unreliable and out-of-date data, inadequate intellectual tools for dealing with complexity, managerial styles that are grossly ill-adapted to the task of environmental management, and many other factors, the current managerial regime is incapable of operating in real time—much less with the 30- to 50-year time horizons that have become necessary. In short, the task of environmental management is *already* running away from us. Moreover, our complex technological systems are making us exceedingly vulnerable to accident, error, and sabotage.[14]

Gregory Minor, one of the three GE engineers who resigned, brings the managerial problems down to earth in commenting on the control room of a nuclear power plant, which he says may be as much as 70 feet long and have more than 50 systems that the operator must interact with. "Experience has shown that there is too much information to read, comprehend, and respond effectively to, particularly in a crisis."[15] That was before Three Mile Island.

Other Policy Questions

In addition to the technological, regulatory, and managerial dilemmas posed by nuclear development, other factors require assessment and political decision. One is the question of *alternatives.*

Ecologist Barry Commoner, in a highly cogent analysis of the energy situation, criticizes the nuclear solution on a number of grounds, including risks, technological obstacles, costs, and even efficiency. "Nuclear power represents a kind of thermodynamic overkill," Commoner says. "The use of nuclear radiation for the relatively mild task of producing steam (for electricity) violates the familiar caution against attacking a fly with a cannon."[16]

Commoner continues with an elaborate review of the benefits of solar energy for most energy purposes, because high temperatures can be achieved through magnification. Others, such as Hans A. Bethe, Nobel Laureate and physics professor emeritus at Cornell University, insist that the costs of solar power will be much higher than for nuclear.[17]

Coal is another alternative, and nuclear enthusiasts are fond of comparing nuclear power's excellent accident record to the deaths and injuries from coal mining. This certainly is a valid point, but these advocates are silent on the causes of these human losses, which include the coal industry's sorry safety efforts and the government's long failure to legislate and effectively enforce mine safety measures. (One might wonder, in fact, if these very failures do not suggest that we also cannot expect continued safe practices and regulation in the nuclear field.)

Closely allied to the analysis of alternative sources of energy is the question of relative *economics*. Commoner foresees a situation in which even conventional nuclear reactors will no longer be able to compete economically with coal-fired plants.[18] As for shifting to plutonium and the fast breeder reactor, development costs are mushrooming. Many examples could be cited, but the starkest involve the nation's efforts to recycle plutonium—that is, build commercial reprocessing plants that take "spent fuel" from existing power plants and recover both uranium *and* plutonium, which can then be recycled back to the power plants for use as new fuel.

The first commercial reprocessing plant, at West Valley, N.Y., operated on a limited scale for some five years, but was shut down in 1972 because of excessive radioactivity emissions and a desire to expand the plant. Another reprocessing plant, built at Morris, Ill., by General Electric, used a different design. But it didn't work properly and, after costs of some $80 million, the whole operation was scratched. Finally, there is the large Allied Chemical Corp. plant near Barnwell, South Carolina, which cost hundreds of millions of dollars more than originally estimated, and on which construction ran years behind schedule.[19]

One major reason for the cost escalation has been design changes to meet more stringent government safety requirements. Cost estimates for the proposed Clinch River plutonium breeder reactor also keep escalating; the initial figure of $700 million in 1973 was later boosted to almost $2 billion.

Other political policy questions involve nuclear facility *siting* difficulties (seen most starkly in the series of major civil disobedience protests at the Seabrook nuclear plant site in New Hampshire), *thermal pollution*, and the *social consequences* of living with nuclear energy. A major consequence often cited is the possible evolution of a garrison state to cope with nuclear dangers.

Waste Management

Meanwhile, as pro- and antinuclear groups beat heads in the political arenas, researchers in and out of government are busily trying to find solutions to unresolved safeguard and waste management problems.

To begin with, the scientists are still wrestling with one of the oldest problems in the cycle—disposal of uranium mill tailings—and this does not inspire confidence that the more difficult problems now at hand will be dealt with adequately.[20]

Speaking of the billions of cubic feet of tailings piled up and still accumulating in 10 western states, NRC Commissioner Edward A. Mason said "old concerns are receiving increased attention" because the tailings contain radioactive isotopes of thorium and radium which, without effective control, "can be spread to the environment by wind and water erosion, groundwater and soil contamination, and deliberate removal and unauthorized use of tailings material." He continued:

> While the resulting radiation dose rates are very low, doses integrated over long times in populated areas must be considered. The control and stabilization of uranium mill tailings is a problem that must be dealt with, but the solution is presently complicated by the lack of clear definition of both the nature and magnitude of the risks to the public and of responsibility for regulation.[21]

In one instance, the government spent an estimated $8 million to help correct a little oversight: Starting 25 or so years ago, people casually used uranium mill tailings in building thousands of homes around Grand Junction, Colo. When the health threat was better appreciated many years later, a "remedial action" program was begun. It involved removal of huge quantities of tailings, mostly from underneath homes and public buildings.[22]

Farther along the cycle, many other wastes are generated, with similarly unsuccessful disposal efforts. An NRC document speaks blandly of the "absence of a suitable regulatory posture for waste management."[23] There is mounting evidence that this is a whopping understatement, including recurrent reports of leakages and mismanagement.

A General Accounting Office report on the burial sites for radioactive wastes stated the problem succinctly:

> Some of these sites have been operating for more than 30 years, yet it is not known what mix of hydrogeological characteristics and engineering features offer the greatest assurance that radioactivity, once disposed of, will not create a possible public health hazard and require extraordinary and costly efforts to correct.[24]

Environmental Protection Agency (EPA) experts have estimated that the bill for all nuclear waste management could reach $1.7 billion per year by the end of the century.[25] This still would be only a very small fraction of the total cost of electricity. But two EPA officials have written, "Until the cost commitments, including the cost of perpetual care, are well understood, the societal commitments involved cannot be evaluated."[26] In fact, they suggested that *interim* waste storage facilities might be made permanent "solely due to the economic costs involved in reprocessing and repackaging the interim stored wastes (if this becomes necessary), their transportation to the ultimate disposal site, and the decommissioning of the interim storage facilities." Such considerations have led the NRC to plan on bypassing as much as possible the interim stage, or retrievable storage, and concentrate instead on the permanent disposal.

Pro-nuclear experts generally believe that all necessary waste management technology already is largely at hand. Hans Bethe says, "It seems to me virtually certain that a suitable permanent storage site will be found." And he elaborates in detail his reasons for concluding that such a site can be safe from "man-made interference" as well as diffusion back to the surface.[27]

But the government's energy experts themselves do not appear so sanguine—at least not when asking Congress for money. In fact, there is a note of urgency and even desperation in their suddenly expanding appropriations requests for research on long-term management of commercial wastes.

The same uncertainties and mushrooming appropriations are evident in the nuclear weapons programs. The government's military-related nuclear installations, which have operated much longer than commercial reactors, are faced with a host of problems, including deteriorating and leaking storage tanks. Since no permanent disposal is available, many expensive procedures must be undertaken: constructing new tanks, emptying old ones, upgrading liquid-waste transfer pipelines, and improving controls for emergency situations.

The operations have taken on a discomforting circularity. For example at the Savannah River, S.C., weapons facility, as the waste management problem intensified, an increasing amount of waste management broke down. Since this equipment in turn becomes highly contaminated, it either turns into radioactive waste itself or must be decontaminated and repaired in a special shielded facility.[28]

Where Else Can It Be Put?

The nation, then, is saddled with large amounts of weapons-related wastes and a commercial waste management problem that will probably be greatly exacerbated in the 1980's. So there is great pressure to find a permanent disposal site to accommodate these wastes. The most likely solution—or at least the one over which industry and government exude much confidence—is putting the wastes in special containers and burying them deep in a huge salt formation. Such formations are prime candidates because they are geologically tight (if there were leaks, the salt would have melted), and their resiliency allows them to seal up after shocks or dislocations.

Time and costs are not the only problems. "There is no sure way of telling from surface geologic indications the conditions existing thousands of feet down," says one high official in the government's nuclear fuel program.[29] So extensive drilling is necessary, with the expectation of some unsuccessful holes.

Current plans call for utilization of New Mexican salt beds. On December 31, 1979, President Carter signed legislation that authorizes the construction near Carlsbad of the nation's first permanent repository for high-level radioactive military wastes. The project is reminiscent of the choice of an abandoned salt mine near Lyons, Kansas, some 10 years ago—a choice that proved premature. It was discovered that an active salt mine nearby had lost a large volume of water that might be migrating toward the disposal site. Also, several dozen old drill holes punctured the area and it was feared that, since they could not all be plugged, they posed another leakage threat. Political and environmental opposition to the project also was strong, and in late 1971 the Lyons site was abandoned.[30]

The government, has looked longingly at the oceans as another possibility. Radioactive wastes from the U.S. were dumped at sea for some 24 years, but the practice was stopped in 1970. However, some countries, particularly European nations, continue dumping such wastes in the ocean.[31]

The government has also been trying to check out the feasibility and costs of burying nuclear wastes *beneath* the seabed. It would like to tuck them into the middle of a tectonic plate (the edges of the plates are associated with high seismic activity) and in a "mid-gyre" area where the bottom water is relatively calm—in hopes they will remain stable and hidden forever.[32]

There is also the possibility of exploding a *nuclear device* to create a very deep underground cavity (20,000 to 30,000 feet) and injecting liquid nuclear wastes into it. The theory is that the hot wastes would melt the underground rock which would then resolidify so as to "encapsulate" the wastes in a very tight formation below the water line.[33] "We know how to make the cavity," said an energy official.

If some of these schemes sound promising, it is not reassuring to recall that there already has been a long history of laborious and unsuccessful attempts to find a final solution to the waste disposal problem.

Safeguards

The safeguards problem is something else again. To capture the flavor of the situation, it helps to consider both the strategies and tactics involved.

Safeguards can be aimed at (a) reducing the likelihood of *attempts* to cause mischief, (b) reducing the likelihood of an attempt being *successful,* and (c) reducing the *consequences* of a successful attempt.

Going a step further, there are two general categories of control. First, there is physical protection of materials, facilities, and transport from outside access, attack, or accident. Second, there is inventory accounting and internal security to protect against theft or sabotage from within.

Much brainpower is being applied to the safeguards problem. In 1975-76, the NRC contracted for several dozen think-tank studies at a cost of $2.5 million.[34] These and other sources have spawned a truly staggering—and chilling—assortment of suggestions to choose from. Some of the measures already are in use. Consider a sample of the work and ideas in the field:

Comprehensive analyses of "potential malevolent events" and the "motivation and resources" of adversary "elements," ranking potential targets and modes of attack, and the use of "threat intelligence."

Patrol cars, radio systems, alarms, closed-circuit TV monitoring, guards armed with automatic weapons and bazookas, fences that release incapacitating gases, voice identification cards for employes, night vision and radiation sensing devices, regular psychiatric interviews at plants to weed out disgruntled employes, elimination of in-plant gambling (to make sure organized crime obtains no leverage over employes), computerized systems for pinpoint inventory control of nuclear materials.

Special shipping containers for truck, rail, and air transportation of nuclear materials and wastes, including huge casks that often cost more than a million dollars each. (Testing the "survivability" of such containers includes staging a collision between a truck and a train, and an airplane crash.)

Heavily armored transport vehicles that follow prescribed routes, that are in constant radio contact with a central control, that operate on an automatic position location system, that are protected by helicopter reconnaissance, and that have axles that fall off when a button is pushed.

A federal police force, a federal "command center," contingency plans, a "retrieval operation," development of "organized rapid response resources."

Two other techniques have been widely discussed and are worthy of special note: One is "spiking" vulnerable weapons-grade material by

adding material that is radioactively highly penetrating, thereby making the combination too hot for thieves to handle. The other is to reduce
shipping risks by grouping facilities, such as reprocessing and fuel
fabrication plants, where feasible. But the environmental and political
problems could be enormous.[35]

What is the prognosis for all these safeguards techniques? Can they
work? Some experts are convinced that the problem is basically insolu-
ble, since there is no accounting for, or countering, all contingencies
that might flow from the fertile minds of terrorist groups, crackpots,
disgruntled employes, and the like. In this view, the safeguards problem
becomes the Achilles heel of the whole worldwide nuclear program.

On the other side, there are plenty of experts who dismiss the safeguards fears, as, at best, unfounded, and, at worst, kneejerk alarmism.
They argue that only small quantities of critical material are involved,
that the vulnerable spots are few, that redundant safeguards already are
more or less available and will provide more than adequate protection,
and even that terrorists already have access to more convenient means to
blackmail or destroy. Two authorities conclude: "A system of safeguards can be developed that will keep the risks of theft of nuclear
weapon materials from the nuclear power industry at very low levels."[36]

John P. Holdren, a physicist and associate professor at the University
of California, Berkeley, says that the effectiveness of safeguards systems
cannot be measured—"the character of the uncertainty does not lend
itself readily to quantification." Thus we can expect unending disagreement on the chances of successful sabotage, etc. Holdren adds
wryly: "I believe this disagreement is not likely to be resolved by further
argument, although it might be resolved by the real-world 'experiment'
that now is in progress."[37]

In the real world there already have been numerous safeguard-related
incidents aside from those related to inadequate safety or waste management. The consequences have not been serious, but the incidents
inspire some lack of confidence in the future. They include thefts of
uranium and fuel rods, arson, a bomb hoax, the explosion of two
terrorist bombs at a reactor under construction in France, and a threat to
crash a hijacked plane into the Oak Ridge reactor.[38]

Of similar concern is the failure to keep complete track of where all
the plutonium and enriched uranium is. It has been charged that
thousands of pounds of the stuff already have been more or less lost in
the shuffle, though no one can say that it necessarily represents a danger
or has been garnered by evil hands.[39] (In the industry, any inventory
discrepancy is called an "MUF," which stands for "material unac-
counted for.")

Various lax safeguard procedures have been the subject of critical reports. The General Accounting Office has scored the Army and Navy for loose protection of nuclear weapons transported on highways, making them vulnerable to terrorist activity.[40] An internal memo by an NRC official expressed concern over the adequacy of safeguards at licensed facilities.[41] Another GAO study pointed to "weaknesses" in the NRC program to control those who use radioactive materials, such as universities, hospitals, and industries.[42]

Finally, but not least, the application of extreme vigilance and tight security measures raises the specter of infringement on civil liberties. The issue is far from academic. In the pessimistic view, the goals of adequate nuclear protection and adherence to democratic principles are incompatible. Already we have had hints of what could be in store. For example, at the time of the mysterious Karen Silkwood case, the Oil Chemical and Atomic Workers Union filed a still unresolved complaint with the National Labor Relations Board charging that Kerr-McGee Corp. asked employes to take lie-detector tests that included questions about contacts with reporters and union officials.[43] In 1974, the Texas Department of Public Safety was found to have created a "subversive" file on an airline pilot because he was active in opposition to a proposed nuclear power plant.[44]

Any government would have to use "every means possible" to locate a nuclear terrorism threat, suggests L. Douglas DeNike, a clinical psychologist and antinuclear operative for the Sierra Club. "This would include brutal interrogations and searches based on the scantiest information." Yet even the tightest domestic controls would not eliminate the possibility of nuclear smuggling from abroad, he adds.[45]

Congressman George E. Brown, Jr., of California has offered this general warning:

> A nuclear energy system meshes, most naturally, with a tightly organized, centralized industrial and political system, with all the potential for coercive and authoritarian tendencies which these systems have historically demonstrated. Adding all the necessary nuclear safeguard and security "solutions" together does not present a picture of the kind of peaceful, stable, and democratic world that I and, I think, most others would like to see.[46]

Administration and Enforcement

There is another important dimension of doubt. Both safeguards and waste-management measures must be tightly *administered and enforced.* This requires that highly capable technicians and managers be available, and that a highly effective regulatory agency be in operation. The Kemeny Commission report on Three Mile Island cast doubt on both these propositions.[47]

Much is made of the fact that the NRC is an *independent* agency, having been spun off, along with parts of ERDA, from the old Atomic Energy Commission in January 1975. (The AEC unhappily had difficulty separating its conflicting roles of regulating nuclear development and fostering it.)

But that move, salutary as it was, still only leaves the NRC in roughly the same position vis-a-vis the nuclear industry as other regulatory commissions are vis-a-vis the industries they are in charge of. So even if one concludes that the NRC can be a reliable, independent, adversary watchdog, can one be confident that it will remain so indefinitely? That it somehow will be able miraculously to stay at arm's length from the industry it regulates—thereby flying in the face of all the lessons of political science that have been spread on the record for decades?

Whatever one's appraisal of the NRC, domestic regulation seems far better than that at the international level. It is most disheartening to realize that, even if the United States were to solve the many dilemmas in the nuclear fuel cycle, other countries around the world might be unwilling or unable to do so. This makes it even more discouraging to contemplate the fact that prospects for halting international nuclear proliferation seem so dismal.

One need only consider the forces at work: *Exporting countries* avidly seek the trade advantages and hefty profits from nuclear materials and facilities. The competition is fearsome and puts in mind the military arms merchants.[48] In some cases, of course, there may be a more altruistic desire to improve productivity and living standards in poorer nations. (The U.S. Atoms for Peace program is an example.)

Importing countries may seek to improve their energy base. Many of them shopped quickly for nuclear plants when confronted with the 1973 oil embargo and climbing oil prices. Or they may buy for prestige purposes. Lincoln P. Bloomfield, a professor of political science at MIT and a former State Department planner, believes that the main thrusts behind proliferation are the desires for prestige and influence, plus national resentment over the fact that the Nuclear Nonproliferation Treaty of 1970 and other antiproliferation efforts discriminate against countries that don't yet have nuclear weapons.[49]

Paul L. Leventhal, a staff member of the Senate Government Operations Committee, has written of the "sure knowledge that even energy-rich nations like Iran and Saudi Arabia are only too ready to pay the price for the stuff that international dreams are made of: ultimate power. . . . Plutonium has become the world's most valuable and coveted substance."[50]

Importing nations may seek to acquire a military capability to keep up with their neighbors or adversaries, as in the case of Pakistan.[51] This

results in what a former head of the U.S. Arms Control and Disarma-
ment Agency called "the iron law of proliferation."[52]

So, if one assumes widespread proliferation,[53] what are the chances of
achieving effective regulation? If a country like the United States—
technologically advanced, resourceful, with a relatively open decision-
making process, and with vast uninhabited spaces in the West—is hard
put to develop adequate safety, safeguards, and waste management
techniques, one can assume that controls in other countries might be
more elusive, primitive, or unenforced. Certainly internal regulation
will vary greatly in quality and effectiveness.

Then there is the umbrella control of the International Atomic
Energy Agency (IAEA), headquartered in Vienna. The United Nations-
affiliated IAEA has some capability to detect what's going on and to
issue warnings. But it unfortunately is rather impotent, a policeman
armed only with little more than a whistle. (Its weaknesses are illumi-
natingly described in a General Accounting Office study[54] and other
appraisals.) The IAEA also seems unlikely to be provided any truly
effective authority, given the chauvinistic—and secretive—atmosphere
of international trade and diplomacy.

Other Institutional Problems

Still other institutional problems affect the way safeguards and waste
management problems are handled. For one thing, the economic forces
are powerful. They involve not only the companies and unions that
manufacture equipment and build plants, but banks, electric utility
companies, and other interests.

A legal brief filed for seven environmental groups says:

> Investments of time, money, and reputation in a technology such as
> plutonium recycle inevitably shift the balance in favor of its ultimate
> application, diminish the opportunity for consideration of environmen-
> tal factors—including preferable alternatives—and thereby frustrate the
> underlying policies of the National Environmental Policy Act.[55]

Government energy spokesmen have made the same point, though
with an unseemly protectionist slant: "Transitions to new systems must
occur without major disruption of existing systems. Existing investment must be paid for and represent an inertial force on the system."[56]

Also, as Commoner and others have indicated, neither solar energy
development, with its localized applications, nor energy conservation,
lend themselves easily to control or profit by existing large energy
companies.[57]

Economic forces can influence the effectiveness of safeguards and
waste management. Harvard's George Wald cites a statement by retired
Rear Admiral Ralph Weymouth about greater safety precautions taken

by the Navy at its nuclear installations than by the nuclear industry. "The point is simple enough," says Wald. "The Navy operates without regard to profit, whereas the industry bends all its efforts to maximize profit, and regularly cuts corners to achieve that end."[58]

David Salisbury, science editor of the *Christian Science Monitor*, says, "Nuclear facilities around the country have adopted tighter security only when ordered to by government regulators."[59]

Is it possible, then, to produce nuclear power safely? Wald replies:

> That is a technical question, and the answer to it may well be *yes*. But that is the wrong way to ask the question. The real question we face is whether nuclear power can be produced safely *while maximizing profit*. The answer to that question is *no*.[60]

A final, but most important institutional problem is providing for reasonable full public understanding and involvement in the great nuclear debate. This means access to adequate, reliable information, as well as a choice and a voice at the points of decision. The nuclear establishment has a long history of stifling reports that it disagrees with and keeping the public in the dark. If the situation has improved recently under citizen pressure, the problem remains ever-present.

II. COAL AND AIR POLLUTION

When utilities switch to coal as a major alternative to the skyrocketing costs of both nuclear plant construction and oil, the future of coal becomes entangled in the costs to public health of sulfur dioxide pollution in the air.

To what extent is a sharp increase in coal combustion likely to undermine the government's long and laborious struggle to keep sulfur dioxide and its derivatives out of the air—and out of the lungs? The Carter Administration has tried to keep the expanded use of coal from taking place at the expense of national ambient air quality standards, which are set at levels designed to protect the public's health. Congress is generally in agreement with that proviso. But there is considerable skepticism that the Administration's coal production forecast of about 1,752 million tons by 1995—almost triple the present level of about 665 million tons—could be met at all, much less in tandem with air quality requirements. Among the problems cited are productivity and mine-safety problems, decrepit railroad transport systems, volatile labor conditions, and economic and legislative uncertainties.[61]

The combustion of coal releases a devilish assortment of pollutants. Most notable are sulfur dioxide and particulates. Also emitted are nitrogen oxides, toxic trace elements (such as mercury, lead, arsenic, and zinc), and radioactivity. The long-term health and environmental effects of most of these pollutants are not well defined. Many also are not regulated and are not susceptible to control even with the best technology.

For a long time, studies have shown that sulfur dioxides from power plants and other sources, in combination with particulates, are the most villainous of pollutants, responsible for increased incidence of bronchitis, emphysema, upper and lower respiratory tract diseases in children,

ELECTRIC PLANT SULFUR DIOXIDE EMISSIONS

Each dot on the map represents 50,000 tons of sulfur dioxide emitted each year by electric power plants (based on 1971 data). Obviously, their locations correlate with heavy concentrations of population. The effects of generally prevailing eastward winds also can be gauged.

and death rates above normal. Scientists have shown that the tiny by-products of sulfur dioxide (SO_2)—the fine sulfate particles and mists of sulfurous and sulfuric acid that form when SO_2 combines with water or with water and oxygen in the atmosphere—are the most damaging.[62]

The chemical transformations take place when the sulfur dioxide remains airborne for days. The sulfates and acid aerosols float easily, and more deeply, into human lungs. They also travel far, settling to earth either dry or as "acid rain," which may be causing serious damage to crops, timber, fish, and materials in the Northeast, Scandinavia, and elsewhere.

Dollar estimates of damage, generally thought to be conservative, are large.[63] One study for the Environmental Protection Agency estimates total damage in 40 metropolitan areas at $5.3 billion to $6 billion per year.[64]

It can be argued that neither money nor technology presents an insurmountable obstacle to a high degree of control over SO_2 emissions.

Effective desulfurization techniques are available, and the costs are by no means exorbitant. However, it is widely agreed that SO_2-related pollution will increase anyway simply because more coal-fired plants will be built to meet energy demands, and also because many plants will violate or avoid air-quality regulations.

Considering the history of noncompliance, the General Accounting Office has concluded that "it is unlikely that all coal-burning installations will adhere to the air quality regulations. . . . Hence, the increase in air emissions from many more planned coal-burning facilities could be highly significant, from a health point of view."[65]

Senator Edmund Muskie of Maine says that "even if the most moderate growth rate is projected (4.8%) and even if the states are most aggressive in the application of technological requirements (as spelled out in legislation), there will still be an increase (by the year 1990) of 2.8 million tons per year of sulfur oxides to the atmosphere nationally."[66] (This would be an 8 percent rise over the 34.3 million tons emitted in 1975.)

It's hard to imagine what sort of increase might result from lax enforcement, which is the norm. At present, the SO_2 ambient standard is being violated in a number of densely populated areas, despite an original compliance deadline of mid-1975. And the Environmental Protection Agency is faced with continued adamant opposition to regulation by major segments of industry.

Although many industries burn coal in their boilers, this discussion will focus on the electric utilities. They probably contribute more than two-thirds of the total national SO_2 load, and their share is rising.[67] They also emit large quantities of suspended particulates. The National Coal Association estimates that utilities in 1977 consumed 480 million tons of coal—75 percent of total domestic consumption and an increase of 7.7 percent over 1976.[68]

Some power plants are being pushed by the government to shift from oil or gas to coal. More significantly, the utility industry, in planning new generating units, is making coal a heavy favorite, principally because of its attractive cost and the shrinking supplies of oil and gas. It is estimated that coal-fired capacity will reach 434,000 megawatts by 1990 (almost double what it was in 1977).[69]

Whatever the extent of coal combustion in the future, it is clear that a heavy burden will be placed on the political and regulatory systems for controlling SO_2 and particulates. If the past is any prologue, the systems will be hard-pressed to reduce the pollution load to a level that safeguards health everywhere.

The Clean Air Act provided for the establishment of a federal ambient SO_2 standard and for the adoption of State Implementation Plans which are supposed to limit emissions from particular sources to whatever extent is necessary to meet the ambient standard. Consider the effects of laggard implementation and enforcement, as of 1977:

Out of 394 coal-fired power plants, some 227 were not in compliance with state plans. This included 56 plants on a schedule to meet requirements.[70] In 1976, an estimated 43 percent of all coal delivered to utilities did not conform to the receiving plants' requirements under State Implementation Plans.[71] (The effects were mitigated to some extent by precombustion blending with lower-sulfur coal and by the use of desulfurization equipment. Also, excessive emissions do not necessarily violate regulations, since some plants operate under approved variances. On the other hand, coal varies greatly in sulfur content, even coal from the same mine, so many plants presumably exceed 24-hour emission limitations more than the limit of once a year.)

Techniques for Reducing Emissions

These techniques are available for reducing SO_2 emissions:

• Simply burn less coal by dampening the demand for electricity or increasing the efficiency of boilers.

• Burn coal with a low sulfur content.

• Wash sulfur from the coal before combustion.

• Build tall smokestacks so the SO_2 is dispersed.

• Use "intermittent" controls, such as reducing combustion or shifting to nonpolluting fuels, when weather conditions foster severe pollution and dictate such measures.

• Use flue-gas desulfurization (FGD) or "scrubbers" to remove SO_2 after combustion.

Other technologies—principally fluidized-bed combustion, coal gasification, and coal liquefaction—have considerable desulfurization potential. But by general agreement they will not be practicable for quite a few years.

As might be expected, all currently available techniques present problems. In many places, including most of the East, low-sulfur coal is hard to get or expensive. Transportation costs from the West—where the most abundant seams of low-sulfur coal lie (and where the need to strip-mine adds a further environmental drawback)—are high.

Physical cleaning of coal can be effective despite an inherent limitation: It removes the pyritic sulfur but not the chemically bound, organic variety, which must be removed by far more expensive chemical cleaning processes.[72] But Frank T. Princiotta, director of EPA's Energy Processes Division, says that coal cleaning has

not received adequate attention. FGD and coal cleaning, singly or in combination must be vigorously and imaginatively applied over the next 10 to 20 years if we are to harmoniously achieve two of the country's major goals: adequate energy supplies at reasonable cost and environmental protection.[73]

Tall stacks and intermittent control systems have been highly popular with industry because they cost virtually nothing compared to other techniques and present virtually no operational problems. However, as EPA has relentlessly pointed out, they do not solve the emissions problem in a consistent way, and they disperse many of the pollutants to other areas, increasing the opportunities for sulfates to form, Richard E. Ayres, of the Natural Resources Defense Council, also has argued that dispersion techniques are "neither reliable nor enforceable."[74]

EPA has had the support of several court decisions for its position,[75] and Congress may have settled the controversial issue at last by legislating against "atmospheric loading through dispersion technology" as a means of meeting the emission limitations in a State Implementation Plan. In 1977 amendments to the Clean Air Act, Congress made clear that "continuous" emission reduction is required, and it disallowed any credit for pollutant reductions achieved with tall stacks.[76]

A still greater controversy has swirled around requirements that utilities install scrubbers to keep SO_2 out of the air. In June 1979, EPA issued final New Source Performance Standards for coal-burning electric generating plants[77], and EPA chief Douglas M. Costle says they will make new plants about seven times as clean as existing ones. He also asserts that, despite greatly increased burning of coal, total SO_2 emissions from power plants will increase only 5 percent by 1990.[78] Whatever the results, SO_2 and sulfate levels will climb higher in some areas of the country then they would have under earlier, more stringent standards.

The new standards require that SO_2 pollution of the atmosphere be limited to 1.2 pounds per million Btu's of heat input, and that a 90 percent reduction in potential emissions be achieved at all times unless emissions would be less than 0.6 pounds per million Btu's. In the latter case, a 70 percent reduction is required. The general effect of this will be to require 90 percent control of coals with higher sulfur content and at least 70 percent control from even the lowest sulfur content coals.

EPA figures that, while the conventional and more expensive "wet" scrubbers will be needed for high-sulfur coal, newer and less complex "dry" scrubbers will be adequate to meet the 70 percent requirements for low-sulfur coal, and perhaps exceed them.[79]

Generally speaking, scrubbers are expensive—though far from prohibitively so—as well as technologically complex and, one might say, unpredictable. "Their performance," says George Erskine, of the Mitre Corporation, "is highly specific to the site, and the type of coal, and the color of the overalls of the guy who's running the boiler." But he adds that operational problems—which include mechanical breakdowns, clogging, corrosion, and scaling—have been ironed out as utilities and manufacturers have gained more experience. (For example, the Kansas City Power & Light Co., after years of difficult effort, said it finally overcame performance hang-ups at its La Cygne plant.[80])

Scrubbers are basically chemical systems, notes Erskine, and therefore quite alien to the mechanics, pipefitters, and others who usually deal with the engineering problems in a power plant. The Louisville Gas & Electric Co. began a commitment to scrubbers years ago and took on a chemical engineer, Robert Van Ness, to develop the program. The company's Paddy's Run plant went into successful operation in 1973, and in 1977 its Cane Run No. 4 plant passed scrubber performance tests.

Princiotta says that "most problems initially encountered . . . have essentially been overcome." He argues that successful performance of scrubbers has been achieved for both high- and low-sulfur coals and for both retrofit and new plants.[81]

Although most of the emphasis has been on lime and limestone scrubbers, a 1977 Federal Power Commission (FPC) study lists no less then seven processes "currently in full-scale commercial use by utility companies."[82]

There have been a number of failures, to be sure.[83] In most such cases, says Samuel J. Biondo, senior fuel and environmental analyst with the FPC and director of the 1977 study, scrubbers didn't work because "not enough money was spent on them, or they didn't put in the kinds of operation and maintenance efforts that are required."

In addition to high construction and maintenance costs, scrubbers use up 4-8 percent or so of a plant's energy. Industry opponents have called the costs exorbitant and unnecessary but studies by EPA, the FPC, and others provide a different perspective at the bottom line.[84] For example, EPA predicts that the new power plant performance standards for SO_2 will increase monthly residential electricity bills in 1995 by a maximum of 3 percent for full control—corresponding to $1.60 per month.[85]

The major environmental drawback of "wet" scrubbers (but not so much "dry" scrubbers) is the large quantity of sludge they leave. This fact, too, has been seized upon by many utilities as a reason to avoid scrubbers. Land for sludge disposal may be scarce. And there is a potential for toxic chemicals to leach into ground-water supplies.

However, various techniques are available or being developed for reducing the volume of sludge, decreasing its capability to pollute, and increasing its strength. These should substantially lower handling costs and land requirements, and should increase the value of the sludge as landfill material. The methods include several types of chemical fixation and dewatering.[86]

Still more promising is a second generation of scrubbers, called "regenerable," that produce byproducts such as sulfur and sulfuric acid which can be sold.[87] Despite claims to the contrary, Biondo's FPC study indicates that several regenerable scrubber processes are commercially available.

To Scrub or Not to Scrub

In choosing a technique to deal with the SO_2 problem, each utility is faced with a different mix of circumstances at each plant site. These involve the characteristics of the coal available, the size of the plant and its age, the capability for dealing with sludge disposal, and the stringency of control regulations.

Louisville Gas & Electric long ago embraced scrubber technology largely because it had a long-term contract to purchase inexpensive but high-sulfur coal. Conversely, a company may have fought hard to rely on low-sulfur coal for several reasons. High fuel costs can be passed on directly to consumers under fuel adjustment clauses permitted in most states. Thus, the major incentive to economize in coal purchases is removed. (A survey said that in 1976, utility consumers paid $12.7 billion more for electric and gas service than in 1975, and that three-fourths of the increase resulted from fuel adjustment clauses—which also can be abused.[88])

By contrast, the large capital investment in a scrubber often must be allowed into a rate base to bring a full financial return, and this can require a lengthy regulatory process.

Many utilities also own "captive" coal companies and coal reserves. In 1975, 11.2 percent of the coal delivered to utilities was captive, and it has been estimated that the share will grow to 18.8 percent by 1985.[89] Without adequate regulatory control, a utility can overprice the coal it delivers to itself and derive the excess profits at the expense of its customers.

The utility companies that have opposed scrubbers—spearheaded by such giants as the American Electric Power Co. (AEP) and the Tennessee Valley Authority—have been hard-nosed and defiant. Industry opposition to scrubbers has taken many forms. Perhaps the most publicly visible was the $3.5 million advertising blitz against them launched in 1974 by AEP and its board chairman, Donald C. Cook.[90]

On the other side, EPA has been very obstinate in its insistence on use of the technology, sometimes even exaggerating claims of scrubber effectiveness. The industry-government clash has weakened the enforcement process. In many areas it has been encumbered by relaxation of regulations, interim permission for alternative control measures, variances, compliance date extensions, and lawsuits.

Some companies no doubt have had genuine concerns over the technology's feasibility, costs, and operational problems. Some probably had a gut resistance to any government intrusion into their affairs. Some may have figured it's cheaper to pay a few lawyers to hamstring and delay, to see if the regulatory wind will blow the other way, or to wait for someone else to perfect the technology.

EPA's Princiotta has made some comparisons between the United States and Japan, which has a number of successful scrubbers (ironically including one, operating since early 1972, which was built using U.S. technology).

> I visited Japan twice, and the utilities there are not crazy about scrubbers either. But the regulations are often more severe, and they are going ahead with it essentially. Reliability is not at all an issue there. The level of technological capability of the U.S. utility industry is quite a bit lower. But the attitudinal differences are greater than the technological differences. In Japan, the law is the law, and they do what has to be done. It's a different mentality. Here, the attitude is, "If it doesn't make sense, to hell with the law."

EPA has fought its battle for scrubbers virtually alone. In prior years, other federal agencies frequently supported the EPA position. (In 1974, former EPA head Russell E. Train publicly chastised John N. Nassikas, then chairman of the Federal Power Commission, because an FPC expert witness went to a state hearing in Kentucky and questioned the reliability of scrubbers.)

But EPA was armed with the Clean Air Act, and the Supreme Court eventually agreed that the law's "technology-forcing" provisions were "expressly designed to force regulated sources to develop pollution control devices that might at the time appear to be economically or technologically infeasible."[91] And the 1977 amendments to the Clean Air Act added some teeth in the form of civil fines for violations and penalties for delayed compliance.

To what extent existing law and regulations will be implemented or enforced is anyone's guess. "These provisions," said Senator Muskie, "seek to put an end to the first round of efforts to circumvent emission control requirements."[92]

Chapter 9

ENERGY ANALYSIS

It's a matter of substituting brains for the
brute force use of energy.

—Clark W. Bullard

For a long time, the chief criteria for decision making in our society have
been economic—values defined in dollars, cost-price mechanisms, profits. But now another measure of value has taken on critical importance:
energy.

We are accustomed to asking: How much will it cost, and how great
will the profit be? Now there are other relevant questions: How much
energy does it use, and how much energy will be saved or returned?
What kind of energy? And with what impacts?

Speaking of nuclear power projects, W. Kenneth Davis, a vice president of Bechtel Power Corp., has said there is "an energy investment just
as there is a financial investment and there is a necessity to show an
energy profit."[1]

A rather specialized methodology has emerged for measuring and
understanding the energy flows in a given project, process, or product.
It is *energy analysis*. It is used, for example, to calculate the energy
inputs and outputs, or the "net energy" derived in a system. It has been
called energy accounting, energy cost evaluation, net energy analysis,
and other labels. (An international group of pioneers in the field has
agreed to stick to the term energy analysis.)

Energy analysis is not viewed as a substitute for economic analysis,
but as a complement to it. In some respects, to be sure, energy and
economic costs are inseparably fused. Rising energy costs have been
permeating the system, generating higher economic costs and inflation.
This is one reason why many companies have balked at going ahead
with grandiose energy projects they planned—oil shale development,
coal gasification, nuclear power plant construction, and the like. And
why some pollution control projects are in trouble as well.

215

How did we drift into our present energy dilemma? In large part because we took for granted an endless supply of cheap fossil fuel energy. As Howard T. Odum, a professor of environmental engineering at the University of Florida, has noted: "Only the last two centuries have seen a burst of temporary growth made possible by the one-time use of special energy supplies that accumulated over long periods of geological time."[2]

These bountiful energy supplies offered a means to boost labor productivity and profitability. So industries were seduced into squandering energy and shifting to capital- and energy-intensive processes at the expense of labor. The United States' highly mechanized agriculture is a conspicuous example. (It has been estimated that the agriculture industry consumes more than five times the energy content of the food it produces.[3])

So we have locked ourselves into an economy heavily dependent on intensive use of energy, and we can expect to have considerable trouble making necessary adjustments.

To understand how energy analysis can aid public and private decision making in these days of energy constriction and rocketing costs, it is important to examine some basic facts about energy. In the first place, an energy transaction can seldom be measured with the same neat precision as an economic transaction expressed in dollars. There are different kinds of energy, different sources, different uses, and different ways of measuring.

For one thing, we have energy stored in structural states—in the chemical structure of a lump of coal, in the cellulose of a piece of wood, in the hydrogen atom, in the water in a reservoir. And we also have energy in kinetic states—such as electricity, heat, and motion.

Energy is constantly being transformed from structural to kinetic states (coal changed into electricity) or vice versa (sunlight embodied in a plant). So energy in a system can be tracked in the form of materials as well as pure energy forms.

Under the First Law of Thermodynamics, the law of conservation, the total amount of energy is constant. But its forms change, and there are differences in the amount of work and types of work that can be done by various forms. Oil is a highly valued energy source. You can run cars on it. Natural gas is even more desirable. It can be easily piped back and forth and can be used for many purposes, including electricity generation, home heating, and industrial processes. Electricity can run computers.

So there are major differences in the value per Btu of energy forms. And, under the Second Law of Thermodynamics, the law of entropy, there will always be, in any energy transaction or transformation, a net overall loss in the *quality* of the energy (even though part of the output, such as electricity generated from coal, may be a higher quality). Entropy can be defined as an increase in the inability to do work.

There is zero entropy in gravitation. But terrestrial waste heat has lost almost all its ability to do work. As changes occur in the universe, energy continually slides down the scale, and entropy increases.[4]

Assessments

The most frequent and well-known use of energy analysis is to calculate the total energy cost of producing and operating something, and then compare it with alternatives. This has been done in analyses of manufacturing,[5] agriculture,[6] transportation[7] and energy production itself,[8] as well as in studies of materials,[9] appliances,[10] bottles (returnable vs. throw-away[11]) and other products.[12]

"In general, a more efficient device will cost more energy to produce," says Milton D. Rubin, of the Raytheon Co. "However, usually it will be found that the extra energy necessary to produce the more efficient device will be paid for very rapidly in the operating savings."[13]

The air conditioner provides a theoretical example: To double the energy efficiency, it would perhaps be necessary to double the weight and thus the energy needed for manufacture; but the extra energy cost might be saved by six months of operation. (The monetary cost could be another matter.) But in the case of the automobile, as Rubin points out, a smaller, lighter car will not only consume less energy in operation, but require much less to manufacture. (And cost less as well.)

Energy analysis has often been used to quantify in energy units the value of natural systems—for example, the calories of sunlight that fall on an area, or that are captured by plants through photosynthesis. But analysts must beware of gross calculations of energy that is not really available or usable, and there is some disagreement among them over methodology. Dwain Winters, a program analyst with the Environmental Protection Agency (EPA), explained in an interview a widely accepted technique, using solar energy and wind as examples:

> Although nature provides us with vast quantities of solar energy every day, this does not necessarily make it an abundant energy source. For this energy to serve the needs of a technological society, it must be subject to concentration and storage. Therefore, the measure of solar energy's availability lies in the relationship between the energy cost of the equipment used to concentrate and store the energy and the gross energy output of that equipment.

He added that analysis now in progress suggests that a significant amount of net solar energy probably will be available. And he continued:

For people who dry clothes on a line, the wind is an important source of energy. You could figure out the total kinetic energy of the wind. But that would not be its energy value to society. What we need to know is its energy opportunity cost. That is the amount of energy that would be needed to do the same work by a substitute method, such as a clothes dryer. So the value of the wind is not fixed, but varies with the energy cost of the technology that is used to replace the wind's function.

The methodology applies equally well to any energy sources.

It has been noted that different energies have different values. One indication of value is the kind and amount of work the energy can do. Another is its relative availability—how abundant is the energy, how easy to extract, and how close to the place where it is needed. Amory B. Lovins, a physicist with Friends of the Earth, has noted that, for an energy technology to be appropriate, it should be "matched in *scale* and in geographic distribution to end-use needs"; and it should use the type or quality of energy best suited to end use. Decrying the use of electricity for space heating, for example, Lovins says that "electricity can do more difficult kinds of work than can the original fuel [used to generate it], but unless this extra quality and versatility are used to advantage, the costly process of upgrading the fuel—and losing two-thirds of it—is all for naught."[14]

This points to one of the problems which must be considered in an energy analysis—the "mixed fuels problem." Said Winters:

> If we take 1,000 Btu's of natural gas and compare it with 1,000 Btu's of oil or coal, we can see that they are not of equal value to society. They are not interchangeable in their work tasks, nor does their use create equal environmental or social costs. In some cases, adding different energy species together raises serious questions about what the results really mean.

The search for higher quality energy can lead to perfectly rational decisions to accept a very small net energy gain or even "negative net energy." For an example, Winters took an imaginary energy analysis of oil shale:

> Suppose it showed oil shale to be a negative net producer. Ignoring for the moment the environmental and economic aspects, we still might want to go ahead with oil shale production if society places a high enough value on the resulting liquid hydrocarbon fuel.
>
> In such a case, oil shale might be particularly attractive if it could be subsidized by an abundant energy source such as coal, and if it represented a more efficient way to convert coal to synthetic oil than direct coal liquification.

It should be remembered, however, that while it may be practical to have a significant net energy loser in an energy system, the system as a whole must deliver a high net yield.

There can be reasons other than energy quality to accept less net energy. As noted by Lovins, one is geographic. Society may justify a heavy expenditure of energy to extract and transport fuel to a distant city where it is most needed. Another consideration is time. Society could condone a net energy loss to gain time to develop a promising new source. Thus, the United States can be viewed as encouraging nuclear power in the hope that it will tide us over until fusion, solar energy, or some other technology is readily available.

Energy for Energy

Much energy analysis, in fact, is focused on the costs of obtaining energy itself. One study concluded that in the United Kingdom, five energy industries (coal mining, oil refining, coke, gas, and electricity generation) jointly consume more than 30 percent of the UK's total energy input.[15]

Of course, the problem is exacerbated in the U.S. as reserves such as oil and gas become increasingly unyielding and costly to extract and as more primary fuels are converted to secondary energy sources (gasification of coal, for example). "Many proposed alternative energy sources would take even more energy feedback than is required in present processes," says Howard Odum.[16]

Winters pointed out that if we are planning on shifting to a solar or nuclear economy:

[W]e need to know to what extent such an economy is self-sustaining and where it is dependent on fossil fuels. If we're going to make these transitions, we want to make sure we've made the appropriate use of our fossil fuels to get us from here to there.

Winters noted that during the planning and construction of any energy production facility, the project is borrowing energy from society:

When the plant begins operation, it starts paying back this debt. If the plant is a net energy producer, eventually it will pay back this debt and then contribute a net energy gain to society until the plant wears out. For any energy process, there is this period during which it is a new energy sink. Just how long the period lasts should be of considerable interest.

The length should be of particular interest with regard to nuclear power technologies. For even if a nuclear plant should turn out to be a substantial net energy gainer, it could still create a net energy problem. If nuclear plants are built in too rapid succession, there might be temporary energy shortfalls because of the immediate demand for energy to build the plants.

A workshop of the International Federation of Institutes for Advanced Study (IFIAS) offers this example (with the figures picked for illustrative purposes):

Consider a country embarked on a program of nuclear reactors. Suppose such reactors to have a 30-year life, and to have a capital energy require-

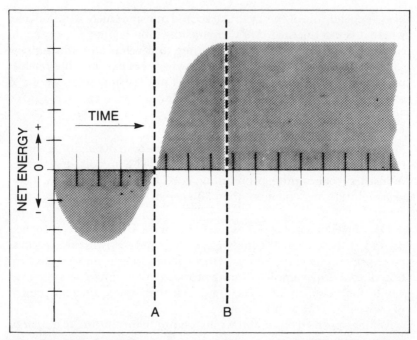

From the start of planning to the completion of construction (at line A), an energy production plant takes a certain amount of energy from society. At some point after the plant has begun operation, it will have paid back an amount equal to what it borrowed. That point is at line B. Thereafter, the net energy gain to society depends on how long the plant is kept in operation.

ment to build them equal to 10% of the total energy production in their life; that it takes six years to build a reactor, and one new reactor is started each year. . . . For many years the country will incur a net energy deficit (11 years), and 20 years will elapse before the cumulative energy production exceeds the cumulative energy investment.[17]

Two parallel debates over nuclear power have been waged—one over its energy efficiency and one over its cost efficiency. Davis, of Bechtel Power, estimates that all the energy invested in a nuclear plant is repaid after 2.3 months of full power operation.[18] Similarly, many utility executives have touted nukes as great cost savers over coal-fired plants.

Nuclear critics, on the other hand, charge that industry calculations are carefully tailored, and don't include all the money and energy costs (or subsidies) associated with mining uranium ore, enriching nuclear fuel, reprocessing, research and development, insurance, safety, plant decommissioning, and long-term waste disposal and safeguarding.

"When all energy inputs are considered," says energy consultant E.J. Hoffman, "the net electrical yield from fission is very low."[19]

Much of the difference between the various estimates lies in what the analysts include in their accounting and what they leave out. In other words, where they draw their system boundaries. And that is a critical decision in any energy analysis. "If you let me draw the system boundaries wherever I want, I can make almost any project look good or bad," said Winters. "That's the nature of the game."

He noted that the boundary is determined in part by the question you're trying to ask:

> You may be interested only in the energy you're borrowing from society as opposed to the amount you're returning. You may be interested in the rate at which you're depleting a resource. . . . In that case, what you do is put the resource that's in the ground within the system boundary of society.

Or, in accounting for the energy cost of an automobile, do you include the gas an assembly line worker uses getting to the job? The energy used to make *his* automobile? The gas used by those who made it? Perhaps the most important thing an analyst can do is make very clear what his boundaries are.

Achievement of Goals

Energy analysis can help identify the most fruitful conservation strategies. It can compare the savings from home insulation with the energy costs of making and installing the insulation. It can pinpoint ways to reduce the energy intensiveness of a manufacturing process and thereby lower the energy input per unit.

Winters commented that an overall conservation strategy is suggested by the fact that some 70 percent of all energy used by a final consumer is in the form of goods and services, rather than species of energy such as electricity and gasoline.

> So if we really want to cut down our consumption, there's probably more room to attack that sector than there is in how much gasoline we use or how much we heat our houses. What this implies is somehow changing the product mix.

Such as shifting to returnable bottles or smaller cars.

Energy analysis, says the IFIAS workshop report, is a means of identifying the constraints of a system:

> For example, by means of thermodynamic calculations one may establish the theoretical energy requirements for a process, and compare them with those of present technology. This gives one a feel for the extent to which a given technology could be developed—a limit not identifiable by economic methods.[20]

Energy analysts certainly don't see their techniques as a replacement for economics—though the limitations and failures in trying to apply economic analysis and operate a market economy have been all too obvious. (One thinks of the widespread anticompetitive practices and arrangements, including OPEC; the natural monopolies like public utilities; the government regulation induced by varied corporate abuses; the distorted flow of information; the failures to account for external effects such as pollution; and the many subsidies provided by taxpayers. The effects include social inequities, environmental degradation, resource scarcities, recession, and inflation.)

Winters suggested that an economic analysis can be made of an individual technology—or a mix of technologies—to check feasibility, and this can be followed by an energy analysis to ascertain efficiency.

The IFIAS group is particularly interested in the use of energy analysis to understand price changes and other factors in the economic system. It can be a "means of injecting physical variables into economic theory," the workshop report said. "It can be a more sensitive indicator than money."[21]

Winters saw at least five "gates" through which a decision-making process must pass to show that a project will work—political, economic, cultural, environmental, and energetic:

> The two primary parameters that are currently being used are what is politically feasible and what is economically feasible. They don't always overlap. These are the two areas in which most of the arguments over weeding out the various energy alternatives take place.

But the constraints of the other three gates must be satisfied in order to conform to human behavior, to maintain the stability of the environment, and to be thermodynamically, or physically, possible.

There is reason to believe that the energy gate is one of the narrowest of all the gates for society's options to pass through. So if limited funds are available to evaluate options, it is logical to ascertain early what will fall through the energy gate.

Winters noted that perhaps environmental considerations should sometimes be grounds for rejecting energy options, but may not carry the necessary political clout. "Whereas, if one took those environmental objections, and at the same time noted that something is energetically impractical, one might be better able to implement environmental criteria."

These days, particularly, there is good reason to factor into energy analysis the effects of employment. Because, typically, reductions in energy use generate more jobs. John P. Holdren, assistant professor at the University of California, Berkeley, says that the energy producing industries themselves comprise the most capital-intensive and least labor-intensive major sector of the economy:

> Accordingly, each dollar of investment capital taken out of energy production and invested in something else, and each personal-consumption dollar saved by reducing energy use and spent elsewhere in the economy, will create more jobs than are lost.[22]

(Whether that dollar helps or hurts the energy situation would depend on where it's spent.)

Much valuable work in this area has been done by Bruce Hannon, of the Center for Advanced Computation, University of Illinois at Urbana-Champaign. One case study showed that returnable bottles demanded less energy *and* more labor than throwaways.[23]

But Hannon has gone much further. He has plotted on graphs the relationships in 363 industries between dollar value added, energy use and employment.[24]

One chart shows the tradeoffs in the economy as a whole resulting from a 10 percent growth in specific industries, if total GNP is held constant. For example, it indicates that growth in railroad-car manufacture would have an overall impact of increasing energy use by almost 4.5 trillion Btu's and decreasing employment by more than 2.5 million jobs. Toward the other end of the scale, a 10 percent growth in making wood furniture would lower energy demand by more than a trillion Btu's while increasing jobs by more than 2.5 million.

Such analyses suggest that it is possible to make intelligent plans to shift from enterprises that are negative in terms of energy consumption, environmental effects, and job formation, to enterprises that better serve society's needs.

In some cases, existing industries, by eliminating waste and altering products, could make desirable transitions. In most cases, perhaps, change would be extremely difficult. Ecologist Barry Commoner has long stressed the need for shifting away from products—such as plastics—that involve heavy pollution and energy consumption. But he notes that with some industries, such as the petrochemical makers, "the intensive use of energy is built into the very design of the enterprise in order to eliminate human labor."[25]

Even if a large net gain in employment is indicated, the type of labor or its location could be radically different and pose an additional dilemma. Of the shift to returnable bottles, Hannon says: "Jobs would be lost in the highly organized, high-wage can makers' plants and gained in the low-wage, relatively non-organized retail sector." Thus the opposition to the plan by organized labor.[26]

"That's something that labor will have to deal with," says Nick Apostola, of Environmentalists For Full Employment (EFFE). He suggests that labor "seize the opportunity to boost up those low-level jobs so they'll be higher paid." In a policy statement, EFFE said:

> Modern technologies that are excessively capital intensive and energy wasteful simultaneously destroy the environment, deplete resources, and cause structural unemployment. These problems must be attacked concurrently and such technologies must be rejected.

Feedback and Diversity

One of the more interesting questions raised by net energy analysis is what are the cybernetic (feedback control) properties of an energy system. If it takes energy to make energy, to what extent does this input influence the functioning of a system outside the control of economic forces?

In the past, such factors may have been minor, but in a period of resource scarcity, their influence could be dominant. To illustrate how we might better understand and manipulate to our advantage these cybernetic functions, Winters used a hypothetical ecosystem as an example (an ecosystem is a highly complex energy system that is governed by its energy cybernetics):

> You can think of any animal as an energy storage. Take, for example, a group of lions in a closed ecosystem. They are in a highly ordered state, tending to go toward disorder—an example of the law of entropy at work. And so they must have an energy source to maintain their order. Otherwise you have fewer lions, or emaciated lions.
>
> Suppose they pick zebras for an energy source. In order to utilize the zebra energy—since zebras don't just walk into the lions' mouth—the lions are going to have to expend some energy to run down the zebras. I used to be a zookeeper and have some appreciation for the task the lion has before him.
>
> If our lions are to survive, they must make sure they get more energy out of zebra hunting then they put in. Let's say they put two energy units in and get 10 out.
>
> A lion will be competing with some other carnivore in that ecosystem for an energy source. Maybe the leopard. And one factor that determines who will win the competition is who has the most efficient return on his investment. If another carnivore in competition with the lion could reinvest at a rate of one unit in for 10 out, then he would end up being the dominant species.
>
> In the ecosystem, no two animals occupy the same niche, competing for the same energy source. There's always at least a slight difference. And the relationship becomes very complex. Finding the niche with the best reinvestment ratio becomes a major key to species survival.
>
> It carries with it a risk, however, for if our lions should become solely dependent on zebras, then what happens when there is a zebra plague? The answer, of course, is that the lions eat something else. To be able to compete for other prey, however, means that the lions have had to maintain an ability to hunt for animals which did not yield a maximum return on their investment. And if we examine lion habits, we see that they have done exactly that.
>
> This makes the problem most interesting, for it implies that there is a force in addition to net energy efficiency directing lion evolution. This force is called diversity. Diversity, in the case of lions, is seen in their varied feeding habits. It enables them to survive environmental changes. So we see two antagonistic forces operating upon lions: one, hunting efficiency strengthening their chance for survival in the present and, two, diversity enhancing chances of survival in the future.

A given organism has to find a compromise between how much energy
it's going to tie up in reinvestment and how much in diversity. If it ties up
in reinvestment, it may become a dominant member of the ecosystem at
any given time, but may also end up the way of the dinosaur.

The application to man's technological system, I think, is direct. We
should choose energy systems which show a good net energy gain, but we
must balance this with a diversity of interchangeable technology which
will help protect us from the unforeseen problems that always interrupt
the best-laid plans of men and lions.

Winters pointed out that man, throughout history, has periodically
improved his reinvestment ratio. He learned to use rocks to break bones
and get the marrow. And there was agriculture, and fire, and so forth, up
through the stream of innovations in the Industrial Revolution. But
after each of the earlier energy crises and innovations, there appears to
have been a long plateau.

Where are we now? At one of the "wrinkles" of a major growth spurt
that will continue for a long time? Or are we at a broad plateau locked in
a situation where we exceed the total productive capacity of our energy
system?

Winters said that to maintain our growth rate in energy supply, the
technological innovations must be bigger and come in more quickly
than in the past. Energy analysis may tell us the theoretical upper limits
of available energy, but physical limits apparently are not the prime
constraint:

> If we look at today, we know we're not at our physical limits in terms of
> what we could do theoretically. It looks as if social and cultural limits
> always begin to impede the system before the technical limits are reached.
>
> The question may not at all be, Can we build a fast-breeder reactor? Or
> can we get nuclear fusion? It may well be, Can we construct social
> institutions which can maintain the dynamic stability of the cultural,
> political, and economic processes that are needed to maintain such a
> technology.

As a matter of fact, Winters suggested, the social structure we have
come to depend on—with its standard of living and complex, centralized system of organization—may itself demand a lot of energy to
maintain:

> There is an interesting paradox—and this is pure supposition and beyond
> the level of measurement. If we believe there is some relationship within a
> given system between the complexity of a social order and the energy base
> (and one culture may require more energy than another), then in order to
> get total cooperation at any larger level of complexity, a broader energy
> base is required. [An example would be the need to achieve affluence
> before people cooperate in population control.]
>
> If it takes affluence to induce cooperation, and you can only do this by
> increasing the energy base (a necessary but not sufficient cause for afflu-
> ence), then it would seem that the only way to increase the energy base is

through greater cooperation. So you've just got yourself in a self-stultifying situation.

Energy Use and the Economy

There is another important field of inquiry in energy analysis, and it turns on this question: To what extent is a high level of energy consumption indispensable to a healthy economy? The question can be put another way: Is extensive energy conservation compatible with economic growth or providing a reasonable standard of living?

A large accumulation of evidence and expert opinion now indicates that there is no tight or predetermined correlation between energy use and economic growth, and that a healthy economy can be maintained with a greatly reduced reliance on energy.

This heretical notion collides head-on with conventional thinking. It also runs contrary to the constant barrage of statements, from industry quarters and elsewhere, attacking environmentalists as antigrowth elitists.

Before turning to the evidence, consider a more careful definition of the issue and its significance. Thus, is it necessary to feed the economy x amount of energy input to produce y dollars of output in return? What is the energy/GNP ratio? What, as one economist puts it, is the "productivity of energy"?[27] Or, in the words of another, the "feedback from constraints on the growth of energy use to the growth of GNP"?[28]

The enormous importance to society of this question is fairly obvious. If the United States can, in fact, develop a strong economy fueled by less energy, this would help alleviate problems of pollution, safety, national security, balance of payments, and high prices associated with oil, coal, and nuclear power. It also could facilitate the timely introduction of more desirable solar energy technologies. Any clarification of the relationship between energy use and economic growth thus could be very helpful in making many policy decisions.

In a secondary way, the issue is part of the important public debate over growth and energy, a debate highlighted by attempts to discredit environmentalists in the eyes of labor, the poor, and other social groups. Here are several samples of statements stressing the economic importance of energy production:

• Randall Meyer, president of the Exxon Company, has spoken of the "very strong correlation between economic growth and energy demand in the United States." He said:

It is essential that the public-at-large have a much better understanding of this relationship. Otherwise, our political leaders are not going to be able to make those difficult decisions which are required to provide the energy supplies needed to sustain long-term economic growth.[29]

• Congressman Mike McCormack of Washington, an important House spokesman on science, technology, and energy, has said:

We cavalierly assume we can decouple energy, gross national product, and employment levels. All the evidence we can find points to the opposite direction. It is irresponsible to think we can decouple these three factors without disrupting the economy. Last year [1976] we had a 4.8% growth, and energy use followed right along. It follows simple laws.[30]

• A report from Chase Manhattan Bank asserted that per capita use of energy varies widely in different parts of the world and that there is an "almost identical variation" in the per capita GNP. Noting a roughly parallel trend in the U.S. in recent years, it said, "There is no sound, proven basis for believing a billion dollars of GNP can be generated with less energy in the future."[31]

• The controversial NAACP statement on the Administration's National Energy Plan said, "We note the historic direct correlation between the level of economic activity and energy availability and consumption." The statement went on to say that the Administration plan's emphasis on conservation and a reduction in the growth of total energy demand and consumption "cannot satisfy the fundamental requirements of a society of expanding economic opportunities."[32]

• Secretary of Energy James R. Schlesinger, in a speech to the AFL-CIO, linked energy and economic growth in a denunciation of the "antigrowth philosophy" which he attributed to environmentalists and others:

We can have nothing to do with that kind of unrestrained attitude which is antigrowth. Restraining growth means restraining the growth of jobs. It means unemployment. It means the failure to provide the best part of the American way of life to a growing number of our citizens. And in this connection, I know that the AFL-CIO has strongly endorsed getting on with creation of new sources of energy and the building of nuclear plants.[53]

Statements such as these are based on an inflexible premise that is widely discredited. Aside from several factual errors, the statements represent, at the very least, a far too simplistic view of a very complex relationship. Broadly speaking, the ratio of energy/GNP is determined by the mixture of goods and services that comprise the Gross National Product *and* the energy intensities with which they are produced. But both of these are constantly changing.

The Natural Selection of Energy

Changes are triggered by new consumer values and choices, by material shortages or supply uncertainties, by rising prices (especially energy prices), by market saturation, by changes in the make-up of the population and the labor force, and by government policies to protect public or private interests (such as controls on natural gas prices, restrictions on the manufacture of aerosol spray cans, or subsidies for waterways).

Once the changes are triggered and signaled to the economic system, they may alter rates of energy consumption. There are several important ways they can *reduce* consumption: (1) conservation practices that cut energy waste, (2) technological innovations that lower energy usage, (3) substitution of other factors of production (capital or labor) for energy, and (4) energy-saving changes in consumer life-styles and purchasing habits.

The automobile market illustrates all these mechanisms of change. Threatened shortages or higher prices of gasoline induce drivers to take buses, drive slower, or forego trips. Federal law forces auto manufacturers to build smaller or more fuel-efficient cars. A decrease in household formations dampens the demand for cars. Manufacturers alter assembly lines to substitute workers or investment for energy-intensive processes. And so forth.

The point is that the gigantic, multifaceted U.S. economy is loaded with possibilities for reducing energy consumption vis-a-vis economic output. That economy—with its great diversification, flexibility, and adaptability—is analogous to the natural world in this regard. During its evolution, the economy can adapt to constraints and external stimuli such as shortages or high prices. Through a kind of natural selection, amidst the constant efforts to compete and survive, it can weed out inefficiencies and components that use energy excessively. And in this process, the economic system can develop mutations—technological mutations in the form of discoveries by which manufacturing and other operations can save energy.

This suggests an important dimension of what might be dubbed the "econergy" issue: the time factor, or the time required for changes to take place. Everyone more or less concedes that abrupt and unforeseen disruptions in energy supplies or prices are likely to have serious ill effects on economic growth and welfare. "With a physical plant structure geared to a high level of energy inputs, there would undoubtedly be plant shutdowns and widespread unemployment in response to unexpected shortfalls in energy supply," say Marc H. Ross, a University of Michigan physics professor, and Robert H. Williams, a research scientist at Princeton University's Center for Environmental Studies. But the long-term situation is "vastly different."[34]

The 1974 report of the Ford Foundation's Energy Policy Project said:

> We believe that the fear of the ripple effect of economic disruption and lost jobs, if we do not continue high rates of energy growth, is unfounded.

This fear confuses the impact of sudden supply disruptions with the quite different longer term effects of a slowdown in the growth of energy demand. . . .[35]

One panel of experts in an elaborate National Academy of Sciences (NAS) study of energy systems concludes that, in the long run and under certain assumptions

> . . . even an actual contraction in energy use could still be absorbed without creating significant unemployment of either capital or labor, as long as it is gradual, and proceeds at a rate no higher than that implicit in the normal retirement cycle of the plant and equipment specialized for energy production and use, and in the normal rate of turnover of the attendant labor.[36]

John H. Gibbons, former director of the University of Tennessee's Environment Center and chairman of another NAS study panel (the Demand/Conservation Panel), concurs that, given time, a great deal can be done to substitute facilities and equipment with much greater efficiencies and at "remarkably small difference in first costs." He also says he feels there is a small amount of flexibility in the GNP, such that even in the short run a 5-10 percent reduction in energy supply could be absorbed without major economic effect.[37]

A wide variety of expertise has been applied to the energy/GNP relationship—including the extrapolation of historical trends, international comparisons, econometric models, and engineering efficiency calculations. As to historical data, it can to some extent be selected and interpreted to suit the eyes of the beholder. But it provides this double-bladed argument for some:

Historical trends do not reflect a close coupling between economic growth and energy consumption. And even if they did, history is a poor guide to that relationship in coming decades. Many of the changes that could take place already have been cited. As Kenneth E.F. Watt, a professor of environmental studies and research systems analyst at the Institute of Ecology, University of California at Davis, puts it, "The future is not what it used to be."[38]

Some historical evidence of the shifting correlation between energy and GNP is presented in the graph, The Role of Energy in Economic Growth. The graph shows the general decline in the energy/GNP ratio, or the amount of energy required to produce a dollar of output in the U.S. economy. It shows further that this decline has occurred despite a drop in relative energy prices, which might have been expected to encourage energy use. Many major industrial transformations contributed to the decline in the ratio and its somewhat erratic zigzags. These included, after World War II, the expanded electrification of industry

The Role of Energy in Economic Growth

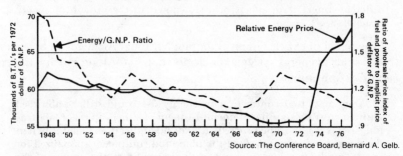

Source: The Conference Board, Bernard A. Gelb.

and the shift to diesel locomotives. (Electrification permitted great production efficiencies. Also, improvements in generation did much to offset electricity's thermal inefficiency.)

The decline slowed down somewhat after 1954 as larger automobiles proliferated, and as petrochemical plants began to devour oil and gas. Part of the sharp increase starting in 1968 is attributed to high sales of appliances and a major boost in air conditioning. Of course, the next plunge in the ratio of energy use to GNP after 1970 was prompted largely by climbing energy prices and conservation efforts. Many experts feel the ratio will continue its helpful decline, particularly considering the likelihood of further energy price increases.

To go back farther in history, the chart does not show two far more precipitous long-term changes in the energy/GNP ratio; compared to which the trend between 1947 and 1977 is relatively flat: From 1880 to 1920, the ratio increased dramatically as energy consumption grew at an average annual rate of 5.6 percent, while GNP rose by only 3.4 percent per year. This was a period of heavy industrialization. The ratio reached its peak in 1920 at 94.2.

Then began an almost equally steep decline in the ratio, in a period of generally decreasing energy prices. From 1920 to 1960, the average annual growth rate of energy consumption was only 2.1 percent while GNP rose at 3.2 percent. Part of the explanation is the shift to services and light manufacturing, along with the other changes mentioned above.

Many variables are at work, of course, but it is interesting that a long-term decline in the energy/GNP ratio took place even while real energy prices were dropping—a circumstance that might have been expected to induce relatively greater energy consumption.

Data Resources, Inc., a consulting firm, estimates that the energy/GNP ratio will continue its decline in coming years, from 57.6 shown on the graph for 1977 to 51.3 in 1990.[39]

To be sure, energy growth and economic growth per se have moved in parallel over long periods. Several explanations have been offered to discount the conventional theory that this reveals a lockstep relationship between the two. For example, Allan Mazur, an associate professor of social science, and Eugene Rosa, then a graduate student, at Syracuse University, suggested that perhaps the energy and economic variables are not really distinct but

> . . . simply different measures of one general variable such as level of industrialization. The high correlations may simply be telling us that highly industrialized countries, as measured by energy consumption, are highly industrialized countries, as measured by GNP or by production of automobiles. In this case the correlations have no causal significance at all.[40]

Watt cites figures on energy consumption per capita in industrialized countries and concludes that the more energy consumed, the *lower* the economic growth rate. "As energy consumption per capita rises, the growth rate in GNP per capita rises up to a maximum, *then falls.*"[41]

Watt reasons that countries such as Sweden and Switzerland have passed the U.S. in GNP per capita because they are not obliged to divert so much capital away from growth-promoting activities to deal with the consequences of excessive energy use:

> In short, beyond about 9,000 pounds of coal equivalents of energy consumption per capita, further energy use is correlated with a decrease, not an increase, in economic growth rate. There are a great many reasons for this, ranging from the consequences of pollution, to the consequences of displacement of expensive labor by cheap energy, with resultant unemployment, crime, police costs, and other problems.

Comparisons with other countries indicate great variations in energy/GNP ratios—but also a complex web of causation. This web has been carefully explored by Joel Darmstadter, of Resources for the Future, who stresses that, while long-term flexibility in energy-intensiveness is probable, many intercountry differences—in social customs, geography, climate, price and tax policies, and economic structure—account for the variations, and some would be difficult to change.[42]

However, Darmstadter and Lee Schipper, of the Lawrence Laboratory at the University of California, Berkeley, have found that comparisons between the United States and other countries do not point to a "unique relationship between a nation's economic growth and its use of energy."[43]

Another way to approach the question is to note that, compared to capital and labor, energy is relatively small potatoes in determining output. Walt W. Rostow, professor of economics and history at the University of Texas at Austin, says that "the total cost of energy in the U.S. economy as a proportion of GNP is a relatively small number, say 5 percent in 1975. Therefore, even a quite substantial rise in the price of energy will yield only a modest dampening in the rate of increase of real GNP" (assuming GNP continues to rise at recent rates).[44]

What the Numbers Show

A number of economists have fashioned models aimed at solving the mysteries of the energy/GNP ratio. These models, too, are instructive, though they tend to suffer from one very soft spot: the general lack of understanding or agreement about price elasticities for energy—for example, the extent to which increases in price will reduce demand. This is a critical variable. Another major area of debate is the extent to which capital and labor can be substituted for energy.

The econometric models also tend to embody assumptions or extrapolations that do not fully account for the many flexibilities in the system. Aggregating figures for dissimilar processes also can be misleading.

Caveats aside, the Modeling Resource Group (MRG) of the National Academy of Sciences study came up with some interesting results.[45] It concluded, in general, that GNP growth in the long run is "relatively independent" of growth in energy consumption, if the long-run energy price elasticity of demand is -0.5 or greater. (That is, if a 10 percent increase in aggregate energy prices relative to other prices would result in a decrease of 5 percent or more in energy use.)

It happens that a study of six developed countries by William D. Nordhaus, a member of the Council on Economic Advisers, indicated that the long-run price elasticity is -0.8. Thus, said Nordhaus, "it appears that relative prices play a crucial role in determining the energy intensiveness across space and time."[46]

The MRG concluded more specifically that, under certain assumptions, an average GNP growth rate of 3.2 percent over the 35 years from 1975-2010 would result in an energy growth rate of between 1.7 percent and 2.9 percent, depending on the model used. However, that only represents "base case" projections in which the GNP growth is considered a "driving variable" that determines energy use. A more dramatic picture emerges if it is assumed that government conservation, pollution control, or other policies that curtail energy use are imposed (gradually), or if it is assumed, as many experts do, that GNP will grow at a rate substantially less than 3.2 percent per year:

• Assuming a set of policies that would reduce energy use by up to 20 percent from the base case in the year 2010, the total aggregated, negative effect on GNP (discounted) over the 35-year period would be only 1 to 2 percent.

• A more drastic across-the-board curtailment—such as a conservation tax on all primary energy which resulted in an energy use reduction of about 50 percent in the year 2010—also would affect the aggregate

GNP by only 1 to 2 percent, according to one model. (This result assumes that the price elasticity of demand for energy is -0.5. However, the model shows that with a price elasticity of -.25, the effect on the GNP would jump up to 30 percent.)

• The panel sums up the results by saying:

We estimate that the negative feedback from a curtailment of energy use below the base path is moderate, in fact small, unless *both* the curtailing is large—say by 50%—*and* the price elasticity of demand is small in absolute terms—say substantially below half.

• A Nordhaus model used by the MRG group shows what might happen looking at the opposite side of the coin—without policy constraints on energy consumption, but under a low rate of GNP growth:

	Average rate of growth (percent per year)		Total energy consumption (in quads)	
	GNP	Energy use	1975	2010
Base case	3.2	1.7	71.6	129.6
Low GNP growth	1.8	0.4	71.6	82.3

The figures show that the drop in energy consumption under the low GNP growth rate would be far more than proportional to the change in GNP itself. Interestingly, the model showed that a combination of energy constraint policies *and* low GNP growth would not reduce energy consumption more than low GNP growth alone.

Another, earlier model was developed by Data Resources, Inc., for the Ford Energy Policy Project. The results of a study based on the model, by Edward A. Hudson, of Data Resources, and Dale W. Jorgenson, of Harvard University, were summarized in the project report.

The study indicates that it is economically efficient, as well as technically possible, over the next 25 years, to cut rates of energy growth at least in half. Energy consumption levels could be 40 to 50% lower than continued historical growth rates would produce, at a very moderate cost in GNP—scarcely 4% below the cumulative total under historical growth in the year 2000, but still more than twice the level of 1975.[47]

More recently, Hudson and Jorgenson reported some less optimistic model results.[48] To oversimplify the outcome under one set of government energy policy assumptions: With energy consumption in the year 2000 reduced to 35 percent less than under a base case scenario with no policy changes, the total GNP would be 7.2 percent lower. Hudson and Jorgenson conclude, generally, that policies to restrict the growth of energy consumption involve "possibly large economic cost in terms of slowed economic growth and output foregone."[49]

These results were criticized on a number of grounds by Clark W.

Bullard, director of the Department of Energy's Office of Conservation and Advanced Energy Systems Policy. For example, he argued in a rebuttal that, in using an energy model to analyze human behavior at the turn of the century, "we must remember that nearly half the population of that year has not yet entered kindergarten; their values and price elasticities of energy demand may be substantially different from our own." Bullard also says it is reasonable to expect engineers to begin substituting capital for energy in modern industrial facilities as energy prices rise. "A substantial trend in this direction could significantly reduce the economic losses forecast by Hudson and Jorgenson."[50]

The Bottom Line on Conservation

The punch line—or the bottom line—for many experts in the energy field is this: Whatever history, econometric models, or other analyses may show, the fact remains that a multitude of energy-saving adjust-

Reprinted by permission of the Chicago Tribune-New York News Syndicate, Inc.

ments in the economy can be made without ill effect on economic or social well-being. This brings us back to the four types of adjustments mentioned earlier—conservation, technological innovation, substitution of inputs, and alterations in life-styles.

The potential impact of conservation on the energy/GNP ratio may be enormous. Ross and Williams have calculated what would have happened in 1973 if the nation had by then completely adopted a set of purely technical conservation measures—those which could be implemented within roughly two decades—while providing the same product. "Fuel consumption would have been less than 60 percent of its actual level," they estimated.[51] (That result does not include the potential savings from either technological innovation or life-style changes.)

Ross and Williams go on to estimate that if the same degree of technical improvement—what one writer called "meticulous engineering"[52]—were accomplished over the rest of the century, the result would be zero energy growth beyond 1985.

Some general forecasts from the Demand/Conservation Panel of the National Academy of Sciences study have been reported by Schipper and Darmstadter.[53] They say that, over the next 30 years or so, "depending on the course of future energy prices and a corresponding pursuit of cost-effective conservation possibilities, a given rate of GNP growth might occur with a wide range of energy growth rates." Comparisons of the combined effects of different increases in GNP growth and prices are made. For example:

With an average annual GNP growth rate of 3 percent per year and prices going up at 2 percent, the consumption of energy in 2010 would reach about 133 quads. But with GNP increasing at 2 percent and prices at 4 percent, the use of energy would total only 80 quads.[54]

Of more immediate relevance was a 1978 report by Anthony J. Parisi in the *New York Times* that "conservation has started to take hold" and was a major factor in a *decline* in oil imports. (The decline was believed to be temporary, with imports then expected to increase at a much slower rate than before.)

Parisi said the Petroleum Industry Research Foundation estimated that in 1977, while GNP was expanding 4.9 percent, the demand for energy grew less than 3 percent. "The experts," he said, "now believe that this new ratio of six or seven units of energy growth for every 10 units of economic growth is becoming the norm."[55]

Schipper and Darmstadter also take note of the Swedish example, in which higher energy prices have been a major factor in stimulating conservation:

> Yet Sweden is by no means an "ideal" energy consumer. This suggests that there is no definable limit to conservation, at least not until we approach both thermodynamic limits and the exhaustion of our ingenuity to modify and refine tasks.[56]

A first cousin to conservation is the kind of technological ingenuity that brings about radical alterations in manufacturing processes, product designs, and provisions of services. Bullard speaks of "the emerging technologies that are now changing the structure of the U.S. economy."[57]

He points out that we can make comfortable, six-passenger cars that travel twice as far on a gallon of gas. He says studies have shown that "it may be possible to gradually reduce the energy required to produce a dollar's worth of GNP to about half or even a third its present level with little or no adverse impact on GNP."

John H. Gibbons says:

> Typically, given time for production changeover, the improvements can increase efficiency by 50% for up to 10% increase in first cost. Such a change is generally cost-effective at present energy prices.[58]

Computers (including the microcomputers that automatically adjust fuel consumption in cars), new forms of electronic communication, advanced steel and aluminum processing equipment, fuel cells, heat pumps—these are the types of technological innovation that keep emerging. Charles A. Berg, former chief engineer of the Federal Power Commission and now a consultant, writes of "fundamental conceptual advances" that typically take place in industry, and that are not necessarily prompted by energy price increases or the need to substitute other inputs for energy: "The history of industrial processes seems to show that each one is susceptible to improvement through basic innovation."[59]

The MRG group says that the recurrence of "spurts" in technological innovation—which go beyond the technical options included in its projections—would diminish still further the negative feedback on GNP from a given curtailment of energy use.[60]

The extent to which capital or labor can be substituted for energy (the "elasticity of substitution") is a very complex question and a matter of disagreement. Suffice it to say that most economists and others at least concur that the potential for substitution depends on many variables, including critical ones involving price elasticity.

Bullard points, for example, to the potential for saving large amounts of energy by requiring deposits on beverage containers. That way, he says, "You don't have to manufacture a beverage container every time someone in the country gets thirsty."[61] He also notes that the NAS study has found that most of the industry potential for saving energy can be realized by substituting capital for energy, in the form of new technologies that cut energy requirements in half, and do so with no significant differences in labor productivity.[62]

A comparable view is expressed by Ross and Williams, who say their calculations suggest that

> . . . energy growth could be sharply curtailed in response to rising energy prices without adversely affecting the economy, because there are considerable opportunities for substituting other inputs for energy throughout the economy.[63]

A Three-Dimensional Problem

Finally, we turn to some aspects of the potential for change in consumer behavior and in the mix of goods and services that makes up the final output and determines the amount of energy needed to produce it. There is wide agreement, for example, that the economy is shifting from goods to services at the consumer end, and from basic materials to fabrication at the manufacturing end.

The growth in electronics is one illustration. Bullard notes, moreover, that if a family saved x dollars by insulating its home, and spent the money on something else—such as going to a restaurant every month—it would inevitably end up with a less energy-intensive activity.[64]

A continuation of the trend toward a "post-industrial economy" should lead to a further gradual reduction in the energy/GNP ratio, say Ross and Williams.[65] (Of course, some services, especially those involving travel, are very energy consumptive.)

The energy/GNP ratio also could decline as a result of market saturation of such energy-demanding consumer items as cars, electric lighting, refrigerators, and the like. Virtually all U.S. households already are equipped with stoves, refrigerators, and TV sets.[66] Ross and Williams say that

> . . . the likely mix of activities in the year 2000 will be intrinsically less energy-intensive, largely because we can drive only so much or heat so much space, two activities that in the past slowed the drop in the energy/GNP ratio considerably.[67]

The gamut of possible life-style changes is large indeed. Nearly 30 percent of U.S. energy demand is in the form of direct consumption for personal use. Public choices are not guaranteed to cut energy use, to be sure. Millions of consumers may decide they want microwave ovens, saunas, and deep-freezes. Darmstadter cautions against the dangers of prescribing supposedly "innocuous" changes in behavior and life-style to save energy. He says it is important to recognize that personal energy consumption represents the " 'proceeds' of economic growth . . . rather than the 'springboard' for growth through its role in the productive process."[68]

In summary, there is little that can be done about some of the factors that determine the amount of energy used to generate a dollar of GNP. Obstacles to reducing the ratio do exist. For example, Mancur Olson, professor of economics at the University of Maryland, speaks of "institutional arthritis" and the incentives of organized interest groups to keep out new entrants, to delay innovations, and to "limit the flow of resources into whatever industries and occupations should be expanding most rapidly."[69]

Yet a wide variety of measures can be taken by government, industry, and the public to improve the energy/GNP ratio or increase the job-intensiveness of economic activities. These include price incentives, tax incentives, elimination of counterproductive subsidies, regulatory controls, changes in cost-benefit analysis and accounting procedures, alteration of advertising messages, educational campaigns, and changes in research and development emphasis.

Bullard has called attention to the question of "whether the nation's R&D talent is directed toward developing energy supply technologies needed for a high energy future, or toward designing efficient industrial equipment for a low energy future."[70]

There also is considerable room for programs to inform industries and individuals of the many opportunities to reduce energy use without incurring economic penalty—opportunities that are not adequately revealed by price changes or other signals. As Gibbons has said, "Conservation, like any other good product, must be sold."

Finally, Darmstadter's comment that personal energy consumption represents the "proceeds" of economic growth raises an important point that has been missing from the foregoing discussion of energy-economic relationships. That is the fact that the GNP itself is not a good measure of economic growth, much less of social welfare and quality of life.

The GNP automatically classifies too many negative effects as positive contributions to the economy (medical costs resulting from pollution, for example) and does not measure other factors at all (such as the value of not having the noise of an SST climbing overhead). As a result, the energy/GNP ratio is likely to *overstate* our society's dependence on energy.

Certainly the connections between economic growth and quality of life are very muddy, particularly since they depend on individual values and perceptions. Among the many relevant questions are: What kinds of growth are at issue? And who is to benefit from them? A group of environmental leaders has said, "We try to distinguish between healthy, positive growth and destructive growth."[71]

A number of energy experts have commented on the complex, three-dimensioned relationships between energy use, GNP, *and* quality of life. Mazur and Rosa, interpreting the results of their study on living standards, said: "Of the life-style indicators examined here, only the economic indicators show a consistently high association with energy consumption." (Indicators more impervious to a reduction in energy use are in the categories of health care, education and culture, and general satisfaction.)[72]

Amory Lovins sums up several points this way:

> Since the energy needed today to produce a unit of GNP varies more than 100-fold depending on what good or service is being produced, and since GNP in turn hardly measures social welfare, why must energy and welfare march forever in lockstep?[73]

And John P. Holdren, of the University of California at Berkeley, says, sweepingly, that "the notion of a one-to-one link between energy use and well-being is the most dangerous delusion in the energy-policy arena."

Chapter 10

APPROPRIATE TECHNOLOGY

> The choice of technology, whether for a
> rich or a poor country, is probably the most
> important decision to be made.
>
> —George McRobie

The wrong technologies, in the wrong places, aggravate the ailments of society. These ailments include severe shortages of capital, enduring unemployment, climbing energy costs, environmental degradation, and a package of social problems such as work alienation, urban migration, and maldistribution of income. There has been increasing recognition of the bad side effects of grandiose, highly technological, automated, capital-intensive apparatus—like agribusiness combines, SST's, nuclear plants, supertankers, or massive dams. Even small technologies, carelessly chosen, can have serious negative impacts.

In their rush to development, many countries and their aid benefactors frequently overlook or ignore the secondary impacts of their projects, which as a result can cause acute environmental and social damage. Consider some examples in the field of water development alone:

In one Third World town, a new water-supply system was installed, thereby making obsolete a well that had long been the focal point of the town's social life. A project to develop a water-supply system in Surabaya, second largest city in Indonesia, has had to confront the fact that providing safe and adequate water would lure people from rural areas—contrary to Indonesian government policy—and thereby exacerbate other urban problems.[1] Wells in Africa's Sahel, equipped with motorized pumps to boost the flow of water, intensified settlement and grazing and magnified the horrendous effects of drought when it came.

The recognition of such problems in the United States and other countries has led to the evolution of an important expertise—"technology assessment." The goal of technology assessment is to evaluate fully the social, environmental, and economic consequences of an existing or proposed technology. This, certainly, is a major step beyond the shopworn practice of judging technology solely by its contributions to productivity, profit, or the gross national product, and hang the externalities and societal consequences. However, technology assessment, by and large, does not address the next critical question: What is to take the place of bad technologies?

Fortunately, answers abound. They have proliferated under the banner of *appropriate technology*—also known as alternative technology, intermediate technology, light capital technology, self-help technology, socially relevant technology, or, in the phrase of the late British economist E.F. Schumacher, "technology with a human face."

Appropriate technology might be a windmill, a solar cooker, a small-scale paper recycler, a nonflush toilet, a pedal thresher, a bicycle-powered pump, a device to capture methane gas from manure, a small hydroelectric turbine, a soap maker. In Asia, it might be hollowed bamboo to carry irrigation water. In the United States, it might be a heat pump or a small car.

Appropriate technology, or AT for short, also involves making these things locally—and making them in small enterprises that are flexible and easily duplicated by other entrepreneurs.

An important dimension of AT is finding the means to utilize and spread the fruits or benefits derived from these technologies. These include management (for example, organizing a cooperative, or bookkeeping), training programs, financial institutions, tax structures, and marketing and distribution methods.

"I believe the marketing side may be the most important," says Edgar L. Owens, an Agency for International Development (AID) official. "All the agencies have concentrated on production and sort of skipped distribution." Thus, the "appropriate technologies" or the so-called green revolution—such as better plant varieties and more sophisticated methods of irrigating and fertilizing—may produce local crop surpluses that never get to market because there is no transport, or roads are impassable.

To spread the word on such technologies, one approach is to establish industrial and agricultural extension services along the lines of the agricultural services in the United States.

Obviously, the appropriateness of a technology depends on the circumstances. "It's a matter of selecting the technologies to fit the political process and social ends you happen to have in mind," says David Elliott, a lecturer at Britain's Open University. "Some advanced technologies can be very liberating." "The basic determination of appropriateness must come from the field," says a study prepared for AID. "Moreover, the potential technology must be tested in the field, in its intended use area."[2]

The Advantages of Alternatives

The potential advantages of appropriate technology are enormous as the following list makes clear. (Most of the advantages cited apply both to Third World countries and developed nations like the United States.)

• From an individual human standpoint, AT can offer more reward-ing work, a chance to be "creatively, usefully, productively engaged with both hands and brains," in Schumacher's words. AT is "com-patible with man's need for creativity."[3] It can promote individual—and community—self-reliance.

• AT usually is far more job-intensive. It might eventually alleviate the widespread unemployment in developed countries, as well as offer a future to the endless millions in poor countries who simply have nothing to do. (This, in turn, could provide hope that the lemming-like migration to cities, and the resultant exacerbation of urban problems, can be stemmed.)

• Some appropriate technologies—a mini-sugar refinery, for ex-ample—are just as sophisticated as any other. They just happen to be small. However, many of them do not demand highly skilled workers or costly training programs. Workplaces can be created fairly quickly, said Schumacher, because they would be within reach of "the more enter-prising minority within the district, not only in financial terms but also in terms of their education, aptitude, organizing skill, and so forth."

• AT typically requires little investment capital. At a time of great capital scarcity, this is important for its own sake. But it also offers opportunities to decentralize, to democratize, and to eliminate bureauc-racy and foreign or monopoly control and exploitation. It is, said Schumacher, a technology "to which everybody can gain admittance and which is not reserved to those already rich and powerful."[4] It generates income at the bottom of the social ladder; it facilitates the more equitable distribution of income. Concurrently, it can encourage group efforts and community cohesiveness.

• Ideally, appropriate technologies use indigenous resources and locally produced inputs in plentiful supply. "Increasingly," says con-sultant George McRobie, "countries realize they should process their own raw materials to the maximum extent possible. So the power will keep shifting toward countries with raw materials."

• AT workplaces are low in cost; the products of appropriate tech-nology are likely to have the same advantage, and thus be accessible to the poor. They can be geared to the local market and emphasize the basic needs of the poor. They also are likely to be far easier to operate, maintain, and repair. ("If you push the wrong gear on a 24-gear trac-tor," said Schumacher, "the owner is between 500 and 1,000 pounds out of pocket."[5])

- It should be "gentle in its use of scarce resources," or nonrenewable resources, said Schumacher.[6] This, of course, includes the sparing use of energy, which now is one of the most valued characteristics of appropriate technology.
- AT is likely to be more environmentally benign—less polluting, less productive of unhealthy chemicals, less noisy.
- Appropriate technology can be compatible with the social values and the cultural constraints of the people in the area.

Many of these advantages are illustrated by a project of the Intermediate Technology Development Group (ITDG), which is based in England. In a rural African area, farmers had been persuaded to shift from their primitive techniques to new seeds and fertilizers. They were highly pleased when a big crop surplus resulted. Since it had long been customary for the women to carry the produce to market, they lugged the new crops there as well. No other means of transport was available— the roads and tracks were full of potholes and rocks, and the farmers' wooden-wheeled oxcarts broke on them. The women had never worked so hard in their lives, and they complained mightily. The next year the farmers abandoned the new seeds and fertilizer.

This unhappy dilemma was discovered by a representative of the ITDG. He thought the problem might be solved if metal rims could be put on the oxcart wheels. But people had stopped bending metal by hand some 200 years before, and there was no electricity in the area to run a metal-bending machine, or likely to be any for a long time.

Tackling the problem back in London, ITDG found, in a county historical museum, a complicated and cumbersome old machine used before the invention of power. It took the specimen to the National College of Agricultural Engineering. Designers there simplified and modernized it, coming up with a device for two people to curve metal bands for wheels. It weighs only about 10 pounds and costs some $15. Now the Africans, and others elsewhere, can use their carts to far greater advantage, and have a small metal-bending enterprise to boot.

ITDG also has developed a machine to manufacture egg cartons, a water-catchment tank, animal-drawn farming equipment, and a variety of other small-scale technologies.

Better Pest Management

On a more elaborate scale, consider the example of pesticides, which are used profusely in the U.S. as well as exported in great quantities. As a technology, these chemicals often have been most inappropriate—they poison the environment, they induce resistance in the targets, and they backfire (for example, by killing of insect predators as well as the insects themselves).

"Worldwide, there presently are at least 266 species of insects, mites, and ticks that possess strains resistant to one or more chemical pesticides," Warren R. Muir, formerly of the Council on Environmental Quality has said. "Resistance in certain rodents and plant pathogens is currently limiting the effectiveness of pesticides against these pests."[7] Of particular concern has been the resistance to DDT developed by some malaria-carrying mosquitoes. "Unfortunately," says David Pimental, of the Department of Entomology at Cornell University, "crop losses from insect pests have increased nearly two-fold from the 1940's . . . in spite of the 10-fold increase in insecticide use."[8]

The late Robert van den Bosch, an entomologist at the University of California, Berkeley, warned that pests may have a resurgence after being sprayed. "You treat them and they come roaring back," he said. Insecticides sometimes "turn them on" through some physiological stimulus. "One insect turned into an egg-laying machine." Another problem is that many pesticides destroy not only the target species but its natural enemies, or another dormant pest's natural enemies. "You may treat for A, but kill B's enemies. Then B abruptly becomes an epidemic."

The various counterproductive side effects of pesticide usage—combined with increasing concern for health, environmental, energy, and financial costs—have led to a number of research break-throughs on alternatives to chemicals. Of principal interest is a wide assortment of natural pest-control tactics that, when used in various combinations, are called integrated pest management (IPM). Many of the techniques themselves have been around a long time. But greater sophistication and flexibility in their use has added an impressive new dimension to the field.

The tactics include importation of predator species, planting more pest-resistant crop varieties, planting crops earlier or later to avoid pest infestations, spacing rows differently, rotation and mixture of crops, changes in cultivation and in water and fertilizer use, distribution of sex pheromones and hormones to disrupt insect behavior, mass introduction of sterile male insects, release of pest viruses, use of crops and other lures to trap insects, and a reliance on more selective pesticides that don't wipe out predators.[9]

With such an arsenal of appropriate, nonchemical technologies, the war against bugs can be waged with considerable finesse. This has been demonstrated by a massive, multidisciplinary IPM research project directed by Carl B. Huffaker, an entomology professor at the University of California, Berkeley. Eighteen universities participated in the effort, which dealt with six major crops.

IPM experts generally are guided by a number of basic principles, of which the following simplified examples are perhaps the most important:

• Don't institute controls at all unless necessary. A certain amount of crop damage is likely to be quite tolerable. The farmer or pest manager should ascertain the "economic injury level" at which it is imperative to act.

"As we had hoped, it kills weevils instantly. It also kills bluebirds, snow geese, peacocks, wolverines, wallabies, anteaters, brown bears. manatees, butterflies, swordfish, sea snakes, and Alaska king crabs. Will that be a problem?"

Shirvarian, *Audubon Magazine*

• Don't attempt to wipe out a pest completely. "Most pests are tremendously adapting, highly reproductive organisms and are not likely to be eradicated," notes Huffaker. "Containment . . . is the logical strategy."[10]

• Use biological and cultural controls, rather than chemicals, whenever possible. Capitalize on the natural mortality factors inherent in every pest population.

• Use chemicals when necessary, for they can be an important and effective tool. But they are more appropriate as a tactic than a strategy. And applications should be as small and infrequent as possible to achieve needed control.

• In evaluating a management technique, include its hidden costs—whether they be borne by the farmer himself, his neighbors, downstream inhabitants, or others, and whether they involve damage to beneficial species, environmental contamination, unfavorable ecosystem disruption, or other disbenefits.

• Pinpoint the critical pest or pests—those that cause intolerable losses. (Obviously, there is no need to lavish attention on those that are induced or reinforced by pesticides themselves.) "It is patently impossible within a reasonable period of time and with allocatable funds to fully evaluate all influencing variables concerning all the pests on a crop," say Huffaker and his colleague at California, Ray F. Smith. "Nor is this necessary."[11]

It may be possible to obviate the need for a complicated, expensive control program by concentrating on a key pest and finding a single management tactic that will reduce that pest's damage to an acceptable level. For example, as Huffaker and Smith note, "Use of a resistant plant variety would also render many other factors irrelevant." Another example might be the simple destruction of neighboring weeds or crop residues that provide the pest a refuge.

Examples of Success

Many examples could be given of these pest management principles put to work and resulting in both increased farmer profits and decreased environmental damage. They illustrate how different an appropriate technology can be from the traditional chemical one. Consider a Huffaker project experimental program with cotton in Texas, where past heavy use of pesticides has proved disastrous:

Field tests had revealed that an early-fruiting genetic variety of cotton rapidly became unattractive to boll weevils. In effect, the weevils came too late for their best feeding. It also was found that this effect is enhanced by greatly narrowing the 40-inch spacing between rows.

In the experiment, directed by Perry L. Adkisson, head of Texas A&M

University's Department of Entomology, irrigation water was cut from the usual 72-80 inches to 30 inches. Nitrogen fertilizer was reduced from 200 to 50 pounds. No late-season pest control was necessary because of early maturation, and applications of pesticide were cut from 12 to virtually none.

The results, in an area where banks balk at lending money to cotton farmers: a per-acre net profit of $364 compared to a loss of $1.88 per acre under the old system. An experiment with a different genetic type resulted in a net of $164.[12] J.R. Phillips, of the University of Arkansas, says the system can be made even more efficient with insect-disease resistant varieties presently being developed.[13]

Another example, described by L.D. Newsom, head of the Department of Entomology at Louisiana State University, involves soybeans, now being widely grown in southern states where the climate is more favorable to pests than in the more northern soybean areas. The experiment found that stink bugs could be controlled adequately by using "trap cropping"—a technique in which most of the pest population is lured to a small section of the total acreage that has been planted early. There the bugs do relatively little damage or can be readily suppressed with an insecticide. "Five percent of the total acreage of soybeans or less can be used to attract and concentrate up to 80% of the overwintering bugs," says Newsom.[14]

Another possibility is the use of pheromones—odorous natural chemicals that insects use to communicate for sex and other purposes— to lure the pests to a small area planted at the same time as the rest of the crop.

Newsom also has reported some other revealing results. He said it was discovered that soybean pods could tolerate nine times as much damage from pod-feeding insects as had been thought. It also was found that a pest predator was far more susceptible to methyl parathion spraying than the pest itself. Applying the insecticide later in the season increased the yield five-fold[15]

While these examples may not be typical, they nevertheless illustrate some of the enormous potentials of integrated pest management.

An Idea on the Move

Appropriate technology is not a new concept. As noted earlier, there already exists a rich assortment of tools and processes and products, with more being developed at a rapid pace. Many dozens of private voluntary organizations have used such technologies in the field—the American Friends Service Committee, CARE, Inc., Oxfam-America, Mennonite Central Committee, among others. Some foreign development experts, notably Edgar Owens, have long touted the advantages of

AT—with no big breakthrough, no broad shift in establishment thinking or in priorities.

Then along came the environmental and other protest movements
with high technologies as their targets. Individuals and groups wanted
new back-to-the-land, do-it-yourself life-styles. On the heels of this
came the energy crunch, which spurred particular interest in energy-
saving technologies. At the same time, it was becoming inescapably
clear that the billions of dollars spent on foreign aid over the last three
decades had not produced very good results—that the "trickle down"
theory of development was discredited because the investments and
incomes from high-technology, capital-intensive projects were not
reaching the large populations of poor.

Into this loose but highly combustible mixture of people, programs,
and ideas, Schumacher tossed a match. It was his book *Small is Beautiful*, published in 1973. After a sluggish start, it suddenly took hold and
became an inspiration for the cause of appropriate technology.

"The environmental movement in the last few years has taken up this
new theme," according to Byron Kennard, a community organizer:

> It transcends old concepts in the economics versus environment dispute. It
> emerges with a broader and brighter synthesis. We used to dimly perceive
> that social justice could be on a collision course with environmental
> concerns. Now we realize that you can talk about both in the same breath
> without being denounced as hopelessly idealistic or naive. *Small is Beau-
> tiful* explained how you could put it all together, how the two goals can be
> pursued in a related fashion. I thought it was too good to be true.

Now the AT movement has been bolstered by establishment of the
National Center for Appropriate Technology in Butte, Montana; by a
proliferation of new and existing periodicals; by a growing number of
appropriate technology organizations in developing countries; and by
groups in England, the U.S., the Netherlands, Canada, and elsewhere
which are busily applying new techniques (for example, the New
Alchemy Institute, in Falmouth, Massachusetts, the Institute for Local
Self-Reliance, in Washington, D.C., and the Farallones Institute, in
Berkeley), or are developing AT tools and generally spreading the word.
Three of the most noteworthy organizations in the last category are
ITDG, Rodale Press publishers, and Volunteers In Technical Assist-
ance (VITA).

Obstacles and Drawbacks

Appropriate technology is not without its drawbacks and problems, to
be sure. Some say that to be effective it desperately needs to be preceded
by land reform in underdeveloped countries.

In some cases, small-scale technologies might not be economically or qualitatively competitive within a country or in the export market (though true comparisons should take into account all the non-economic social and environmental costs and benefits).

Big imported technologies often have an appeal that is difficult to surmount. As a World Bank study puts it:

> Broadly speaking, such technologies are familiar and relatively well-tested, and can be purchased in packaged, guaranteed form, installed with relatively little risk or delay, implemented and maintained with external technical assistance, and controlled from a central point.[16]

Government regulations and pricing policies may mitigate against adoption of AT. Another obstacle is a reluctance to experiment with innovative techniques in organizing and financing projects.

It is relatively easy to make a mistake and inadvertently introduce an intermediate technology that clashes with a social or cultural custom. Similarly, a product may not be in tune with consumer preferences, which are linked in turn to income levels. Says an AID report: "If consumers demand drip-dry, color-fast, cotton-dacron shirts, the scope for substitution of technology in a labor-intensive direction is more restricted than if consumers will accept cotton shirts."[17]

It is argued that a commitment to small-scale and less capital-intensive technologies will bring lower productivity and lower living standards than more advanced development. Such results would be politically unpopular in the United States, of course, though it should be remembered that there are different ways of evaluating both productivity and living standards.

As with the chicken and the egg, there is a dispute among economists about whether capital or labor must come first in developing countries. Says one economist:

> As to Schumacher's argument that if you have no capital you can put people to work making capital goods—not so. There has to be *some* capital. It takes more capital per worker to make capital goods than to make consumptive goods. Creating capital out of nothing—as Russia did after the Revolution—means the sacrifice of a generation or more of people.

Perhaps the appropriate technologists do not really disagree; they suggest that minimal inputs of capital, in the form of small technologies put within reach of a huge and idle labor force, can create the necessary capital.[18] As Edgar Owens stated in an interview:

> The traditional view is that you have to have machines to do it. But suppose you have a bunch of people digging with shovels, and they make an irrigation ditch. The benefit comes from increased agricultural production and the income you get out of it. You often find this kind of work is done free. So how do you evaluate it?

Finally, there is certain to be considerable resistance to appropriate technology from strong vested interests. As Congressman Clarence D. Long of Maryland has put it:

> Heavy capital aid is the only kind of assistance most of the aid bureaucrats understand . . . it is profitable to politically influential groups in the receiving nations. Ruling elites of the developing contries welcome heavy capital investment because of the money to be made on port development, airport construction, dams, steel mills, and similar projects.

Long said the traditional pressure to boost exports and foreign exchange have only increased the poor countries' dependency, in large degree because the foreign exchange has been used "to increase luxury buying, to build roads to airports, to raise the incomes of the well-to-do whose assets wind up in foreign banks."[19]

Many of the technocrats and economists in poorer nations have been educated at western universities that tout the benefits of large-scale, high-technology engineering and capital development. At the same time, many of their government leaders view the more humble technologies as second-rate or hand-me-down items designed to keep the Third World dependent on modern imports. The AID proposal states:

> There is a substantial group of skeptics who see appropriate technology as "technological imperialism," a way in which western nations are trying to keep poor countries in their place so that they can retain access to the energy and resources needed to maintain high consumption western life styles.[20]

Yet many experts discern a fast-growing realization by developing countries that AT is necessary to get their poor people, and their countries as a whole, off the dead center of poverty. One observer says there is a "tremendous amount of posturing in public by people who privately support appropriate technology."

In any case, the problems with AT seem pale compared with its promise. And the resistance to it seems unlikely to last, considering the critical underlying needs for which AT seems to offer help. It would not be surprising, in fact, if the general drift toward appropriate technology became a wave. The fermentation is there.

Chapter 11

VALUES

> The environment is not just one more factor to be
> considered along with dozens of others in making
> social and economic decisions. The environment is not
> a crisis or a problem at all. Rather, it is the context in
> which all crises and problems have to be analyzed and
> judged.
>
> —William V. Shannon

One astonishing result of the Environmental Revolution over the last
decade has been the development and propagation of a comprehensive
environmental philosophy. The movement has succeeded in planting
new values in the consciousness of millions of people, so that now
nearly everyone finds it natural (or expedient) to feel and express concern about environmental quality.

Part of the environmental philosophy is a humane value system
which recognizes the ties that bind—the commonality of interests
between humans and the other species that inhabit the earth, as well as
the intertwined fate of all humans in the face of increasingly severe
resource pinches. These two interactions—humans among themselves
and humans among the other creatures of nature—will determine
whether environmental values can help to prevent a degeneration of our
society and to lead us into a self-sufficient future with plenty of room for
the full expression of human potential. Such results depend on the
desire and ability of enough people to take the new-found environmental consciousness and use it in shaping the future.

Consider first the interactions of humans with the other species that
share the lifeboat earth.

Developing a Wildlife Ethic

For centuries, most human societies and individuals have had a disturbing ambivalence toward the other creatures that share the earth. The
result has been a serious identity crisis for the humans, and worse for the
animals.

With varying degrees of affection and respect, disdain and cruelty,
humans have treated animals as sacred and have sacrificed them. They

have hunted and trapped them. They have kept them as pets and
abandoned them. They have caged and raised them to slaughter and eat
them. And they have used or abused them in every conceivable way for
medical experiments.

Some Eastern, primitive, and other societies developed cultures in
which people lived in a structured harmony with the rest of nature. But
in our modern civilizations, there is much inconsistency and confusion.
With few limitations, each human has been left to himself or herself to
decide how to view and treat the other claimants to the earth's thin
biological mantle of support. Despite the pleas of history's great defend-
ers of wildlife—Plutarch, Montaigne, Leonardo da Vinci, Voltaire,
Hume, Bentham—mankind has not developed a coherent, responsible,
wildlife ethic.

Drawing by H. Martin; © 1979 The New Yorker Magazine, Inc.

Typically, we use animals to serve whatever purposes we pursue, rationalizing as necessary. "Their interests are allowed to count only when they do not clash with human interests," says author Peter Singer.[1]

Yet the environmental movement and the expanded understanding of ecology have broadened and deepened humanity's concern for wildlife. This is particularly true when the irrevocable loss of a whole species is at stake. In that context, passage of the no-nonsense Endangered Species Act in 1973 can be considered a milestone in the development of thinking about wildlife.

To be sure, the meaning and implications of the act were later disputed;[2] it was argued by many who sought successfully to amend the act that Congress did not realize what it was doing, that it did not intend minor species such as the minnow-like snail darter to hamstring major human endeavors like the Tellico dam. Perhaps not. But Congress did list six types of value that endangered fish, wildlife, and plants have for the nation and its people: aesthetic, ecological, educational, historical, recreational, and scientific.

These values by and large are utilitarian in nature. Notably absent from the list are the *ethical* values in species protection.[3] Yet in the last analysis, it may be ethical considerations that bring the strongest public pressures to bear on behalf of threatened or endangered wildlife. "We must instill the morality and ethics of conservation in the fiber of contemporary consciousness," said Roger Caras, vice-president of the Humane Society of the United States, at a Yale University symposium. "Then it will bear fruit."[4]

Wildlife values are subjective, complex melanges of purposes and attitudes. But the key questions at issue here are these: How substantial are the values claimed for wildlife species? How much evidence is there to support the arguments for saving species from decimation or extinction?

Pragmatic Wildlife Values

The rationales for conservation fall into only two broad categories: the pragmatic and the moralistic. The pragmatic category can in turn be broken into four wildlife values—ecological, scientific, economic, and human enrichment. But in assessing those values, it is important to remember two things. First, present knowledge is severely limited, and new values for species will continue to be discovered. Second, the loss of a species is irrevocable.

"Species are becoming extinct today before they are known to man," says Thomas Lovejoy, program director of the World Wildlife Fund (U.S.). "Usually we remain in eternal ignorance of what we have lost.

Who on receiving a package would toss it out before looking inside? Yet that is what we are doing with our biological heritage."[5]

Similarly, Michael Berger, of the National Wildlife Federation, reminds us that "the evolution of a single species is a process which may take millions of years and which can never be duplicated."[6]

Following is a discussion of the four pragmatic values of wildlife:

1. The ecological arguments for species run like this: Most forms of wildlife are part of finely tuned, dynamic ecosystems. Mankind depends on healthy ecosystems for its biological sustenance. The disruption and degradation of ecosystems, through the extirpation of species and their habitats, can undermine this life-supportiong value. Says Lovejoy: "I submit that a nation which cannot afford to protect its endangered species has already overreached itself biologically."[7]

Still, we do not know much about the effects of species losses, so ecological arguments tend to be vague and unconvincing. Charles Warren, former chairman of the Council on Environmental Quality (CEQ), has warned against pushing such arguments too far. Though making a strong case in defense of endangered species on other grounds, Warren noted:

> By the time a species is as reduced in population as the California condor or the snail darter, it is doubtful that its ecological function is important to anything except itself—and, perhaps, to an ecosystem already on the verge of extinction.[8]

William T. Conway, director of the New York Zoological Park, concurs that an endangered population no longer is ecologically significant, though a threatened species, such as the African elephant, may be.[9] It is argued, too, that the loss of a species at the top of the food chain—like the condor, the grizzly bear, and the bald eagle—is not likely to affect the underlying ecosystem or man.

Paul Shepard, a professor of human ecology at Pitzer College, writes that:

> . . . in our present state of knowledge one cannot show that wolves, bears, tigers, eagles, green sea turtles, orioles, bullfrogs, monarch butterflies, olive baboons, red kangaroos, bottle-nosed dolphins, or a thousand other big species are really indispensable to their ecosystems. Indeed, the domino theory is just opposite the true metaphor of the web of nature. If one small strand goes, the whole does not fall, and in fact the survivors adjust to the break. . . .
>
> What is lost is not absolute for the ecosystem but relative. In spite of the dynamic balance of nature, "trade-offs" are possible. . . . To kill an ecosystem you must burn it up, plow it under, or poison it. Only at the level of its plant life, its microbes and its invertebrate fauna, is the natural system itself vulnerable.[10]

Of course, the burning, the plowing, and the poisoning are taking place on a grand scale. So an ecological judgment about a particular species must depend on the nature of the threat.

Then, too, ecologist Raymond Dasmann, professor of environmental studies at the University of California at Santa Cruz, notes that while no single creature may be essential to man's existence, in nature's overall scheme a species may have far more importance than suspected.[11]

Certainly the pursuit of ecological knowledge is full of surprises. For example, it had been assumed that in the Amazon the disappearance of fish-devouring caimans would greatly increase the native's fish catch. It is now asserted that the reverse is true—the more profuse the caiman excrement, the more nutrients for the production of fish in the aquatic system.[12]

Or consider the sacred cow in India, which outsiders have long considered a religious extravagance in a land plagued by hunger. Recent ecological perceptions seem to confirm what the Indians probably knew or sensed all along—that only by being strictly protected have their sacred cows been able to contribute in many more valuable ways to India's fragile human and agricultural ecosystem.[13]

Little is known, too, about the importance of species to the evolution of ecosystems and man himself.

How do we want the processes of evolution and species loss to continue, considering that man is intimately connected to all changes? Is it wise to permit the extinction of species before they are able to make their natural contributions to the fine threads of evolution?

It seems evident, finally, that damage or loss of a species, including those at the top of the food chain, can signal an unhealthy or dangerous condition in time to do something about it. Perhaps the most dramatic example is the way in which the withering of peregrine falcon and brown pelican populations revealed the insidious permeation of DDT and other chlorinated hydrocarbons.

2. Many hundreds of animal and plant species have provided substances of great scientific value to the medical, agricultural, and industrial operations of both primitive and modern societies. There is no reason to doubt that many other benefits will turn up in the future.

A natural storehouse of diverse genetic materials could be of inestimable value, permitting the breeding of crops or animals that give high yields and are resistant to pests and disease; the extraction of chemicals that repel or attract insect pests; and the exploitation of highly desirable wild food plants.

An estimated 80,000 edible plants enrich the earth, but man is believed to have used only about 3,000 for food, and few of those on a significant scale.[14] Efforts are being made to collect and store a large variety of seeds on a global basis. However, a CEQ report notes that seed collections "can never match nature's genetic wealth, and invariably involve seed mortality and cataloguing mistakes. Moreover, varieties in a collection do not continue to evolve as they would within a natural environment."[15]

Despite limited investigation, plant and wildlife species already have made enormous contributions to medical science. It is estimated that as many as half of all prescriptions written in the U.S. contain plant extracts as their main ingredients.[16] Plants, which have been called "chemical factories," often have been used as models for synthesized drugs, such as quinine.

An important group of drugs derived from plants are the alkaloids, some of which are used to treat leukemia and cardiac problems. Others show promise for use against several types of cancers and hypertension. Tropical plants are the source of the corticosteroids used in contraceptive pills and the chemicals that have greatly helped victims of Parkinson's disease.[17] Two drugs being tested for anticancer properties are derived from the mayapple herb, which the Penobscot Indians of Maine once applied to cancerous growths.[18] A molluscide recently found in pokeweed appears to have potential for controlling the snail that transmits schistosomiasis, one of the world's most widespread and debilitating diseases.[19]

To be sure, it is difficult to link medical benefits to particular endangered species. This make the scientific argument on their behalf somewhat speculative. However, says Edward S. Ayensu, a botanist at the Smithsonian Institution, "There is *no* plant that is unimportant. The genetic information contained in the germ plasm of each species is unique and cannot be reproduced once the last living tissue is gone."[20]

And only about 5 percent of all plant species have been screened for active pharmacological substances.[21] "Most plant species," says Siri von Reis Altschul, honorary curator of ethnobotany at the New York Botanical Garden, "including those long put to practical use by primitive societies, have never been scrutinized from the viewpoint and with the techniques of modern science."[22]

"Despite limited knowledge about genetic reservoirs," says conservation scientist Norman Myers, "it seems a statistical certainty that tropical forests contain source materials for many pesticides, medicines, contraceptive and abortifacient agents, potential foods, beverages, and industrial products." Myers, author of *The Sinking Ark*,[23] adds:

> Of particular value for human purposes are the specialized genetic characteristics of many localized species—yet these attributes are associated in many instances with restricted range, precisely the factor that makes them vulnerable to destruction.[24]

As Ayensu puts it:

Many of our rare and threatened species are especially valuable since they are able to grow in difficult habitats, such as cedar and shale barrens, islands, sand dunes, ocean and estuary shorelines, rock faces, mountaintops, bogs, and other unstable areas.[25]

Animals, too, have contributed greatly to the study of physiology and the testing of drugs for human use. (The advisability of this in terms of inhumane treatment is a critical question which must be sidestepped at this point.)[26]

Chimpanzees are used to test the safety of hepatitis vaccine. The cottontopped marmoset has been employed in a search for anticancer vaccines. The potential of the golden lion marmoset, now squeezed into a small habitat in Brazil, is unknown. Rhesus monkeys are used to test smallpox, measles, mumps, and most particularly, live polio vaccine.

The drug thalidomide was tested on rats and guinea pigs, then marketed. Tests on monkeys, performed later, would have shown in advance that the drug caused birth defects. The study of armadillos could lead to the development of a way to combat leprosy, since it is the only species other than man that contracts the disease. (Oddly, nine-banded armadillos also give birth only to quadruplets with identical genes.)

The list could go on and on. A final example is the tiny Devil's Hole pupfish, a species that survives only in a cavern pool in Nevada, where its status was protected after a dispute that went all the way to the Supreme Court.[27] The pupfish and its relatives thrive in hot or salty water, and a National Science Foundation report says:

[S]uch extreme conditions tell us something about the creatures' extraordinary thermoregulatory system and kidney function—but not enough as yet. . . . They can serve as useful biological models for future research on the human kidney—and on survival in a seemingly hostile environment. . . . Man, in the opinion of many ecologists, will need all the help he can get in understanding and adapting to the expansion of arid areas over the earth.[28]

As with the plants, the potential future benefits of preserving animal species are impossible to gauge.

3. The economic value of a wildlife species is hard to assess, but in some cases clearly is considerable. Many industries use natural substances from marine organisms, trees, fruits, flowers, and other species. New uses undoubtedly will be found. As Myers has noted "Today it is difficult for us to believe that, only 100 years ago, the rubber tree's value was not even remotely recognized."[29]

Overexploitation of the sardines off California's coast was a major and enduring economic setback, since they never returned to revive Cannery Row. The loss of elephant and other animal populations in

Africa also would have economic consequences for those countries which derive sizeable tourism revenues from them. In general, the legions of bird watchers, whale watchers, nature photographers, and others comprise a major part of the recreation and tourism industries.

After a stay in Africa, *New York Times* reporter Boyce Rensberger said that many wildlife conservation experts believe that only economic incentives have any promise of wide acceptance in developing countries. These would have to be based on revenues from tourism, or on controlled harvesting of animals and sale of their products. The profits from such harvesting, he said, would have to be distributed more evenly.[30]

An alternative, or supplementary, technique for making wildlife protection palatable would be for richer countries to subsidize it. Much of the responsibility for "preserving the earth's genetic heritage falls to poorer countries," notes the CEQ report:

> Those concerned about the depletion of species are, in effect, asking tropical countries to leave untapped the economic potentials of sizeable areas and to pass up possible development projects—for example, a dam that would destroy a unique habitat but would produce needed power and food. . . . [This predicament] could be partially untangled through global sharing of the costs of habitat protection. . . . If the world's extant species and gene pools are the priceless heritage of all humanity, then people everywhere may need to share the burdens of conservation according to their ability to do so.[31]

Of course, if a water, deforestation, or other project is environmentally or economically unsound overall, no outside incentive should be needed. Sometimes a project can be modified to serve wildlife needs. The proposed Kafue hydroelectric project in Zambia would have upset the water cycles and threatened the Lechwe, a small antelope species unique to the area. But to compensate for the loss of natural flooding, the dam was redesigned to allow additional reservoir storage and the discharge of water needed by wildlife during critical dry months.[32]

"The real problem," says William Conway, "is that man can get along economically without the overwhelming majority of animals and plant life, for some period of time. The economic trade-offs will not be consciously made. They are being made every day by fishermen, pastoralists, and farmers, in no orderly way."[33] Conway says he is not sanguine about the long-term potential of ethical rationales for protecting species. "Very few Latin American countries have any such ethical constraints in their cultures yet," he says. Some Asian countries have taken protective measures, "but ethical considerations sometimes fall by the wayside." In parts of Africa such as Kenya, Conway says, wildlife soon may be unable to compete with agriculture as a generator of dollars. "On the other hand, maybe by then there will have developed an ethos whereby the Kenyans come to value their bird life and animal life more highly."

4. In many ways, the glorious profusion and diversity of nature contributes immeasurably to the enrichment of human life and culture. The emotional enjoyment and sheer fascination of plants and animals is an ever-available tonic for the human psyche.

Botanist Anthony Huxley writes of the world of plants "whose diverse beauties help to keep us sane."[34] Uberto Tosco says that plants should be regarded as "Jewels in the devalued currency of our world environment."[35]

The educational and scientific investigation of species also contributes to the enrichment of the human mind. For example, the study of evolution, aside from its possible medical or other pragmatic benefits, fertilizes human thought and enlarges the understanding of homo sapiens itself.

Wayne Grimm, a malacologist with the National Museum of Canada, says that endangered species "are the key to the evolutionary process of all living things in an area; they demonstrate the process of isolation, genetic drift, the emergency of hybrids. . . ."[36]

The Socorro isopod, in fact, could conceivably be of great significance to the study of evolution. It is one of only two freshwater species in a family of marine isopods. Its ancestors presumably dwelled in the oceans that covered much of the west, and as the oceans receded, it adapted to life in a warmwater spring.[37]

Enormous sums of money are spent on an avid search for life in outer space. If a three-inch snail darter—or even an amoeba—had been found on Mars or the moon, the scientific community would have reveled in intellectual ecstasy. Here at home, the excitement is subdued.

In his book *Thinking Animals*, Paul Shepard constructed an elaborate and provocative thesis that the prime rationale for saving species— at least the major, visible species of animal—is that they are indispensable to human growth and thought.[38] Shepard identifies and explores the countless ways in which animals infuse our cultural and learning experiences; his purpose is to "identify and explore the ways in which the human mind needs animals in order to develop and work." Shephard says animals "have a very large claim on the maturing of the individual and his capacity to think and feel."

Although it is necessary to refer to the book for specifics on animals in literature, religion, sport, psychiatry, and other fields, Shepard summarizes part of his argument thus:

Human intelligence is bound to the presence of animals. They are the means by which cognition takes its first shape and they are the instruments for imagining abstract ideas and qualities, therefore giving us consciousness. . . . They are the means to self-identity and self-conscious-ness as our most human possession, for they enable us to objectify quali-ties and traits . . . they further, throughout our lives, a refining and mat-uring knowledge of personal and human being.

An Environmental Ethic Rediscovered

How persuasive are these reasons for protecting species? Even a wildlife scientist recently said that "some of the utilitarian arguments don't wash." Yet when all the pragmatic values are viewed together—with some allowance for the knowledge we still don't have—they constitute a forceful rationale.

Even so, in the long run, it is possible, if by no means certain, that all the utilitarian arguments will count for less than the potentially power-ful appeal of ethics and morality. This involves not only an insistence on humane behavior toward other species, but concepts of moral responsibility, reverence for life, animal rights, and human self-respect.

While such concepts apply to wildlife in general, feelings are sharp-ened when the total and irreversible loss of a species is at stake.

Roderick Nash, professor of history and environmental studies at the University of California, Santa Barbara, says that, from an ethical rather than an economic perspective, the conservation of species "is justified because, in the last analysis, it is right. The explosive force of this idea is only now beginning to be felt." Nash writes:

> It is intriguing to dwell on the possibility that the quest today for an environmental ethic is an effort to recover something that has been lost rather than to discover something new. Primitive man may well have possessed an ethic that extended well beyond his fellow men, one which embraced plants and animals, even mountains and rivers, all seen as members of his community and subject to ethical restraints. It is possible that, under the pressures of individualism, competition, technology, nationalism, and capitalism, mankind gradually lost this broad ethical perspective. Today, under the countervailing pressures of international-ism, exhaustion of resources, revision of priorities, and a growing under-standing of ecological reality, we may be recovering—or rediscovering—something which our ancestors instinctively grasped.[39]

Much has been said and written throughout history about the moral and legal rights of animals—as well as trees, plants, and other compo-nents of the natural world.[40] Some of the more recent statements have been legalistic, others more philosophical, such as this by Peter Singer:

> It can no longer be maintained by anyone but a religious fanatic that man is the special darling of the whole universe, or that other animals were created to provide us with food, or that we have divine authority over them, and divine permission to kill them.[41]

There is at the moment considerable disagreement among experts in the field about whether a strong ethic for species protection exists in this country now, and whether it is likely to blossom in the future.

"It bothers me that society has no ethic for dealing with animals," says John R. Clark, a marine ecologist with The Conservation Foundation:

> We have a few rules. Kill them humanely. Don't torture them. About two years ago, I thought we were really moving to an ethic by which people could have a respectful relationship with the other species on earth. But now I'm not sure. It doesn't seem to be happening.

On the other hand, the public has expressed considerable anxiety about the welfare of whales and eagles, and even smaller creatures like pupfish and snail darters.

Whether this represents a discernible trend is difficult to say. Shepard belittles the possibility that a new morality can be marshaled to save animals:

> Ethically, there have been discourses against the enslavement, torture, and killing of people since civilization began without ending war, tyranny, or cruelty. There is no evidence that crime, brutality, or murder have diminished at all. If human behavior is not improved by the incorporation of such ethics into the dominant religions, what reason is there to suppose that such a new ethic can save animals?[42]

Warren concurs that the ethical argument "will not take root in our society soon, if ever" and will "convince only those who are already disposed to accept it."[43]

In contrast to this view is the belief that endowing animals with rights is both indispensable and quite feasible—as an extension of the process of liberation for minority and other groups. At one time, blacks had no rights, and women no rights, points out Michael Fox, director of the Institute for the Study of Animal Problems, a division of the Humane Society. "So we're dealing with a broadening really, of our framework of moral reference."[44]

Roger Caras contends that wildlife cannot be saved "unless we can instill our beliefs in the people of our time and those to follow as moral and ethical issues. That they will buy." He cites two major precedents for such a major shift in thought: cannibalism and slavery. Slavery, he notes, "has in less than a century become morally and ethically repugnant."[45]

A final dimension to the argument is the thought—first expressed centuries ago—that cruelty or disrespect for other species can induce a callousness toward other humans. Or that if you can't respect the fellow creatures of the earth, you won't respect yourself.

Herbert Spencer said, "The behavior of men to the lower animals, and their behavior to each other, bears a constant relationship."[46] Feodor Dostoevsky, in *The Brothers Karamazov*, took the concept a few steps further:

> Love the animals, love the plants, love everything. If you love everything,
> you will perceive the divine mystery in things. Once you perceive it, you
> will begin to comprehend it better every day. And you will come at last to
> love the whole world with an all-embracing love.

Preserving Values in an Age of Scarcity

As environmental limitations and resource scarcities continue to take
their toll of society, the way we deal with them will determine, in large
measure, the very nature of our political and economic systems, and the
kind of civilization we leave to future generations.

For two centuries, philosophers and politicians have warned of the
many dangers that jeopardize the freedoms rooted in the United States'
democratic system. And the nation seems to have survived—without a
crippling, permanent erosion of these freedoms—such internal and
external threats as the Civil War, the Great Depression, Hitlerian fas-
cism, communism, racism, the Vietnam war, and Watergate.

But there is a new and lingering menace. It is not inherently political;
it is not caused chiefly by people and their malevolent behavior. It is
ecological and economic. It is caused by escalating demands on land,
air, water, energy, and other natural resources that support the political
and economic systems.

The result of environmental limitations is an increasing constriction
of those systems and of the governmental, individual, and corporate
freedoms that derive from them and that comprise our way of life.

Scarcities can be caused, and their effects exacerbated, not only by
growth in demand and population, but by manipulations and distribution and prices. The most obvious and serious examples so far, of
course, are the world food problem and the Arab oil embargo and
price-fixing agreements, with their dire economic effects in the U.S. and
elsewhere.

There are many other less blatant, or more localized, manifestations
of a long-term dilemma—the land and housing crunch, the transportation mess, the large array of pollution and other chemical hazards.
These are thorny to deal with politically. For the laws of ecology and
economics cannot be amended. And the race to forestall their effects by
applying more and more technology may be counterproductive.

There is a Greek chorus of warnings from many of our most perceptive thinkers about the insidious nature of this new dilemma. Their
theme is distressingly consistent:

• "The future austerity will be perennial," says historian Arnold
Toynbee, "and it will become progressively more severe. What then?
. . . Within each of the beleaguered 'developed' countries there will be a
bitter struggle for the control of their diminished resources." The struggle will have to be stopped, he says; therefore "a new way of life—a

severely regimented way—will have to be imposed by a ruthless authoritarian government."[47]

In a siege economy, Toynbee adds, such a government will have to
impose a scale of subsistence payments, and most private property
might have to be nationalized.

• A healthful and attractive urban environment "might have to be
sustained to a considerable degree by coercion," write Martin and Margy
Meyerson, both experts on urban planning. Most qualitative improvements in the environment—including pollution control, better transportation, more open space and recreation, decent housing—depend on
public, collective actions, including not only taxation and funding
support, but "regulation of behavior," or "requiring individuals or
firms or agencies to refrain from previous practices—practices they have
come to regard from habitual usage as freedoms."[48]

• Says William Ophuls, a political scientist and writer:

> The problem that the tragedy of the commons forces us to confront is, in
> fact, the core issue of political philosophy: How to protect or advance the
> interests of the collectivity as a whole when the individual that make it
> up . . . behave in a selfish, greedy and quarrelsome fashion. The only
> answer is a sufficient measure of coercion.
>   In a situation of ecological scarcity . . . the individualistic basis of
> society, the concept of inalienable rights, the purely self-defined pursuit
> of happiness, liberty as maximum freedom of action, and laissez-faire
> itself all require abandonment or major modification if we wish to avoid
> inexorable environmental degradation and perhaps extinction as a civili-
> zation. We must thus question whether democracy as we know it can
> survive.

Ophuls notes that the historic responses to scarcity have been war,
oppression, and "great inequality of wealth and the political measures
needed to maintain it."[49]

Nor is Ophuls sanguine about the potential for technological
answers:

> If the optimists are right in supposing that we can adjust to ecological
> scarcity with economics and technology, this effort will have, as we say,
> "side effects." For the collision with physical limits can be forestalled only
> by moving toward some kind of steady-state economy—characterized by
> the most scrupulous husbanding of resources, by extreme vigilance
> against the ever-present possibility of disaster should breakdown occur,
> and therefore, by tight controls on human behavior.[50]

• In his book *An Inquiry Into the Human Prospect*, Robert L.
Heilbroner repeatedly sounds a similar theme, and speculates on the
probably inadequate responses of both capitalist and socialist societies.
He suggests that we must be prepared to face the fact that "values and
beliefs precious to us may be assaulted by overriding claims of human
survival."

Heilbroner, an economics professor, wonders whether the "exigencies of the future . . . point to the conclusion that only an authoritarian, or possibly only a revolutionary, regime will be capable of mounting the immense task of social reorganization needed to escape catastrophe."

He speaks of enormous inflationary pressures that could "require the imposition of much stronger control measures than any that capitalism has yet succeeded in introducing," and of "intolerable strains on the representative democratic political apparatus." He warns of "the need to exercise a much wider and deeper administration of both production and consumption," of "psychological insecurity," of sharpened feelings of nationalism, of "wars of redistribution."[51]

What's at Stake

One could cite many other such warnings about the dangers of conflict, and of increasingly autocratic, overbearing government. For there can be no doubt that man's needs—not to mention his expectations—are outrunning the environment's ability to satisfy them. Individuals, nations and other entities are likely to be fighting more and more over the division of shrinking natural resources, incomes, and gross national products, and over competing values, freedoms, and amenities.

In fact, visible portents seem to be confirming the pessimistic prognoses. At the international level, we have seen cartels, embargoes, restrictions on immigration, fishing wars, disputes over access to the oceans—as well as increasing talk of coercive trade barriers and even the war over Middle Eastern oil. Many nations are pushing exports hard to cover their outlays for oil and reduce their trade deficits. The United States has furiously sold military equipment, with Middle East oil countries among the major buyers. The nation's surplus foods have sometimes been used for international economic and political leverage. "To a far greater degree than many Americans realize," notes Dan Morgan of the *Washington Post*, "the U.S. now depends on massive commercial exports of agricultral commodities in seeking a trade balance."[52] Five international economists have wondered whether oil-importing countries, "as they reach desperately for each other's markets, will also erect more menacing barriers against each other's exports." They speak of the possibilities of currency devaluations, defaults by business and banking firms, debt moratoria—and political revolution and debt repudiation.[53]

In this country, in addition to serious economic ills, we are witness to fuel allocations, disputes over the construction and location of energy facilities and waste disposal sites, efforts to restrain community growth, and many other confrontations over jobs, growth, and the protection of health and the environment.

In all these cases, someone's freedoms and privileges are at stake. But if the ecological-economic noose continues to tighten as expected, and we must brace ourselves for new restrictions on individual and corporate activity, then it will be useful to keep in mind that there are many *kinds* of freedoms and rights involved. Some are more critical to the welfare of the democratic system, and to the people, than others. Some, in fact, could more accurately be described as *privileges* that have come to be regarded as rights.

Consider a rough and perhaps arbitrary categorization of those rights and privileges that reflect the range of human values:

1. *Civil liberties.* Under this heading are the various political rights that are essential to democracy—the rights of free speech, assembly, due process of law, privacy, and security. One might add the right to play a role in political decision making, not just by voting but through direct participation in open government.

2. *Human rights.* The right to have enough to eat; the right to health and safety through sufficient protection from unsafe drinking water, polluted air, radioactivity, and hazardous chemicals in consumer products and in the workplace; and the right to reasonable space and quiet.

3. *Social rights.* Some of these might also be considered privileges or amenities. But the category could include the right to procreate; the right to have a job; the right to travel freely (to foreign lands? in a big car without expensive pollution controls? for unlimited mileage?); the right to own one's own home (a detached dwelling? with plenty of yard space? a second home, too?); the right to have access to an aesthetic environment, open space, and recreation opportunities.

4. *Economic freedoms or privileges.* For the individual, there is the right to earn a decent living, or the right to a guaranteed minimum income; the right to profit in business or in the sale or development of land; and the right to indulge one's material wants, what Heilbroner calls the "freedom of acquisition."

For corporations, there is the right to earn a profit; to use, and possibly pollute, common air, water, or land resources; to be free of price controls, export controls, burdensome taxes and other governmental interference with the marketplace; to withhold certain information from the public and the government; to obtain government subsidies; and to protect property from unfair confiscation.

5. *National rights.* A nation can be seen as entitled to freedom from unreasonable political, economic, or environmental aggression by other nations.

What is the status of environmental "rights" or "privileges"? Rene Dubos, the microbiologist and Pulitzer Prize-winning author, has said: "The new fact is that the right to a good environment has come to be regarded as a natural right of man for which the community is responsible." And he adds that "there has never been a lasting retreat from the recognition of a natural right of man."[54]

Nevertheless, the many rights and privileges at work in society are frequently antagonistic, and there are many conflicting perceptions of which are most important, as a few examples serve to illustrate:

• Rene Dubos said, "Privacy, space and quietness may not be essential for survival, but they are needs deeply rooted in human nature, and the demand for them increases with prosperity." (He added that with labor, energy and open land becoming more and more scarce and expensive, "the isolated freestanding house will become an economic burden too heavy for the average person, as well as becoming socially unacceptable."[55])

• Citing examples of Environmental Protection Agency (EPA) interference with development projects and with efforts to increase energy supplies, Irving Kristol, professor of urban values at New York University and co-editor of *The Public Interest*, says that Congress and the public

> . . . certainly never intended to give a handful of bureaucrats such immense powers. If the EPA's conception of its mission is permitted to stand, it will be the single most powerful branch of government, having far greater direct control over our individual lives than Congress, or the Executive, or state and local government. . . . [N]or are the American people likely to permit it to endure. Clean air is a good thing—but so is liberty, and so is democracy, and so are many other things.[56]

• Edmund K. Faltermayer, an editor of *Fortune* magazine, has written that it is important to keep free enterprise as unfettered as possible, but added this:

> Only in one area—in the determination of land-use patterns—need there be any curtailment of laissez-faire. But land use has never been determined solely by the market mechanism anyway; government has always intervened to some extent, in order to prevent a state of total anarchy.[57]

• In a 1974 attack on gasoline rationing, increased gasoline taxes, and wage-price controls, the *Dallas Morning News* said it is disturbing to hear officials "talk so blandly of coercive, totalitarian economic measures." It said that, "with more equanimity than is advisable, the American people are listening to a host of politicians demand that they be stripped of some basic liberties."[58]

• Paul W. McCracken, former chairman of the Council of Economic Advisers, wrote that it's logical to encourage people to save energy by switching to smaller cars, but added:

> On the other hand, availability of personal transportation will continue to be a jealously-prized freedom in the American setting and an energy policy which involves a drastic curtailment of that freedom is not apt to have staying power.[59]

On Shifting Gears

The relationships between people and automobiles are particularly illuminating when it comes to a discussion of values. While industry and government scratch for answers to the automobile problem, the people are out there doing their own motorized thing. Is the public passion for cars on the wane? Can American drivers be weaned from their cars? Should they be?

There is no agreement on the answers, of course, just as there is none between the sociologists and economists who extol cars and those who excoriate them. At least some observers believe the nation is growing out of the "American Graffiti" stage. But there is enough contrary evidence to deduce that cars will still be running around after all their drivers have expired.

There may be less reliance on the car as a status symbol. The conspicuousness of the automobile played a part in its early development, notes Joseph F. Coates, of the Office of Technology Assessment, U.S. Congress:

> It was good to have the first, or have the best, or the only, of an outstanding machine. This is a traditional characterization of American behavior in regard to gadgets, at least until a gadget becomes fully integrated in society.
>
> One still sees conspicuous consumption via the automobile, particularly among the nouveaux riches and in the ghettos.

But, he told an annual meeting of the American Association for the Advancement of Science, its importance diminishes as one moves up the socio-economic ladder. "This may be an important long-term trend."

In fact, says Coates, there is an "anti-conspicuous consumption attitude on the part of the middle class," what with the adoption of blue jeans and other "marks of calculated informality." And there are many new routes to conspicuous consumption—travel, electronic equipment, cameras, etc.

Similarly, Coates thinks the automobile is needed less for another kind of psychic support: "the manliness and independence" associated with wheels and power and other factors with a "juvenile orientation." He sees "less association between machismo, manliness and the car." Besides, adds Coates, "For those with the machismo hang-up there is a far better instrument—the motorcycle."

Related to this are the effects on automobile usage of the change in sexual mores. The car "seems to be of declining popularity as a portable bedroom. The openness of sex now makes other facilities more readily available and convenient." Coates further thinks the emphasis on cars may diminish as Americans lean more on individuality, health, and self-sufficiency, and as they take more to walking, bicycling, and other active pursuits.

But there are many reasons to suspect that automobiles in some form will continue to hold the nation in their clutches, shaping both its economy and its whole culture, for decades. As of 1979, the number of cars on the road was estimated to be more than 120 million. It is not hard to imagine that this number will climb significantly—considering (1) the steadily growing population, (2) the likelihood of increasing affluence, (3) the new recreational and other uses to which cars and other vehicles are put, and (4) the potential market for more cars per family.

The following Census Bureau figures for 1970 indicate the nature of this potential, assuming that those families with on or more cars are happy to have them:

Percentage of households with

| No car — 17.5 | Two cars — 29.3 |
| One car — 47.7 | Three or more cars — 5.5 |

Of course, many people without cars are unable to drive for various reasons.

The automobile's staying power in our society is partly explained by its functional values—its convenience, flexibility, and privacy. It is a source of mobility not only in the narrower sense, says Coates, but "in a larger sense of carrying us out of our neighborhoods, out of our milieu, out of our environment. . . . [I]t gives us choices and options regarding employment and recreation which go beyond the short-term immediate flexibilities of a day-to-day, work-a-day world."

Ironically, as people take up more outdoor activities such as boating, camping and skiing, they become more dependent on cars to get them there, beyond urbanization. And so there are mounting sales of both cars and recreational vehicles. Author Edward Ayres says this indicates that "even people who love the outdoors are growing to like the idea of rolling through the wilderness on wheels." Ayres added that, "in all this automania, there lurks the danger of a slowly diminishing quality of existence, of a fading appreciation of the experiences cars have usurped from the bodies and senses of men."[60] In a similar vein, San Diego columnist Neil Morgan has written that the freeway driving experience is "chillingly impersonal, suicidally frenetic, and so vacuous as to make [Los Angeles] inhabitants appear as the robots of a city that has become a puppet of technology."[61]

Yet for all the putdowns of the driving experience, there are many who sing its praises. And they seem to voice a sort of public consensus when they note that driving, in addition to its obvious convenience, induces euphoric feelings of motion and control, of purpose, of peace, of liberation. This peace, which derives from the privacy of the car, is otherwise hard for many people to find.

"It's the only time we're really disengaged," says one driver. Another says he gets into his car when he has trouble working. "My whole mind opens up, I'm so aware of things. It's a strange kind of highway narcosis."[62]

Even in the madding maze of city rush-hour traffic, these feelings may be at work. Speaking of privacy in mass society, sociologist Edward McDonagh said: "You find it driving to work, alongside all those other people, but alone with your thoughts. The car has become a secular sanctuary for the individual, his shrine to the self, his mobile Walden Pond."[63]

Conflicting Interests

In a time of tightening scarcities, private and public decisions can have a magnified effect on the distribution of resources, of economic benefits, and of freedoms and privileges. The recurring question will be: Who has the political or economic power to sustain their preferences? "The future," says Leonard J. Duhl, of the University of California's College of Environmental Design, "will be shaped by the outcome of the struggle of competing values."[64]

In that struggle, the conflicts and compromises—the trade-offs of rights and privileges—will be between various interests, broken down somewhat arbitrarily as follows:

1. *Individual vs. individual.* One person wants his property rezoned to allow development; his neighbor wants to protect his environmental advantages. Everyone wants to have wastes dumped, or an oil refinery located, in someone else's state or community.

A person living on a fixed income wants to see government brake inflation; another, laid off from his job, wants an antidote to recession. "Inflation makes spending decisions for us that we once were free to make ourselves," said the magazine *Skeptic*. "Inflation has narrowed our choices and options. In the end, it threatens to eliminate them entirely."[65] But the person out of a job is similarly without options.

The dilemma was put another way by Maurice Barbash in a letter to the *New York Times*: "A limitation on growth as our society is currently structured would impose a crushing sentence on the presently disadvantaged. We still operate under the terms of a 'trickle down' philosophy, where the poor get a little something only when the rich get richer."

2. *Individual vs. community.* A builder and a would-be homeowner are stymied by a community-imposed sewer moratorium. Or the government insists on purchase of an automobile pollution control device to safeguard the community's air resource.

3. *Individual, or community, vs. corporation.* The public wants a company to stop polluting a stream; but the company is anxious to avoid the high cost. To put it another way, a corporate activity that

benefits stockholders and company managers may be in conflict with the interests of residents, workers, or consumers, or a government acting in their behalf, or vice versa.

4. *Corporation vs. corporation.* With shortages of oil and natural gas, companies clash over their allocations. The same goes for places in the West where water is in limited supply.

5. *Nation vs. nation.* Export controls and other trade barriers are obvious examples of friction between developed and less-developed countries. These are unlikely to diminish with greater scarcity and greater conflict between environmental and development goals. "Mankind has still found no organized system for reconciling the driving demands and ambitions of national statehood with the wider unities of a shared planet," wrote Barbara Ward and Rene Dubos.[66]

Richard H. Gardner, law professor at Columbia University and a former State Department official, has suggested a "mutual survival pact," with developed nations agreeing to conserve energy, food, and other resources, and to provide needed access to markets, technology, and capital, while undeveloped countries agree to change some of their "suicidal" population, food, and environmental practices.[67]

6. *Present vs. future generations.* To what extent shall today's population husband its natural resources in the interests of tomorrow's, which has no say in the decisions? Heilbroner suggests that if we can acquiesce in the destruction of those contemporaries who rot in prison or starve to death, we are not likely to take the "painful actions" needed to protect future generations:

> Worse yet, will [we] not curse these future generations whose claims to life can be honored only by sacrificing present enjoyments; and will [we] not, if it comes to a choice, condemn them to nonexistence by choosing the present over the future.[68]

Allen V. Kneese, of Resources For the Future, notes that one of the questions is whether society should strike what Alvin M. Weinberg called the Faustian bargain with atomic scientists and engineers.

> If so unforgiving a technology as large-scale nuclear fission energy production is adopted, it will impose a burden of continuous monitoring and sophisticated management of a dangerous material, essentially forever.[69]

Columnist Anthony Lewis writes that one of society's greatest problems is the absence of

> . . . adequate mechanisms for weighing long-term interests against the immediate. Our system grew on the principle of the market. . . . The market ideal has given us wealth and much freedom. But its emphasis is necessarily on immediate gain. . . . We look to government to weigh the immediate against the distant, but our government is desperately short of people with the training and the vision to make such judgments.[70]

The absence of such vision has been most starkly revealed in the energy crisis of the 1970's. Fortunately, however, there are many reasons to believe that the energy problem can be turned into a substantial, albeit disguised, blessing. For it offers an unprecedented opportunity to examine some questionable traditions, and to plan for the future with a deeper economic, social, and ecological understanding. Suddenly the nation can no longer afford the luxury of leisurely, ivory-tower discussion. The current state of urgency can force the country and the world to face key issues squarely and with new awareness. For the first time, every move a corporation or government agency makes, everything a consumer buys, is being assessed almost instinctively in terms of energy consumption. We have a sharpened perception of many issues, from economic growth to foreign affairs, from transportation and city planning to individual and community life-styles.

The energy crisis, perhaps more than anything else in all of history, should engrave certain facts onto the world's generally numbed consciousness. These are: that vital resources are unevenly distributed; that because they are vital, they can be manipulated in politically dangerous ways; that as shortages become more binding, resources will be shared only through unprecedented multinational cooperation; and, most importantly, that all nations are in the same rather leaky, overloaded boat.

Individual Goals

The energy crisis has given us a golden opportunity to reexamine our social and personal aims, to reassess our way of life. William Bolitho put the internal conflict succinctly in *Twelve Against the Gods* in 1929: "The adventurer is within us, and he contests for our favor with the social man we are obliged to be. . . . We are born as wasteful and unremorseful as tigers; we are obliged to be thrifty, or starve, or freeze."

It's more than a question of simply cutting out waste and doing the same things more frugally. It involves a basic, revolutionary challenge to the present, blatantly materialistic society—a society seemingly absorbed by motorcycles for 10-year-olds, foppish shoes, and quadrasonic sound.

There have been countless acid comments about America's materialism—from economists and sociologists as well as poets and philosophers. It has been blamed, increasingly, for making us more selfish and inhumane, and for fostering delinquency, family alienation, and crime.

Mancur Olson, an economist at the University of Maryland, has referred to our "increasingly ambiguous luxuries."[71] Admiral Hyman G. Rickover is blunter: "The American public has been brainwashed during recent decades into the belief that progress means introducing into our lives everything we know how to produce." This, he says, leads to "a senseless consumption of electricity to create a more artificial life."[72]

Swedish economist Staffan Burenstam Linder has argued that the so-called "leisure class" is in fact the most harried, because it purchases and maintains so many goods it is unable to enjoy real leisure.[73] Similarly, columnist James Reston wrote that it is not our shortages but our surpluses that are hurting us. "Too much gas, too much booze, too much money, talk, noise. . . . We need to cut down, slow up, stay home, run around the block, eat vegetable soup, call up old friends and read a book once in a while."[74]

Many view things differently. For example, John B. Connally, when he was Secretary of the Treasury, spoke of a beautiful island he had visited:

> [It was] an artist's dream of a landscape. Pastures rimmed with rock walls, put there lovingly by hand without mortar . . . wildflowers growing in abundance, wild roses growing along every road, beautiful to behold. I looked at these beautiful white stucco houses with the red tile roofs and I thought how wonderful it was. And I began to drive through the villages and I asked about them. And of all the islands and of all the villages, only two of these lovely villages have our modern conveniences. The rest have no indoor plumbing. They have no bathroom facilities. They have no electricity. They have no running water. . . .
>
> Why should we be apologetic for what we have done? Name anybody, anywhere, anyplace on the face of this earth that has done as much. Why should we want to turn our backs on it?[75]

President Richard Nixon, in a 1973 energy speech, referred to the fact that per capita energy consumption in the U.S. is far higher than elsewhere in the world. He then said:

> That isn't bad; that is good. That means we are the richest, strongest people in the world, and that we have the highest standard of living in the world. That is why we need so much energy, and may it always be that way.

Fortunately, studies indicate that a reduction in the seemingly insatiable material desires of our more affluent citizens, at least, need involve little hardship, even to the psyche.

Richard A. Easterlin, a professor of economics at the University of Pennnsylvania, has analyzed several dozen surveys of the relationship between happiness and income. He finds the evidence pointing to these paradoxical conclusions:

> In all societies, more money for the individual typically means more individual happiness. However, raising the incomes of all does not

increase the happiness of all. . . . Richer countries are not typically happier than poorer ones. In the United States, the average level of happiness in 1970 was not much different from that in the late 1940's, though average income, after allowances for taxes and inflation, could buy over 60% more.

How can this be explained? Easterlin says that the satisfaction we get from our material well-being is not gauged by an absolute measure of goods we have, but according to how this compares with what we think we need. What we think we need derives, in turn, from our perceptions and experiences in society. "What one 'needs' as he reaches adulthood typically depends on the impressions he has formed of 'how to live' from observing life around him and in his society while growing up." People in the same society tend to have similar perceptions, thus establishing, in effect, a "social norm."[76]

It is a basis of "adaptation-level" theory that familiarity leads to decreasing satisfaction. Philip Brickman and Donald T. Campbell have written that we may be condemned to live on a "hedonic treadmill"—seeking "new levels of stimulation merely to maintain old levels of subjective pleasure." A more optimistic theme, they said, is that "society is overdue to undertake an explicit, experimental commitment to maximize the greatest subjective good for the greatest number."[77]

Harry Helson, retired professor of psychology at the University of Massachusetts, said: "The presence of extreme contrasts has accentuated the dissatisfactions and disequilibria that are found in our society today." These contrasts are perceived by "every individual who watches television, goes to the movies, or looks into the popular magazines."[78]

There are "nonrelativistic elements" of happiness, such as eating, noted Brickman and Campbell, and there may be a purely physical or physiological solution to the problem of happiness:

> Short of this, however, there may be no way to permanently increase the total of one's pleasure except by getting off the hedonic treadmill entirely. This is of course the historic teaching of the Stoic and Epicurean philosophers, Buddha, Jesus, Thoreau, and other men of widsom from all ages.

Unfortunately, they added, it is very difficult to do unless one has "travelled the full path from innocence to corruption."[79]

Despite all the stark warnings about the advent of authoritarian controls, we need not indulge ourselves in unbridled pessimism about the nation's future. The late British ecologist Sir Frank Fraser Darling once said, "Ecologists can scarcely afford to be optimists. But an absolute pessimist is a defeatist, and that is no good either."

Heilbroner, for all his gloom, says:

> The human prospect is not an irrevocable death sentence. It is not an inevitable doomsday toward which we are headed, although the risk of

enormous catastrophes exists. The prospect is better viewed as a formidable array of challenges that must be overcome before human survival is assured, before we can move *beyond doomsday*. . . . And the fact that the collective destiny of man portends unavoidable travail is no reason, and cannot be tolerated, as an excuse for doing nothing.

He maintains that intellectuals, with their "privileged roles as sentries for society," have the task of preparing their fellow citizens for the necessary sacrifices. Also, he says they must

. . . take the lead in seeking to redefine the legitimate boundaries of power and the permissible sanctuaries of freedom, for a future in which the exercise of power must inevitably increase and many present areas of freedom, especially in economic life, be curtailed. . . .
    What we do not know, but can only hope, is that future man can rediscover the self-renewing vitality of primitive culture without reverting to its levels of ignorance and cruel anxiety.[80]

Garrett Hardin, in his famous essay "The Tragedy of the Commons," wrote:

To many, the word coercion implies arbitrary decisions of distant and irresponsible bureaucrats; but this is not a necessary part of its meaning. The only kind of coercion I recommend is mutual coercion, mutually agreed upon by the majority of the people affected.[81]

Says Toynbee:

A society that is declining materially may be ascending spiritually. . . . The loss of our affluence will be extremely uncomfortable and it will certainly be difficult to manage. But in some respects, it may be a blessing in disguise, if we can rise to this grave occasion.[82]

A very good life is possible without our present profligacy, Ophuls concurs. He says we could achieve "a life of simple sufficiency that would yet allow the full expression of the human potential. Having chosen such a life, rather than having had it forced on us, we might find it had its own richness."[83]

In any case, most of the stark warnings of the Environmental Revolution are not intended to signal hopelessness, but to encourage us to make positive adjustments to changing realities. In doing this, the most important tasks are to protect the resources essential to life and to safeguard those freedoms that are truly important to us.

NOTES

THE ENVIRONMENTAL REVOLUTION

1. Max Nicholson, *The Environmental Revolution* (London: Hodder and Stoughton, 1970).
2. Wendell Phillips, speech, January 28, 1852.
3. Henry David Thoreau, "Walking" (1862).
4. Garrett Hardin, "The Tragedy of the Commons," in *Science,* December 13, 1968.
5. Lynton K. Caldwell, *Environment: A Challenge for Modern Society* (Garden City, N.Y.: Natural History Press, 1970).
6. Richard L. Means, *The Ethical Imperative* (New York: Doubleday, 1969).
7. William H. McNeill, *Plagues and People* (New York: Anchor Press, 1976).
8. Henryk Skolimowski, in *Ecologist Quarterly,* Autumn 1978.
9. *Ibid.*
10. Roger Starr, in *New York Times Magazine,* August 19, 1979.
11. Paul Shepard, *The Subversive Science,* ed. Paul Shepard and Daniel McKinley (Boston: Houghton Mifflin, 1969).
12. Henryk Skolimowski, in *The Ecologist,* October 1977.
13. Max Lerner, "Liberalism," *Encyclopedia Britannica* (Chicago: Encyclopedia Britannica, Inc., 1969).
14. Lynton K. Caldwell. See above, footnote 5.
15. *Scenic Preservation Conference* v. *FPC,* 354 F.2d 608.
16. Donnella Meadows, et al., *The Limits to Growth* (New York: Universe Books, A Potomac Associates Book, 1972).
17. Paul and Anne Ehrlich, *Population, Resources, Environment* (San Francisco: W.H. Freeman, 1972).
18. Neil H. Jacoby, in *Center Magazine* (Center for the Study of Democratic Institutions), November-December 1970.
19. California Environmental Quality Study Council, progress report, February 1971.
20. Ian McHarg, *Design with Nature* (Garden City, N.Y.: Natural History Press, 1969).
21. The June 1974 issue of *Conservation Foundation Letter* dealt with "carrying capacity" analysis.
22. Barry Commoner, *The Closing Circle* (New York: Alfred A. Knopf, 1971).
23. Samuel T. Dana, in *Conservation Foundation Letter,* February 23, 1968.
24. Jay W. Forrester, at the second general assembly of the World Future Society, June 2, 1975.

25. Nicholas Georgescu-Roegen, "U.S. Economic Growth from 1976 to 1986: Prospects, Problems, and Patterns" Joint Economic Committe, December 17, 1976.

26. Russell E. Train, at Earth Day '80 press conference, January 18, 1980.

27. Ronald G. Ridker, in *Science*, December 28, 1973.

28. SRI International, "City Size and Quality of Life," a report to the Senate Agriculture and Forestry Subcommittee on Rural Development, June 13, 1975.

29. Herman Daly, *Steady-State Economics* (San Francisco: W.H. Freeman, 1977).

30. The concept is discussed in S.C. Ciriacy-Wantrup, *Resource Conservation Economics and Policies* (Berkeley: University of California Press, 1952); Daniel Fife, in *Environment*, April 1971; and Colin W. Clark, in *Science*, August 17, 1973.

31. 15 U.S. Code 2601.

32. *In re Stevens Industries, Inc.*, June 14, 1972.

33. *Ethyl Corp.* v. *EPA*, U.S. Court of Appeals for the District of Columbia, 541 F.2d 1.

34. See, especially, *The Closing Circle*.

35. For example, Barry Commoner, *The Poverty of Power* (New York: Alfred A. Knopf, 1976); Amory B. Lovins, *Soft Energy Paths* (Cambridge, Mass.: Ballinger, 1977).

36. A detailed account of the air-pollution battle in Pittsburgh is given in Charles O. Jones, *Clean Air: The Policies and Politics of Pollution Control* (Pittsburgh: University of Pittsburgh Press, 1975).

37. *Federal Register,* January 17, 1969.

38. Letter from Sydney Howe, then president of The Conservation Foundation, to John T. Middleton, September 2, 1969.

39. "Don't Leave It All to the Experts," Environmental Protection Agency, November 1972.

40. Gladwin Hill, *New York Times,* December 30, 1979.

41. William K. Reilly, radio interview on FOCUS, December 1979.

42. *Washington Post,* December 31, 1979.

43. *New York Times Magazine,* November 4, 1979.

44. Douglas M. Costle, in *EPA Journal,* January 1980.

45. G. Keith Rogers, in *Time,* December 3, 1979.

46. Nuclear Regulatory Commission, program summary report, July 20, 1979.

47. See Rice Odell, *The Saving of San Francisco Bay* (Washington, D.C.: The Conservation Foundation, 1972).

48. Council on Environmentql Quality, *Our Nation's Wetlands,* an interagency task force report (Washington, D.C.: 1979).

49. Council on Environmental Quality, *Annual Report* (Washington, D.C.: 1978).

50. William E. Shands, et al., *National Forest Policy: From Conflict Toward Consensus* (Washington, D.C.: The Conservation Foundation, 1979).

51. U.S. Department of Interior, "Environmental Impact of the Big Cypress Swamp Jetport" (Washington, D.C.: 1969).

52. National Academy of Sciences, "Jamaica Bay and Kennedy Airport" (Washington, D.C.: 1971).

53. *EPA Journal,* January 1980.

54. Russell E. Train. See above, footnote 26.

55. House Interstate and Foreign Commerce Committee, *House Report 1491, 1976.* For a full discussion of hazardous waste regulatory problems, see House Commerce Committee Subcommittee on Oversight and Investigations, "Hazardous Waste Disposal," September 1979.

56. *Washington Post,* January 3, 1980.

57. Michael Goodwin, in *New York Times,* October 21, 1979.

58. William K. Reilly. See above, footnote 41.

59. See *Conservation Foundation Letter,* November 1978.

60. Juan Cameron and Richard I. Kirkland, Jr., in *Fortune,* January 14, 1980.

61. Douglas M. Costle, in *EPA Journal,* November/December 1979.

62. Eugene Kennedy, in *New York Times Magazine,* December 2, 1979.

63. Herman Kahn, *World Economic Development* (Boulder, Colo.: Westview Press, 1979).

64. Jean-Francois Revel, *Without Marx or Jesus* (New York: Dell, 1974).

CHAPTER I: HISTORICAL FAILURES

1. Vernon Gill Carter and Tom Dale, *Topsoil and Civilization,* rev. ed. (Norman, Okla.: University of Oklahoma Press).

2. See, for example, George F. Carter, *Man and the Land* (New York: Holt, Rinehart and Winston, 1964).

3. William H. McNeill, *Plagues and Peoples* (Garden City, N.Y.: Anchor/ Doubleday, 1976).

4. Paul B. Sears, in *Environmental Geomorphology and Landscape Conservation,* ed. Donald R. Coates, vol. 1 (Stroudsburg, Pa.: Dowden, Hutchinson, & Ross, 1972).

5. Thorkild Jacobsen and Robert M. Adams, in *Science,* November 21, 1958. See also Erik P. Eckholm, *Losing Ground* (New York: W.W. Norton, 1976).

6. J. Donald Hughes, *Ecology in Ancient Civilizations* (Albuquerque, N.M.: University of New Mexico Press, 1975).

7. The words are those of geographer Donald R.Coates, who so characterized Professor Bell's theme. See above, footnote 4.

8. Fernand Braudel, *The Mediterranean,* vol. 1 (New York: Harper & Row, 1972).

9. Reid A. Bryson and David A. Baerreis, in *Bulletin of the American Meteorological Society,* March 1967. See also Stephen H. Schneider, *The Genesis Strategy* (New York: The Plenum Press, 1976).

10. Georg Borgstrom, *Too Many* (New York: Macmillan,1969).

11. Vernon Gill Carter and Tom Dale. See above, footnote 1.

12. William H. McNeill. See above, footnote 3.

13. George Perkins Marsh, *Man and Nature,* ed. David Lowenthal (Cambridge, Mass.: Harvard University Press, 1965).

14. Walter Clay Lowdermilk, in *Smithsonian Institution Annual Report,* 1943. See also above, footnote 4.

15. Edward Goldsmith, "The Fall of the Roman Empire," in *The Ecologist,* July 1975.

16. Fernand Braudel. See above, footnote 8.

17. Vladimir G. Simkhovitch, "Rome's Fall Reconsidered," in *Political Science Quarterly,* June 1916. See also above, footnote 10.

18. Vernon Gill Carter and Tom Dale. See above, footnote 1.

19. Donald R. Coates, interview, October 1977.

20. B.L. Turner II, "Prehistoric Intensive Agriculture in the Mayan Lowlands," in *Science,* July 12, 1974.

21. Karl A. Wittvogel, in *Man's Role in Changing the Face of the Earth,* ed. W.L. Thomas (Chicago: University of Chicago Press, 1956). See also Karl W. Butzer, *Early Hydraulic Civilization in Egypt* (Chicago: University of Chicago Press, 1976).

22. Harry Walters, *Ecology, Food and Civilization* (London: Charles Knight & Co., 1973).

23. Walter Clay Lowdermilk. See above, footnote 14.

24. *Population Bulletin,* Population Reference Bureau, September 1977.

25. See Otis L. Graham, Jr., Garrett Hardin, and Ronald M. Green, "Immigration Ethics," in *World Issues,* Center for the Study of Democratic Institutions (Santa Barbara, Calif.), February/March 1978. See also David Gordon, in *The Economist,* April 22, 1978; Richard R. Fagen, in *Foreign Affairs,* July 1977; and *Environmental Action,* June 1979.

26. Daniel Bell, "Future World Disorder: The Structural Context of Crises," in *Foreign Policy,* Summer 1977.

27. Thomas A. Sloan, in *The Global Predicament,* eds. David W. Orr and Marvin S. Soroos (Chapel Hill, N.C.: University of North Carolina Press, 1979).

28. A fascinating example—the worldwide impact of volcanic eruptions around 1815—is detailed in John Dexter Post, *The Last Great Subsistence Crisis in the Western World* (Baltimore: The Johns Hopkins University Press, 1977).

29. J. Donald Hughes, "Deforestation and Erosion in Greece and Rome," paper prepared for The Conservation Foundation, Washington, D.C., November 1978.

30. Donald R. Coates, ed., *Environmental Geomorphology and Landscape Conservation.* See above, footnote 4.

31. McGuire Gibson, paper prepared for UNITAR conference on desert development and management, Sacramento, Calif., June 1977.

32. William H. McNeill, *The Rise of the West* (Chicago: University of Chicago Press, 1963).

33. *Washington Post,* October 1, 1979.

34. Josef Eisinger, in *Trends in Biochemical Sciences,* July 1977.

35. For example, see S.C. Gilfillan, in *Journal of Occupational Medicine,* February 1965.

36. *Washington Post,* November 3, 1979

37. *The Futurist,* April 1979.

38. *Chemical and Engineering News,* October 22, 1979.

39. Robert Strausz-Hupe, in *Philadelphia Inquirer*, 1968.

40. Arnold J. Toynbee, *A Study of History* (Oxford: Oxford University Press, 1947).

41. Denis Goulet, *The Uncertain Promise* (New York: IDOC/North America, 1977).

42. *Chemical Week*, November 8, 1978.

43. *The New Yorker*, October 15, 1979.

CHAPTER 2: FOOD

1. Senator George McGovern, *Congressional Record*, August 3, 1973.

2. Lester R. Brown, in *Wall Street Journal*, March 26, 1973.

3. Louis Thompson, speech to Soil Conservation Society of America, October 1, 1973.

4. Willard Cochrane, testimony before the Congressional Joint Economic Committee, July 30, 1973.

5. Norman Borlaug, testimony before two Senate Agriculture and Forestry subcommittess, October 17-18, 1973.

6. *Ibid.*

7. Lester R. Brown. See above, footnote 2.

8. Addeke H. Boerma, statement to United Nations Economic and Social Council, Geneva, Switzerland, July 5, 1973.

9. United Nations Food and Agriculture Organization, *The State of Food and Agriculture 1977* (New York: 1978).

10. Edgar Owens, testimony before the House Foreign Affairs Committee, May-June 1973.

11. Alan Berg, "Nutrition, Development, and Population Growth," in *Population Bulletin*, vol. 29, no. 1, Population Reference Bureau, 1973.

12. Willard Cochrane. See above, footnote 4.

13. Georg Borgstrom, interview.

14. *Washington Post* editorial, August 23, 1973.

15. Interview.

16. Georg Borgstrom, interview.

17. Lester R. Brown, interview.

18. Lester R. Brown and Gail W. Finsterbusch, *Man and His Environment: Food* (New York: Harper & Row, 1972).

19. President's Science Advisory Committee, *The World Food Problem*, vol. 2 (Washington, D.C.: Government Printing Office, 1967).

20. National Academy of Sciences, *Resources and Man* (San Francisco, Calif.: W.H. Freeman & Co., 1969).

21. President's Science Advisory Committee. See above, footnote 19.

22. Raymond F. Dasmann, et al., *Ecological Principles for Economic Development* (New York: John Wiley & Sons, 1973); *Tropical Forest Ecosystems in Africa and South America* (Washington, D.C.: Smithsonian Institution Press, 1973).

23. Walter H. Pauley, "Possibilities of Increasing World Food Production," United Nations Food and Agriculture Organization, 1963.

24. *Ibid.*

25. Addeke H. Boerma, speech to International Development Conference, Washington, D.C., October 23, 1973.

26. U.S. Department of Agriculture Soil and Water/Conservation Service, "National Inventory of Soil and Water Conservation Needs, 1967," *Statistical Bulletin*, No. 461 (Washington, D.C.: 1971).

27. *Science*, November 16, 1973.

38. James I. Middleswart, interview.

29. Harry M. Caudill, in *Atlantic Monthly*, September, 1973.

30. David M. Gates, in *Scientific American*, September 1971.

31. William Paddock and Paul Paddock, *Famine 1975!* (Boston: Little, Brown & Co., 1967).

32. Roy W. Simonson, interview.

33. Lester R. Brown, "Why Hunger?", Overseas Development Council communique, April 1971.

34. Darnell M. Whitt, interview.

35. See, for example, *The Careless Technology* (Garden City, N.Y.: Natural History Press, 1972).

36. Georg Borgstrom, interview.

37. Robert S. McNamara, address to Board of Governors, World Bank Group, Nairobi, Kenya, September 24, 1973.

38. See, for example, H. Garrison Wilkes and Susan Wilkes, "The Green Revolution," in *Environment*, October 1972.

39. "Farming With Petroleum," in *Environment*, October 1972; see also Eric Hirst, "Food Energy Requirements," and David Pimental, et al., "Food Production and the Energy Crisis," in *Science*, November 2, 1973.

40. Quentin M. West, speech at Oklahoma State Fair Energy Forum, Oklahoma City, Oklahoma, September 29, 1973.

41. Lester R. Brown and Gail W. Finsterbusch. See above, footnote 17.

42. Roy W. Simonson. See above, footnote 32.

43. National Academy of Sciences. See above, footnote 20.

44. Edgar Owens, see above, footnote 10; Penny Lernoux, "Illusions of Agrarian Reform," in *The Nation*, October 15, 1973; and Robert S. McNamara, see above, footnote 37.

45. Lester R. Brown, in *Population Bulletin*, vol. 29, no. 2, Population Reference Bureau, 1973.

46. Georg Borgstrom, interview.

47. "Lives in Peril," United Nations Food and Agriculture Organization, 1970.

48. Alan Berg. See above, footnote 11.

49. "Lives in Peril." See above, footnote 47.

50. Alan Berg. See above, footnote 11.

51. Georg Borgstrom, in *Science and Public Affairs*, October 1973.

52. Lester R. Brown and Gail W. Finsterbusch. See above, footnote 17.

53. Robert H. Boyle, in *Sports Illustrated*, September 24, 1973.

54. Alan Berg. See above, footnote 11.

55. United Nations Food and Agriculture Organization, *The State of Food and Agriculture 1973* (New York: 1974).

56. United Nations Protein Advisory Group, Statement no. 20, 1973.

57. Addeke H. Boerma. See above, footnote 25.

58. Georg Borgstrom. See above, footnote 51.

59. Georg Borgstrom, interview.

60. Paul Simon and Arthur Simon, *The Politics of World Hunger* (New York: Harper's Magazine Press, 1973).

CHAPTER 3: WATER

1. Gilbert F. White, in *Natural Resources Journal*, October 1976.

2. *Montana Outdoors*, vol. 8, no. 2, 1976.

3. John F. Griffiths, in *Mosaic*, National Science Foundation, January/February 1977.

4. These and other droughts were described by L. Dean Burk, a climatologist at the Kansas Agricultural Experiment Station, at the American Association for the Advancement of Science meeting in Denver, Colorado, February 21, 1977.

5. Gary D. Weatherford and Gordon C. Jacoby, "Impact of Energy Development on the Law of the Colorado River," in *Natural Resources Journal*, January 1975.

6. *Ibid.*

7. Stephen H. Schneider, testimony before Senate Public Works Subcommittee on Water Resources, March 31, 1977.

8. Among many excellent discussions of climate problems is Stephen H. Schneider, *The Genesis Strategy* (Garden City, N.Y.: The Plenum Press, 1976).

9. Stephen H. Schneider. See above, footnote 7.

10. See Senator Frank E. Moss, *The Water Crisis* (New York: Praeger, 1967).

11. Figures are from the 1973 report of the National Water Commission, Washington, D.C.

12. Among the comprehensive reports on the Colorado River situation: *Natural Resources Journal*, January 1975; "Colorado Water," League of Women Voters of Colorado, 1975; *Water and Choice in the Colorado Basin*, National Academy of Sciences, 1968; and T.H. Watkins, *The Grand Colorado* (New York: American West/Crown, 1969).

13. Water Resources Council, "Task Force Report on Water Requirements," for Project Independence, Washington, D.C., November 1974.

13a. Gary D. Weatherford and Gordon C. Jacoby. See above, footnote 5.

14. *New York Times*, March 3, 1977.

15. Colorado River Basin Project Act of 1968, 943 U.S. Code 1511.

16. Gary D. Weatherford and Gordon C. Jacoby. See above, footnote 5.

17. "Water Resources of the Missouri River Basin," report of the Senate Interior Subcommittee on Energy Research and Water Resources, November 1976.

18. Much has been written about minimum stream flows. A specific and enlightening discussion is Liter Spence, "Montana's New Water Law," in *Montana Outdoors*, January/February 1977.

19. The key case was *Federal Power Commission* v. *Oregon*, 349 U.S. 435 (1955).

20. *Winter* v. *U.S.*, 207 U.S. 564 (1908).

21. *Arizona* v. *California*, 373 U.S. 546 (1963).

22. Most references on water resources or water projects contain discussions of Indian rights.

23. *Arizona Republic*, February 26, 1977.

24. Colorado River Basin Project Act. See above, footnote 15.

25. *Daily Astorian*, December 20, 1976.

26. Robert F. Vining, in newsletter of "1,000 Friends of Oregon," February 1977.

27. See discussion earlier in this chapter.

28. General Accounting Office, "Problems Affecting Usefulness of the National Water Assessment," March 23, 1977.

29. Under the Water Resources Planning Act of 1965, 42 U.S. Code 1962a-1.

30. See discussion earlier in this chapter.

31. These were prepared for the Water Resources Council by the Bureau of Economic Analysis of the Commerce Department and the Economic Research Service of the Agriculture Department. Federal regulations (40 C.F.R.1500.8) say that federal agencies, in preparing environmental impact statements, "should give consideration" to the WRC projections.

32. A full set of recommendations for dealing with water problems is contained in the National Water Commission report of 1973 and the summary volume, *New Directions in U.S. Water Policy*.

33. Stephen H. Schneider. See above, footnote 7.

34. Helen Ingram, in *Values and Choice in the Development of an Arid Land River Basin*, eds. D.F. Peterson and A.B. Crawford (Tucson, Az.: University of Arizona Press, 1977).

35. Jack Shepherd, "A New Environment at Interior," in *New York Times Magazine*, May 8, 1977.

36. See discussion earlier in this chapter.

37. James P. Sterba, *New York Times*, March 23, 1977.

38. Harold Faber, *New York Times*, March 6, 1977.

39. *Environmental Science and Technology*, March 1976, p. 226.

40. Aaron Weiner, testimony before Senate Public Works Subcommittee on Water Resources, March 31, 1977.

41. Some are analyzed in G.L. Dugan and P.H. McGauhey, "A Second Look at Water Re-Use," in *Water Pollution Control Federation Journal*, February 1977.

42. *Environmental Science and Technology*, February 1977, p. 126, and June 1976, p. 524.

43. See below, Chapter 5: Climate Modification. A brief report on these issues is contained in *Nature*, February 24, 1977.

44. *Rocky Mountain News*, February 23, 1977.

45. *New York Times* editorial, March 9, 1977.

46. *Time*, March 7, 1977; and *New York Times* editorial, November 11, 1976.

47. Grace Lichtenstein, *New York Times*, January 20,1977.

48. General Accounting Office, "Better Federal Coordination Needed to Promote More Efficient Farm Irrigation," June 22, 1976.

49. Thomas Barlow, testimony before Senate Public Works Subcommittee on Water Resources, March 31, 1977.

50. See above, footnote 32.

51. *Irrigation Age,* September 1976, p. 37.

52. General Accounting Office. See above, footnote 48.

53. *Congressional Record,* April 19, 1977,p.E2261.

54. Ruth Lahav, "Water in Israel: The Bottomless Pitcher," article distributed by Consulate General of Israel, April 1977.

55. See above, footnote 32.

56. Water Resources Council, *The Nation's Water Resources,* 1968.

57. As with energy, much practical information on water conservation techniques is contained in various grass-roots and other publications—for example, *RAIN,* April 1977, and *Econews,* March 1977.

58. American Association for the Advancement of Science, annual meeting, Denver, Colorado, February 21, 1977.

59. See *The Conservation Foundation Letter,* June 1974, on carrying capacity.

60. *Planning,* April/May 1977.

61. *Washington Post,* March 26, 1977.

62. Paul Castro, testimony before House Appropriations Subcommittee on Public Works, March 28, 1977.

63. Frank Quinn, in *Geographical Review,* January 1968.

64. Congressional Research Service, "Water Resources of the Missouri River Basin," in report of Senate Interior Subcommittee on Energy Research and Water Resources, November 1976, p. 1-34a.

65. Gilbert F. White. See above, footnote 1.

CHAPTER 4: POPULATION

1. U.S. Bureau of the Census, "World Population: 1977," report prepared for the Agency for International Development (advance summary, 1978).

2. W. Parker Mauldin, in *Studies in Family Planning,* The Population Council, April 1978.

3. Amy Ong Tsui and Donald J. Bogue, in *Population Bulletin,* Population Reference Bureau, October 1978.

4. *New York Times,* November 20, 1978.

5. *Washington Post,* November 26, 1978.

6. *New York Times,* November 30, 1978.

7. *The Futurist,* October 1978.

8. Marshall Green and Robert A. Fearey, in *New York Times,* January 10, 1979.

9. U.S. Bureau of the Census. See above, footnote 1.

10. *Population Bulletin,* vol. 29, no. 5, Population Reference Bureau, 1974.

11. Amy Ong Tsui and Donald J. Bogue. See above, footnote 3.

12. U.S. Bureau of the Census. See above, footnote 1.

13. Population Reference Bureau, "1978 World Population Data Sheet," March 1978.

14. Marshall Green and Robert A. Fearey, "Silent Explosion," reprint of articles in the October, November, and December 1978 *Department of State Bulletin.*

15. W. Parker Mauldin and Bernard Berelson, in *Studies in Family Planning*, The Population Council,May 1978.

16. *Washington Post*, December 2, 1978.

17. Amy Ong Tsui and Donald J. Bogue. See above, footnote 3.

18. Davidson R. Gwathkin and James P. Grant, Overseas Development Council, Paper for Fifth International Health Conference, New York, May 14-17, 1978.

19. *Wall Street Journal*, October 24, 1978.

20 John J. Gilligan, speech before Planned Parenthood Federation of America, October 26, 1978.

21. John Passmore, *Man's Responsibility for Nature* (New York: Charles Scribner's Sons, 1974).

22. Joseph Kraft, in *Washington Post*, December 5, 1978.

23. "Domestic Consequences of United States Population Change," House Select Committee on Population, December 1978.

24. "Legal and Illegal Immigration to the United States," House Select Committee on Population, Serial C, December 1978. Figures on immigration are also contained in "Questions and Answers on U.S. Immigration and Population," Zero Population Growth, September 1978, and in "Projecting the U.S. Population to the Year 2000," The Environmental Fund, May 1978.

25. Lester R. Brown, *Worldwatch Paper 20*, Worldwatch Institute, May 1978.

26. George J. Beier, in *Population Bulletin*, Population Reference Bureau, December 1976.

27. Alexander Shakow, testimony before House Select Committee on Population, in "Population and Development Assistance" report, December 1978.

28. Report of House Select Committee on Population, December 1978.

29. *Intercom*, Population Reference Bureau, May 1977.

30. See above, footnote 28.

31. Amy Ong Tsui and Donald J. Bogue. See above, footnote 3. See also Ronald Freedman and Bernard Berelson, in *Studies on Family Planning*, The Population Council, January 1976.

32. See, for example, *Population Bulletin*, Population Reference Bureau, November 1977; and Bill Peterson in *Washington Post*, May 18, 1978.

33. A.R. Omran and M.N. El-Khorazaty, paper presented to annual meeting of Population Association of America, St. Louis, Mo., April 1977.

34. W. Parker Mauldin and Bernard Berelson. See above, footnote 15.

35. The issues are debated in many books and documents. For a brief discussion, see "World Population: Myths and Realities," Report of House Select Committee on Population, October 1978. Agency for International Development (AID) policy is reviewed at some length in the report "Reducing Population Growth Through Social and Economic Change in Developing Countries—New Direction for U.S. Assistance," General Accounting Office, April 5, 1978.

36. Selwyn Enzer, et al., in *The Futurist*, October 1978. For an excellent commentary on the nature and dangers of income maldistribution, see Richard R. Fagen, in *Foreign Affairs*, February 1979.

37. Emilio Casetti, in *Journal of Developmental Studies*, April 1977.

38. Emilio Casetti, chapter for book, *Dimensions of Geography*, published in India. The point is discussed as it relates to Mexico by Ansley J. Coale, in *Foreign Affairs*, January 1978.

39. William Pfaff, in *The New Yorker*, February 19, 1979.

40. Marshall Green and Robert A. Fearey. See above, footnote 14.

41. Selwyn Enzer, et al. See above, footnote 36.

42. See William Branigan, in *Washington Post*, December 29, 1978.

43. Quoted by David Vidal, in *New York Times*, February 4, 1979.

44. Lawrence C. Stedman, in *Foreign Affairs*, Winter 1978/79.

45. Robert Repetto, in *Journal of Developmental Studies*, July 1978.

46. Robert S. McNamara, address at Massachusetts Institute of Technology, April 1977. See also William Rich, *Smaller Families Through Social and Economic Progress*, Overseas Development Council, 1973.

47. National Security Council Ad Hoc Group on Population Policy, Second Annual Report, January 1978.

48. Kariba J.C. Munio, speech to American Association for the Advancement of Science, annual meeting, Philadelphia, Pa., December 1971.

49. Reuters News Service, in *New York Times*, January 18, 1979.

50. Hobart Rowen, in *Washington Post*, November 11, 1978.

51. Leo A. Orleans, in *Current Scene*, February/March 1978.

52. *Time*, January 15, 1979.

CHAPTER 5: CLIMATE

1. Charles F. Cooper, in *Foreign Affairs*, April 1978.

2. Jim Norwine, in *Environment*, November 1979.

3. *Ibid.*

4. G. Callendar, in *Quarterly Journal of the Royal Meteorological Society*, vol. 64, 1938.

5. Roger Revelle and Hans E. Suess, in *Tellus*, no. 1, 1957.

6. News release, National Oceanic and Atmospheric Administration, May 29, 1979.

7. Minze Stuiver, in *Science*, January 20, 1978.

8. C.F. Baes Jr., et al., in *American Scientist*, May/June 1977.

9. Lester Machta, interview.

10. "Summary of the Carbon Dioxide Effects Research and Assessment Program," Department of Energy, April 2, 1979.

11. Wil Lepowski, in *Chemical and Engineering News*, October 17, 1977.

12. George M. Woodwell, et al., in *Science*, January 13, 1978. See also Woodwell in *Scientific American*, January 1978.

13. National Academy of Sciences, "Energy and Climate," 1977.

14. Wil Lepkowski. See above, footnote 11.

15. C.F. Baes, Jr., et al. See above, footnote 8.

16. National Academy of Sciences. See above, footnote 13.

17. Charles F. Cooper. See above, footnote 1.

18. Earthscan Press Briefing Document no. 13, January 1979.

19. Wallace C. Broecker, in *Technology Review*, October/November 1977.

20. C.F. Baes, Jr., et al. See above, footnote 8.

21. John Dexter Post, *The Last Great Subsistence Crisis in the Western World* (Baltimore: The Johns Hopkins University Press, 1977).

22. Wallace C. Broecker. See above, footnote 19.

23. Dewey M. McLean, in *Science*, August 4, 1978.

24. Charles F. Cooper. See above, footnote 1.

25. William W. Kellogg, in *Climatic Change*, ed. John Gribbin (Cambridge: Cambridge University Press, 1978).

26. National Academy of Sciences. See above, footnote 13.

27. Office of Technology Assessment, "The Direct Use of Coal," April 1979.

28. *Washington Post*, May 21, 1978.

29. Earthscan. See above, footnote 18.

30. "The Long-Term Impact of Atmospheric Carbon Dioxide on Climate," JASON Report, SRI International, April 1979.

31. *Washington Post*, June 21, 1979.

32. *New York Times*, July 12, 1979.

33. *Washington Post*, July 11, 1979.

34. Denis Hayes, *Rays of Hope* (New York: W.W. Norton & Co., 1977).

35. Stephen H. Schneider, *The Genesis Strategy* (Garden City, N.Y.: The Plenum Press, 1976).

36. Quoted in Wil Lepkowski. See above, footnote 11.

37. *Ibid.*

38. Department of Energy "Summary." See above, footnote 10.

39. Cesare Marchetti, International Institute for Applied Systrems Analysis, 1976.

40. M.I. Budyko, in *Climatic Changes*, American Geophysical Union, 1977 (Soviet Union edition, 1974).

41. Charles F. Cooper. See above, footnote 1.

42. William W. Kellogg. See above, footnote 25.

43. *Science News*, April 14, 1979.

44. Seymour M. Hersh, in *New York Times*, May 19, 1974.

45. Richard A. Frank, testimony before Senate Commerce subcommittee on science, technology, and space, October 24, 1979.

46. "A National Program for Accelerating Progress in Weather Modification," Interdepartmental Committee for Atmospheric Sciences, Report no. 15a, June 1971.

47. National Advisory Committee on Oceans and Atmosphere, First Annual Report, June 30, 1972.

48. Gordon McDonald, testimony before Senate Foreign Relations Subcommittee on Oceans and International Environment, July 27, 1972.

49. Walter Orr Roberts, testimony before Senate Commerce Committee, February 21, 1966.

50. Walter Orr Roberts, speech to American Meteorological Society, annual meeting, 1965.

51. "A National Program . . . " See above, footnote 46.

52. Of particular interest is an article by David Howell in *Environmental Action*, May 12, 1973.

53. *Southwest Weather Research Inc.* v. *Jones*, 327 S.W. 2nd 417 (1950), cited

by Ray J. Davis in *Controlling the Weather*, ed. Howard J. Taubenfeld (Port Washington, N.Y.: Dunellen Publishing Co., 1970).

54. *Slutsky* v. *City of New York*, 97 N.Y.S. 2nd 238 (1950).

55. Howard J. Taubenfeld, speech to American Association for the Advancement of Science, annual meeting, Washington, D.C., December 1972.

56. "Human Dimensions of the Atmosphere," National Science Foundation, 1968.

57. Robert L. Hendrick, "Human Dimensions of Weather Modification," University of Chicago Department of Geography, Research Paper no. 105, 1966.

58. Adrian Chamberlain, testimony before Senate Commerce Committee, February 21, 1966.

CHAPTER 6: CHEMICALS AND PUBLIC HEALTH

1. "Environmental Pollution and Cancer and Heart and Lung Disease," first annual report to Congress of five-agency task force, including Environmental Protection Agency, August 7, 1978.

2. Figure from Manufacturing Chemists Association.

3. Barry Commoner, "The Promise and Perils of Petrochemicals," in *New York Times Magazine*, September 25, 1977.

4. National Academy of Sciences, *Pest Control: An Assessment of Present and Alternative Technologies*, February 5, 1976 (vol. I, p. 244). This five-volume study contains a wealth of information on all aspects of pesticides. Of particular interest are volumes I (an overview report) and V (dealing with public health). The other three volumes deal, respectively, with pest control for corn and soybeans, cotton, and forests.

5. "EPA Pesticide Cancellations/Suspensions: A Survey of Economic Impacts on Users," September 1975.

6. *Pesticide Chemical News*, November 27, 1974.

7. See, for example, *Environmental Science & Technology*, March 1973, on results of EPA studies; various EPA position papers; studies of the National Academy of Sciences; congressional hearings; and regular issues of journals listed herein, as well as of *Environment, Medical World News, Environmental Health Letter*, and the American Lung Association newsletter *Air Conservation*, among others.

8. *Journal of Environmental Health*, January/February 1974.

9. *Chemicals and Health*, report of panel of President's Science Advisory Committee, September 1973.

10. *Archives of Environmental Health*, September 1973; see also "Tobacco Smoke Emissions," fact sheet of American Lung Association of Southeast Florida, West Palm Beach.

11. *Environmental Pollution and Mental Health* (Washington, D.C.: Information Resources Press, 1973).

12. Leroy Schieler, report to regional meeting of American Chemical Society, Pullman, Wash., June 15, 1973.

13. World Health Organization, "Safe Use of Pesticides," WHO Technical Report, ser. no. 513, 1973.

14. W.J. Hayes, cited in *Federal Register*, July 3, 1975, p. 28528.

15. *Health Effects of Energy Systems,* study by American Public Health Association task force for Energy Policy Project, March 1974, draft; see also *Environmental Science & Technology,* December 1973.

16. *New York Times,* March 10, 1974.

17. *Business Week,* May 11, 1974.

18. A comprehensive, if slightly dated, source of information is *Health Hazards of the Human Environment,* World Health Organization, 1972. Also see eighth annual report, Council on Environmental Quality, 1977. Information on occupational carcinogenesis is provided in "Cancer and the Worker," New York Academy of Sciences, 1977, and *Federal Register,* October 4, 1977, part VI.

19. Luther L. Terry, in "Health Effects of Environmental Pollution," Environmental Protection Agency pamphlet, May 1973.

20. See, for example, *Washington Post,* May 4, 1974;*New Republic,* May 4, 1974; and *Wall Street Journal,* May 13, 1974.

21. See Paul Brodeur, "Annals of Industry," in *The New Yorker,* October 29 through November 26, 1973.

22. See H.H. Hiatt, J.D. Watson, and J.A. Winsten, eds., *Origins of Human Cancer,* Cold Spring Harbor Conference on Cell Proliferation, vol. 4, Cold Spring Harbor Laboratory, 1977. Also of interest is Herman T. Blumenthal, "The Cancer Lottery," in *Harper's,* September 1978, and hearings of the Senate Agriculture subcommittee on nutrition, June 1978.

23. American Public Health Association. See above, footnote 15.

24. Gregory J. Ahart, Hearings of House Interstate and Foreign Commerce Subcommittee on Oversight and Investigations, September 20, 1976.

25. Harold M. Schmeck, Jr., in *New York Times,* November 19, 1972.

26. Charles F. Wurster, in *Environmental Defense Fund Letter,* January 1973; see also Health Research Group, "Cancer Prevention and the Delaney Clause," undated, Washington, D.C.

27. Gregory J. Ahart. See above, footnote 24.

28. Council on Environmental Quality, sixth annual report, December 1975, chapter 1.

29. William D. Ruckelshaus, orders and findings of fact, Environmental Protection Agency, April 13, 1972.

30. David P. Rall, quoted by Morton Mintz, in *Washington Post,* October 24, 1976.

31. Joseph F. Fraumeni Jr., Hearings of House Interstate and Foreign Commerce Subcommittee on Consumer Protection and Finance, June-July 1975.

32. *Time,* August 11, 1975.

33. Summary of Proceedings, National Academy of Sciences Conference on Health Effects of Air Pollution, October 3-5, 1973, printed by Senate Public Works Committee, ser. no. 93-13.

34. National Environmental Research Center, "Status Report on Sulfur Oxides," Environmental Protection Agency, April 17, 1974.

35. John F. Finklea, "Conceptual Basis for Establishing Standards," paper for National Academy of Sciences conference. See above, footnote 33.

36. National Environmental Research Center. See above, footnote 34.

37. Results of January 19, 1973, study under EPA's Community Health and Environmental Surveillance System program, reprinted in *Congressional Record*, April 4, 1973.

38. John B. Moran, paper for congress of Society of Automotive Engineers, Detroit, Mich., February 25, 1974.

39. *Journal of Environmental Health*, March/April 1973.

40. Nicholas A. Ashford, *Crisis in the Workplace: Occupational Disease and Injury* (Cambridge, Mass.: MIT Press, 1975).

41. Richard Doll, in *Origins of Human Cancer*. See above, footnote 22.

42. Herman S. Bloch, hearings of House Interstate and Foreign Commerce Subcommittee on Oversight and Investigations, September 20, 1976.

43. American Public Health Association. See above, footnote 15.

44. Paul G. Rogers, speech to Third Annual Conference on Health Policy, sponsored by *National Journal*, May 22, 1978.

45. Donald Kennedy, speech at commencement, Stanford University, June 18, 1978.

46. Barry Commoner, et al., in *Science*, September 8, 1978.

47. David Brinkley, radio editorial, May 23, 1978.

48. William Tucker, "Of Mites and Men," in *Harper's*, August 1978.

49. Liebe F. Cabalieri, letter to *New York Times*, August 8, 1978.

50. Gus Speth, in *Sierra*, February/March 1978.

51. *Federal Register*, October 4, 1977, p.54151.

52. Daniel S. Martin, in *New York Times*, July 17, 1978.

53. Liebe F. Cavalieri. See above, footnote 49.

54. John F. Schmutz, speech to National Symposium on Chronic Hazards, November 29, 1977.

55. Barry Commoner, et al. See above, footnote 46.

56. David A. Hamburg and Sarah Spaght Brown, in *Science*, May 26, 1978.

57. *BASF Wyandotte Corp., et. al.* v. *Costle*, First Circuit U.S. Court of Appeals, May 7, 1979, 598 F. 2nd 637.

58. Hearings of House Agriculture Committee on extension of FIFRA, May 16, 1975.

59. Hearings of Senate Labor and Public Welfare subcommittees on Health and Administrative Practice and Procedure, April 9, 1976.

60. Ernest Saward and Andrew Sorenson, in *Science*, May 26, 1978.

61. William H. Glazier, in *Scientific American*, April 1973. See also John McKnight, in *The New Ecologist*, July/August 1978; and Hugh Drummond, in *Mother Jones*, December 1977.

62. Merril Eisenbud, quoted by Michael Sterne, in *New York Times*, May 12, 1978.

63. See James C. Hyatt, in *Wall Street Journal*, August 2, 1977; and David Burnham, in *New York Times*, March 14, 1976.

64. Douglas E. Costle, at Public Citizens Forum, Washington, D.C., August 3, 1978.

65. Nicholas A. Ashford, speech to International Conference on Public Control of Environmental Health Hazards, New York Academy of Sciences, New York, N.Y., June 28-30, 1978.

66. Ralph Nader, at Public Citizens Forum, Washington, D.C., August 3, 1978.

67. *Business Week*, November 3, 1973.

68. Office of Science and Technology, "Cumulative Regulatory Effects on the Cost of Automotive Transportation," February 28, 1972.

69. Ralph Nader, Center for Auto Safety news release, March 1972.

70. National Highway Traffic Safety Administration, "Societal Costs of Motor Vehicle Accidents," April 1972.

71. Paul G. Rogers, in Environmental Study Conference, *Weekly Bulletin*, June 26, 1978.

72. Paul G. Rogers. See above, footnote 44.

73. See *Conservation Foundation Letter*, August 1978; and *Washingtonian*, October 1977.

74. John Cairns, in *Origins of Human Cancer*. See above, footnote 22.

75. *Ibid.*

76. Jane E. Brody, in *New York Times*, August 2, 1977.

77. *Chemical and Engineering News*, July 17, 1978; and Jane E. Brody, in *New York Times*, June 30, 1978.

78. John Cairns. See above, footnote 74.

79. Council on Environmental Quality, sixth annual report, 1975.

80. Ernest Wynder, in *New York Times*, June 30, 1978.

81. Jean L. Marx, in *Science*, August 11, 1978.

82. R. Saracci and J. Cooper II, letter to *Chemical and Engineering News*, July 17, 1978.

83. See, for example, Samuel S. Epstein, "Polluted Data," in *The Sciences*, New York Academy of Sciences, July/August 1978; and Samuel S. Epstein, *The Politics of Cancer* (San Francisco, Calif.: Sierra Club Books, 1978), rev. and exp. ed. (Garden City, N.Y.: Anchor Press, 1979).

84. See above, footnote 61.

85. John H. Knowles, in *Science*, December 16, 1977.

86. Jane E. Brody, in *New York Times*, December 11, 1977.

87. *Wall Street Journal*, July 6, 1978.

88. George F. Will, in *Newsweek*, August 7, 1978.

89. Ernest Saward and Andrew Sorenson. See above, footnote 60.

CHAPTER 7: ENERGY RESOURCES

1. Robert Stobaugh and Daniel Yergin, eds., *Energy Future* (New York: Random House, 1979). Also see *Energy in Transition*, a report of the National Academy of Sciences, January 1980.

2. An article in the *Wall Street Journal* of June 13, 1979, is among the more interesting of the many that summarize various factors contributing to 1979's gasoline shortages.

3. Geoffrey Kemp, in *Foreign Affairs*, January 1978.

4. Harold D. Hoopman, quoted in *Oil and Gas Journal*, March 26, 1979.

5. Lester R. Brown, *Worldwatch Paper 29*, Worldwatch Institute, May 1979.

6. John M. Blair, *The Control of Oil* (New York: Pantheon, 1977).

7. National Energy Plan II, May 7, 1979.

8. *Resources*, March 1978, a special issue of the Resources For The Future publication, provides a lucid discussion of oil and gas resource estimating problems.

9. United States Geological Survey, "Geological Estimates of Undiscovered Recoverable Oil and Gas Resources of the United States," Circular 725, 1975.

10. M. King Hubbert, testimony before House Interior Subcommittee on the Environment, June 4, 1974.

11. *Washington Post*, January 6, 1979.

12. Charles D. Masters, speech to American Association for the Advancement of Science, annual meeting, Houston, Texas, January 1979.

13. See above, footnote 7.

14. American Petroleum Institute, news release from Committee on Reserves, April 30, 1979.

15. *Resources*, March 1978. See above, footnote 8.

16. Charles D. Masters. See above, footnote 12.

17. See also *Science*, January 19, 1979.

18. Robert Stobaugh and Daniel Yergin, in *Foreign Affairs*, Spring 1979.

19. United States Treasury Department, report of investigation Under Section 232 of the Trade Expension Act, March 14, 1979.

20. John M. Blair. See above, footnote 6.

21. John D. Moody, in *Petroleum Economist*, June 1975.

22. *Resources*, March 1978. See above, footnote 8.

23. Bernardo F. Grossling. "A Critical Survey of World Petroleum Opportunities." January 20, 1977.

24. *Wall Street Journal*, November 13, 1978; *Washington Post*, May 6, 1979; and *Washington Star*, June 1, 1979.

25. *Washington Post*, December 23, 1978.

26. Congressional Budget Office, "A Strategy for Oil Proliferation," staff working paper, February 23, 1979.

27. Energy Supply Act, S. 1308, introduced June 11, 1979.

28. *Washington Post*, May 6, 1979.

29. Senate Committee on Energy and Natural Resources, "Energy: An Uncertain Future," December 1978.

30. *Ibid.*

31. Congressional Research Service, "Mexico's Oil and Gas Policy: An Analysis," report for Senate Committee on Foreign Relations and Joint Economic Committee, December 1978. See also *Washington Post*, October 27, 1978.

32. J. Lopez Portillo, message to Mexican Congress, September 1978.

33. See *Foreign Affairs*, Summer 1979.

34. Andrew R. Flower, in *Scientific American*, March 1978.

35. See above, footnote 33.

36. Walter J. Levy, in *New York Times*, June 21,1979.

37. Alberto Quiros Corradi, in *Foreign Affairs*, Summer 1979.

38. *World Oil*, February 15, 1979; and *Oil and Gas Journal*, December 25, 1978.

39. *Wall Street Journal*, June 20, 1979.

40. *Business Week*, June 18, 1979.

41. *New York Times*, June 21, 1979.

42. The Petroleum Economics study, prepared for the Department of Energy, was reported at length in *Chemical and Engineering News*, September 4, 1978.

43. *Washington Post*, July 13, 1979.

44. *Washington Post*, July 29, 1979.

45. See, for example, *New York Times*, February 13 and 18, 1979.

46. Central Intelligence Agency, "The International Energy Situation: Outlook to 1985," April 1977.

47. *Washington Post*, April 23, 1978; and *Wall Street Journal*, May 8, 1978.

48. Congressman Les Aspin, statement, July 29, 1979.

49. For example, see Marshall I. Goldman, associate director of Harvard University's Russian Research Center, in *Washington Post*, August 19, 1979.

50. *Wall Street Journal*, May 8, 1978.

51. Robert Stobaugh and Daniel Yergin. See above, footnote 18.

52. Alberto Quiros Corradi. See above, footnote 37.

53. James E. Akins, testimony before House Government Operations Subcommittee on Environment, Energy, and Natural Resources, June 20, 1979.

54. Federal Energy Administration, "National Energy Outlook," February 1976.

55. Council on Wage and Price Stability, "A Study of Coal Prices," staff report, March 1976.

56. *Ibid.*

57. *Coal Week*, November 10, 1975.

58. *Federal Register*, June 11, 1979.

59. Douglas M. Costle, quoted in *Journal of the Air Pollution Control Association*, July 1979.

60. For example, see *Environment Reporter*, December 28, 1979.

61. Arnold Miller, in *New York Times*, June 6, 1976.

62. Federal Energy Administration. See above, footnote 54.

63. Matthew J. Kerbec, letter to President Ford, July 23, 1976, reprinted in *Congressional Record*, August 3, 1976, p. E4297. There are many discussions of restraints on competition. Among the more interesting: a speech by Senator Floyd K. Haskell of Colorado on July 20, 1976 (*Congressional Record*, p. S11938) and an editorial in *Electrical World*, December 15, 1974.

64. See "Electric Utility Automatic Fuel Adjustment Clauses," report of House Interstate and Foreign Commerce Subcommittee on Oversight and Investigations, October 1975.

65. Federal Energy Administration. See above, footnote 54.

66. For a detailed discussion, see the series of articles on coal research by Allen L. Hammond, in *Science*, August 20 through September 3, 1976.

67. Barry Commoner, *The Poverty of Power* (New York: Alfred A. Knopf, 1976).

68. Energy Supply and Environmental Coordination Act of 1974 (P.L. 93-319) and Energy Policy and Conservation Act of 1975 (P.L. 94-163).

69. A detailed report on the conversion program's status, issued in April 1976 by FEA's Office of Coal Utilization, is reprinted in the *Congressional Record* of April 26, 1976, p. S5897.

70. To comprehend the pervasive environmental and social impacts in a given area, it is helpful to consult the relevant environmental impact statements. An example is vol. 1 of the draft EIS for Northwest Colorado Coal prepared by the Bureau of Land Management.

71. Council on Economic Priorities, *Leased and Lost*, 1974.

72. National Academy of Sciences, *Rehabilitation Potential of Western Coal Land*, study done for the Ford Foundation's Energy Policy Project, (Cambridge, Mass.: Ballinger, 1974).

73. *Ibid.*

74. Congressional Research Service, "Factors Affecting Coal Substitution for Other Fossil Fuels in Electric Power Production and Industrial Uses," study done for Senate Interior Committee, no. 94-17, 1975.

75. *Ibid.*

76. Calculated from *Weekly Coal Report*, Bureau of Mines, November 21, 1975.

77. Office of Fossil Energy, "Energy From Coal," Energy Research and Development Administration, 1976.

78. Russell Boulding, "What Is Pure Coal?" in *Environment*, January/February 1976.

79. United States Bureau of Mines, "The Reserve Base of U.S. Coals by Sulfur Content (East of the Mississippi)," 1975.

80. See above, footnotes 70 and 74.

81. Raymond Gold, "Final Report: A Study of the Social Impact of Coal Development in the Decker-Birney-Ashland Area," Institute for Social Research, University of Montana, May 31, 1975.

82. Council on Economic Priorities. See above, footnote 71.

83. George Szego, president of InterTechnologyCorp.,quoted in *Environmental Science & Technology*, September 1976.

84. William E. Heroemus, in *Center Report*, February 1975.

85. An excellent, brief survey of these solar energy sources in contained in "Energy: The Solar Prospect," *Worldwatch Paper 11*, Worldwatch Institute, March 1977.

86. Theodore B. Taylor, at "The Unfinished Agenda" symposium, Washington, D.C., February 2, 1977.

87. Raymond W. Bliss, from an illuminating discussion of the subject in the March 1976 issue of the *Bulletin of the Atomic Scientists*, one of a series on solar energy published in that magazine. Also see *Solar-Oriented Architecture*, AIA Research Corp., 1975, and articles by Norma Skurka, *New York Times Magazine*, November 30, 1975, and Paul Goldberger, *New York Times*, May 22, 1977.

88. *Bulletin of the Atomic Scientists*, April 1976.

89. *Bulletin of the Atomic Scientists*, May 1977.

90. See for example, Peter E. Glaser in *Physics Today*, February 1977; and Arlen J. Large, *Wall Street Journal*, March 23, 1976.

91. Among these are "The Economics of Solar Home Heating," Joint Economic Committee, March 13, 1977, and "An Economic Analysis of Solar Water

& Space Heating," prepared by the Mitre Corp. for the Energy Research and Development Administration, November 1976. A good, concise summary is David Morris, "Solar Economics," in *Self-Reliance*, January 1977. The economics of solar electricity generation are discussed in *Self-Reliance*, November 1976, and the May 1977 and April 1976 issues of *Bulletin of the Atomic Scientists*.

92. *Business Week*, May 16, 1977.

93. Most of these forecasts and others are discussed at length in Frank M. Shooster, "The Potential Impact of Solar Energy on U.S. Energy Requirements," August 1976, printed in part 2a (Appendices) of hearings of the Senate Select Committee on Small Business, October-November 1975. The 1976 ERDA figure was cited in a letter to Senator Henry Jackson, September 28, 1976.

94. A rather complete range of criticisms is contained in Angus McDonald, "Solar Energy in Washington," a report to the Midwest Electric Consumers Association, July 1976, printed in hearings cited in footnote 93. Also see "Jobs and Energy," Environmentalists for Full Employment, Spring 1977, and various issues of *Solar Energy Intelligence Report*.

95. Amory Lovins, "Energy Strategy: The Road Not Taken?" in *Foreign Affairs*, October 1976.

96. Barry Commoner, in *Washington Post*, May 29, 1977. See also Commoner, *The Politics of Energy* (New York: Alfred A. Knopf, 1979).

97. A comprehensive description of what major firms have been doing in the solar field is contained in Stewart H. Herman and James S. Cannon, *Energy Futures* (Cambridge, Mass.: Ballinger, 1977). Utility company activities are described in *Electrical World*, June 1, 1976. Also see *Bulletin of the Atomic Scientists*, October 1976, and *Solar Energy Intelligence Report*, April 25, 1977.

98. Les Gapay, in *Wall Street Journal*, May 25, 1977, and *Solar Energy Intelligence Report*, November 8, 1976.

99. Gerald M. Schaflander, of Idaho Solar Power Inc., in letter to *New York Times*, January 31, 1977.

100. For example, see Mobil ad in *Wall Street Journal*, October 5, 1976, and statements by Exxon in article in that paper on May 25, 1977.

101. Hearings of Senate Select Committee on Small Business, October-November 1975.

102. Senator Gaylord Nelson, hearings of Senate Select Committee on Small Business, October-November 1975.

103. A provocative, if sometimes undocumented, treatise on such problems is John Keyes, *The Solar Conspiracy* (Dobbs Ferry, N.Y.: Morgan & Morgan, 1975).

104. *Engineering News Record*, February 24, 1977.

105. Environmental Law Institute, *Legal Barriers to Solar Heating and Cooling of Buildings*, March 1977. This report for ERDA is an excellent survey of the many legal issues related to solar energy.

106. This invasion was thoroughly outlined by William Greider, in *Washington Post*, May 22, 1977.

107. John B. Goodenough, in *Technology Review*, October/November 1976.

108. *Engineering News Record.* See above, footnote 104.

109. Joint Economic Committee, "The Economics of Solar Home Heating," March 13, 1977.

110. See Bernard Wysocki, Jr., in *Wall Street Journal*, April 28, 1977.

111. See above, footnote 109.

112. *Bulletin of the Atomic Scientists*, February 1976. This contains an excellent, wide-ranging discussion of system components, uses, efficiencies, and economics.

113. See above, footnote 105; see also 6 *Environmental Law Reporter* 50039; and *Science*, February 4, 1977. A proposal to prohibit discriminatory utility rates was dropped from President Carter's energy program in 1977.

114. Alan S. Miller, 6 *Environmental Law Reporter* 50039.

115. Environmental Law Institute. See above, footnote 104.

116. See above, footnote 105; see also Alan S.Hirshberg in *Bulletin of the Atomic Scientists*, October 1976.

117. For example, see Sheilah Kast, in *Washington Star*, June 6, 1977.

118. Roger Noll, Environmental Law Institute. See above, footnote 104.

119. Energy Research and Development Administration, "Solar Program Assessment: Environmental Factors," March 1977.

120. Richard S. Caputo, in *Bulletin of the Atomic Scientists*, May 1977.

121. Stanford Research Institute, "A Preliminary Social and Environmental Assessment of the ERDA Solar Energy Program, 1975 to 2020," draft, printed in "Alternative Long-Range Energy Strategies," joint hearings of Senate Select Committee on Small Business and Senate Interior Committee, December 9, 1976. A revised, final version of the report is "Solar Energy in America's Future," ERDA, March 1977.

122. *Bulletin of the Atomic Scientists*, May 1977.

123. William E. Heronemus. See above, footnote 84.

124. Richard S. Caputo. See above, footnote 120.

125. See above, footnote 105.

126. Solar Rights Act, Laws of New Mexico 1977, Chapter 169.

127. Amory Lovins. See above, footnote 95.

128. "Jobs and Energy." See above, footnote 94.

129. Andrew Tobias, in *New York Magazine*, May 31, 1977.

CHAPTER 8: ENERGY PROBLEMS

1. James J. Glackin, in *Bulletin of the Atomic Scientists*, February 1976.

2. Robert O. Pohl, letter to *New York Times*, November 14, 1975.

3. *Wall Street Journal*, October 23, 1975.

4. Testimony before Joint Committee on Atomic Energy, February 18, 1976.

5. *Fortune*, December 1975.

6. George Wald, in *Progressive*, December 1975.

7. Congressman John Young, comment during Joint Committee on Atomic Energy hearing on waste disposal, November 19, 1975.

8. John McPhee, *The Curve of Binding Energy* (New York: Farrar, Straus, and Giroux, 1973).

9. *Technology Review*, December 1975.

10. "Common Sense About Nuclear Electricity," a flyer issued by the Committee for Nuclear Responsibility, reprinted in *Congressional Record*, March 2, 1976, p. S2617.

11. Alvin M. Weinberg, in *American Scientist*, January/February 1973.

12. Natural Resources Defense Council, "The Plutonium Decision," September 1974.

13. Henry Kendall, Critical Mass convention, Washington, D.C., November 1974.

14. William Ophuls, conference on Limits to Growth '75, The Woodlands, Texas, October 1975.

15. Gregory Minor, testimony before Joint Committee on Atomic Energy, February 18. 1976.

16. Barry Commoner, "The Poverty of Power," in *The New Yorker*, February 2, 9, and 16, 1976; published as *The Poverty of Power* (New York: Alfred A. Knopf, 1976).

17. Hans A. Bethe, in *Scientific American*, January 1976.

18. Barry Commoner. See above, footnote 16.

19. *Wall Street Journal*, February 17, 1976; *Atlanta Constitution*, February 12, 1976.

20. For example, see Union of Concerned Scientists, *The Nuclear Fuel Cycle*, rev. ed. (Cambridge, Mass.: MIT Press, 1975), chapter 3; David Dinsmore Comey, "The Legacy of Uranium Tailings," in *Bulletin of the Atomic Scientists*, September 1975; John W. Gofman, "Alice in Blunderland," Committee for Nuclear Responsibility, reprinted in *Congressional Record*, March 11, 1976, p. S3319, and H.W. Ibser, "The Nuclear Energy Game: Genetic Roulette," in *Progressive*, January 1976.

21. Edward A. Mason, speech at annual conference of Atomic Industrial Forum, November 17-18, 1975.

22. See General Accounting Office, "Controlling the Radiation Hazards of Uranium Mill Tailings," May 21, 1975. See also John Fialka, in *Washington Star*, series from February 29 to March 2, 1976.

23. Nuclear Regulatory Commission, program statements in support of fiscal 1977 budget requests, January 1976, and interviews with agency officials.

24. General Accounting Office, "Improvements Needed in the Land Disposal of Radioactive Wastes—A Problem of Centuries," RED-76-54, January 12, 1976.

25. Testimony before Joint Committee on Atomic Energy, November 19, 1975.

26. William D. Rowe and William F. Holcomb, in *Nuclear Technology*, December 1974.

27. Hans A. Bethe. See above, footnote 17.

28. Nuclear Regulatory Commission. See above, footnote 23.

29. Frank P. Baranowski, testimony before Joint Committee on Atomic Energy, November 19, 1975.

30. See Philip Boffey, *The Brain Bank of America* (New York: McGraw-Hill, 1975), chapter 5.

31. Testimony before Joint Committee on Atomic Energy, November 19, 1975.

32. Nuclear Regulatory Commission. See above, footnote 23.

33. *Ibid.*

34. Among them: "The Threat to Licensed Nuclear Facilities" (Mitre Corp.) and "Analysis of the Terrorist Threat to the Commercial Nuclear Industry" (BDM Corp.). Another recent research paper is Brian M. Jenkins, "Will Terrorists Go Nuclear?" (Rand Corp.). A wide range of safeguards problems were the subject of hearings before the House Interior subcommittee on energy and environment, February 26-27, 1976. For more optimistic view, see above, footnotes 1 and 17.

35. *Critical Mass*, May 1975; and *New York Times*, February 20, 1976.

36. Mason Willrich and Theodore B. Taylor, *Nuclear Theft: Risks and Safeguards*, Report to the Ford Froundation Energy Policy Project (Cambridge, Mass.: Ballinger, 1974). This is a comprehensive study of the safeguards problem.

37. John P. Holdren, in *Bulletin of the Atomic Scientists*, March 1976.

38. See above, footnote 34.

39. *Critical Mass*, September 1975; *Washington Star*, February 24, 1976; *New York Times*, December 28, 1975 and January 3, 1974.

40. Unclassified digest of General Accounting Office report, April 23, 1975.

41. *Wall Street Journal*, February 3, 1976.

42. General Accounting Office, "Management of the Licensing of Users of Radioactive Materials Should Be Improved," February 11, 1976.

43. *Wall Street Journal*, March 5, 1975.

44. *Not Man Apart*, mid-October 1974. For many other examples, see *Environmental Action*, January 1980.

45. *Sierra Club Bulletin*, November/December 1975.

46. Congressman George E. Brown Jr., speech to American Association for the Advancement of Science, Boston, Mass., February 20, 1976.

47. "Report of the President's Commission on the Accident at Three Mile Island," October 30, 1979.

48. See, for example, *Portland Oregonian*, February 17 and 18, 1976, reprinted in *Congressional Record*, March 3, 1976, p. E1035 and April 7, 1976, p. E1885.

49. Lincoln P. Bloomfield, "Nuclear Spread and World Order," in *Foreign Affairs*, July 1975.

50. Paul L. Leventhal, in *New York Times*, July 14, 1974.

51. *New York Times*, February 26, 1976 and *Christian Science Monitor*, March 8, 1976.

52. Testimony before Senate Foreign Relations Subcommittee on Arms Control, International Organizations, and Security Agreements, February 23, 24, 1976.

53. Much information and many statistics are contained in "Facts on Nuclear Proliferation," Senate Government Operations Committee (prepared by Library of Congress), December 1975.

54. General Accounting Office, "Role of the International Atomic Energy Agency in Safeguarding Nuclear Material," July 3, 1975.

55. *Natural Resources Defense Council et al.* v. *Nuclear Regulatory Commission*, U.S. Court of Appeals, Second Circuit, nos. 75-4276 and 75-4278.

56. Testimony before Senate Small Business Committee, hearing on solar energy, October 7, 1975.

57. Barry Commoner. See above, footnote 16.

58. George Wald, in *New York Times*, February 29, 1976.

59. David Salisbury, in *Technology Review*, December 1975.

60. George Wald. See above, footnote 58.

61. General Accounting Office, "An Evaluation of the National Energy Plan," July 25, 1977.

62. The literature is extensive. For example, "Clean Air Act Amendments of 1977," report of House Interstate and Foreign Commerce Committee, May 12, 1977, no. 95-294; J. F. Finklea et. al., "Status Report on Sulfur Oxides," Environmental Protection Agency, April 17, 1974; and "Sulfates and the Sulfur Oxide/Particulate Complex," American Lung Association, April 1976.

63. Thomas E. Waddell, "The Economic Damages of Air Pollution," Environmental Protection Agency, May 1974.

64. Physical and Economic Damage Functions for Air Pollutants by Receptors," Midwest Research Institute for the Environmental Protection Agency, Environmental Research Laboratory, Corvallis, Oregon, September 1976 (released September 2, 1977).

65. General Accounting Office. See above, footnote 61.

66. Senator Edmund Muskie, *Congressional Record*, June 8, 1977, pp. S9164 and 9183.

67. National Academy of Sciences, *Air Quality and Stationary Source Emission Control*, report to Senate Public Works Committee, March 1975.

68. *Public Utilities Fortnightly*, August 4, 1977.

69. Estimate of Environmental Protection Agency's Office of Policy and Planning.

70. Environmental Protection Agency, Office of Enforcement, January 1976.

71. Federal Power Commission, "Annual Summary of Cost and Quality of Electric Utility Plan Fuels," May 1977.

72. *Environmental Science & Technology*, August 1977. See also, Jim Montgomery, *Wall Street Journal*, June 14, 1977.

73. Frank T. Princiotta, paper for Energy Technology IV conference, Washington, D.C., May 1977.

74. Richard E. Ayres, testimony to Senate Public Works subcommittee on enviroment, May 16, 1974.

75. For example, *Big Rivers Electric Corp.* v. *Environmental Protection Agency*, Sixth Circuit U.S. Court of Appeals, (1975).

76. Public Law 95-95, printed in *Congressional Record*, August 3, 1977, p. H8507.

77. *Federal Register*, June 11, 1979.

78. *Journal of the Air Pollution Control Association*, November 1979.

79. *Journal of the Air Pollution Control Association,* July 1979. Also see *Public Utilities Fortnightly,* December 20, 1979.

80. The story is told by George Getschow, in *Wall Street Journal,* June 14, 1977.

81. Frank T. Princiotta. See above, footnote 73.

82. Federal Power Commission, *The Status of Flue Gas Desulfurization and Applications in the United States: A Technological Assessment,* July 1977.

83. *Ibid.*

84. James Herlihy, "Flue Gas Desulfurization in Power Plants," Environmental Protection Agency, April 1977; Council on Wage and Price Stability, "A Study of Coal Prices," March 1976; and see above, footnotes 67 and 82.

85. *Federal Register,* June 11, 1979.

86. See above, footnotes 82 and 84.

87. Electric Power Research Institute, *EPRI Journal,* June/July 1977.

88. Congressional Research Service, "Electric and Gas Utility Rate and Fuel Adjustment Clause Increases, 1976," report to two Senate Governmental Affairs subcommittees, July 1977.

89. Federal Power Commission, "Electric Utilities Captive Coal Operations," June 1977.

90. *Environmental Law Reporter* 10009; and Paul H. Weaver, "Behind the Great Scrubber Fracas," in *Fortune,* February 1975.

91. *Union Electric Co.* v. *Environmental Protection Agency,* U.S. Supreme Court, June 25, 1976.

92. Senator Edmund Muskie, in *Congressional Record,* August 4, 1977, p. S13697.

CHAPTER 9: ENERGY ANALYSIS

1. W. Kenneth Davis, quoted in Atomic Industrial Forum, "Info," March 1975.

2. Howard T. Odum, in *Not Man Apart,* mid-August 1974.

3. New York Academy of Sciences, *The Sciences,* October 1973.

4. Entropy is discussed at length by Nicholas Georgescu-Roegen in *Ecologist,* June 1975, and at greater length in his book, *The Entropy Law and the Economic Process* (Cambridge, Mass.: Harvard University Press, 1971).

5. The Conference Board, *Energy Consumption in Manufacturing,* a report of the Ford Foundation's Energy Policy Project (Cambridge, Mass.: Ballinger, 1974).

6. For example, John S. Steinhart and Carol E. Steinhart, "Energy Use in the U.S. Food System," in *Science,* November 2, 1973; Malcolm Slesser, "Energy Subsidy as a Criterion in Food Policy Planning," in *Journal of the Science of Food and Agriculture,* November 1973.

7. "Conservation and Efficient Use of Energy," report of joint hearings of House Government Operations Subcommittee on Conservation and Natural Resources and Science and Astronautics Subcommittee on Energy, part 2, July 10, 1973; and Robert H. Williams, ed., *The Energy Conservation Papers,* a report of the Ford Foundation's Energy Policy Project (Cambridge, Mass.: Ballinger, 1975).

8. Thomas A. Robertson, "Systems of Energy and the Energy of Systems," in *Sierra Club Bulletin*, March 1975; P.F. Chapman, et al., "The Energy Cost of Fuels," in *Energy Policy*, September 1974.

9. P. F. Chapman, "The Energy Costs of Materials," in *Energy Policy*, March 1975

10. David B. Large, "Hidden Waste," The Conservation Foundation, 1973.

11. League of Women Voters Educational Fund, "Reduce," 1975; Bruce M. Hannon, "Bottles, Cans, Energy," in *Environment*, March 1972.

12. For example, David J. Wright, "Goods and Services," in *Energy Policy*, December 1974.

13. Milton D. Rubin, speech to American Association for the Advancement of Science, annual meeting, January 30, 1975.

14. Amory Lovins, "Energy Strategy: The Road Not Taken," in *Foreign Affairs*, October 1976.

15. P.F. Chapman, et al., "The Energy Cost of Fuels," in *Energy Policy*, September 1974.

16. Howard T. Odum. See above, footnote 2.

17. International Federation of Institutes for advanced Study (IFIAS), "Energy Analysis," Workshop Report no. 6, Guldsmedshyttan, Sweden, August 25-30, 1974.

18. W. Kenneth Davis. See above, footnote 1.

19. E.J. Hoffman, quoted in Wilson Clark, "It Takes Energy to Get Energy," in *Smithsonian*, December 1974.

20. IFIAS. See above, footnote 17.

21. *Ibid.*

22. John P. Holdren, in *New York Times*, July 23, 1975.

23. Bruce M. Hannon, "Bottles, Cans, Energy," in *Environment*, March 1972.

24. Bruce M. Hannon, "Options for Energy Conservation," reprinted in *Technology Review*, February 974.

25. Barry Commoner, "The Energy Crisis—All of a Piece," in *Center Magazine*, March/April, 1975.

26. Bruce M. Hannon, "Energy Conservation and the Consumer," Center for Advanced Computation, University of Illinois, October 1974.

27. John G. Meyers of New York University, in *Business Week*, April 15, 1977.

28. Tjalling C. Koopmans of Yale University, at Tokyo Congress of International Economic Association, August 29 to September 3, 1977.

29. Randall Meyer, speech to Economic Club of Memphis, January 27, 1977.

30. Congressman Mike McCormack, quoted in *Chemical and Engineering News*, May 30, 1977.

31. Chase Manhattan Bank, "Energy, the Economy, and Jobs," in *Energy Report from Chase*, September 1976.

32. National Association for the Advancement of Colored People (NAACP), "Energy, Jobs, and Black America," report of NAACP's National Energy Con-

ference, January 9, 1978. (A contrary view was presented by Vernon E. Jordan, Jr., president of the National Urban League, at a Northern States Power Company conference, Minneapolis, Minn., January 20, 1978).

33. James R. Schlesinger, speech to AFL-CIO convention, Los Angeles, Calif., December 9, 1977. (A letter of reply by 18 environmental leaders was reprinted in the *Congressional Record*, March 7, 1978, p. E1095.)

34. Marc H. Ross and Robert H. Williams, "Energy and Economic Growth," study for the Joint Economic Committee Subcommittee on Energy, August 31 1977.

35. Ford Foundation's Energy Policy Project, *A Time To Choose* (Cambridge, Mass.: Ballinger, 1974).

36. Modeling Resource Group, "Energy Modeling for an Uncertain Future," Committee on Nuclear and Alternative Strategy Systems, National Academy of Sciences, final draft, July 1, 1977. The final report of the full NAS study called *Energy in Transition*, was released on January 14, 1980.

37. John H. Gibbons, interview.

38. Kenneth E.F. Watt, et al., "The Long-Term Implications and Constraints of Alternate Energy Policies," Institute of Ecology, University of California at Davis, January 1976.

39. Reported by Anthony J. Parisi, *New York Times*, January 8, 1978.

40. Allan Mazur and Eugene Rosa, in *Science*, November 15, 1974.

41. Kenneth E.F. Watt, et al. See above, footnote 38.

42. Joel Darmstadter, *How Industrial Societies Use Energy*, (Baltimore: The Johns Hopkins University Press, 1977).

43. Joel Darmstadter and Lee Schipper, in *Technology Review*, January 1978.

44. Walt W. Rostow, speech to American Association for the Advancement of Science, annual meeting, Washington, D.C., February 14, 1978.

45. Modeling Resource Group. See above, footnote 36.

46. William D. Nordhaus, in proceedings of the Workshop on Energy Demand, International Institute for Applied Systems Analysis, May 1975.

47. Ford Foundation's Energy Policy Project. See above, footnote 35. See also James O'Toole, *Energy and Social Change*, University of Southern California Center for Futures Research (Cambridge, Mass.: MIT Press, 1976).

48. Edward A. Hudson and Dale W. Jorgenson, paper presented to American Economics Association, New York, N.Y., December 1977.

49. An interesting discussion of the same points is in a paper by Alan S. Manne, of Stanford University, for the 1978 AAAS annual meeting, Washington, D.C. Also see Hamilton Treadway, in *Public Utilities Fortnightly*, September 15, 1977.

50. Clark W. Bullard, paper presented to American Economics Association, New York, N.Y., December 1977.

51. Marc H. Ross and Robert H. Williams. See above, footnote 34.

52. Tom Alexander, in *Fortune*, May 1977.

53. Joel Darmstadter and Lee Schipper. See above, footnote 43.

54. See Institute for Energy Analysis, "U.S. Energy and Economic Growth, 1975-2010," Oak Ridge Associated Universities, September 1976.

55. Anthony J. Parisi, in *New York Times*, March 14, 1978.

56. Joel Darmstadter and Lee Schipper. See above, footnote 43.

57. Clark W. Bullard, speech to University of Michigan Conference on Energy Conservation, November 1-2, 1977.

58. John H. Gibbons, testimony to House Interstate and Foreign Commerce subcommittee on energy and power, June 1977.

59. Charles A. Berg, in *Science*, February 10, 1978. An excellent and comprehensive discussion of the many possible adjustments in the economic system is a study of productivity by Edward F. Renshaw, economics professor at the State University of New York, Albany, contained in Joint Economic Committee report, vol. 1, "Productivity," October 1, 1976. The importance of technological change is described in Sam H. Schurr, ed., *Energy, Economic Growth, and the Environment*, Resources For The Future, Inc. (Baltimore: The Johns Hopkins University Press, 1972), appendix A, by Joel Darmstadter.

60. Modeling Resource Group. See above, footnote 36.

61. Clark W. Bullard, interview.

62. Clark W. Bullard. See above, footnote 57.

63. Marc H. Ross and Robert H. Williams. See above, footnote 34. On the question of substitution, see footnotes 36 and 47; Thomas Veach Long II and Lee Schipper, "Resource and Energy Substitution," a study for the Joint Economic Committee, in vol. 4, "Resources and Energy," November 16, 1976; James W. McKie, paper at International Ex-Students' Conference on Energy, University of Texas at Austin, April 26-30, 1976; and William W. Hogan and John P. Weyant, paper at the 1978 AAAS annual meeting, Washington, D.C.

64. Clark W. Bullard, interview.

65. Marc H. Ross and Robert H. Williams. See above, footnote 34.

66. Institute for Energy Analysis. See above, footnote 54.

67. Marc H. Ross and Robert H. Williams. See above, footnote 34.

68. Joel Darmstadter, speech to American Association for the Advancement of Science, annual meeting, Washington, D.C., February 14, 1978. See also footnote 26, for an excellent analysis of the implications of consumer choices.

69. Mancur Olson, study for Joint Economic Committee, in vol. 2, "The Factors and Processes Shaping Long-Run Economic Growth," November 10, 1976. See also footnote 47, and Environmentalists for Full Employment, "Jobs & Energy," Spring 1977.

70. See above, footnote 49.

71. Letter of reply to James R. Schlesinger by 18 environmental leaders, reprinted in *Congressional Record*, March 7, 1978, p. E1095.

72. Allan Mazur and Eugene Rosa. See above, footnote 40.

73. Amory Lovins. See above, footnote 14.

CHAPTER 10: APPROPRIATE TECHNOLOGY

1. *Natural Resources Defense Council* v. *Export-Import Bank*, 9 *Environmental Law Reporter* 20145.

2. Program of Advanced Studies in Institution-Building and Technical Assistance Methodology of the Midwest Universities Consortium for International Activities, study for Agency for International Development (AID), printed in AID's "Proposal For a Program in Appropriate Technology," and transmitted to the House Committee on International Relations, July 27, 1976.

3. E.F. Schumacher, *Small Is Beautiful*, (New York: Harper & Row, 1973).

4. *Ibid.*

5. E.F. Schumacher, in *The Center Magazine*, January/February 1975.

6. E.F. Schumacher. See above, footnote 3.

7. Warren R. Muir, at symposium on Pest Control Strategies, Cornell University, Ithaca, N.W., June 22-23, 1977. Leading pest management authorities participated in the symposium, which was organized by Cornell, the Environmental Defense Fund, and the Center for Science in the Public Interest, and sponsored by the Council on Environmental Quality and the Environmental Protection Agency.

8. David Pimental, at symposium on Pest Control Strategies. See above, footnote 7. See also W.B. Ennis, Jr., et al., in *Science*, May 9, 1975.

9. The literature on integrated pest management is plentiful. A good, full roundup is Entomological Society of America, *Integrated Pest Management: Rationale, Potential, Needs and Implementation*, August 1975. A number of texts are available, such as Carl B. Huffaker and P. S. Messenger, *Theory and Practice of Biological Control* (New York: Academic Press, 1976); and Robert L. Metcalf and William Luckmann, *Introduction to Insect Pest Management* (New York: John Wiley & Sons, 1975). A more popular discussion of viruses, by Keven Shea, is in *Environment*, May 1977, and of hormones and pheromones, by Anthony Wolff, in *New York Times Magazine*, November 28, 1976.

10. Carl B. Huffaker, at state-of-the-art research seminar on integrated pest management (IPM), Environmental Protection Agency, March 16, 1977.

11. Carl B. Huffaker and Ray F. Smith, proceedings of Annual Tall Timbers Conference on Ecological Animal Control by Habitat Management, February 24, 1972.

12. Research Seminar on IPM. See above, footnote 10.

13. J.R. Phillips, in proposal for a national integrated pest management development project, February 1977.

14. L.D. Newsom, at symposium on Pest Control Strategies. See above, footnote 7.

15. L.D. Newsom. See above, footnote 14.

16. World Bank, "Appropriate Technology in World Bank Activities," July 19, 1976, draft.

17. AID Proposal. See above, footnote 2.

18. See, for instance, footnote 2, for the proposal that includes Lawrence J. White, "Appropriate Factor Proportions for Manufacturing in Less Developed Countries: A Survey of the Evidence."

19. Congressman Clarence D. Long, testimony before House Committee on International Relations, July 12, 1975.

20. AID Proposal. See above, footnote 2.

CHAPTER 11: VALUES

1. Peter Singer, *Animal Liberation* (New York: Avon Books, 1975).

2. See *Conservation Foundation Letter*, April 1978.

3. Stephen R. Kellert, senior research associate at Yale's School of Forestry and Environmental Studies, arrived at nine classifications, roughly matching the six put forth by Congress, in his extensive survey of American attitudes toward animals.

4. Roger Caras, at symposium on "The Endangered Species Act: A Case Study in Biopolitics," Yale School of Forestry and Environmental Studies, April 10-11, 1978.

5. Thomas Lovejoy, in *Smithsonian*, July 1976.

6. Michael Berger, address to American Association for the Advancement of Science, annual meeting, Washington, D.C., February 17, 1978.

7. Thomas Lovejoy, at symposium on "The Endangered Species Act: A Case Study in Biopolitics." See above, footnote 4.

8. Charles Warren, address to American Association for the Advancement of Science, annual meeting, Washington, D.C., February 17, 1978.

9. William T. Conway, interview.

10. Paul Shepard, *Thinking Animals* (New York: Viking Press, 1978).

11. Raymond Dasmann, quoted by Edward Flattau, syndicated colmnist, October 9, 1976.

12. *New Ecologist*, January/February 1978.

13. Marvin Harris, in *Human Nature*, February 1978.

14. *Natural Resources Defense Council Newsletter*, January/February 1977.

15. Worldwatch Institute, "The Global Environment and Basic Human Needs: Trends and Problems," report for Council on Environmental Quality, January 1978.

16. See above, footnote 14.

17. Peter Gwynne, in *International Wildlife*, July/August 1976.

18. Richard D. Lyons, in *New York Times*, August 28, 1977.

19. Edward S. Ayensu, quoted by Hank Burchard, in *Washington Post Magazine*, January 22, 1978.

20. *Ibid.*

21. See above, footnote 14.

22. Siri von Reis Altschul, in *Scientific American*, May 1977.

23. Norman Myers, *The Sinking Ark* (Elmsford,N.Y.: Pergamon Press, 1979).

24. Norman Myers, in *Science*, July 16, 1976.

25. Edward S. Ayensu, in *Smithsonian*, January 1975.

26. See above, footnote 1.

27. *Cappaert* v. *U.S.*, June 23, 1975, 5 *Environmental Law Reporter* 20494.

28. National Science Foundation, *Mosaic*, January/February 1977.

29. Norman Myers, in *Natural Resources Defense Council Newsletter*, January/February 1977.

30. Boyce Rensberger, *The Cult of the Wild* (Garden City, N.Y.: Anchor Press, 1977).

31. Worldwatch Institute. See above, footnote 15.

32. World Bank, "Environment and Development," June 1975.

33. William Conway, interview.

34. Anthony Huxley, *Plant and Planet* (New York: Viking Press, 1974).

35. Uberto Tosco, *The World of Wildflowers and Trees* (Bounty Books, 1973).

36. Wayne Grimm, quoted by Constance Holden, in *Science*, June 24, 1977.

37. Fish and Wildlife Service, *Endangered Species Technical Bulletin*, January 1978; United Press International dispatch, December 28, 1977.

38. Paul Shepard. See above, footnote 10.

39. Roderick Nash, in *The Center Magazine*, November/December 1977.

40. See above, footnotes 1 and 10; John Passmore, *Man's Responsibility for Nature* (New York: Charles Scribner's Sons, 1974); Christopher D. Stone, *Should Trees Have Standing? Toward Legal Rights for Natural Objects* (New York: Avon Books, 1975); Tom Regan and Peter Singer, *Animal Rights and Human Obligation* (New York: Prentice-Hall, 1976); Stanley Godlovitch, Roslind Godlovitch, and John Harris, eds., *Animals, Men and Morals*(New York: Taplinger, 1972); Michael W. Fox and Richard K. Morris, eds., *On the Fifth Day: Animal Liberation and Human Ethics* (Washington, D.C.: Acropolis, 1977); and Emily Stewart Leavitt, *Animals and Their Legal Rights*, Animal Welfare Institute, new edition forthcoming.

41. Peter Singer. See above, footnote 1.

42. Paul Shepard. See above, footnote 10.

43. Charles Warren. See above, footnote 8.

44. Michael Fox, interview, in *Washington Star*, April 28, 1978.

45. Roger Caras. See above, footnote 4.

46. Herbert Spencer, *Social Statics*,1951.

47. Arnold J. Toynbee, in *London Observer*, April 14, 1974.

48. Martin Meyerson and Margy Meyerson, in Harvey S. Perloff, ed., *The Future of the U.S. Government* (New York: George Braziller, 1971).

49. Stuart S. Nagel, ed., *Environmental Politics* (New York: Praeger, 1974).

50. William Ophuls, in *Harper's*, April 1974. See also Ophuls, *Ecology and the Politics of Scarcity* (San Francisco, Calif.: W. H. Freeman, 1977).

51. Robert L. Heilbroner, *An Inquiry into the Human Prospect* (New York: W.W. Norton, 1974).

52. Dan Morgan, in *Washington Post*, January 12, 1975.

53. Robert V. Roosa, et al., in *Foreign Affairs*, January 1975.

54. Rene Dubos, in *Saturday Review/World*, August 24, 1974.

55. *Ibid.*

56. Irving Kristol, in *Wall Street Journal*, December 16, 1974.

57. Edmund K. Faltermayer, *Redoing America* (New York: Harper & Row, 1968).

58. *Dallas Morning News*, editorial, December 22, 1974.

59. Paul W. McCracken, in *Wall Street Journal*, December 26, 1974.

60. Edward Ayres, *What's Good for GM* (Nashville, Tenn.: Aurora Publishers, 1970).

61. Neil Morgan, quoted by Steven V. Roberts, "Ode to a Freeway," in *New York Times Magazine*, April 15, 1973.

62. Quoted by Steven V. Roberts. See above footnote 61.

63. *Time*, May 10, 1963.

64. Leonard J. Duhl, in Harvey S. Perloff, ed., *The Future of the U.S. Government* (New York: George Braziller, 1971).

65. *Skeptic*, no. 3, 1974.

66. Barbara Ward and Rene Dubos, *Only One Earth* (New York: W.W. Norton, 1972).

67. Richard H. Gardner, in *New York Times*, November 11, 1974.

68. Robert L. Heilbroner. See above, footnote 51.

69. Allen V. Kneese, in *Resources*, Resources For The Future, September 1973.

70. Anthony Lewis, in *New York Times*, January 13, 1975

71. Mancur Olson, in *Daedalus*, Fall 1973.

72. Hyman G. Rickover, hearings of House Appropriations Subcommittee on Defense, June 19, 1973.

73. Staffan Burenstam Linder, *The Harried Leisure Class* (New York: Columbia University Press, 1970).

74. James Reston, in *New York Times*, November 11, 1973.

75. John B. Connally, speech to White House Conference on the Industrial World Ahead, Washington, D.C., February 8, 1972.

76. Richard A. Easterlin, in *The Public Interest*, Winter 1973.

77. Philip Brickman and Donald T. Campbell, in M.H. Appley, ed., *Adaptation-Level Theory* (New York: Academic Press, 1971).

78. Harry Helson in M.H. Appley, ed., *Adaptation-Level Theory* (New York: Academic Press, 1971).

79. Philip Brickman and Donald T. Campbell. See above, footnote 77.

80. Robert L. Heilbroner. See above, footnote 51.

81. Garrett Hardin, "The Tragedy of the Commons," in *Science*, December 13, 1968.

82. Arnold J. Toynbee. See above, footnote 47.

83. William Ophuls. See above, footnote 50.

BIBLIOGRAPHY

Considering the explosion of books and studies that has fueled the environmental movement, this selective bibliography necessarily excludes countless fine volumes, including many nature and wildlife books and academic works. It includes only a few of the important government publications on environmental problems. It also does not contain many of the books referenced in footnotes, of which most are highly recommended.

General

Ayres, Robert U. *Resources, Environment and Economics.* New York: John Wiley & Sons, 1978.

Brown, Harrison. *The Challenge of Man's Future.* New York: Viking Press, 1954.

Caldwell, Lynton Keith. *Environment: A Challenge to Modern Society.* Garden City, N.Y.: Natural History Press, 1970.

Commoner, Barry. *The Closing Circle.* New York: Alfred A. Knopf, 1971.

Council on Environmental Quality. *Annual Reports.* Washington, D.C.: Government Printing Office, 1971-79.

Daly, Herman E. *Steady-State Economics.* San Francisco: W.H. Freeman, 1977.

Darling, Sir Frank Fraser, and Milton, John, eds. *Future Environments of North America.* Garden City, N.Y.: Natural History Press, 1966

Darling, Sir Frank Fraser, *Wilderness and Plenty.* Boston: Houghton Mifflin, 1970.

Dasmann, Raymond F. *A Different Kind of Country.* New York: MacMillan, 1968.

Dasmann, Raymond F. *Environmental Conservation.* New York: John Wiley & Sons, 1959.

Ehrlich, Paul R., et al. *Ecoscience.* San Francisco: W.H. Freeman, 1977.

Farb, Peter. *Face of North America: The Natural History of a Continent.* New York: Harper & Row, 1963.

Freeman, A. Myrick. *Benefits of Environmental Improvement.* Baltimore: Johns Hopkins University Press, 1979.

Freeman, A. Myrick, et al. *The Economics of Environmental Policy.* New York: John Wiley & Sons, 1973.

Leopold, Aldo. *A Sand County Almanac.* New York: Oxford University Press, 1949.

Maddox, John. *The Doomsday Syndrome*. New York: McGraw-Hill, 1972.

Marsh, George P. *Man and Nature*. Edited by David Lowenthal. Cambridge, Mass.: Harvard University Press, 1965.

Meadows, Donnella, et al. *The Limits to Growth*. New York: Universe Books, A Potomac Associates Book, 1972.

Mesarovic, Mihajlo, and Pestel, Edward. *Mankind at the Turning Point*. New York: Signet, 1971.

Nash, Hugh, ed. *Progress as if Survival Mattered*. San Francisco: Friends of the Earth, 1977.

Nicholson, Max. *The Environmental Revolution*. New York: McGraw-Hill, 1970.

Odum, Howard T. *Environment, Power and Society*. New York: Wiley-Interscience, 1971.

Osborn, Fairfield. *Our Plundered Planet*. New York: Pyramid, 1948.

Orr, David W., and Soroos, Marvin S., eds. *The Global Predicament*. Chapel Hill, N.C.: University of North Carolina Press, 1979.

Sansom, Robert L. *The New American Dream Machine*. New York: Doubleday, 1976.

Shepard, Paul. *Man in the Landscape*. New York: Alfred A. Knopf, 1967.

Shepard, Paul, and McKinley, Daniel, eds. *The Subversive Science*. Boston: Houghton Mifflin, 1969.

Singer, S.F., ed. *The Changing Global Environment*. Hingham, Mass.: D. Reidel, 1975.

Thomas, William L., Jr., ed. *Man's Role in Changing the Face of the Earth*. Vols. 1 and 2. Chicago: University of Chicago Press, 1966.

Ward, Barbara, and Dubos, Rene. *Only One Earth*. New York: W.W. Norton, 1972.

Wilson, Carroll L. *Man's Impact on the Global Environment*. Cambridge, Mass.: The MIT Press, 1970.

Energy

Brown, Lester R., et al. *Running on Empty*. New York: W.W. Norton, 1979.

Commoner, Barry. *The Poverty of Power*. New York: Alfred A. Knopf, 1976.

Energy Policy Project of the Ford Foundation. *A Time to Choose*. Cambridge, Mass.: Ballinger, 1974.

Faulkner, Peter, ed. *The Silent Bomb*. New York: Vintage Books, 1977.

Hayes, Denis. *Rays of Hope*. New York: W.W. Norton, 1977.

Landsberg, Hans, et al. *Energy: The Next Twenty Years*. Cambridge, Mass.: Ballinger, 1979.

Large, David B. *Hidden Waste*. Washington, D.C.: The Conservation Foundation, 1976.

Lovins, Amory. *Soft Energy Paths*. Cambridge, Mass.: Ballinger, 1977.

Morgan, Richard. *Nuclear Power: The Bargain We Can't Afford*. Washington, D.C.: Environmental Action Foundation, 1977.

Mostert, Noel. *Supership*. New York: Alfred A. Knopf, 1974.

Murphy, Arthur W., ed. *The Nuclear Power Controversy*. Englewood Cliffs, N.J.: Prentice-Hall, 1976.

Nader, Ralph, and Abbotts, John. *The Menace of Atomic Energy.* New York: Grossman, 1977.
Sawhill, John C., ed. *Energy Conservation and Public Policy.* Englewood Cliffs, N.J.: Prentice-Hall, 1979.
Schurr, Sam H., et al. *Energy in America's Future.* Baltimore: Johns Hopkins University Press for Resources for the Future, 1979.
Stobaugh, Robert, and Yergin, Daniel. *Energy Future.* New York: Random House, 1979.
Willrich, Mason, and Raylor, Theodore B. *Nuclear Theft: Risks and Safeguards.* Cambridge, Mass.: Ballinger, 1974.

International Development

Bosselman, Fred P. *In the Wake of the Tourist.* Washington, D.C.: The Conservation Foundation, 1978.
Dasmann, Raymond F.; Milton, John P.; and Freeman, Peter H. *Ecological Principles for Economic Development.* New York: John Wiley & Sons, 1973.
Fravar, M. Taghi, and Milton, John P., eds. *The Careless Technology.* Garden City, N.Y.: Natural History Press, 1972.
Goulet, Denis. *The Uncertain Promise.* New York: IDOC/North America, 1977.
Myrdal, Gunnar. *The Challenge of World Poverty.* New York: Pantheon, 1970.
Nobel, John H.; Banta, John S.; and Rosenberg, John S. *Groping Through the Maze.* Washington, D.C.: The Conservation Foundation, 1977.
Overseas Development Council. *The United States and World Development.* New York: Praeger, 1979.
Schumacher, E.F. *Small Is Beautiful.* New York: Harper & Row, 1973.

Land and Water Management

Berkman, Richard L., and Viscusi, W. Kip. *Damming the West.* New York: Viking Press, 1973.
Caudill, Harry. *Night Comes to the Cumberlands.* Boston: Little Brown & Co., Atlantic Monthly Press, 1963.
Conservation Foundation. *National Parks for the Future.* Washington, D.C.: The Conservation Foundation, 1972.
Hanrahan, John, and Gruenstein, Peter. *Lost Frontier: The Marketing of Alaska.* New York: W.W. Norton, 1977.
Laycock, George. *The Diligent Destroyers.* Cambridge, Mass.: Ballinger, 1970.
Marx, Wesley. *The Frail Ocean.* New York: Coward McCann, 1967.
Moss, Frank E. *The Water Crisis.* New York: Praeger, 1967.
National Water Commission. *Water Policies for the Future.* Huntington, N.Y.: Water Information Center, 1973.
Natural Resources Council of America. *What's Ahead for Our Public Lands?* Tracys Landing, Md.: Natural Resources Council of America, 1970.
President's Council on Recreation and Natural Beauty. *From Sea to Shining Sea.* Washington, D.C.: Government Printing Office, 1968.
Public Land Law Review Commission. *One Third of the Nation's Land.* Washington, D.C.: Government Printing Office, 1970.

Schnepf, Max, ed. *Farmland, Food and the Future.* Ankeny, Iowa: Soil Conservation Society of America, 1979.
Shands, William E., and Healy, Robert G. *The Lands Nobody Wanted: Policy for National Forests in the Eastern United States.* Washington, D.C.: The Conservation Foundation, 1977.
White, Gilbert F. *Strategies of American Water Management.* Ann Arbor: University of Michigan Press, 1971.
Wood, Nancy. *Clearcutting.* San Francisco: Sierra Club, 1971.

Land-Use Control

Baldwin, Pamela L., and Baldwin, Malcolm F. *Onshore Planning for Offshore Oil: Lessons from Scotland.* Washington, D.C.: The Conservation Foundation, 1975.
Clark, John R. *Coastal Ecosystem Management.* New York: Wiley-Interscience, 1977.
Council on Environmental Quality. *The Costs of Sprawl.* Washington, D.C.: Government Printing Office, 1974.
Frieden, Bernard J. *The Environmental Protection Hustle.* Cambridge, Mass.: The MIT Press, 1979.
Healy, Robert G., and Rosenberg, John S. *Land Use and the States.* Baltimore: Johns Hopkins University Press for Resources for the Future, 1979.
Healy, Robert G., ed. *Protecting the Golden Shore.* Washington, D.C.: The Conservation Foundation, 1978.
Lefcoe, George. *Land Development in Crowded Places.* Washington, D.C.: The Conservation Foundation, 1979.
McHarg, Ian. *Design With Nature.* New York: Doubleday, 1969.
Moss, Elaine, ed. *Land Use Controls in the United States.* New York: Dial Press, 1977.
Reilly, William K., ed. *The Use of Land.* New York: Thomas Y. Crowell, 1973.
Urban Land Institute. *Management and Control of Growth.* Vols. I-IV. Washington, D.C.: Urban Land Institute, 1975-78.
Whyte, William H. *The Last Landscape.* New York: Doubleday, 1968.

Law

Anderson, Frederick R. *NEPA and the Courts.* Baltimore: Johns Hopkins University Press for Resources for the Future, 1973.
Baldwin, Malcolm, and Page, James K., Jr., eds. *Law and the Environment.* New York: Walker, 1970.
Liroff, Richard A. *A National Policy for the Environment: NEPA and its Aftermath.* Bloomington: Indiana University Press, 1976.
Mandelker, Daniel R. *Environmental & Land Controls Legislation.* Indianapolis: Bobbs-Merrill Law, 1977.
Rodgers, William H., Jr. *Handbook on Environmental Law.* St. Paul: West, 1977.
Sax, Joseph L. *Defending the Environment.* New York: Alfred A. Knopf, 1971.

Nature & Wildlife

Abbey, Edward. *Desert Solitaire*. New York: Ballantine, 1968.

Anderson, David D., ed. *Sunshine and Smoke*, Philadelphia: J.B. Lippincott, 1971.

Bates, Marston. *The Forest and the Sea*. New York: Vintage Press, 1965.

Carson, Rachel. *The Edge of the Sea*. Boston: Houghton Mifflin, 1955.

Krutch, Joseph Wood. *The Great Chain of Life*. Boston: Houghton Mifflin, 1957.

Myers, Norman. *The Sinking Ark*. Elmsford, N.Y.: Pergamon Press, 1979.

Nash, Roderick. *Wilderness and the American Mind*. New Haven: Yale University Press, 1973.

Passmore, John. *Man's Responsibility for Nature*. New York: Charles Scribner's Sons, 1974.

Singer, Peter. *Animal Liberation*. New York: Avon Books, 1975.

Stone, Christopher D. *Should Trees Have Standing?* Los Altos, Calif.: William Kaufmann, Inc., 1974.

Politics and Citizen Action

Cahn, Robert. *Footprints on the Planet: A Search for an Environmental Ethic*. New York: Universe Books, 1978.

Caldwell, Lynton K., et al. *Citizens and the Environment: Case Studies in Popular Action*. Bloomington: Indiana University Press, 1976.

Haefele, Edwin T. *Representative Government and Environmental Management*. Baltimore: Johns Hopkins University Press, 1974.

Leonard, H. Jeffrey, et al, eds, *Business and Environment: Toward Common Ground*. Washington, D.C.: The Conservation Foundation, 1978.

McPhee, John. *Encounters with the Archdruid*. New York: Farrar, Straus & Giroux, 1971.

Mitchell, John G., and Stallings, Constance. *Ecotactics*. New York: Simon & Schuster, 1970.

Ophuls, William. *Ecology and the Politics of Scarcity*. San Francisco: W.H. Freeman, 1977.

Pollution, Chemicals, and Health

Ashford, Nicholas A. *Crisis in the Workplace: Occupational Disease and Injury*. Cambridge, Mass.: The MIT Press, 1975.

Ayres, Robert U., and McKenna, Richard P. *Alternatives to the Internal Combustion Engine*. Baltimore: Johns Hopkins University Press, 1972.

Baron, Robert Alex. *The Tyranny of Noise*. New York: St. Martin's Press, 1970.

Boyle, Robert H., and Environmental Defense Fund. *Malignant Neglect*. New York: Alfred A. Knopf, 1979.

Carson, Rachel. *Silent Spring*. Boston: Houghton Mifflin, 1962.

Davies, J. Clarence. *The Politics of Pollution*. New York: Pegasus, 1970.

Eckholm, Erik P. *The Picture of Health*. New York: W.W. Norton, 1977.

Eisenbud, Merril. *Environment, Technology, and Health: Human Ecology in Historical Perspective*. New York: New York University Press, 1978.

Epstein, Samuel S. *The Politics of Cancer.* 2nd ed. New York: Doubleday, 1979.

Esposito, John C. *Vanishing Air.* New York: Grossman, 1970.

Kneese, Allen V., and Schultze, Charles L. *Pollution, Prices and Public Policy.* Washington, D.C.: Brookings Institution, 1975.

Lave, Lester B., and Seskin, Eugene P. *Air Pollution and Human Health.* Baltimore: Johns Hopkins University Press for Resources for the Future, 1978.

National Academy of Sciences. *Pest Control: An Assessment of Present and Alternative Technologies.* Washington, D.C.: National Academy of Sciences, 1976.

Quarles, John R. *Cleaning up America.* Boston: Houghton Mifflin, 1976.

Rudd, Robert L. *Pesticides and the Living Landscape.* Madison: University of Wisconsin Press, 1964.

Shurcliff, William A. *S/S/T and Sonic Boom Handbook.* New York: Ballantine, 1970.

Van Den Bosch, Robert. *The Pesticide Conspiracy.* New York: Doubleday, 1978.

Wallick, Franklin. *The American Worker: An Endangered Species.* Cambridge, Mass.: Ballinger, 1972.

Zwick, David, ed. *Water Wasteland.* New York: Grossman, 1971.

Population, Food & Climate

Berg, Alan. *The Nutrition Factor.* Washington, D.C.: Brookings Institution, 1973.

Borgstrom, Georg. *Focal Points: A Global Food Strategy.* New York: MacMillan, 1971.

Brown, Lester R., and Eckholm, Erik P. *By Bread Alone.* New York: Praeger, 1974.

Brown, Lester R. *In the Human Interest.* New York: W.W. Norton, 1974.

Brown, Lester R. *The Twenty-Ninth Day.* New York: W.W. Norton, 1978.

Bryson, Reid, and Murray, Thomas. *Climates of Hunger.* Madison: University of Wisconsin Press, 1977.

Eckhold, Erik P. *Losing Ground.* New York: W.W. Norton, 1976.

Ehrlich, Paul R. *The Population Bomb.* New York: Ballantine, 1968.

Gribbin, John, ed. *Climatic Change.* Cambridge, Eng.: Cambridge University Press, 1978.

Lamb, Hubert. *Climate: Present, Past and Future.* London: Methuen, 1978.

Lappe, Frances Moore, and Collins, Joseph. *Food First.* New York: Ballantine, 1977.

Osborn, Fairfield, ed. *Our Crowded Planet.* New York: Doubleday, 1962.

Paddock, William, and Paddock, Paul. *Famine 1975!* Boston: Little, Brown & Co., 1967.

Schneider, Stephen H. *The Genesis Strategy.* New York: Plenum Press, 1976.

Simon, Paul, and Simon, Arthur. *The Politics of World Hunger.* New York: Harper's Magazine Press, 1973.

Vogt, William. *People!* New York: William Sloane Associates, 1960.

Urban

Jacobs, Jane. *The Death and Life of Great American Cities.* New York: Vintage Books, 1961.

Leavitt, Helen. *Superhighway—Superhoax.* New York: Doubleday, 1970.

Little, Charles E., and Mitchell, John G. *Space for Survival.* New York: Pocket Books, 1971.

Mumford, Lewis. *The City in History.* New York: Harcourt Brace Jovanovich, 1961.

Owen, Wilfred. *The Accessible City.* Washington, D.C.: Brookings Institution, 1972.

Rudofsky, Bernard. *Streets for People.* New York: Anchor Press, 1969.

Whyte, William H. *The Social Life of Small Urban Spaces.* Washington, D.C.: The Conservation Foundation, 1980.

INDEX

Rice Odell &
The Conservation Foundation Letter

Rice Odell is editor of the *Conservation Foundation Letter*, an eight-page newsletter that each month analyzes a single environmental topic. A staff member of The Conservation Foundation since 1967, Odell is the author of *The Saving of San Francisco Bay* and numerous articles that have appeared in *Audubon, Smithsonian, World, Nation's Business*, and *The Washingtonian*. From 1953 to 1967, he was a reporter and columnist at the *Washington Daily News*, specializing in legal, business, and consumer affairs.

Environmental Awakening: The New Revolution to Protect the Earth is drawn from Odell's writings over the last decade. His continuing investigation of emerging environmental issues is available monthly in the *Conservation Foundation Letter*, published by The Conservation Foundation, 1717 Massachusetts Avenue, N.W., Washington, D.C. 20036. (Subscription rates in the United States are: $10 a year, $18 for two years, $25 for three years. All other countries: $12 a year, $22 for two years, $31 for three years.)